AMARETTO, APPLE CAKE AND ARTICHOKES

Anna Del Conte was born in Milan and lived there until 1943, when she and her family evacuated to Emilia Romagna. She read History and Philosophy at Milan University but left in 1949 to learn English in London, where she also met her husband.

In 1975 her first book, *Portrait of Pasta*, was published. After the acclaim the book received she became the first cookery writer in England to specialise in Italian food. Her books have won many prizes: *Gastronomy of Italy* received the Duchessa Maria Luigia di Parma award, *Entertaining All'Italiana* was shortlisted for the Andre Simon Award, *The Classic Food of Northern Italy* won awards from the Guild of Food Writers and from the Accademia Italiana della Cucina.

In 1994 Anna Del Conte was awarded the Verdicchio d'Oro prize for 'having contributed to the diffusion of the right and documented knowledge of Italian food and cooking'. She contributes regularly to *Sainsbury's Magazine* and received the Glenfiddich award for her articles in 1999.

Anna Del Conte lives in Dorset with her husband, close to her daughter and her beloved grandchildren.

ALSO BY ANNA DEL CONTE

Portrait of Pasta
Good Housekeeping Italian Cookery
Pasta Perfect
Gastronomy of Italy
Secrets from an Italian Kitchen
Entertaining All'Italiana

ANNA DEL CONTE

Amaretto, Apple Cake and Artichokes

The Best of Anna Del Conte

VINTAGE BOOKS
London

Published by Vintage 2006

8 10 9

These recipes were previously published in *Secrets from an Italian
Kitchen* in 1989 and *Entertaining All'Italiana* in 1991 by Bantam Press

Vintage
Random House, 20 Vauxhall Bridge Road,
London SW1V 2SA

The Random House Group Limited Reg. No. 954009
www.randomhouse.co.uk/vintage

A CIP catalogue record for this book
is available from the British Library

Line drawings by Elizabeth Carpenter

ISBN 9780099494164 (from Jan 2007)
ISBN 0099494167

Penguin Random House is committed to a sustainable future for
our business, our readers and our planet. This book is made from
Forest Stewardship Council® certified paper.

Printed and bound in Great Britain by Clays Ltd, St Ives plc

Typeset in Sabon by Palimpsest Book Production Limited,
Grangemouth, Stirlingshire

contents

acknowledgements

I am particularly grateful to my agent, Vivien Green – always my champion. My thanks also go to Rachel Cugnoni and Elizabeth Foley at Vintage. Finally I thank Julia Matheson for coming to my rescue with her skills on the electronic side.

introduction

Each chapter in this book is dedicated to an ingredient or a group of related ingredients. The ingredients I have chosen are those which feature most prominently in Italian cooking, ingredients that Italians use with particular success. In each chapter you will find recipes in which the ingredient in question is either the main ingredient, or is the one that gives the dish its particular character.

There are two reasons why the book is arranged in this way. Firstly it enables me to pay due respect to the fundamental importance of the ingredients in Italian cooking – of which more later. Secondly this arrangement resolves the problem that arises when you say, 'Let's use what's in the larder' (or the fridge, or the garden) or indeed 'Let's use what looks good in the shops'. If you have bought too many lemons, or peaches are in season, if your tomatoes have all ripened at once or a particular fish or vegetable is in season, then you can turn to the right chapter and find a choice of recipes using that ingredient.

In the index at the back of the book recipes are listed by name as well as by principal ingredient, in the usual way, so that you can easily locate a recipe without knowing in which chapter it appears.

To allay my suspicions that the real secret of Italian cooking is to buy your ingredients in Italy, I must make it clear that in testing the recipes in this book I have always used ingredients that I have bought in the UK.

Some of the recipes are ones that I have created, some come from my family's or my friends' recipe books and others are derived from the inexhaustible store of Italian local cooking. A few come from restaurants, although most are dishes that I connect with homes. Restaurant dishes may dazzle in their theatrical presentation and puzzle by their complexity; home cooking should never do that, except on special occasions: otherwise it becomes pretentious.

What I hope to have achieved in this book is to have brought into focus the basic characteristics of Italian cooking. After that, I hope my recipes will inspire you to improve them, following your own creativity, inspiration and palate.

Some of my earliest memories are of watching our cook Maria at work in the kitchen. As she worked Maria sang the Communist songs that were forbidden during the Fascist years, while I watched, fascinated by the speed with which she filled the ravioli or by her dexterity in flicking potato gnocchi down the prongs of a fork. It was listening to her discussing with my mother what to do with the mountain of *porcini* on the kitchen table, or pointing out how the beautiful slices of *prosciutto di Parma* had just the right amount of fat around them that laid the foundations of my knowledge of cooking.

So when, years later, I had to cook for my family in London, I knew by instinct – or so it seemed – when to stop adding flour to the pasta dough, what a *battuto* should be like, or when and how you add the stock to the rice in making a risotto. The sad part of this story is that when I arrived in London, in the early fifties, the culinary scene was so bleak that I had little chance to practise my skills. The only vegetables in the shops were root vegetables, limp lettuce and cabbage and cabbage and cabbage.

In my resolve to make the best of the situation, the basic instincts and the thriftiness of an Italian asserted themselves. I bought horsemeat from the butcher in the Fulham Road, and with this I made *polpette* or *polpettoni* which I finished off in a tomato sauce or in an egg and lemon sauce like a fricassee. My friends, little knowing, roundly declared that they would never touch horsemeat or offal, and then tucked into my meat balls flavoured with dried porcini with great enthusiasm.

Slowly through the years the gastronomic scene has improved, so that nowadays you can find everything in most British towns and it is quite easy to produce *un buon pranzo all'Italiana*.

the characteristics of italian cooking

Italian cooking at its best is made up of traditional dishes to which a cook has given his or her own imprint. It is a cuisine of few surprises but of deep satisfaction, of few innovations but of innumerable variations. It is basically home cooking of great simplicity, where the only important elements are good ingredients and love.

The best Italian cooking consists of dishes that enhance the flavour of the ingredients from which they are made, never swamping them with flamboyant side effects such as sauces and garnish. People sometimes comment on the lack of sauces in an Italian meal, but in fact food is usually served in the juice in which it has cooked, this being its 'sauce'. Separate sauces are used to dress plain foods such as pasta or polenta which, in their turn, become an instrinsic part of the sauce. Sauces are sometimes added to give the main ingredient a different dimension, but the respect for each ingredient is always there, a respect due to the ingredients because of their excellence. Fish, for instance, is usually grilled or boiled; no need to disguise its flavour in a pool of some cream sauce. A few drops of the best olive oil are all that is needed.

Fish, vegetables and cereals are the mainstays of this healthy cooking. Meat, traditionally, comes second in most regions; pork, a poor man's meat, being the most popular. The Italians have mastered the best ways of getting the most out of it by making prosciutti, sausages and salami of all kinds.

the importance of the seasons

Some years ago I visited the Renaissance cities of northern Italy in order to plan a gastronomic tour. On the last day I was in Mantua, possibly my favourite provincial city, and before leaving I went to the market in the Piazza delle Erbe to buy my favourite vegetables, so that I could cook them that evening when I got back to my mother's house in Milan. It was a perfect September morning, sunny and warm, yet cool enough to enjoy strolling among the vegetable stalls.

My first stop was to buy some free-range eggs from a man who was very insistent that I should also buy an *anitra muta*, a barbary duck. We discussed its merits at length, and it seemed that the chief point in its favour was that it was just the right time of year for buying such a duck. In various cages there were small chicks, bigger chicks, chicken, guinea-fowl, ducks and geese, plus a lonely young white rabbit trapped in a tiny cage for which even I, the unsentimental Latin, felt very sorry. I was reminded of the writer Colin Thubron who, when in a food market in Canton, was able to assuage his sorrow at the fate of the animals there by buying an owl – regarded as a delicacy and therefore commanding a high price – with the sole object of setting the poor creature free. But a tame rabbit would hardly have found its freedom in the middle of Mantua, nor could I arrive in Milan with a white rabbit for my mother. So on I went to the fruit and vegetable stalls.

There were still some *pesche da vigna* – vine peaches, small and scented, with their beautiful greenish-pink bloom, as well as some *prugne a fiaschetto* – flask-shaped plums. The grapes were perfect and kept me happy during the journey back to Milan. The season's first pumpkins were on display, but a group of local women judged they were not yet ready. They decided to postpone the making of the famous *tortelli di zucca* for which, partly because of the excellence of the local pumpkins, Mantua is famous. I next bought a kilo of tomatoes and a kilo of large meaty yellow peppers, both being in full season, to make a *peperonata*. Then, giving way to the acquisitive passion that grips me in such a market, and without really thinking, I asked a stall-holder if she had some fennel. '*Finocchi*?!? *Ma, signora, finocchi in settembre*!' and she shook her head, looking at me with a mixture of surprise and pity. For a moment I had forgotten where I was: in Italy they still have seasons!

Fruit and vegetables, fish and farm cheeses are sold when they are at their best, especially in provincial towns. I remember the Easters spent at our flat in Venice, when I would go to the market at Rialto to buy the first small artichokes, pale green and so young that we ate them raw, dipped in oil. There were tender small peas from Torcello for the *risi e bisi* – rice with peas – and an incredible variety of local salads, both cultivated and wild. Even in Milan there is the joy of witnessing the first appearance of the various fruits: the small *fragoline di bosco* – wild strawberries – the cherries, the Japanese medlars, followed by the apricots and the peaches, the real glories of full summer. I still make a wish when I eat the first fruit of the year, an old superstition. And I still use up the past year's dried beans, lentils and chick-peas in warming and comforting soups to make way for the new crop, which reaches the shops at the beginning of autumn.

The use of seasonal foods, such an important element in the cooking of Italy, can – to a lesser extent – be observed in Britain. When November comes, for instance, buy the last grapes, the first chestnuts and the juicy pears. Fennel can replace the tired courgettes, and the local celeriac will be the perfect accompaniment to all the game that begins to be plentiful in the shops. Steer clear, when you can, of the produce that is imported out of season from quite different climates, so that your dishes can relate to the time and place where they are cooked.

Just as there were seasonal vegetables, so there were seasonal dishes. In Italy there still are. In April, *brasati* and *umidi* – braised meats – are forgotten in favour of roasts and sautéed meat. Polenta slowly gives way to the more frequent appearance of pasta, and by the summer it has disappeared from the table, as have the *risotti* and pasta dishes with heavy meaty sauces. I remember the joy of seeing, again in April, the first peas of the season, and at Easter the *soncino* – lamb's lettuce. These were followed by all the glories of the summer fruit and vegetables.

As much as the food itself, the expectation of the *primizie* – new season's produce – was a keen pleasure. But although there is little of that left, we can still prepare a dinner suitable for the season.

It is, I am sure, not necessary to introduce pasta as if it were some novel foodstuff, yet its relative novelty has allowed one or two popular misconceptions to go unchallenged. One concerns the difference between fresh pasta and dried pasta, and has arisen partly from the use of those words 'fresh' and 'dried'. For, by implication, that which is not fresh is stale, or is second-best in some way, so that the phrase 'fresh pasta' implies that the other kind is not all that it might be. This is simply not so. There is no doubt in my mind that good brands of dried pasta are better than most of the fresh pasta sold in shops in Britain. Fresh pasta has become something of a fad here and in the United States, and yet in Italy – undeniably the home of pasta – most people eat dried pasta most of the time. My advice is that you should either make your own, a quick and easy job with the cheap hand-cranked machine, or buy dried egg pasta of a good Italian brand.

Another misconception is that pasta should be well drained. It is a great mistake to drain pasta too much; as soon as it is *al dente* you should tip it all into a large colander, give the colander a couple of shakes and – while the pasta is still wet and slippery – quickly turn it into a heated dish or into the frying pan with the sauce. In Naples, in fact, long pasta is lifted from the water with a long wooden fork instead of being drained through a colander, and a long-handled wicker strainer is used for draining short pasta. They say '*gli spaghetti devono avere la goccia*', meaning that the spaghetti should still be thoroughly wet when it goes into the dish. When serving some types of pasta dressed in a thick and creamy sauce, the Neapolitans fill an earthenware jug with the water in which the pasta has cooked, to be poured on the pasta at the table if required.

Another rule is summed up in the saying '*gli spaghetti amano la compagnia*' – spaghetti and all pasta loves company. You will need to stay around while it is cooking, unless, that is, you prefer to use the method I learnt from the late Vincenzo Agnesi, the Ligurian pasta manufacturer, a method suitable only for dried pasta. When I went to see him in 1974 for my first book, *Portrait of Pasta*, he was the fittest octogenarian I have come across, 'due', he said, 'to eating 100 grams [3 1/2 ounces] of pasta every day of my life'. He told me how he cooks his pasta, the advantage being that the goodness is not boiled out of it. This is the Agnesi method: bring a large saucepan of water to the boil, add salt to taste and then add the pasta and stir vigorously. When the water has come back to the boil cook for 2 minutes, stirring frequently. Turn off the heat, put a turkish towel cloth over the pan and close with a tight-fitting lid. Leave for the same length of time that the pasta would take to cook by the normal method, i.e. if it were still boiling. When the time is up, drain the pasta. The water will be much clearer than usual, and you will have a dish of pasta that has retained the characteristic flavour of semolina. The other advantage is that it does not become overcooked if you leave it one minute too long in the pot.

All pasta needs to be cooked in a large pot in plenty of water – Italians calculate 1 litre (1 3/4 pints) per 100 grams (3 1/2 ounces) of pasta. The salt must be added before the pasta in the ratio of 5ml (1 teaspoon) per litre of water. Add the pasta all at once when the water boils rapidly and stir with a wooden spoon.

The cooking time for pasta is, to a certain extent, a matter of taste. A dish of pasta in Naples would seem undercooked to a traditional English palate. I was amused to see this piece of advice in a 1900 edition of Baedeker: 'the Maccaroni [sic] of Naples is much esteemed, but is generally hard, and should therefore be ordered *ben cotti*.'

My last piece of advice – or should I say commandment? – is to dress the pasta immediately after you drain it. If, by an error in timing, the sauce is not ready, toss the pasta with some butter or oil; never leave any kind of pasta sitting undressed in a colander or a bowl.

pasta with fennel and cream
pasta coi finocchi

Fennel has a distinct, positive flavour that combines well with the simple uncomplicated flavour of pasta. The shape of pasta I like to use for this dish is shells or farfalle, but other short shapes are good too. I wouldn't use long pasta such as spaghetti, although tagliatelle are very suitable.

Cut off and discard the tops and any wilted or bruised parts of the fennel. Reserve the green feathery leaves and wash and chop them coarsely. Cut the fennel bulbs into quarters and then into wedges about 5 mm (1/4 in) thick. Wash thoroughly in cold water and dry with kitchen paper.

Heat half the butter in a large, heavy sauté pan until it begins to foam. Add the fennel and sauté for 5 minutes. Add the milk and sprinkle with salt. Reduce the heat to very low, cover the pan, and cook until the fennel is tender, about 30 minutes, stirring from time to time. Add a little hot milk or water if the fennel gets too dry.

When the fennel is very tender, break it up with a fork to make a coarse purée. Stir in the cream and season with plenty of pepper. Cook over a very gentle heat for 2 minutes, stirring very often, then blend in half the Parmesan. Cover the pan and set aside.

Meanwhile cook the pasta in plenty of boiling salted water until done. Drain, then immediately return it to the pan in which it was cooked. Toss with the remaining butter and with the sauce. Turn the pasta into a heated serving dish and sprinkle with the reserved fennel leaves. Serve at once, with the rest of the Parmesan separately in a bowl.

Serves 8
4 large fennel bulbs, total weight about 1 kg (2 lb)
90 g (3 oz) unsalted butter
300 ml (1/2 pint) full-fat milk
sea salt and freshly ground black pepper
300 ml (1/2 pint) double cream
90 g (3 oz) freshly grated Parmesan
700 g (1 1/2 lb) shells or other medium-sized tubular pasta

pasta with butter bean purée
gnocchetti alla puré di fagioli bianchi

Serves 8
**250 g (9 oz) dried
butter beans**
**1 celery stick,
preferably with its
leaves**
1 medium onion
8 garlic cloves
2 bay leaves
2 rosemary sprigs
sea salt and pepper
**120 ml (4 fl oz) extra
virgin olive oil**
**large bunch of flat-
leaf parsley,
chopped**
**700 g (1 1/2 lb)
gnocchetti,
conchiglie or other
medium-sized pasta**
**freshly grated
pecorino or
Parmesan for
serving**

Pasta and pulses are a staple in southern Italy and Sicily. What is new is to purée the pulses, and what is mine is to do it with butter beans instead of broad beans or lentils.

My husband being something of a pulse addict, all sorts of beans appear regularly at our table. One day I had run out of my usual stock of chick-peas, lentils and borlotti, but it so happened that I had some butter beans in the larder. Having soaked and cooked them, I began to taste them and immediately, in my mind, I could taste them with pasta. I removed the tough skin, as I always do with chick-peas and broad beans, and then puréed them. The final result was quite delicious, creamy, delicate and buttery, even though the dish contained no butter. A perfect dressing for the pasta.

Gnocchetti sardi *are a good shape of pasta to go with this sauce. They are available at Italian shops, but if you cannot find them, use shells,* ditali *or any medium-sized shape. The grated cheese ideally should be a mature pecorino because it has a stronger flavour than Parmesan.*

Rinse the beans, cover them with water and leave to soak for 6–8 hours or overnight. Alternatively, cover them with boiling water and soak for 1 hour.

Drain the beans and put them in a pot with the celery, onion, garlic, bay and rosemary. Cover with water to come about 2.5 cm (1 inch) above the beans. Bring to the boil, add 1 teaspoon of salt, lower the heat and simmer gently until the beans are tender. Drain, reserving the liquid.

Now you can either peel the beans by hand and purée them with the flavouring vegetables in a food processor, or you can purée the beans and the vegetables though a food mill, in which case you do not need to peel the beans. Return the purée to the saucepan and add enough of the reserved cooking liquid to make a thin purée. Bring back to the simmer and pour in half the oil in a thin stream, while beating vigorously to incorporate it. Draw off the heat, add half the parsley, a generous amount of pepper and salt if necessary. Cover the pan and keep warm.

Cook the pasta in the usual way or use the Agnesi method described on pages 15–16. I find this much easier when I have friends to supper, as you can leave the kitchen, quite confident that the pasta will cook beautifully without needing to be watched. When it is ready, drain, reserving a cupful of the pasta water.

Transfer the pasta into a large heated bowl. Toss immediately with the remaining oil and dress with the bean purée. Add enough reserved pasta water to give the dish the right fluidity and bring the rest of the water to the table in a jug. This sauce dries out pretty quickly and it may be necessary to add a drop or two of the water later on. Mix very thoroughly, sprinkle with the remaining parsley and serve at once. Hand round a bowl of grated pecorino or Parmesan.

preparation
The bean purée can be prepared up to 2 days in advance and refrigerated. It also freezes well. Add the oil when you reheat it.

pasta with a garlicky béchamel
gli ziti con la besciamella all'aglio

I discovered this recipe when I was doing the research for my Gastronomy of Italy; *it is in a book by the Duke Alberto Denti di Pirajno, called* Il gastronomo educato, *which has since become one of my favourites. The flavour of garlic is just enough to give an edge to the béchamel. Denti di Pirajno was a Sicilian, and* ziti *are one of the shapes of pasta much favoured in Sicily. They are ideal for this dish. It is best to make this dish in the spring, when the new, sweet garlic is in the shops.*

Roughly peel the garlic cloves and put them in a small saucepan. Add about 250 ml (9 fl oz) of water and bring to the boil. Cover the pan with a tight-fitting lid, turn the heat down to minimum (I use a flame disperser) and simmer for 1 1/2 hours. Check every now and then that the water has not evaporated and add more boiling water if necessary. By the end of the cooking time you should have about 150 ml (1/4 pint)

Serves 3–4
2 heads of garlic
a thin béchamel sauce
   made with 30 g (1
   oz) unsalted butter,
   20 g (3/4 oz) flour
   and 50 ml (3/4 pint)
   full-fat milk
350 g (12 oz) *ziti,*
   penne **or other**
   large tubular pasta
30 g (1 oz) unsalted
   butter
20 g (3/4 oz) plain
   flour

continued over >>

sea salt and freshly ground black pepper
45 g (1 1/2 oz) freshly grated Parmesan, plus extra grated Parmesan for serving

of liquid still in the pan. Put the contents of the pan in a food processor and whiz to a purée, then spoon it back into the pan.

Make a very thin béchamel (see page 489).

If you are using *ziti*, break them into 6 cm (2 1/2 inch) lengths. Cook the pasta in the usual way in plenty of boiling salted water.

Return the garlic purée pan to the heat.

Blend the butter and flour together with a fork and add, a little at a time, to the garlic purée, while beating with a small metal whisk. Cook for a minute or two and then add to the béchamel. Season with salt and pepper if desired.

Drain the pasta (but do not overdrain it) and transfer immediately to a heated bowl. Toss well with the sauce and with the Parmesan and serve immediately, with more Parmesan handed round separately.

fusilli and green beans with tomatoes
fusilli e fagiolini al pomodoro

Serves 6
600 g (1 1/4 lb) green beans
salt
1 onion, finely chopped
8 tbsp extra virgin olive oil
8 medium-sized ripe tomatoes, blanched and skinned
pepper
600 g (1 1/4 lb) *fusilli*
a dozen basil leaves
freshly grated Parmesan for serving

A pasta dish for the summer when green beans and tomatoes are at their best.

Top and tail the beans and wash well. Cook in plenty of boiling salted water for 5 minutes. Drain and refresh under cold water. Do remember that green beans need to cook in water that is quite salty, more so than any other vegetable. Cut the beans into pieces of the same length as the *fusilli*, and set aside.

Put the onion and half the oil in a sauté or frying pan large enough to contain the beans and the pasta. If necessary use 2 smaller pans, dividing the ingredients in half and using a little more oil. Add a sprinkling of salt, which will help the onion to release its moisture, thus preventing it from burning. Cook for about 10 minutes, stirring frequently and pressing the onion down to squeeze out its juices, then add the beans.

Cut the tomatoes in half and squeeze out and discard the seeds and water. Chop the flesh coarsely and add to the onion and beans. Season with plenty of pepper and cook over a very low heat until the beans are tender, adding a couple of tablespoons of hot water twice during the cooking, which will take about 20–25 minutes. Stewed beans should be cooked until they are tender; they should not be crunchy.

While the beans are cooking, cook the pasta in plenty of boiling salted water. Drain well – *fusilli* keep enough water in their spirals – and transfer to the pan with the beans. Add the rest of the oil and stir-fry for a minute or two. Serve at once, preferably from the pan. Hand a bowl of Parmesan round separately.

preparation
The beans can be cooked in the tomato sauce up to 2 days in advance and kept covered in the refrigerator. Heat slowly before you add the oil and the pasta, which must be cooked at the last minute.

thin spaghetti with garlic, oil and chilli
spaghettini aglio, olio e peperoncino

This is possibly the easiest and best spaghetti dish, an ideal choice for a lunch party in the summer. When you cook pasta for a large number of people, I find it easer to use the Agnesi method, as described on pages 15–16.

Cook the pasta in plenty of boiling salted water.

Meanwhile put the oil, garlic and chillies in a frying pan large enough to hold all the pasta. Cook for 1 minute over a low heat. As soon as the garlic aroma rises, the sauce is ready. Draw off the heat immediately or the garlic may burn, and this would ruin the taste.

Serves 6
**450 g (1 lb) thin
 spaghettini**
sea salt
**150 ml (1/4 pint)
 extra virgin olive oil**
**6 garlic cloves,
 peeled and sliced**
**2 or 3 dried chillies,
 according to taste,
 seeded and
 crumbled**

When the pasta is ready, drain it through a colander, reserving a cupful of the water. Transfer the pasta immediately to the frying pan. Stir-fry for a minute or so, lifting the *spaghettini* high into the air so that every strand is beautifully glistening with oil. Add a couple of tablespoons of the reserved pasta water if the dish seems a bit too dry. Serve at once, preferably straight from the pan.

No cheese is needed for this typically Neapolitan quick pasta.

preparation

This dish, like every pasta dish, must be made at the last minute. *Spaghettini* cook in about 6 minutes.

spaghetti with tuna and tomato sauce
spaghetti al tonno

Serves 3–4
1 or 2 garlic cloves, according to taste
5 tbsp extra virgin olive oil
6 peeled tomatoes, coarsely chopped
10 black olives, stoned and cut into strips
1 tbsp capers, rinsed and dried
12 fresh basil leaves, torn
sea salt and pepper
300 g (10 oz) spaghetti
200 g (7 oz) good tuna, packed in olive oil

This recipe differs from the usual one for a sauce with tuna in that here the tuna is not cooked. As a result the taste of the tuna comes through more clearly.

Peel and cut the garlic into thick slices. Put it in a small saucepan with half the oil, the tomatoes, olives and capers. Bring to the boil and then add the basil and half a teaspoon of salt, and cook for 5 minutes.

Cook the pasta as usual in plenty of boiling salted water.

Meanwhile drain the tuna, flake it and put into a serving bowl. Mix in the remaining oil and plenty of pepper.

When the spaghetti are done lift them out of the water with a wooden fork or a spaghetti lifter, or drain through a colander, and transfer to the bowl with the tuna. If you use a colander, reserve a cup of the water in which the pasta cooked. Mix in the tomato sauce and toss very thoroughly. If the dish seems too dry, add a little of the reserved water, and serve at once.

radicchio leaves filled with thin spaghetti
conchiglie rosse ripiene di spaghettini in insalata

Remember that cold pasta must be more al dente than hot pasta. This is a perfect antipasto for a summer party. I prefer olives with the stone to the pitted sort, because they have more flavour, but if your guests don't like spitting, buy good pitted olives without any stuffing and with as little dressing as possible. The dressing must be made by you.

Cut the core of the radicchio heads and unfurl the outside leaves very gently so that they remain whole. Keep the rest of the radicchio for a salad. Wash the leaves, dry very thoroughly and place them on one or two large dishes. You will need 12 large leaves.

Cook the *spaghettini* in plenty of salted water. It cooks quite quickly, and when serving it cold you should drain it when you think it is still on the undercooked side. Drain and refresh it under cold water. Drain again and then transfer to a large bowl. Pat dry with kitchen paper. Toss with half the oil and allow to cool.

About 2 hours before you want to serve the pasta, chop together, by hand or in a food processor, the parsley, garlic and chillies. Add the mixture to the *spaghettini* and toss thoroughly with the rest of the oil. Taste and add salt and pepper if necessary.

Fill each radicchio leaf with a forkful or two of *spaghettini*. Sprinkle the olives and the capers over it. Cut the eggs in segments and garnish each leaf and the dish with them.

preparation
The radicchio leaves can be prepared up to 1 day in advance and kept in the fridge in a covered container. The pasta can be cooked and partly dressed with the oil up to 8 hours ahead, but it must be finished off no longer than 4 hours in advance.

Serves 12
2 or 3 large radicchio heads
450 g (1 lb) spaghettini
sea salt
120 ml (4 fl oz) extra virgin olive oil
60 g (2 oz) flat-leaf parsley
2 garlic cloves, peeled
2 dried chillies
freshly ground black pepper
225 g (8 oz) black olives
5 tbsp capers, rinsed
8 hard-boiled eggs

baked pasta and grilled peppers
pasta e peperoni al forno

Serves 3–4

700 g (1 1/2 lb)
mixed yellow, red
and green peppers

1 tsp oregano

sea salt and freshly
ground black
pepper

6 tbsp extra virgin
olive oil

1–2 garlic cloves,
according to taste,
peeled and finely
sliced

2 tbsp dried
breadcrumbs

2 tbsp chopped flat-
leaf parsley

a few leaves of fresh
basil, torn

1/2 dried chilli or 1
fresh chilli, seeded
and chopped

12 black olives,
stoned and cut into
strips

1 tsp anchovy paste

300 g (10 oz) *penne*

This robust dish epitomises the flavour and aroma of southern Italian cooking. The recipe is from Basilicata, where chilli is a favourite spice. Buy very fresh, meaty peppers – the heavier they are, the more pulp they have – and use the best extra virgin olive oil. The grilling and peeling of the peppers is rather laborious, but quite necessary so as to release their flavour and rid them of the skin. Use dried pasta, not fresh, and preferably a medium-sized tubular shape such as penne.

Wash and dry the peppers. Grill them under a preheated gas grill or on a wire rack directly over a gas flame. (I find the latter method easier.) Cook them, turning them from time to time until the skin is black and charred on all sides, and top and bottom. Allow the peppers to cool. I find there is no need to put them in bags while they are cooling, as is sometimes recommended: if properly charred, the skin is very easily removed.

Peel the peppers with the help of kitchen paper and a small knife if necessary. Do not wash them as the lovely taste will wash away too. Cut in half, discard the seeds and remove the white ribs. Cut into strips of about 1 cm (1/2 inch) width. Place the strips in a bowl and sprinkle with the oregano and some salt and pepper. You can do this the day before: keep the peppers covered in the refrigerator.

Now put a large pan with 4 litres (7 pints) of water on the heat to boil, and meanwhile prepare the sauce.

Heat 2 tablespoons of the oil in a small frying pan and then add the garlic, the breadcrumbs, parsley, basil, chilli, olives and the anchovy paste, and cook, stirring constantly, for about 2 minutes. Taste and check the salt.

Heat the oven to 200°C (400°F) mark 6.

When the water for the pasta is boiling fast, add about 1 1/2 tablespoons of cooking salt. Bring the water back to a fast boil and then add the *penne*. Stir and cook until *al dente*. Scoop out of the pan about half a mug of boiling water and reserve. Drain the pasta and return it to the pan. Toss with 3 tablespoons of the oil and add

2 or 3 tablespoons of the reserved water and the breadcrumbs mixture. Mix thoroughly. If the pasta seems too dry, add a little more reserved water.

Grease a medium-sized ovenproof dish and put about half the pasta into it.

Cover with half the peppers, then with the rest of the pasta, and top with the other half of the pepper strips, taking care that all the pasta is covered by the peppers. Pour over the remaining oil in a thin stream. Place the dish in the oven for about 15 minutes. Allow to stand out of the oven for at least 5 minutes before serving.

preparation
This dish can be prepared a few hours in advance. Before serving, place in the oven for about 30 minutes so that it can heat through.

chick-pea and pasta soup
minestra di pasta e ceci

Soups are easy to serve at a large dinner party. You can prepare them totally in advance and forget about the first course. This soup can be served hot in winter or warm or even cold – not chilled – in the summer. I am afraid you cannot use tinned chick-peas for this recipe because you need the liquid in which the chick-peas have cooked. You have to buy dried chick-peas, soak them and cook them yourself, which, frankly, is not a great problem, since you just put them on and let them simmer slowly until they are properly cooked, not al dente, please.

Put the chick-peas in a bowl and cover with plenty of water.

Mix together the bicarbonate of soda, flour and salt and add enough water to make a thin paste. Stir this mixture into the bowl with the

Serves 10–12
600 g (1 1/4 lb) dried chick-peas, preferably the large ones
1 tbsp bicarbonate of soda
3 tbsp flour
3 tbsp sea salt
4.5 litres (7 3/4 pints) vegetable stock
4–5 fresh rosemary sprigs
12 garlic cloves, chopped

continued over >>

**180 ml (6 fl oz) extra
virgin olive oil
600 g (1 1/4 lb)
skinned fresh
tomatoes, seeded
sea salt and pepper
400 g (14 oz) small
tubular pasta such
as *ditalini*
Parmesan for serving
(optional)
freshly ground black
pepper**

chick-peas and leave to soak for at least 12 hours. It helps to soften the skin of the chick-peas.

When the chick-peas have doubled their weight they are ready to be cooked. Drain and then rinse them. Put them in a large stockpot, or 2 smaller stockpots, and add the vegetable stock.

Tie the rosemary sprigs in a muslin bag and add to the stockpot. (This will make it possible to remove the rosemary without leaving any needles to float in the soup.)

Add the garlic to the stockpot and pour in half the oil. Cover the pan tightly and bring to the boil. Lower the heat and cook over the lowest simmer until the chick-peas are tender, which can take 2–4 hours. Do not uncover the pan for the first 1 1/2 hours or the chick-peas will harden. For the same reason do not add any salt until the chick-peas are nearly ready.

When the chick-peas are tender, remove the rosemary bundle. Purée the tomatoes in a food processor and add to the soup with their juice. Stir well, add salt and pepper to taste and cook for a further 10 minutes or so.

Before you add the pasta, check that there is enough liquid in the pan. You may have to add some boiling water. Now add the pasta and cook until *al dente*. Ladle the soup into soup bowls and pour a little of the remaining oil in the middle of each bowl. Serve immediately, handing the Parmesan round separately (if used).

preparation

You can prepare the soup 2 days in advance (but do not add the pasta) and chill. You can also freeze it. Add the pasta when the soup is reheated.

home-made egg pasta

Here is my recipe for making the traditional pasta from Emilia Romagna. This is the pasta Italians like best to make because it is the best pasta. It is a pasta you can bite into and one that holds its cooking point well. Use the best free-range eggs for a stronger flavour. It is not possible to give an exact quantity for the flour because it varies according to the flour's absorption capacity, the size of the eggs and the humidity of the atmosphere.

Makes enough pasta for 3–4 people
2 large free-range eggs
approximately 200 g (7 oz) Italian 00 flour

Put the flour on the work surface and make a well in the centre. Break the eggs into the well. Beat them lightly with a fork and draw the flour in gradually from the inner wall of the well. When the eggs are no longer runny, draw in enough flour to enable you to knead the dough with your hands. You may not need all the flour; push some to the side and add only what is needed. Alternatively you might need a little more from the bag, which you should keep at hand. Work until the flour and eggs are thoroughly amalgamated and then put the dough to one side and scrape the work-top clean. Wash and dry your hands.

Proceed to knead the dough by pressing and pushing with the heel of your palm, folding it back, giving it half a turn and repeating these movements. Repeat the movements for about 7–8 minutes if you are going to make your pasta by hand, or 3–4 minutes if you are going to use a machine. Wrap the dough in clingfilm and let it rest for at least 30 minutes, though you can leave it for up to 3 hours.

rolling out pasta by hand
Unless you have a *mattarello* – a long thin Italian rolling pin – and a lot of practice you will find this a difficult task. If you do not have a *mattarello*, roll out the dough in 2 or more batches, keeping the unrolled dough wrapped in a clean cloth. It is particularly hard in humid places or in a draughty or overheated kitchen. Here I condense a very long process into a short paragraph of instructions.

Dust the work surface and the rolling pin with flour. Stretch the dough, working away from you, while turning the widening circle of dough so that it keeps a circular shape. The *sfoglia* – the sheet of rolled-out dough – must be rolled out until it is no thicker than 1 mm (1/16 inch). In theory it should be transparent. This thinning process must be done very quickly, in 8–10 minutes, or the *sfoglia* will dry out, lose its elasticity and become impossible to roll thin.

rolling out pasta by machine
The hand-cranked type of machine is very good and inexpensive. I strongly advise you to buy one and you will be amply repaid within a few weeks. You will be able to produce good tagliatelle for 6 people in half an hour at a quarter of the price of shop-bought fresh pasta and of a quality you could never find in a shop. I prefer the old fashioned hand-cranked machine to the sophisticated but noisy electric ones, of which there are several at various prices.

Follow the manufacturer's instructions, but do remember to knead the dough by hand for at least a few minutes, even if the instructions say that the machine can do that for you.

Tagliatelle and *tagliolini* can be cut by hand or in the machine. There is also an attachment for ravioli which is quite good, although I prefer to make them by hand. Other shapes must be made by hand and I have explained how to make them in the relevant recipes. When making tagliatelle and *tagliolini*, the *sfoglia* – the rolled-out dough – must be allowed to hang a little to dry, or the strands will stick to each other. It is difficult to say how long it needs, as it depends on the temperature and humidity of the atmosphere, but it should be dry to the touch and just beginning to become leathery. Stuffed pasta must not be left to dry.

Lasagne are easy to prepare. Cut out the pasta into rectangles of about 12 x 8 cm (5 x 3 inches) and cook them, no more than six or seven pieces at a time, in a large shallow pan of boiling salted water to which you have added a tablespoon of oil to prevent them sticking to each other. As soon as the lasagne are cooked, lift them out of the water and plunge them into a bowl of cold water which you have placed near the burner. Fish them out of the bowl and lay them on clean tea-towels. Pat them dry with kitchen paper. When all the lasagne are done, assemble the dish.

preparation
As for the cooking of fresh egg pasta, remember that it takes far less time to cook than dried pasta.

tagliatelle with artichokes
tagliatelle coi carciofi

This is a lovely dish for a party. It is easy to make, the only laborious part being the cleaning of the artichokes.

If you are making your own tagliatelle, turn to page 27 and follow the instructions.

Trim and prepare the artichokes as directed on page 240. Cut them into quarters lengthwise and remove the beard and the prickly purplish leaves at the base. Slice the artichokes into very thin wedges, about 5 mm (1/4 inch) thick, so that the cut-up leaves remain attached to the bottom. Put in a bowl of acidulated water. Remove all the tough outside part of the stalks, keeping only the tender marrow inside. Cut it into rounds and add to the bowl. Now at last the artichokes are ready to be cooked.

Thread a wooden cocktail stick through the garlic cloves. (This is to make it easier to fish them out when the artichokes are cooked.) Put them in a large sauté pan with the oil and add the artichokes. Fry them gently for about 5 minutes, turning them over to *insaporire* – make them tasty – and then add enough water to come one-third of the way up the side of the pan. Season with salt and pepper.

Put the lid on the pan tightly and cook over a very low heat for 35–45 minutes, until the artichokes are very tender. Add a little more water whenever all the liquid has evaporated.

Set aside while you cook the tagliatelle in plenty of boiling salted water. Remember that if the tagliatelle are fresh they take no longer than 2 minutes to cook.

Heat the oven to 190°C (375°F) mark 5.

While the pasta is cooking, heat the cream. Drain the tagliatelle, but do not overdrain, and put immediately back into the pan. Toss with the butter and the hot cream. Add the artichokes and the Parmesan and mix thoroughly.

Butter a large and shallow oven dish and pour the tagliatelle into it. Before baking, heat the milk and pour it over the tagliatelle. You may not need to add it all, but remember that the dish will dry while baking.

Serves 8
tagliatelle made with
  500 g (1 lb 2 oz)
  flour and 5 free-
  range eggs, or
  500 g (1 lb 2 oz)
  dried egg tagliatelle
6 or 7 globe
  artichokes,
  depending on size
10 garlic cloves,
  peeled
4 tbsp olive oil
sea salt and pepper
450 ml (3/4 pint)
  single cream
60g (2 oz) unsalted
  butter
6 tbsp freshly grated
  Parmesan
250 ml (8 fl oz) full-
  fat milk

Put the dish in the oven and bake for about 20 minutes. Let it rest out of the oven for a few minutes before you bring it to the table, so that the flavours will settle and combine, and to ensure that your guests will be able to appreciate the delicacy of this dish without burning their mouths.

preparation

The tagliatelle can be made up to 2 days in advance. Leave them on trays to dry and cover them with a cloth as soon as they are thoroughly dry. The artichokes can also be cooked 1 or 2 days in advance and refrigerated, covered with clingfilm. The whole dish can be prepared up to 1 day in advance, covered with clingfilm and refrigerated. Bring back to room temperature before baking, and add the hot milk before you put the dish in the oven, and then, of course, you have to bake it for about 20 minutes longer.

tagliatelle with pumpkin sauce
tagliatelle al sugo di zucca

Serves 4
tagliatelle made with 3 free-range eggs, 300 g (10 oz) Italian 00 flour or 250 g (9 oz) dried egg tagliatelle
120 g (4 oz) shallots or onion
60 g (2 oz) unsalted butter
pinch of sea salt
800 g (1 3/4 lb) butternut squash
good pinch of grated nutmeg

continued over >>

When I was in the Cilento peninsula, south of Paestum, in late September years ago, I saw some long yellowish marrows with a pale green pulp, a type of vegetable that I could not remember having seen before. It was a zucca, *I was told, with which the locals made a superb sauce for pasta. This variety of pumpkin is rather watery in consistency, yet full of the concentrated flavour given by the hot sun of southern Italy. Here in England I find that the common or garden orange pumpkin lacks any depth of flavour. So I use winter squashes, of which I find butternut and onion are my favourites. With these squashes I also make gnocchi or ravioli* mantovani. *These rich ravioli also contain* amaretti, mostarda di Cremona *and* grappa – *a delicious legacy from the kitchens of the Gonzagas.*

First make the tagliatelle, as instructed on page 27. Roll out the dough to the last but one notch of the hand-cranked machine, or as thin as you can if you are doing it by hand.

Peel and chop the shallots or onion. They should be chopped really finely, so that they become like a granular purée. A food processor is ideal for this job.

Put the butter and the shallot or onion in a heavy pan and heat very slowly until the butter has melted. Sprinkle with a little salt. This will make the shallot or onion release its moisture and thus cook without browning. Cover the mixture with a piece of buttered paper (I use the butter's wrapping paper) and put a lid on top. Cook over a very low heat for about half an hour, stirring frequently, until the shallot or onion is *very* soft.

Meanwhile cut the squash into chunks, discard the seeds and the cottony pulp and peel it. Cut it into short matchsticks.

Add the squash to the shallot or onion, sprinkle with the nutmeg and cover the pan. Cook very gently for 40 minutes or so, until the pumpkin has become a purée. Stir in the parsley, the cream, the cheese and the black pepper, check the salt and then draw off the heat.

Cook the pasta as usual in plenty of salted water, remembering that if it is home-made it will take no longer than 2 minutes to cook.

Drain, reserving about a cupful of the pasta water. Transfer the pasta immediately to the pan with the sauce, add a couple of tablespoons or more of the reserved water and heat for 1 minute, lifting it out of the pan to stir so that the sauce does not become too thick. Serve at once with the rest of the Parmesan in a bowl.

preparation

When I am doing a pasta dish, such as this one, that calls for a quick frying in the pan in which the sauce has been cooked, I serve it straight from the pan. Ideally the sauce should be made in an earthenware pot of the kind you can put directly on the heat, as should all slow-cooking dishes when browning is not required.

2 tbsp chopped flat-leaf parsley
200 ml (7 fl oz) double cream
4 tbsp freshly grated Parmesan
freshly ground black pepper
extra Parmesan for serving

tagliatelle with mozzarella, anchovy fillets and parsley
tagliatelle di guido

Serves 6–8

tagliatelle made with
5 free-range eggs
and 500 g (1 lb 2
oz) Italian 00 flour,
or 500 g (1 lb 2 oz)
dried egg tagliatelle
300 g (10 oz) Italian
mozzarella
4 free-range eggs
150 ml (1/4 pint)
single cream
sea salt and pepper
12 anchovy fillets or
6 salted anchovies
large bunch of flat-
leaf parsley
3 garlic cloves,
peeled
120 ml (4 fl oz) extra
virgin olive oil

My brother Guido was a great gourmet; never one to follow recipes slavishly, he always improved on them, or so he claimed. This dressing for the tagliatelle is one of his creations. It certainly needs no further improvements, and yet it is simplicity itself. The strong aromatic flavour of the parsley *soffritto* is softened by the addition of the delicate egg mixture. If you can, buy salted anchovies as they have more flavour than tinned anchovy fillets. It is a delicious sauce that takes less time to make than the pasta takes to cook.

If you are making your own tagliatelle, do this first, following the instructions on page 27.

Put a large saucepan full of salted water on the heat and while the water is coming to the boil prepare the sauce. Grate the mozzarella though the coarse holes of a grater or cut into small cubes. Put it in a bowl and add the eggs, one at a time to incorporate thoroughly. Stir in the cream and add a good deal of pepper. Set aside.

If you are using anchovy fillets, let the oil drip away and pat them dry with kitchen paper. Salted anchovies must be cleaned, rinsed under cold water and dried with kitchen paper. Chop together the anchovies, parsley and garlic and put them in a frying pan that will be large enough to hold all the pasta. Add the oil and sauté for 1 minute, stirring very frequently.

When the tagliatelle are *al dente*, drain them through a colander or use a spaghetti lifter to transfer them directly into the frying pan. If you use the colander, reserve a cupful of the water in which the pasta has cooked.

Stir-fry for 1 minute and then add the egg mixture. Fry for a further minute, lifting the tagliatelle high into the air so that the strands of pasta coat evenly. Taste and check the seasonings. If the dish appears too dry, add a little of the reserved water.

If your pan is presentable, serve straight from it at the table, otherwise transfer the pasta into a heated bowl and serve at once. For this type of pasta I bring a small jug full of pasta water to the table – pasta dressed with eggs, and especially home-made pasta, tends to become very dry while it cools, and the jug of hot pasta water is the ideal solution, as any Neapolitan knows.

preparation
You can grate the mozzarella and chop the parsley, anchovies and garlic in advance, but no more than that. The dish must be made shortly before eating.

tagliolini ring in a creamy courgette sauce
anello di tagliolini in salsa di zucchine

Tagliolini *are a sort of narrow tagliatelle and are not an easy shape to cook. You must be careful not to cook them too long, not to drain them too much and not to leave them undressed. With these three 'nots' in mind you can try, or you can use the safer tagliatelle. Do not buy fresh* tagliolini *from a shop, they cook badly and go totally mushy. Make your own – a tall order for 12 people, I must admit – or buy dried egg pasta of a good Italian brand.*

This ring is beautiful, festive and fresh looking, and it just happens that it is also extremely good. You will need a very large saucepan of no less than 5 litres (8 3/4 pints) capacity to cook all these tagliolini *which, like all home-made pasta, need to cook in even more water than dried pasta. If your pot is not large enough, cook and drain the* tagliolini *half at a time, dressing the first lot with half the butter and cheese.*

First make the *tagliolini*, following the instructions on page 27.

For the sauce, wash the courgettes thoroughly and boil them in plenty of salted boiling water until just tender. Process to a very coarse purée or put through a food mill fitted with a large-hole disc. Set aside.

Melt the butter in a saucepan, blend in the flour and cook for 1 minute, stirring constantly. Add the wine and cook for a further

Serves 10
tagliolini made
with 600 g (1 1/4 lb)
Italian 00 flour
and 6 free-range
eggs, or 800 g
(1 3/4 lb) dried
egg *tagliolini* or
tagliatelle
100 g (3 oz)
unsalted butter,
cut into small
pieces
100 g (3 1/2 oz)
freshly grated
Parmesan
a dozen chive blades,
snipped

For the sauce
600 g (1 1/4 lb)
fresh young
courgettes
sea salt
100 g (3 oz) unsalted
butter
1 1/2 tbsp flour

continued over >>

**120 ml (4 fl oz) dry
white wine
2 tsp vegetable
bouillon powder
600 ml (1 pint)
double cream
freshly ground black
pepper**

minute and then add the bouillon powder. Add 150 ml (1/4 pint) of hot water while you continue stirring to prevent lumps forming. Blend in the cream and then the purée of courgettes. Add pepper and salt to taste, bring to the boil and simmer very slowly while you cook the pasta.

Generously butter a large ring-mould of 2 litres (3 1/2 pint) capacity or two ring-moulds of 1 litre (1 3/4 pints) capacity each.

Boil the *tagliolini* in plenty of salted water. If they are home-made they will cook in less than 1 minute. Scoop out a cupful or so of the water and reserve. Drain the pasta and put it quickly back in the saucepan. Dress with the butter, Parmesan and the chives and pour over about half a cupful of the reserved pasta water. Spoon the pasta into the prepared moulds and press down with a spoon.

Put a heated round platter over the mould, turn the mould upside-down and give the platter a shake. Remove the mould, which should lift away easily.

If the sauce looks too thick, thin it down with a few tablespoons of the reserved pasta water.

Spoon some of the sauce into the hole in the middle of the ring and hand the rest round in two heated sauce-boats or pretty small bowls.

preparation

The *tagliolini* can be made well in advance, allowed to dry thoroughly and stored in tins or plastic containers. The courgettes can be puréed up to 1 day in advance and refrigerated, but the sauce, which takes only a few minutes, is better when made no more than 3 or 4 hours in advance. Reheat it slowly in a bain-marie.

tonnarelli in a crab, tomato and cream sauce
tonnarelli alla polpa di granchio

This is one of the best dishes served at the Ristorante Ciccio in Bocca di Magra, a seaside resort at the southern extremity of Liguria, from which one looks across the valley of the Magra to the magnificent Apuan Alps. These are the mountains where Carrara marble is quarried. Because of the huge quarries, the mountain-sides change colour with the changing light of the day, varying from deep green-blue in the morning to the most delicate pink in the evening.

We first went to Ciccio 40 years ago when it had just been opened and Bocca di Magra was a delightfully sleepy little village with one *pensione* and one restaurant, Ciccio. Now there are several hotels and scores of yachts in a newly built harbour, but Ciccio is still most pleasant and offers some very good dishes.

When we were there in the Spring of 1988 there was a big lunch party to celebrate a golden wedding. *La sposa d'oro* – the golden bride – and her 40 guests managed to eat their way through seven mixed antipasti, a seafood risotto, *tonnarelli* with crab (as in this recipe), daurades in a salt crust, *fritto misto*, salads of rocket, wild plants and tomatoes, fruit salad with ice-cream, the wedding cake (a *mille-feuille* with *crème chantilly*) and coffee. My husband and I felt ashamed only to be able to manage a two-course meal, after which we withdrew to the beach for a siesta. But when we walked back past the restaurant at half-past four, the adults were still sitting round the table in a somewhat dazed condition, while the children were careering around the tables, free at last from parental discipline.

preparing a live crab

I buy live crab, being lucky enough to live a relatively short distance from the south coast of England. If you cannot find a live crab, make sure that it has been freshly boiled. In this case the fishmonger will open it for you and discard the inedible part. If you manage to obtain a live creature, put it in a sink or a bowl and pour over it enough boiling water to cover. When no more bubbles float to the surface – it takes no longer than 5 minutes – the crab is ready to be prepared.

Twist off the legs and claws. Scrub the body and legs with a hard brush. Crack the claws and the legs with a hammer or a nutcracker, trying not to mash the meat. Scoop out the meat. Hold the crab with

Serves 4–6
home-made *tonnarelli* made with 300 g (10 oz) Italian 00 flour and 3 free-range eggs or 350 g (12 oz) dried egg tagliatelle
1 crab weighing about 500 g (1 lb 2 oz)
4 tbsp extra virgin olive oil
2 garlic cloves, chopped
2 shallots or 1/2 onion, very finely chopped
sea salt
1 tbsp tomato purée
stock made from the crab's carapace
200 ml (7 fl oz) double cream
225 g (8 oz) prawns
freshly ground black pepper
30 g (1 oz) unsalted butter

the underneath towards you and pull the underneath away from the body by lifting the flap and pulling hard; this will also remove the intestine. Now tear away the inner rim and then pick out the orange, brown and white meat, using the pointed handle of a teaspoon. Discard the grey sack of the stomach, the mouth and the gills. The female crab, recognisable by a wider flap, may also contain the delicious coral, which, with the creamy tomalley, is the best part.

When you have picked out as much meat as you can, put the carcass in a pan, cover with water and boil for 15 minutes. Remove the remaining meat which you could not detach when the crab was uncooked. Keep the cooked meat apart from the raw meat. Now the hard work is done, and the sauce is quick and easy. *Tonnarelli* are square spaghetti, but made with an egg dough; they have the perfect texture for this sauce.

First prepare the *tonnarelli*, following the instructions on page 27. Knead it and roll it out through the machine, stopping at the last notch but two. The strips of pasta should be equal in thickness to the width of the narrow grooves on the machine's cutting roller.

Prepare the fresh crab, as described above.

Put the oil and the garlic in a saucepan over a low heat and, when the garlic begins to become golden, add the shallots or onion with some salt, cover the pan and cook over a very low heat until soft. Do not let the shallots or onion brown; if necessary add a tablespoon or so of the crab stock.

Add the tomato purée and cook for 1 minute, stirring constantly. Pour in about 4 tablespoons of the stock and bring to the boil. Simmer for 10 minutes and then add the cream and bring to the boil. Add the raw crab meat, cook for 2 minutes and, at the very end, mix in the cooked meat. Draw off the heat and process the sauce to a smooth thin purée. Return the sauce to the pan.

Shell the prawns, cut the larger ones in rings and add to the sauce together with a generous grinding of black pepper. Taste and check the seasoning. The sauce is now made and can be warmed up in a bain-marie ready for dressing the pasta.

Cook the pasta in plenty of salted water. Scoop out a mug of the water in which the pasta has cooked; you will need it for thinning the sauce. Drain the pasta, but do not overdrain, and turn it into a heated bowl. Toss immediately with the butter and then mix in the sauce very thoroughly. Add 3 or 4 tablespoons of the reserved water; the pasta should be well coated with the sauce, but not thickly coated. Bring to the table together with the mug of cooking water, in case the sauce becomes too thick as it cools. I do not serve Parmesan with this dish because its taste is too strong for the delicate flavour of the crab sauce.

fish ravioli
ravioli di pesce

Until 20 years ago ravioli were seldom other than di grasso, *filled with meat, or* di magro, *filled with ricotta and spinach. With the advent of the* nuova cucina, nuovi ravioli *appeared everywhere, some more successful than others. Ravioli di pesce* are to my mind the best of the newcomers, combining in a very Italian way three basic ingredients in the best tradition: pasta, fish and ricotta. The only catch is that they are none too quick to make. But ravioli never were everyday cooking. In my home in Milan, tortellini *and ravioli were made no more than three or four times a year; always at Christmas, for* Sabato Grasso *(the last Saturday in Carnival) and around November, when pumpkins were in season for the delicious* ravioli di zucca, *large ravioli filled with a purée of pumpkin,* mostarda di Cremona *and a touch of crumbled* amaretti. *And at home there was usually a cook to make them!*

First prepare the filling. Heat the butter and the shallot and cook for 5 minutes, stirring and pressing the shallot against the side of the saucepan to release the flavour. Meanwhile clean, trim and cut the fish into very small pieces and add to the pan together with the anchovy

Serves 6
home-made pasta made with 200 g (7 oz) Italian 00 flour, 2 large free-range eggs and 1 tbsp olive oil

For the filling
60 g (2 oz) unsalted butter
1 shallot, very finely chopped
300 g (10 oz) white fish fillet, such as Dover sole, turbot, John Dory, sea bass or sea bream
1 tbsp anchovy purée
100 ml (3 1/2 fl oz) dry white wine

continued over >>

150 g (5 oz) ricotta
4 tbsp double cream
3 tbsp freshly grated
Parmesan
2 free-range egg
yolks
sea salt and pepper

For the sauce
90 g (3 oz) unsalted
butter
3 tbsp chives, very
finely cut
freshly grated
Parmesan for
serving

purée. Cook until the fish becomes opaque – no longer then 2 minutes. Turn the heat up and splash with the wine, then boil rapidly until the wine has totally evaporated. Flake the fish coarsely, transfer to a bowl and allow to cool for a few minutes. Add the ricotta, cream, Parmesan and egg yolks. Season with salt and pepper and mix very well. Set aside while you make the pasta, following the instructions on page 27.

Cut off a quarter of the dough, leaving the rest wrapped in clingfilm. Thin the dough down in the pasta machine notch by notch as far as the last notch. If you are rolling out by hand, roll the dough out as thin as you possibly can. Cover all but a strip of the *sfoglia* (pasta dough) with a tea-towel to prevent it drying out.

Place small teaspoon dollops of the filling in a straight line along the length of the strip of *sfoglia*, spacing them about 4 cm (1 3/4 inches) apart and the same distance from the edge. Fold the *sfoglia* over the filling and, using a pastry wheel, trim the edges where they meet. Then cut the *sfoglia* into squares between each mound of filling. Separate the squares and squeeze out any air. Seal them tight with moistened fingers. In dry climates or hot kitchens I recommend applying a narrow strip of cold water with a pastry brush all round the edges, and in between each dollop of filling, before folding the *sfoglia* over the filling.

Place the ravioli on clean dry tea-towels. Do not let them touch or they will stick together. Cut off a second quarter of the dough, knead in any trimmings from the previous batch and thin the strip down as before. If you are rolling out by hand, keep the *sfoglia* you are not working on well covered or it will dry up and become brittle. Continue making more ravioli until you have used up all the filling and/or all the dough. Leave them uncovered until they are properly dry; you can then cover them with another cloth.

Bring a large saucepan full of water to the boil. Add 1 1/2 tablespoons of salt and 1 tablespoon of olive oil. Drop the ravioli gently into the pan and bring the water back to the boil. Adjust the heat so that the water boils gently; if it boils too fast the ravioli might break. Cook until they are done, about 2 minutes, stirring gently every now and then. The best way to tell if they are done is to try one: the pasta should be still firm to the bite – *al dente* – at the edge. Lift the ravioli out with a slotted spoon, pat dry with kitchen paper, and transfer them immediately to a heated and buttered bowl.

While they are cooking, melt the butter for the sauce in a small saucepan. Add the chives and pour over the ravioli. Serve at once, handing round some Parmesan in a separate bowl if you want.

preparation

The ravioli can be prepared up to 1 day in advance and refrigerated. They must be placed, sprinkled with semolina, in plastic containers between sheets of greaseproof paper. You can cook the ravioli just before the meal and keep them in a very low oven while you eat the first course. They should be lightly covered with foil, so that they can breathe but will not dry out too much.

pappardelle

Of all home-made pasta, *pappardelle* are my favourite. For one thing, they are large, so that you can really feel them between your teeth. Then they have another advantage over the other long shapes of home-made pasta. Living in a country where the humidity is frequently high, as it is here in England, I find that the sheets of pasta you lay out to dry can take much too long before they are ready to be cut into tagliatelle. You have to hang about, feel, wait, feel again, and even then, out of impatience, you begin to put them through the machine when they are still damp. Next, unless you cook the tagliatelle straight away, another problem arises. How can you spread them out so that they won't touch each other? You need lots of space. And if you roll them in pretty nests you are likely to finish up with soggy bundles that look most unappealing.

As for hanging tagliatelle over the backs of chairs, it might look very decorative and impart a highly festive air to the occasion, but it is not practical. Because of their weight, the tagliatelle may well break when they are dry, or even while they are drying.

With *pappardelle*, none of these problems arises. To make *pappardelle*, roll out each sheet of pasta to the same thickness as for tagliatelle (see page 28). Wait 10 minutes and then cut it into ribbons about 12–15 cm (5–6 inches) long and 2 cm (3/4 inch) wide, using a pastry wheel. Lay the *pappardelle*, not touching each other, on a clean cloth. You can cook them straight away or leave them until you are ready.

pasta ribbons with broad beans
pappardelle con le fave

Serves 3–4

pappardelle made with 2 free-range eggs and 200 g (7 oz) Italian 00 flour or 250 g (9 oz) dried egg pappardelle or tagliatelle

1 kg (2 lb) broad beans or 350 g (12 oz) frozen broad beans, thawed

2 shallots

100 g (3 1/2 oz) unsmoked pancetta

4 tbsp extra virgin olive oil

150 ml (1/4 pint) vegetable stock

sea salt and pepper

2 tbsp chopped flat-leaf parsley

Pappardelle are one of the few shapes of pasta traditionally made in Tuscany. Here they are combined with another Tuscan favourite, broad beans. The dish is much improved if you peel the broad beans. For the stock I use Marigold Swiss Vegetable Bouillon powder.

Make the pasta dough as directed on page 27 and then cut your *pappardelle* as instructed above.

Shell the broad beans. Plunge them into a saucepan of boiling water for about 3 minutes and then drain them. Peel them and set aside. If you are using frozen broad beans you can peel them easily once they are thawed, without blanching them.

Make a little *battuto* (a finely chopped mixture) with the shallot and the pancetta. I do this in the food processor, pulsating the machine so that the mixture is chopped evenly. Heat the mixture with half the oil in a pan, sauté for 1 minute or so and then sprinkle with a little salt and add a couple of tablespoons of the stock. Cover the pan and cook gently for 10 minutes, adding a little more stock if necessary. Stir frequently.

Add the broad beans, the parsley, half the remaining stock, salt and plenty of pepper. Cook very slowly in a covered pan until the beans are tender, Keep a watch on the pan and add a little stock if the beans get too dry. There should be some liquid left in the pan when the beans are cooked. Taste and check the seasoning.

Cook the pasta in plenty of salted water. Remember that if the *pappardelle* are fresh they will take only 1 1/2–2 minutes to cook.

When the pasta is ready, lift it out of the water and transfer straight to the pan with the beans, using a spaghetti lifter or a long wooden fork. If you prefer, you can drain them through a colander, but remember to reserve 1 cupful of water. Stir-fry for a minute or two and add a little of the reserved water if the pasta seems too dry. Draw the pan off the heat and pour the remaining oil over the pasta. Mix well and serve straight away.

spinach and pasta roll with melted butter and parmesan
rotolo di spinaci al burro e formaggio

This is a lovely vegetarian dish consisting of a roll of home-made pasta stuffed with spinach and ricotta, the most traditional of all vegetarian pasta fillings. The pasta must be rolled out by hand, but it is not too difficult to handle, being made with only 2 eggs. I recommend adding a teaspoon of oil to the dough to make it easier to stretch and roll thin. For the same reason I also suggest making a dough that is slightly more moist than the dough you would roll out by machine.

Once cooked, allow the *rotolo* to cool, if you have time, because like any other food it becomes easier to slice. I use an electric carving knife, which I find one of the most useful tools. It is invaluable for slicing a roulade like this, or a stuffed fish, or a piece of braised meat that would otherwise tend to crumble.

Serves 6
500 g (1 lb 2 oz) baby spinach leaves or 1 kg (2 lb) fresh bunch spinach
sea salt
2 tbsp shallots, finely chopped
150 g (5 oz) unsalted butter
200 g (7 oz) fresh ricotta

continued over >>

100 g (3 1/2 oz) freshly grated Parmesan
1/4 tsp nutmeg
1 free-range egg yolk
sheet of home-made pasta dough made with 2 free-range eggs, 200 g (7 oz) Italian 00 flour and 1 tsp olive oil
2 garlic cloves, peeled and bruised
small sprig of fresh sage

After experimenting with different sauces to serve with the *rotolo*, I have come to the conclusion that the best, as so often, is the simplest: melted butter and Parmesan. However, if you should prefer a more positive-tasting sauce, I suggest the fontina and cream recipe on the next page. If you cannot find fontina, use Swiss raclette, which is similar both in its flavour and its melting properties.

If you are using bunch spinach, discard any wilted or discoloured leaves, the roots and the long stems. Wash very well in a basin in several changes of cold water. The baby leaves only need one wash. Cook with just the water that clings to the leaves in a covered pan with salt until tender, then drain. Squeeze the spinach lightly in your hands to remove most of its moisture. Set aside.

In a frying pan, sauté the shallot with 45 g (1 1/2 oz) of the butter over a medium heat. Chop the spinach coarsely by hand and when the shallot turns pale gold in colour, add it to the pan. Sauté for 5 minutes, turning the spinach over and over to *insaporire* – take up the flavour. You will find that all the butter has been absorbed.

Transfer the contents of the frying pan to a mixing bowl, and add the ricotta, half the grated Parmesan, the nutmeg, and, last of all, the egg yolk. Mix all the ingredients with a fork until they are all well blended. Taste and check seasoning.

Make the pasta dough (see page 27) and roll out a rectangle of roughly 30 x 25 cm. Spread the filling over the pasta, starting about 5 cm (2 inches) in from the edge near you. The filling should cover all but a 5 mm (1/4 inch) border all round the sheet, and the larger border near you. Fold this border over the filling, and continue to fold until you have rolled up all the pasta. Wrap the pasta roll tightly in muslin, tying the 2 ends securely with string.

Use a fish kettle or other long, deep pan that can hold the roll and 3–4 litres (5–7 pints) of water. Bring the water to the boil, add 1 tablespoon of salt, then put in the pasta roll and cook at a gentle but steady simmer for 25 minutes after the water has come back to the boil. Lift the roll out, using the fish retriever in the kettle or 2 fish slices, and place on a wooden board. Unwrap the roll as soon as you can without burning your hands and set aside to cool a little, which will make slicing easier.

Heat the oven to 200°C (400°F) mark 6.

Cut the roll into 1 cm (1/2 inch) slices. Generously butter a large oven dish and lay the slices on it, overlapping a little.

Heat the butter in a heavy frying pan with the garlic cloves and the sage. When the butter begins to turn a lovely golden colour, draw off the heat. Remove and discard the garlic and the sage and then spoon the sauce evenly over the roll.

Cover the dish with foil and place in the oven until the roll is hot, about 10–20 minutes, depending on how hot it was when it went in the oven. Remove the dish from the oven and uncover it. Serve, handing the remaining Parmesan round separately.

preparation
The *rotolo* can be made up to 2 days in advance and refrigerated, wrapped in foil.

Here is the alternative sauce:

fontina and cream sauce

Bring the cream slowly to the simmer in a heavy-based saucepan and simmer over a low heat for 2 minutes. The cream must not boil; only a few bubbles should occasionally break the surface.

Meanwhile slice the cheese into very thin slices. Add the cheese to the cream and stir constantly until it is dissolved. Stir in 4 tablespoons of boiling water, which will dilute the sauce to the right consistency. Taste and add seasonings. The sauce should be very creamy and glossy.

To complete the *rotolo* recipe, spread 2 or 3 tablespoons of the sauce over the bottom of a large buttered oven dish. Cover with the sliced *rotolo* and then spoon the remaining sauce all over it. Cover the dish with foil and heat for 10–20 minutes in the oven, as above, depending on whether the *rotolo* was warm or cold when it went in the oven. Serve with the rest of the Parmesan in a bowl.

600 ml (1 pint) single cream
200 g (4 oz) fontina or raclette cheese
sea salt and freshly ground black pepper

one egg ravioli in clear broth
il gran raviolo

Serves 10
350 g (12 oz) cooked spinach or frozen leaf spinach, thawed
100 g (3 1/2 oz) unsalted butter
300 g (12 oz) fresh ricotta
100 g (3 1/2 oz) freshly grated Parmesan
1/2 nutmeg, grated
sea salt and freshly ground black pepper
pasta dough made with 5 free-range eggs and 500 g (1 lb 2 oz) Italian 00 flour and 1 tsp olive oil
yolks of 10 small free-range eggs
2.5 litres (4 1/2 pints) chicken stock (see page 485)

The first time I had this soup was in Naples, at the most memorable New Year's Eve supper I ever had. It was not long after the end of the war, when the scars were healing and people were beginning to enjoy life again.

New Year's Eve in southern Italy is a major event. Fireworks go off in all directions and car horns hoot mercilessly, but even then I was not prepared for what happened just a few minutes after we had toasted in the New Year. Our friend Mariarosa got up from the table, picked up her chair, went over to the window, opened it, and proceeded to throw her chair down on to the street below. Her brother and sister did the same with some of the crockery on the table, which I hasten to add was not their best Capodimonte. I ran to the window to witness the spectacle of Neapolitans hurling their oldest chattels into the street; they were having a good clean-up to welcome in 1948. Later in the night the poor people from *i bassi* – the slums – would come around and pick what could be salvaged from the rubble. I am told that nowadays this custom, which also existed in Rome, is dying out, with only a few old crocks being thrown out.

But back to this soup which, as a matter of fact, has nothing in the least Neapolitan about it. It hails from the North, from Emilia Romagna, the motherland of all the best stuffed pasta. This *Gran Raviolo* is a simplification of the local ravioli. It is lovely to look at: a large raviolo floating in a pool of clear broth. It is quite easy to make; the only hurdle is the timing of the cooking so that the pasta at the edges is properly cooked and the egg yolk is still runny.

Squeeze all the liquid out of the spinach with your hands and chop it finely.

Melt the butter in a sauté or frying pan and add the spinach. Turn it over and over until it has absorbed all the butter, and cook for about 5 minutes. Transfer to a bowl and to it add the ricotta, 8 tablespoons of Parmesan, the nutmeg and salt and pepper to taste. Mix very thoroughly with your hands. Taste and check the seasoning.

Now make the pasta dough following the instructions on page 27. Roll it out thinly. If you are rolling out by hand and you are not an experienced pasta maker, you should divide the dough into 5 balls and roll out one ball at a time, while keeping the rest of the dough wrapped in a clean cloth.

Cut the rolled-out dough from each ball into four 10 cm (4 inch) rounds using a saucer or a tartlet tin. Fill these two ravioli before you proceed to roll out more dough, or the dough will dry out and you will not be able to seal the ravioli. Place about 2 tablespoons of the spinach and ricotta mixture on each of two rounds. Shape the mixture into a ring, leaving a 1.5 cm (2/3 inch) clean edge all round, and room for the egg yolk in the middle. Tip the yolk gently, and without breaking it, into the clear centre of the ring of spinach mixture. Using a pastry brush, moisten the edges of the round with cold water and place one of the unfilled rounds on top, making sure that no air is trapped inside. Seal the edges tightly together by pressing down with your fingers.

Roll out more dough, fill it and continue until you have prepared all 10 large ravioli.

Divide the stock between two large sauté pans and bring to the boil. Using a fish slice, transfer as many ravioli as you can into the pans without them overlapping. Cook for 5 minutes after the stock has come back to the boil. Keep the stock simmering rather than boiling fast, or the ravioli may break.

Lift each raviolo out of the stock very carefully and place in a heated soup bowl. Cover with a little of the stock and keep warm while you finish cooking all the ravioli. Top up each bowl with the remaining stock and serve with the remaining Parmesan handed round in a bowl.

preparation

Make the ravioli about 1 hour in advance, but not more or the pasta will dry up and take too long to cook for the yolk to be still runny. Cook at the last minute.

cappelletti stuffed with herbs and ricotta
cappelletti alle erbe

Serves 4
15 g (1/2 oz) flat-leaf
parsley
15 g (1/2 oz) of a
mixture of these
fresh herbs:
rosemary, sage,
thyme, marjoram,
basil and borage (2
leaves) if available
15 g (1/2 oz)
unsalted butter
1 garlic clove, peeled
and bruised
180 g (6 oz) fresh
ricotta
2 tbsp grated
pecorino
3 tbsp freshly grated
Parmesan
1/4 tsp grated
nutmeg
sea salt and black
pepper
1 free-range egg yolk
1 tbsp olive oil
pasta made with 2
eggs and 200 g
(7 oz) Italian 00
flour

For the dressing
200 ml(7 fl oz)
double cream
20 g (3/4 oz)
unsalted butter
salt and pepper
60 g (2 oz) Parmesan

Cappelletti *are not all that easy to shape, but they are great fun to make with the children. If you prefer, make ravioli instead.*

Chop all the herbs by hand or in a food processor. Heat the butter with the garlic in a small frying pan, add the herbs and sauté for a minute. Remove and discard the garlic. Transfer the herbs to a bowl, scraping up all the lovely bits stuck to the bottom of the pan. Add the ricotta, pecorino, Parmesan and nutmeg to the bowl. Add salt, if necessary, and a good grinding of pepper. Mix very thoroughly and then blend in the egg yolk. Mix again so that everything is properly amalgamated. Cover the bowl with clingfilm and refrigerate while you make the pasta.

Prepare the basic dough as directed on page 27. If you are rolling out by hand, roll out about one third of the dough as thin as you can, keeping the rest of the dough, covered by a bowl, to use later. If you are using a hand-cranked machine, cut and stuff each strip of pasta as soon as you have thinned it out, stopping at the last notch.

Cut into strips of about 3.5 cm (1 1/2 inches) and then cut the strips across to form 3.5 cm (1 1/2 inches) squares. Put about half a teaspoon of the filling in the centre of each square, then fold the square across diagonally to form a triangle. Press the edges down firmly to seal them, moistening them with a little cold water if necessary. (If you are making *cappelletti* in a very dry atmosphere, moisten a narrow strip all round the edges with a wet pastry brush before you fold the dough to form the triangle.) Pick the triangle up by one end, with the centre point of the triangle pointing upwards, and wrap it round your index finger. Press the 2 ends firmly together. The peaked part of each cappelletto should stand upright. As you make them, place them in rows on a clean tea-towel. They are now ready to be cooked in plenty of salted boiling water, with a tablespoon of oil added to prevent them sticking to each other. Fresh *cappelletti* take about 4 minutes to cook, but if you have made them beforehand and they have dried out, they will take 10 minutes.

While the *cappelletti* are cooking, heat half the cream with the butter in a large, heavy, sauté pan. Simmer gently for 1 minute to thicken the sauce. Season with a little salt and plenty of black pepper. Draw off the heat while you drain the pasta.

Lift the *cappelletti* out of the water with a large slotted spoon or a large metal sieve and transfer to the pan containing the cream. Put the pan back on the heat, add the remaining cream and half the Parmesan and sauté for a couple of minutes, turning the *cappelletti* over and over to coat them evenly with the sauce. Transfer to a heated bowl and serve, handing the remaining Parmesan round separately in a small bowl. You can keep them warm in a low oven, covered with foil.

preparation

You can make the dish a day in advance, but no more, because of the perishable ricotta.

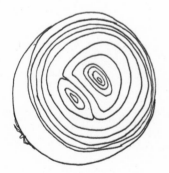

Thomas Jefferson loved Italian rice so much that, in contravention of a local law, he smuggled two sacks out of Piedmont so that he could plant the rice on his estate in Virginia. By the time Jefferson tasted it, rice was already quite popular in northern Italy, thanks primarily to the Sforza, the Dukes of Milan, who had succeeded in developing an excellent variety from the rice first brought to southern Italy by the Aragonese in the fifteenth century. Rice found the ideal climatic conditions in northern Italy, and it became the staple food of northern Italians, just as pasta was of the South.

Italian rice does not have such long grains as patna rice, and it has the property of absorbing the liquid in which it cooks. This is the rice from which was created one of the most successful dishes in the Italian culinary repertoire, the warming, comforting, creamy risotto. Rice is also used in Italy to thicken vegetable soups and as a stuffing, but hardly ever as an accompaniment to meat or fish, as is done in other cuisines.

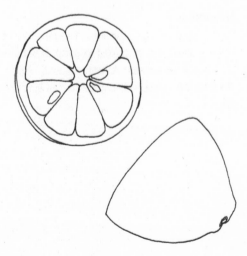

soufflé of rice and lobster
soffiato di riso all'aragosta

Serves 4
1 cooked lobster
200 g (7 oz) long-
   grain rice
sea salt
45 g (1 1/2 oz)
   unsalted butter
100 ml (3 1/2 fl oz)
   double cream
3 free-range eggs,
   separated
2 tbsp chopped dill
4 tbsp freshly grated
   Parmesan
pepper
1 tbsp dried
   breadcrumbs

This soufflé is not difficult to make since it is not a real soufflé; the rice and the lobster keep the mixture up so that you don't have to worry about ending up with a soufflé tombé.

Ask the fishmonger to split the cooked lobster in half. Remove all the meat from the lobster carapace, not forgetting the small claws. Do this over a bowl so as to collect the juices. Cut the lobster meat into small cubes.

Meanwhile cook the rice in boiling salted water. As soon as it is ready, drain and refresh under cold water. Put it back into the saucepan and add the butter, cream, egg yolks, dill and all but 1 tablespoon of the Parmesan. Mix thoroughly, then gently mix in the lobster and its juices. Taste and add salt and pepper.

Heat the oven to 200°C (400°F) mark 6.

Butter a 2 litre (3 1/2 pint) soufflé dish generously and sprinkle with the remaining Parmesan mixed with the breadcrumbs.

Whisk the egg whites until stiff but not dry, and fold them gently into the rice mixture with a metal spoon. Spoon the mixture into the dish and bake for 25–30 minutes.

preparation
You can prepare the lobster meat 1 day in advance and refrigerate it. The rice should not be cooked longer than 6–8 hours in advance and must not be refrigerated. As with potatoes, chilling alters its flavour. The dish can be assembled about half an hour before it goes into the oven.

risotto

Although it is a peasant dish in origin, risotto is not a dish that can easily be mastered. I was weaned on it, and yet it was a long time before I dared cook a risotto for my mother or my critical brothers. The standard I had to reach represented quite a challenge, since I have tasted few *risotti* better than my mother's.

The first thing to remember is that risotto is prepared according to a well-defined method. It is not just a mixture of rice and other ingredients, and it is certainly not a dish that Italians make from an assortment of left-overs. Rice is often the only ingredient, apart from flavourings. When there are other ingredients they are almost always cooked with the rice, so that the flavours fuse together. Although there are certain rules that must be observed, the making of a good risotto can only be achieved with practice.

Rule number one is that the rice must be Italian white rice, which absorbs the liquid in which it cooks, and which swells up without breaking or becoming mushy. There are three varieties of Italian rice easily available in Britain: Carnaroli, Arborio and Vialone Nano. Carnaroli has the biggest grains and is very suitable for a basic risotto, for the risotto with saffron and for rich meaty *risotti*. Arborio has slightly smaller grains, but it can be used instead of Carnaroli, and Vialone Nano with its stubbier grains is suitable for most vegetable *risotti*.

Secondly, the choice of saucepan is crucial to the success of the dish. You need a large squat pan with a heavy round base. A heavy copper pan or an enamelled cast-iron one would be ideal. The pan must be large enough to contain the rice when it has finished cooking, by which time it will have increased its volume by nearly three times.

Thirdly, risotto requires a generous amount of butter and, usually, cheese. It is the butter and the Parmesan that give the risotto that lovely creamy consistency. I allow 60 g (2 oz) of butter to 350 g (12 oz) of rice, which is the right amount for 4 people.

Another important factor is the quality of the stock. It should be a good, but light, meat stock, made with a piece of veal, beef, a chicken joint and very few bones, all flavoured with vegetables, herbs and seasonings (see page 485). Pork and lamb are too strong for this kind of stock. Vegetable stock (see page 487) is also very suitable for a vegetable or fish risotto. If you have not got any stock already prepared, use good-quality meat bouillon cubes, vegetable granules or Marigold Swiss Vegetable Bouillon powder.

Finally, the *mantecatura*. This happens at the very end when the risotto is taken off the heat. A knob of butter and, when required, a few tablespoons of grated Parmesan are added. The lid is put firmly on and as soon as the butter has melted the risotto is stirred vigorously so that it becomes well *mantecato*, which means beaten to a creamy consistency.

A risotto should always be made just before being served. However, if you have guests and do not want to spend the last half hour in the kitchen, you can try the following method. Prepare the *soffritto* (see page 488), sauté the rice and add about 200 ml (7 fl oz) of the stock. As soon as the stock is boiling again give it a good stir, turn off the heat and leave with a lid firmly on. When you go back to finish the dish you will find that the rice will have absorbed all the stock and will be half done. Add a knob of butter and proceed with the cooking, which will now only take about 10 minutes.

There are as many different kinds of risotto as there are ways of dressing pasta. The number of dishes that can be produced from these two basic ingredients has been greatly increased by the creativity of the new generation of chefs, who have combined unlikely flavours and textures in a risotto or in a pasta sauce. We have seen *risotti* with radicchio (perfect), with lobster (very chic), with champagne (strictly for weddings), with lemon (see page 56) or with rosemary.

All the traditional *risotti* are from northern Italy, which is where the rice grows. Lombardy, Piedmont and Veneto compete in offering magnificent *risotti*. The one that wins the prize, at least for me, is the risotto with truffles made in southern Piedmont. It is a plain *risotto in bianco* (see page 54) over which the local white truffles are grated at the table. From Venice come the *risotti* with fish and seafood, some of which are difficult to reproduce because of the difference in the fish available here. Vegetable *risotti* are also mainly from Veneto. And Milan offers the best-known risotto, the *risotto giallo*, with saffron. It is one of the few

Italian dishes to have been described in lyrical terms by a Frenchman. Edouard de Pomiane wrote, '*On vous apporte une préparation que le soir, à la tombée du jour, vous paraîtra de grains d'or. Une bonne odeur vous énivre petit à petit et on se délecte déjà, rien qu' à regarder ce riz aux grains bien séparés et bien dorés.*'

risotto with gorgonzola
risotto al gorgonzola

Warming, comforting risotti *are for chilly days, so I would not serve this dish in the height of summer. Also, it is easier to make in small quantities. For this reason I suggest that, if you are not an experienced risotto maker, you start by making it for 4 people before attempting larger quantities. This risotto from Lombardy is a favourite of mine for its creamy consistency and its assertive flavour.*

Chop the shallots very finely and sauté them in the butter, using a large, heavy saucepan. Add a pinch of salt to release the moisture in the shallots, thus preventing them from browning. Cook gently for about 7 minutes, stirring frequently.

Meanwhile heat the stock in a separate saucepan to simmering point.

Add the rice to the shallots and stir well for a minute or two, coating the grains in the butter. Turn the heat up and pour over the wine. Let it bubble away and then begin to add the stock little by little. As each ladleful of the stock is absorbed, add another ladleful and continue gradually adding it until the risotto is ready.

Halfway through the cooking mix in the Gorgonzola, cut into small pieces. Stir constantly until the cheese has melted and then continue cooking the rice, adding the simmering stock little by little. If you have

Serves 4
4 shallots
60 g (2 oz) unsalted butter
sea salt
1.2 litres (2 pints) vegetable or chicken stock
350 g (12 oz) Arborio, or other Italian risotto rice
150 ml (1/4 pint) dry white wine
180 g (6 oz) mild Gorgonzola, such as Dolcelatte, cut into small pieces
freshly ground black pepper
bunch of flat-leaf parsley, chopped

used up all the stock, use hot water to finish the cooking. When adding stock towards the end of the cooking, add only a very little at a time, in case the rice is cooked before it has absorbed all the stock. The rice should cook at a lively simmer, but not too much so.

When the rice is done, tender yet with an inner firmness – about 20 minutes – season with plenty of pepper. If necessary season also with salt, although the saltiness in the cheese may be enough.

Transfer to a heated bowl and sprinkle with the parsley.

preparation
The *soffritto* – sautéing of the onion – can be prepared in advance and reheated. Apart from that, for a perfect result, you should cook the risotto just before serving it. However, there is a way round that as described on page 52, which, I must admit, works quite well.

risotto with parmesan
risotto in bianco

Serves 3–4
1–1 1/4 litres (1 3/4 – 2 1/4 pints) meat stock
2 shallots or 1 small onion
60 g (2 oz) unsalted butter
300 g (10 oz) Italian rice (Carnaroli or Arborio)
45 g (1 1/2 oz) freshly grated Parmesan

This is the basic risotto and, as such, the purest of any. It is the one which, during the truffle season, is crowned with slivers of white truffle. I prefer to serve this risotto, rather than the Milanese saffron risotto (page 62), both with my Ossobuco (page 142) and the Costolette (page 145).

Bring the stock to a gentle simmer.

Meanwhile chop the shallots very finely and put them in a heavy saucepan with half the butter. Sauté until translucent and soft.

Add the rice and stir until well coated with the butter. Sauté, stirring constantly with a wooden spoon, until the outside of the grains becomes translucent and the rice begins to stick to the bottom of the pan.

Now pour over about 150 ml (1/4 pint) of the stock. Let the rice absorb it and then add another ladleful. Continue to add stock gradually and in small quantities, so that the rice always cooks in liquid but is never drowned by it. Stir constantly at first; after that you need to stir frequently but not all the time. The heat should be moderate, so as to keep the rice at a lively simmer.

When the rice is cooked (Carnaroli and Arborio rice take about 20 minutes) draw the pan off the heat, add the rest of the butter cut into small pieces, and the Parmesan and put the lid firmly on the pan. Leave for 1 minute, until the butter and the Parmesan have melted and then give the risotto a vigorous stir. This is to *mantecare* – cream – the risotto. Serve at once, with more Parmesan handed round separately.

variation

This can easily become a risotto with dried porcini. Pour some boiling water over 30 g (1 oz) of dried porcini. Leave them for 15 minutes and then lift them out and rinse under cold water. Chop them finely and add them to the shallots or onion. Sauté them for 1 minute before you add the rice and proceed according to the recipe above. Filter the liquid in which the porcini have soaked and add it to the rice while it is cooking.

Another attractive and convenient way to serve this risotto is to put it into ramekins, to be unmoulded on to individual plates. Butter generously four 300 ml (10 fl oz) ramekins and sprinkle with dried breadcrumbs. Shake off the excess crumbs and then fill the ramekins with the risotto, pressing down to get rid of any air bubbles. Put in a hot oven for 5 minutes or so, then unmould on to the plates.

preparation

This variation can successfully be made in advance, in which case the ramekins should be placed in a bain-marie of boiling water and heated in the oven until the risotto is hot through.

risotto with lemon
risotto al limone

Serves 3–4

60 g (2 oz) unsalted
butter

1 tbsp extra virgin
olive oil

2 shallots, very finely
chopped

1 celery stick, very
finely chopped

300 g (10 oz) Italian
rice, such as
Arborio

1 litre (1 3/4 pints)
light meat stock or
vegetable stock

1 organic lemon

5 or 6 fresh sage
leaves

a small sprig of
rosemary

1 free-range egg yolk

4 tbsp freshly grated
Parmesan

4 tbsp double cream

sea salt and freshly
ground black
pepper

For this excellent recipe I am indebted to Romana Bosco, a talented cook who runs a cookery school in Turin. She, for her part, owes it to Giovanni Goria, a member of the Accademia Italiana della Cucina. *The first time I made it, my husband looked very dubious at the idea of a risotto with lemon. He thought it sounded 'rather white and insipid'. From the first mouthful, however, he was a convert, and later declared it his favourite risotto. It is indeed delicious: creamy and yet so light.*

Heat half the butter, the oil, the shallots and the celery in a heavy saucepan and cook until the *soffritto* of shallot and celery is done (about 7 minutes). Mix in the rice and continue cooking and stirring until the rice is well coated in the fats and partly translucent.

Meanwhile heat the stock and keep it simmering all through the preparation of the dish.

When the rice becomes shiny and partly translucent, pour in about 150 ml (1/4 pint) of the stock. Stir very thoroughly and cook until the rice has absorbed most of the stock. Add another small ladleful of simmering stock, and continue in this manner until the rice is ready. You may not need all the stock. Good-quality Italian rice for risotto takes about 20 minutes to cook.

While the rice is cooking chop up together the rind of half the lemon and the herbs, and mix them into the rice halfway though the cooking.

In a small bowl, combine the egg yolk, the juice of half the lemon, the Parmesan, cream and a very generous grinding of black pepper. Mix well with a fork.

When the risotto is *al dente* draw the pan off the heat and stir in the egg and cream mixture and the remaining butter. Cover the pan and leave to rest for 2 minutes or so. Then give the risotto an energetic stir, transfer to a heated dish or bowl and serve at once, with more grated Parmesan in a little bowl if you wish.

risotto with seafood
risotto alla marinara

This delicious risotto, originally from Venice, should contain a good selection of seafood which can be varied according to what you find in the shops. Whatever seafood you buy, buy only the freshest and avoid the frozen sort. Freezing destroys much of the delicate flavour, and the final result would not be the same.

Clean and prepare the mussels and clams with the garlic and lemon as described on page 129. Strain the liquid left at the bottom of the pan through a sieve lined with a piece of muslin, and reserve.

Clean and prepare the squid. If you do not know how, read the method on page 136. Cut the squid into very small pieces.

Wash the prawns. Bring about 1.5 litres (2 1/2 pints) of water to the boil, add the vinegar and the prawns and cook for about 2 minutes after the water has come back to the boil. Drain, cool slightly and then peel the prawns, reserving the heads and shells, and cut into rounds.

Put the heads and shells of the prawns in a piece of damp muslin and, with your hands, squeeze out all the juices into the reserved mussel liquid. You may find it easier to put the little bag in a mortar, bash it with the pestle a few times and then squeeze out all the juices. These juices, and the liquid from the molluscs, give the risotto the necessary fish flavour.

Bring the stock slowly to a simmering point.

Reserve 2 tablespoons of the oil and heat the rest with the shallot or onion in a heavy-based saucepan and sauté gently until it is soft but not brown. Stir in half the parsley and the garlic and sauté for about 1 minute. Add the squid and cook for 5 minutes, stirring very frequently. You will notice that the squid will change from being translucent and become opaque and white.

Add the rice and stir well for about 1 minute. Turn the heat up to high and pour over the wine. Boil for about 1 minute to reduce, stirring the whole time.

Turn the heat down to medium and add about 200 ml (7 fl oz) of the simmering stock to the rice. Cook, stirring constantly, until nearly all the stock has been absorbed, then add another 150 ml (1/4 pint) of stock.

Serves 6
450 g (1 lb) mussels in their shells
450 g (1 lb) clams in their shells
5 garlic cloves
1 organic lemon
450 g (1 lb) squid
225 g (8 oz) prawns in their shells
2 tbsp wine vinegar
1.5 litres (2 1/2 pints) vegetable or fish stock
120 ml (4 fl oz) olive oil
1 shallot or 1/2 small onion, very finely chopped
2 tbsp chopped flat-leaf parsley
1 garlic clove, peeled and chopped
400 g (14 oz) Italian rice, such as Arborio
120 ml (4 fl oz) dry white wine
3 large scallops
sea salt and freshly ground black pepper

Continue adding small amounts of simmering stock as soon as the rice dries out. You may not need the whole amount of stock. The rice needs to be stirred every now and then, but not the whole time so that you can do something else in the kitchen while the rice is cooking.

Halfway through the cooking (Italian rice takes about 20 minutes to cook) wash and dry the scallops. Remove and discard the hard muscle and slice into 2 or 3 rounds. Add to the rice with the reserved liquid from the molluscs, and then about 2 minutes before the risotto is ready add the molluscs and the prawns. Stir well and add salt and pepper to taste.

Draw the pan off the heat and stir in the 2 remaining tablespoons of olive oil and the remaining parsley. Mix well, transfer to a warm dish and serve immediately.

risotto with artichokes
risotto coi carciofi

Serves 4
3 artichokes
sea salt
organic lemon
2 tbsp olive oil
1 garlic clove,
    chopped
2 tbsp chopped flat-
    leaf parsley
freshly ground black
    pepper
900 ml (1 1/2 pints)
    light meat or
    vegetable stock
2 shallots or 1 small
    onion, chopped
60 g (2 oz) unsalted
    butter

continued over >>

This recipe from my mother's recipe book works well even with the older, tougher specimens of artichoke we have in Britain. This is because you cook all the tough woody parts separately and then purée them.

Prepare the artichokes according to the instructions on page 240. You must be sure to remove all the hard part of the leaves, because they would stay woody however long you cook them and would spoil the final dish. Remove all the outer part of the stalk until you reach the marrow in the middle. Put all the uneatable tough green leaves and the outer stalk in a saucepan. Cover with water, add half a teaspoonful of salt and bring to the boil. Simmer for about 50 minutes, and then purée through a food mill into a bowl. (I am afraid this is rather a hard job.) You cannot use the food processor for this operation because the woody and stringy parts must be eliminated. Put the purée aside.

Now cut the cleaned artichokes in half, scoop out and discard the fuzzy choke and then cut each half into very thin vertical slices. Put these slices, and the inside of the stalks cut into rings, in another basin containing 2 slices of lemon.

While the outer parts of the artichoke are cooking, heat the oil with the garlic and the parsley in a sauté pan. Add the artichoke slices and the stalk rings and sauté over a moderate heat for 10 minutes, stirring very frequently. Add 120 ml (4 fl oz) of boiling water, and salt and pepper to taste. Turn the heat down, cover the pan tightly and cook for 20 minutes or so, until the artichoke is tender.

Meanwhile begin to cook the risotto. Heat the stock and add the liquid in which the outer parts of the artichoke have cooked. Keep this liquid to a low simmer.

Sauté the shallots or onion in the butter until soft. Add the rice and sauté for 2 minutes until the rice becomes transparent. Add 1 ladleful of simmering stock and cook until it has been absorbed. Add another ladleful and continue in this way until the rice is cooked. If you run out of stock, add hot water. Remember to stir the rice often, but not the whole time since you want the risotto to form a slight crust at the bottom of the pan – the best part.

Halfway through the cooking of the risotto add the artichoke purée. When the rice is nearly done add the sliced artichokes with all their juices. Stir very well.

When the rice is cooked, turn off the heat and add the cream and 4 tablespoons of the cheese. Taste and check the seasoning. Spoon the risotto on to a heated deep dish and serve at once, with the rest of the Parmesan in a bowl on the side.

preparation

If you are short of time you can eliminate the purée. Boil the tough artichoke leaves and stalks and add the drained liquid to the meat stock.

300 g (10 oz) Arborio rice
4 tbsp double cream
60 g (2 oz) freshly grated Parmesan

pumpkin risotto
risotto con la zucca

Serves 8
**700 g (1 1/2 lb)
pumpkin, rindless
and cleaned**
**2.5 litres (4 1/2
pints) home-made
meat or chicken
stock (page 485)**
**90 g (3 oz) unsalted
butter**
**8 shallots, very finely
chopped**
sea salt
1 tsp sugar
**1 large bunch of flat-
leaf parsley**
**600 g (1 1/4 lb)
Italian risotto rice**
**freshly ground black
pepper**
**150 ml (1/4 pint)
double cream**
**90 g (3 oz) freshly
grated Parmesan**

A light buttery risotto is the ideal autumnal dish, especially when flavoured with pumpkin or squash. The Hallowe'en pumpkins, the most commonly available, are not good to eat, as they have practically no taste. I have used the long trumpet-shaped Cyprus pumpkin, the sweet dumpling squash, the butternut or the onion squash and they are quite good. But the best pumpkin for the risotto is a large, squat pumpkin with very tough green rind and bright orange pulp, often sold in halves, quarters or segments in ethnic markets. This pumpkin is similar to the *zucca Mantovana*, Mantua and its neighbouring countryside being the motherland of pumpkins and the best pumpkin recipes, such as this risotto.

It is quite difficult to choose a good squash or pumpkin. The fruit should be ripe, yet not old, heavy for its size, with a green stem showing no blackening at the foot. The rind should be hard with a bright colour, either yellow, green or mottled, depending on the variety, without any blemish, soft spots or dried ridges. In fact it is easier to buy pieces so that you can see and even taste the inside, which should be bright in colour, fresh looking and thick. Pumpkins and squashes have an elusive, sweet flavour which is hard to capture. When they are good, this flavour comes to life in a risotto such as this. For me it rates as one of the best dishes of the Lombard tradition, as interpreted here, in my mother's recipe.

In the recipe I give the quantity of the cleaned pumpkin because some, such as the trumpet-shaped one, have hardly any seeds and cottony pulp, while others have a lot of waste.

Here the method is for cooking the risotto in 2 stages. If you don't need to do this, follow the method for Risotto with Parmesan on page 54.

Cut the cleaned and prepared pumpkin into 1 cm (1/2 inch) cubes.

Heat the stock to simmering point.

Heat the butter and the shallots in a large, heavy saucepan and add 1 teaspoon of salt, which will help the onion to soften without browning, and the sugar. Cook for about 5 minutes. Chop the parsley, add half of it to the pan and continue cooking for a further 5 minutes, stirring very frequently.

Now add the pumpkin and cook until just tender. I cannot give a time for this as it depends on which variety of pumpkin or squash you are using. Some take 5–10 minutes, while others take 20 minutes, in which case you will have to add a ladleful of hot stock to the pan. When the pumpkin is just tender right through when pricked with the point of a knife, stir in the rice and sauté for 1–2 minutes until the grains are well coated in the butter. Pour over about 450 ml (3/4 pint) of simmering stock and stir very thoroughly. Bring the liquid to a lively boil, turn off the heat and cover the pan tightly. You can now leave the rice, and return to the kitchen about a quarter of an hour before you want to serve dinner.

Bring the broth back to simmering point. Add a knob of butter to the rice, which will have absorbed all the broth and be half cooked. Mix 2 ladlefuls of hot broth into the rice and continue cooking and gradually adding a ladleful of broth at a time until the rice is ready. If you finish the broth before the rice is cooked, add boiling water. This risotto should be more creamy and runny than other risottos, halfway between a thick soup and the usual risotto. Season with pepper and check the salt.

Add the cream and half the Parmesan. Turn the heat off and leave for 1 minute for the cheese to melt and the flavours to blend.

Give the risotto a vigorous stir and heap it up on a heated round dish. Sprinkle the remaining parsley all over the steaming golden mound and serve at once, handing the remaining cheese round separately in a bowl.

saffron risotto
risotto giallo

Serves 4
**1.5 litres (2 1/2
pints) chicken
stock (page 485)**
**1 small onion, very
finely chopped**
**60 g (2 oz) beef
marrow, chopped,
or unsmoked
pancetta, chopped**
**60 g (2 oz) unsalted
butter**
**350 g (12 oz)
Arborio, or other
Italian risotto rice**
**150 ml (1/4 pint) dry
white wine**
**1/4 tsp powdered
saffron, or about
1/2 tsp saffron
threads dissolved in
1/2 cup of boiling
stock**
**sea salt and freshly
ground black
pepper**
**30 g (1 oz) freshly
grated Parmesan**

Also called Risotto alla Milanese, *this risotto was one of the first risottos made in Lombardy in keeping with the local fashion for golden food. This started during the Renaissance, when there was a belief that gold, consumed with one's food, was good for the heart. Thus, at the wedding feast given in 1368 for the marriage of a Visconti lady to the Duke of Chiarenza, all the birds and the fish were served covered with gold leaf. Apart from the imagined therapeutic effects of gold, its use by the nobility and the wealthy meant that it became very fashionable to serve golden food. The problem was, of course, that few families were as rich as the Visconti, Dukes of Milan, so they had to content themselves with the pretence rather than the reality; they created dishes that looked as though they were coated with gold, or contained gold powder.*

I have devised this unorthodox method of making a risotto for when I have friends to dinner so as to cut down on the last-minute cooking. It works quite well, but, of course the traditional method gives a better result – see recipe for Risotto with Parmesan on page 54.

Bring the stock to simmering point and keep it at a very low simmer.

Put the onion, the beef marrow or pancetta and half the butter in a large, wide saucepan. Sauté until the onion is soft and translucent, and then add the rice and stir for about 2 minutes until well coated with fat. Pour in the wine, boil for 1 minute, stirring constantly, then pour in 300 ml (1/2 pint) of the stock. As soon as the stock is boiling again, turn off the heat and cover firmly with a lid. You can now leave it for half an hour while you go and have a drink with your guests.

When you go back to finish the dish you will find that the rice will have absorbed all the stock and will be half done. Reheat the stock to simmering point. Add a knob of the butter to the rice and pour in about 200 ml (7 fl oz) of the stock.

Mix the saffron infusion thoroughly and add to the rice. Continue cooking and adding stock in small quantities, especially when the rice is nearly cooked. Do not add too much at a time or you may finish with perfectly cooked rice swimming in too much stock. The rice should cook at a steady, lively simmer the whole time.

When the rice is ready – *all'onda* as we say, i.e. soft and creamy – turn off the heat and add the rest of the butter and the Parmesan. Leave, covered, for 1 minute and then give the risotto a vigorous stir to mix in the butter and the cheese – to *mantecare* the risotto, to make it creamy. Taste and check the seasoning.

Transfer the risotto to a round dish, previously warmed, piling it in a golden mound in the centre of the dish

moulded risotto with vegetables
risotto con le verdure in forma

This risotto is made entirely with spring vegetables. If you want to make it later in the year, use French beans and whatever other vegetables are in season. Choose vegetables with the same type of flavour and avoid a clash such as, for instance, peppers or cauliflower would produce. I make the risotto in a mould because in this way I can cook it beforehand, put it in the mould and reheat it in the oven for 20 minutes. It looks great and it tastes good.

Boil the fresh peas in lightly salted water until just tender. If you are using frozen peas, blanch for about 2 minutes. Blanch the courgettes, drain and cut into small cubes. Cut the tomatoes in half, squeeze out the seeds and discard and then cut the flesh into short strips.

Heat the stock until just simmering. Keep it simmering all through the cooking.

Meanwhile put half the oil with the parsley and the garlic in a sauté pan, sauté for 1 minute and then stir in all the vegetables. Season lightly with salt and sauté over low heat for 2 minutes. Remove and discard the garlic.

Serves 6
150 g (5 oz) fresh peas, podded or frozen peas, thawed
150 g (5 oz) courgettes
300 g (10 oz) firm ripe tomatoes, peeled
1.5 litres (2 1/2 pints) vegetable stock
5 tbsp extra virgin olive oil
large bunch of parsley, chopped
2 garlic cloves, peeled and bruised
75 g (2 1/2 oz) unsalted butter
3 shallots, chopped

continued over >>

350 g (12 oz) Arborio
or other Italian
risotto rice
150 ml (1/4 pint) dry
white wine
half a dozen basil
leaves, torn
45 g (1 1/2 oz)
freshly grated
Parmesan
sea salt and pepper
500 g (1 lb 2 oz)
asparagus

For the mould
15 g (1/2 oz)
unsalted butter
3 tbsp dried
breadcrumbs

Put the rest of the oil and about a third of the butter in another heavy saucepan. Add the shallots and sauté until tender. Add the rice, cook for 2 minutes and then splash with the wine. Boil rapidly, stirring constantly, until the rice has absorbed the wine. Add 1 ladleful of stock and let the rice absorb it while you stir constantly. Continue to add the stock gradually, while you stir, until the rice is nearly, but not quite, cooked – about 15 minutes from the moment you begin to add the stock.

Draw the rice off the heat and add the vegetables, the basil, half the remaining butter cut into small pieces and the Parmesan. Stir thoroughly but gently, then taste and check seasonings. Spread the risotto on a cold surface to cool.

Snap off all the tough butt ends of the asparagus. For this dish you only want the tips, plus about 5 cm (2 inches) of the stalks. Remove any tiny leaves sprouting below the tips. Wash the asparagus and place it in a large sauté pan. Cover it with boiling water, season with a little salt and add the rest of the butter. Cook until tender but firm. Drain and transfer to a dish. Cover with foil and keep warm. (Do not throw away the asparagus cooking water; you can use it to make a soup with the rest of the stalks.)

Heat the oven to 200°C (400°F) mark 6.

Generously butter a 1 litre (1 3/4 pint) ring-mould and sprinkle the breadcrumbs all over the surface. Shake off the excess crumbs. Spoon the cold risotto into the mould and place in the oven. Bake for 20 minutes until the risotto is heated through.

To unmould, run a palette knife round the sides, place a round dish over the mould and turn it upside-down. The mould should lift off quite easily.

Place the asparagus tips in the central hole and around the risotto. Serve at once.

preparation
Both the risotto and the asparagus can be cooked a few hours in advance. Reheat the risotto in the oven, as directed above, and the asparagus in the microwave oven.

rice cake
torta di riso

Rice cakes are as typically Italian as rice puddings are English. They are both based on the same ingredients but these are treated differently to produce a different result. Torta di riso, of which there are as many variants as there are of rice puddings, is a real cake, firm yet moist. It is served unmoulded and cold, maybe tepid, never hot. It is made with Italian rice, a superior quality of 'pudding' rice, which has the property of absorbing the milk, and it is flavoured with characteristic Italian flavourings.

Put the milk, 30 g (1 oz) of the sugar, the lemon peel, vanilla, cinnamon and a pinch of salt in a saucepan and bring to the boil.

Add the rice and stir well with a wooden spoon. Cook, uncovered, over a very low heat for about 40 minutes, until the rice has absorbed the milk and is soft and creamy. Stir frequently during the cooking. Set aside to cool.

While the rice is cooking, heat the oven to 180°C (350°F) mark 4.

Spread the almonds and the pine nuts on a baking tray and toast them in the preheated oven for about 10 minutes. Shake the tray once or twice to prevent them burning. Cool a little and then chop them coarsely by hand or in the food processor, but do not reduce them to powder.

Remove the lemon peel, the vanilla pod and the cinnamon stick from the rice and spoon the rice into a mixing bowl.

Incorporate one egg yolk at a time into the rice, mixing well after each addition. Add the remaining sugar, the nuts, candied peel, grated rind of the lemon and the rum to the rice and egg mixture and combine everything thoroughly.

Whip the egg whites stiffly and fold into the rice mixture.

Butter a 25 cm (10 inch) spring-clip tin, line the base of the tin with greaseproof paper and butter the paper. Sprinkle all over with the breadcrumbs and shake off the excess crumbs.

Spoon the rice mixture into the prepared tin and bake for about 45 minutes, until a thin skewer or toothpick inserted in the middle of the

Serves 8–10

- 750 ml (1 1/4 pints) full-fat milk
- 180 g (6 oz) caster sugar
- strip of organic lemon peel, yellow part only
- piece of vanilla pod, 2.5 cm (1 inch) long, split in half
- piece of cinnamon stick, 5 cm (2 inches) long
- sea salt
- 150 g (5 oz) Arborio rice
- 120 g (4 oz) almonds, blanched and peeled
- 60 g (2 oz) pine nuts
- 4 free-range eggs, separated
- 30 g (1 oz) candied orange, lemon and citron peel, chopped
- grated rind of 1/2 organic lemon
- 3 tbsp rum
- butter and dried breadcrumbs for the tin
- icing sugar for decoration

cake comes out just moist. The cake will also have shrunk from the side of the tin.

Leave the cake to cool in the tin and then remove the clipped band and turn the cake over on to a dish. Remove the base of the tin and the paper, place a round serving dish over the cake and turn it over again. Sprinkle lavishly with icing sugar before serving.

preparation
The cake must be made at least 1 day in advance. It can be kept for a few days in the refrigerator, wrapped in foil. Remove from the refrigerator at least 2 hours before serving, to bring it back to room temperature.

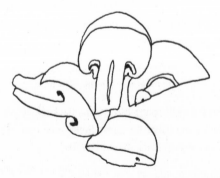

The classic polenta is a mixture of maize flour and water, although in some areas of northern Lombardy buckwheat flour is also included. In antiquity, however, polenta – *puls* or *pulmentum* in Latin – was made from spelt, a kind of wheat, and other cereals, while in the Middle Ages and the Renaissance millet, chestnut and even acorns provided the flour from which polenta was made. Maize was introduced to Europe by Columbus, who wrote in the diary he kept after landing in the New World: 'Maize has a pleasant flavour and all the people of this country live on it.'

Within Europe maize was first cultivated in Spain, and the Spanish began to enjoy it so much that Charles V, who thought that wheat was the right food for Christians, promoted the cultivation of wheat rather than maize by means of various incentives to farmers. From Spain, maize reached Italy, arriving first in Venice at the Rialto market. The bridge was not yet built, but the market was there as it is now, and it was there that goods from abroad were unloaded.

This yellow grain was soon christened *granoturco* – Turkish grain – but why it was given this name is still the subject of dispute. Was it called *granoturco* because of the similarity between the ear of the cob and the beard of a Turk? Or was it, as Pianigiani wrote in his eighteenth-century Etymological Dictionary 'because of a mistake in the translation of the name the English gave to the cereal – turkey wheat – that is to say food for the turkey, a bird so called because of a certain likeness between the bird's neck and the Turkish turban?' To my mind the only credible explanation of the name is that in the sixteenth century so many things of foreign origin came (or were thought to come) from Turkey that *turco* became synonymous with foreign.

In Italy, *granoturco* was first cultivated in the Polesine, an area of marshy land between Padova and Ferrara around the Po delta. It was soon found to flourish where no other plant would grow, in hot and very humid places similar to its native land. For this reason *granoturco* became a very popular crop, and from it the first yellow polenta was made. This polenta had a far more pleasant taste than those made from other cereals, and before long, in northern Italy, it became the staple food of the poor. Indeed, so good was this new polenta that in 1556 an aristocrat from Cremona sent a bag of seeds to Duke Ferdinando de' Medici in Florence, explaining to him that 'it makes very good polenta'. From the tables of the poor, polenta had reached the tables of the rich.

Here a sad episode in the history of polenta has to be recorded. By the early eighteenth century a strange new disease began to be noticed and written about. Characterised by red skin lesions, digestive disturbances, weakness and even mental and physical degeneration, the disease acquired the name of pellagra, from *pelle agra*, meaning rough skin. The symptoms occurred in the spring of each year, after a winter of eating little else but polenta. In 1786, Goethe wrote in his *Italian Journey*: 'Their features spoke of misery and their children looked just as pitiful . . . I believe the unhealthy condition is due to their constant diet of maize and buckwheat or, as they call them, yellow and black polent.' Not unnaturally, polenta was blamed, and before long its consumption was forbidden by law. There followed widespread suffering as a result of malnutrition and hunger; in a few years the food that had been the main nourishment of many thousands of people had been taken away and declared fit only for animals.

It was not until the beginning of the twentieth century, when vitamins were discovered, that the truth emerged. Pellagra was not due to any substance contained in the maize, but rather to a serious deficiency of protein and vitamins that occurs when maize is the principal, or indeed the only, source of nourishment.

Polenta has been acclaimed, written and sung about and altogether celebrated more than any other Italian food. Societies were formed in Italy and abroad, some of which concealed political movements behind the pretence of discussions on the merits of a dish of polenta. The most famous society was the *Ordine dei Polentoni*, formed in Paris in the second half of the nineteenth century. The order numbered many well-known people among its members, including the painter de Nittis, the writers Emile Zola and Edmond de Goncourt and the musician and librettist Arrigo Boito, who wrote a long poem in Venetian dialect on the art of stirring polenta. Polenta also inspired artists such as Magnasco and Longhi who, when representing a country interior, showed golden polenta being poured out of a copper *paiolo* on to a white tablecloth as the centrepiece of their paintings, a *paiolo* being the vessel in which, traditionally, polenta is made. It has the shape of a wide, round-bottomed bucket, with a bucket handle, and it is made of unlined copper.

The actual making of polenta is a ritual, described by Giovanni Arpino, a twentieth-century writer, in nostalgic mood. 'Between the stirring of the polenta, the eating and the next unavoidable hunger, you had to devote a day to it. In the slower world, in the world that ignored frenzies, polenta acted as a clock. Can you seek, or find, these virtues in a lobster or a soufflé or even a raviolo? It is the unique, golden, refuge-food.' And Alessandro Manzoni, in *I Promessi Sposi*, wrote that when smoking polenta was turned out on to the board it 'looked like a harvest moon in a large circle of mist'.

The golden moon is a very versatile food; it is so ready to be matched with others that in the province of Cuneo in Piedmont they call it *La Traviata*. It goes with butter and cheeses, with rich stews, with game and with salt cold. Left over, polenta makes rich layered dishes – *polenta pasticciata* – or it is fried or grilled to accompany many meat and fish dishes. Polenta is to an alpine Italian what pasta is to the southerner. Sadly it has lost ground to the all-conquering pasta, and this is partly because, for all its virtues, polenta is certainly not fast food.

how to make polenta

First you will need the ground maize, of which there are two kinds: finely ground for a soft, thin polenta, and coarsely ground maize, with glassy-looking grains, from which a harder and tastier polenta is made. The disadvantage of the latter is that it needs a longer cooking time to break down the harder outside casing of the grain. Then as you are unlikely to have a *paiolo* – the copper pot for polenta – hanging in your chimney, you will need a large saucepan, a long and stout wooden spoon, a strong arm and some 45 minutes at your disposal. (Which explains why, in Italy, you can now buy a gadget that you plug in and set to stir for the prescribed time.)

Next fill the saucepan with 1.75 litres (3 pints) of water and bring to the boil. Add 1/2 tablespoon of salt and remove the pot from the heat. Add 300 g (10 oz) of ground maize in a thin stream, while stirring constantly. When you have added all the flour, return the pot to the heat and bring the polenta to the boil. Continue stirring for at least 10 minutes and then you can attend to other little jobs in the kitchen, as it is enough if you give the polenta a strong hard stir every minute or so. You should let it cook for at least 40 minutes.

When the polenta is done, turn it out on to a wooden board on which you have laid a large white napkin. The polenta is now ready to be served with the dish of your choice, or to be allowed to cool before being cooked again to make other dishes.

To remove the polenta that is stuck to the bottom of the pan (never an easy job), fill the pan with enough water to cover the polenta that is sticking and leave it for up to 24 hours, after which it should come away easily. In the country of my youth this polenta from the bottom of the pan was given to the chickens. I now give it to my dog, Poppy.

What I have described above is the traditional time-honoured method of making polenta. There are, however, two others. The first is to make polenta in a pressure cooker.

Put 1.5 litres (2 1/2 pints) of water and 1/2 tablespoon of coarse salt in the pressure cooker and bring to the boil. Turn the heat down until the water is just simmering. Add 400 g (14 oz) of ground maize in a very thin stream, letting it run through your clenched fist, while with the other hand you stir rapidly with a long wooden spoon, always in the same direction. When you have added all the flour, turn the heat up and bring to the boil, stirring constantly. Fit the lid on the pressure cooker and bring to pressure. Put the weight in position and cook for 20 minutes. The polenta is now ready.

The second method is to make polenta in the oven. Start off in the traditional way and cook the polenta for 10 minutes or so. After that transfer it to a generously buttered oven dish, cover it with buttered foil and place it in a preheated oven (190°C/375°F/mark 5) for 1 hour.

The easiest method, however, is to buy '*Polenta Istantanea*' – precooked polenta, that can be made in 5 minutes flat. It compares quite well with the real McCoy.

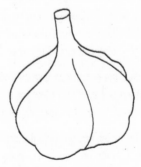

baked polenta with cheeses
polenta pasticciata in bianco

Serves 8
**polenta made with
400 g (14 oz) maize
flour and 2 litres
(3 1/2 pints) water
béchamel made with
1 litre (1 3/4 pints)
full-fat milk, 75 g
(2 1/2 oz) Italian 00
flour and 100 g
(3 1/2 oz) unsalted
butter
1/2 tsp grated
nutmeg
120 g (4 oz)
Gorgonzola, cut into
small pieces
120 g (4 oz)
Emmental, cut into
small pieces
120 g (4 oz) Taleggio,
cut into small
pieces
60 g (2 oz) freshly
grated Parmesan
freshly ground black
pepper**

When I was in Milan for a brief visit recently it was cold and foggy after months of warm sunny weather. My friends seemed quite pleased with the change and I knew why, since I remembered how I felt when I lived there. After a summer that seemed to consist of an endless succession of scorching days, you really long for the winter with its bright piercing cold, the wet snow and the long evenings when you stroll from one inviting warm shop to the next. Cold weather suits Milan, and Milanese cuisine excels in dishes made for winter nights.

During my recent visit I had this polenta dish twice, once for lunch, when it was the *piatto unico* – the only course – and another time for dinner. Traditionally this is the most wintry of all polenta dishes, since it contains Taleggio and Gorgonzola, two cheeses that used to be made in the autumn. They were made when the cows came down from their Alpine pastures, back to their winter sheds in the plains near Bergamo, for the Taleggio, and near Milan for the Gorgonzola. Alas, there are no longer any cows in Gorgonzola; they had to make way for the pink, green and blue high-rise flats of the sprawling suburbs of Milan. But the cheese is still made in many places in Lombardy, as, also, is Taleggio. Both cheeses are produced industrially all year round, and both are subject to strict controls as to their origins, similar to the DOC applied to wine. Gorgonzola and Taleggio are table cheeses, but they are used in cooking too because of their melting properties. In this recipe they add creaminess as well as flavour to the béchamel, into which they are mixed together with Emmental and Parmesan.

Make the polenta as directed on page 69, using the baked method, which is easier and ideal for this recipe. The polenta must be prepared at least 3 hours in advance so that it can cool through.

When cold, cut the polenta into 5 mm (1/2 inch) slices. If a hard crust has formed at the top, cut it away with a sharp knife.

Now make the béchamel. Heat the milk to simmering point. Melt the butter in another pan and blend in the flour. Cook for 30 seconds or so and then draw off the heat and begin to add the milk, a couple of tablespoons at a time. Continue beating and adding the hot milk until all the milk has been properly incorporated. Put the pan back on the heat and bring to the boil, stirring constantly. Season with the nutmeg.

Now continue cooking the sauce for about 10 minutes either in a bain-marie or using a flame disperser. Add the Gorgonzola, Emmental and Taleggio. Stir until dissolved and then mix in the Parmesan and the black pepper. Taste and add salt if needed; this may not be necessary, since the cheeses may have seasoned the sauce enough. Continue the cooking and stirring until the sauce is smooth and creamy once again. The sauce should be of the same consistency as thin double cream. Add a little more hot milk if it has dried too much during the cooking.

Heat the oven to 200°C (400°F) mark 6.

Butter a large, shallow oven dish. Spread 2–3 tablespoons of the cheese sauce over the bottom and cover with polenta slices, then spread some more cheese sauce over. Make another layer of polenta slices and dress with cheese sauce. I prefer to choose an oven dish in which the polenta will fit in 3 layers. Do not pile the polenta into too many layers or the dish will become stodgy.

Bake for about 15–25 minues, depending on the number of layers and on whether the dish has been prepared totally in advance and is therefore cold when you put it in the oven. When ready, the top should show patches of golden crust here and there.

preparation
The dish can be prepared up to 1 day in advance and covered tightly. It does not need to be kept in the fridge.

grilled polenta and fried polenta
polenta alla griglia e polenta fritta

The two most usual ways of cooking left-over polenta in northern Italy are grilling and frying. If you prefer to grill it, cut the cold polenta into slices 1–2 cm (1/2–3/4 inch) thick and place them on the grill rack. Brush each slice with olive oil and put under a preheated grill until a crust forms.

Alternatively, left-over polenta, cut as above, can be fried in a little butter or oil in a very heavy-based pan. Fry the slices until a translucent crust forms, then turn them over and fry the other side.

Polenta alla griglia and *polenta fritta* are used as accompaniments to many dishes, including game and *fritto misto* – fried fish.

polenta with pizza topping
pizzette di polenta

This is another excellent way to use left-over polenta. Cut the cold polenta into 5 cm (2 inch) squares. Dribble a little olive oil over each square, cover with a slice of mozzarella and top that with a dollop of well-drained, peeled and chopped tomatoes. Sprinkle some oregano over the *pizzette*, add plenty of pepper and dribble some more olive oil. Bake in a hot oven until the cheese has melted – about 5 minutes.

If you make smaller squares you can serve the *pizzette* with drinks. They are good either hot or at room temperature. You can cover the polenta slices with different toppings, to make *polenta bruschetta*.

baked polenta with dried porcini and truffle flavouring
polenta pasticciata alla piemontese

Serves 4–6
**polenta made with
300g of maize
flour
45 g (1 1/2 oz) dried
porcini**

continued over >>

Here the cold polenta is cut into slices and pasticciata *– layered – with other ingredients. This can either be done by layering the polenta with a bolognese* ragù *and béchamel sauce, as with lasagne, or in the way described in this recipe. This same sauce can also be used in layers with lasagne.*

An optional ingredient here is the white truffle which is the gastronomic jewel of Piedmont. Nowadays white truffles are too precious to be

*cooked, but there is an excellent truffle paste which gives the dish a
delicious truffle flavour.*

Make the polenta at least 2 hours – or, if you like, 1 day – in advance,
as directed on page 69. It must be cold before you can prepare the
dish. To cool it, pour the polenta on to a board and shape it into a
rectangle that is about 5 cm (2 inches) thick, or pour it into a
rectangular dish previously rinsed with cold water.

Soak the dried porcini in a small bowl of warm water. I find that the
recommended half hour is often not enough to reconstitute them fully,
and I prefer to leave them for 1 hour. Lift them out gently, rinse them
under cold water and dry them very thoroughly. Chop them coarsely.

Strain the liquid of the porcini though a sieve lined with a piece of
muslin or some kitchen paper. Pour gently and you will find that any
sand or grit will be left at the bottom of the bowl.

Heat the milk until simmering.

Heat the oven to 220°C (425°F) mark 7.

Melt the butter in a heavy saucepan, add the chopped porcini and
sauté them gently for 10 minutes, adding a couple of tablespoons of
their liquid during the cooking, whenever necessary.

Stir in the flour and cook for 1 minute, stirring the whole time. Draw off
the heat and incorporate the milk gradually, as you do for a béchamel.
Add salt and pepper. Return the pan to the heat and bring to the
simmer. Put the saucepan in a larger pan half-filled with hot water, or
put a flame disperser under the pan (the easiest method), and continue
cooking the sauce for at least 15 minutes. I find that this slow cooking
is essential for a delicate and well-blended sauce. At the end mix in
the truffle paste. Check the seasonings.

Cut the cold polenta vertically into slices 10mm wide.

Lightly butter a 25 cm (10 inch) rectangular ovenproof dish or lasagne
tin. Spread 2 tablespoons of the mushroom sauce over the bottom.
Cover with a layer of polenta slices and then place some cheese slices
here and there. Sprinkle with some Parmesan and with a grinding of
pepper. Spread some sauce over the cheese and then cover with

**750 ml (1 1/4 pints)
full-fat milk**

**60 g (2 oz) unsalted
butter**

**50 g (1 3/4 oz) flour
sea salt and pepper**

**1 tbsp truffle paste
(optional)**

**120 g (4 oz) Italian
fontina, cut into
thin slices**

**100 g (3 1/2 oz)
Gruyère, cut into
thin slices**

**60 g (2 oz) freshly
grated Parmesan**

another layer of polenta. Repeat these layers until you have used up all the ingredients, finishing with the sauce.

Bake in the preheated oven for 15–20 minutes. Remove from the oven 5 minutes before you want to serve the dish.

preparation
The dish can be prepared totally in advance, even the day before. Bake it for a little longer so that it can heat through.

polenta english style
polenta all'inglese

The simplest of all polenta dishes, which used to be our Sunday supper when my children were young, is polenta with egg and bacon, a dish they used to compare to themselves – half Italian, half English and wholly remarkable! Cook your polenta in the usual way. Mix in a good lump of butter and serve topped with fried eggs and surrounded by bacon rashers, crisply fried.

The Italians are said to eat more bread than any other nation in the world. They prefer their bread fresh, which often means bread baked the same day, yet their education, culture and innate thrift have never allowed bread to be thrown away. So it happened that, once the animals had been fed with the stale bread, other ways of using it had to be found. Thus some of the best recipes of the *cucina povera* were created, *cucina povera* meaning not poor cooking but cooking as done by the poor. It is in fact a cooking rich in flavour, originality and local aromas. Try the *pancotto* on page 79, one of the innumerable versions of this soup made up and down the country, and you will see what I mean. The bread used is usually white, but it is the thick, coarse, grey country bread and not the light airy rolls usually eaten at the table.

I keep a loaf of white bread, cut in half, in the freezer for the many times I need bread in my recipes. Brown bread has a nutty, malty taste that would often interfere with the dish I want to make.

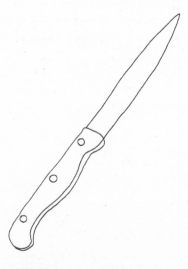

grilled bread with olive oil, garlic and tomato
bruschetta toscana

Serves 6–8

6 ripe firm tomatoes, preferably plum tomatoes

a handful of fresh basil leaves

8 slices good crusty bread, about 1 cm (1/2 inch) thick

4 garlic cloves, peeled and crushed

sea salt and black pepper

4 tbsp extra virgin olive oil

Bruschetta *is the millennium dish* par excellence *in Great Britain. But in Rome, its place of origin, it has been made for ever. The name derives from* bruscare, *which in the local dialect means to burn slightly.*

The Roman bruschetta *is usually made without tomatoes, while the original Tuscan version has a few ripe tomatoes sprinkled on top. This is the version I prefer, provided I can find good tomatoes. A 'good' tomato should be ripe but not mushy, juicy but not watery, with plenty of firm pulp, few seeds and a tomatoey scent.*

Nowadays bruschetta *is topped with all sorts of things, although to my great relief I haven't yet come across a* bruschetta *of pineapple and ham, as on a pizza. I'm sure it will come.*

Blanch and skin the tomatoes, cut them in half lengthwise, and remove as many seeds as you can. Dice the tomatoes into 1.5 cm (3/4 inch) cubes.

Wash and dry the basil. Tear the leaves into small pieces.

Grill the bread slices on both sides and then rub them on each side with the garlic. Cut each slice in half, to make them easier to eat.

Spoon some tomato cubes and some basil leaves over each slice and sprinkle with a little salt and a generous grinding of pepper. Dribble the olive oil over the bread and serve at once.

bread soup
pancotto

Every region, town, village and family in Italy has a favourite pancotto, *and here is mine. It is the best way to use up left-over white bread.*

Break the bread up into pieces and process for a few seconds.

Put half the oil, the chilli, garlic and parsley in a heavy stockpot (earthenware is best) and sauté for about 1 minute, stirring constantly. Add the bread and coat it in the oil for about 5 minutes, until it begins to become golden and then pour on the stock and simmer for 35–40 minutes, uncovered. Taste and adjust the seasonings.

Ladle the soup into individual bowls and divide the rest of the oil between them. Serve with the cheese handed round separately in a bowl.

I prefer to serve this soup at room temperature, especially in the summer.

Serves 4
200 g (7 oz) good quality white bread, stale and with the crust removed
4 tbsp extra virgin olive oil
1 dried chilli, or more according to taste, crumbled
3 garlic cloves, peeled and chopped
3 tbsp chopped flat-leaf parsley
1.5 litres (2 1/2 pints) vegetable or light meat stock
sea salt and freshly ground black pepper
freshly grated pecorino or Parmesan for serving

bread and tomato soup
pappa col pomodoro

This thick bread and tomato soup is well known to the Chiantishire contingent, and is so good that it should be popular with everyone. The best bread to use is pan pugliese, *which is now available from delicatessens, Italian shops and large supermarkets.*

When I was in Tuscany not long ago I had this soup served in hollowed-out michette – *bread rolls – a very attractive presentation. It is a perfect soup for an informal festive party, especially in the summer when the best tomatoes are in the shops.*

Break the bread into small pieces and put in a large bowl.

Bring the stock slowly to the boil and pour over the bread. Leave for 15 minutes, stirring occasionally to break up the bread.

Serves 12
700 g (1 1/2 lb) good-quality stale white bread, with the crust removed
4.5 litres (7 3/4 pints) home-made vegetable stock (page 487), or 6 vegetable bouillon cubes dissolved in the same quantity of water

continued over >>

225 ml (8 fl oz) extra
virgin olive oil
3 onions, chopped
sea salt
2 tsp sugar
a dozen garlic cloves,
peeled and very
finely chopped
2.25 kg (5 lb) fresh
tomatoes, skinned
and coarsely
chopped
4 tsp tomato purée
45 g (1 1/2 oz) fresh
basil leaves
freshly ground black
pepper

Heat the oil with the onion in a saucepan, preferably earthenware, which retains the heat and prevents the onions from burning. Add a teaspoon of salt to the onion to release the moisture, and the sugar. When the onion is soft but not brown, add the garlic, tomatoes and tomato purée. Cook, stirring frequently, for 5 minutes and then add the bread and stock mixture. Cook over a gentle heat for 40 minutes, stirring occasionally.

Five minutes before the soup is ready, add the basil and a generous grinding of black pepper. Serve warm or at room temperature, not piping hot.

preparation

You can prepare the soup up to 2 days in advance and keep it in the fridge.

bread gnocchi
canederli

Serves 4 as a first
course or 6 as an
accompaniment
to a stew

300 g (10 oz)
wholemeal bread
and good-quality
white bread
about 300 ml (1/2
pint) milk
200 g (7 oz) smoked
bacon
75 g (2 1/2 oz)
unsalted butter
1 medium onion, very
finely chopped

continued over >>

These gnocchi are, like their name, the Italian version of the Austrian knödel. They can be made with wholemeal or coarse white bread – any bread, in fact, as long as it is good – and they can be as large as oranges or as small as walnuts. When they are big they are served with goulash, which is the traditional way, or with other meat stews. I prefer small canederli, dressed with butter, melted until it becomes just lightly nutty, flavoured with a little sprig of rosemary and a few fresh sage leaves or with caraway seeds. I use stale left-over wholemeal and white bread mixed together, with the crust left on. It is one of the most successful dishes one can make from the old pieces of bread at the bottom of the bread bin.

The canederli are boiled in stock.

You can make bread gnocchi di magro, for vegetarians, by leaving out the bacon and putting in more onion, parsley and Parmesan.

Break the bread into small pieces and put in a bowl.

Heat the milk and pour over the bread to cover it. Leave for about 3 hours. You might have to add a little more milk after a while; it is difficult to be exact, but what you should have at the end is a moist yet solid mixture. Break it up very thoroughly with a fork. It is important to incorporate as much air as you can while beating, and for this reason you should not use a food processor, which would mash the mixture and make it gluey. After you have broken up the larger lumps of bread, however, you can use an electric beater. The mixture should not be puréed but should appear like wet cracked wheat.

Fry the bacon in a non-stick pan until it changes colour and part of the fat has run out. Cut the bacon into tiny cubes and add to the bread mixture. You can use a food processor to do the bacon, but keep an eye on it and stop it as soon as the bacon is coarsely chopped.

Pour off the bacon fat from the frying pan and put in 15 g (1/2 oz) of butter and the onion. Sauté very gently for 5 minutes, stirring very frequently, and then add the parsley. Continue to cook for a further minute. Mix in 3 tablespoons of the Parmesan and add the contents of the pan to the bread mixture, together with 2–3 tablespoons of flour.

Lightly beat the eggs and add to the mixture together with the nutmeg and salt and pepper to taste. Now mix everything together very thoroughly, lifting it lightly, using a large metal spoon.

Before you make the gnocchi, shape one dumpling and slide it into a small saucepan of boiling water. If it holds its shape, proceed to make all the dumplings; if it breaks, add a little flour to the mixture and test once more.

Put some flour on the work surface. Pluck out small spoonfuls of the mixture, shape them into ovals or balls and coat them lightly in the flour. This sticky job is much easier to do with moist hands: I keep a damp cloth nearby and wipe my hands whenever necessary.

Put the gnocchi on a tray lined with a clean tea-towel and put the tray (or trays) in the fridge for at least 30 minutes. It does not matter if you leave them longer.

3 tbsp chopped flat-leaf parsley
45 g (1 1/2 oz) freshly grated Parmesan cheese
several tablespoons of Italian 00 flour
2 free-range eggs
pinch of grated nutmeg
sea salt and freshly ground black pepper
3 litres (5 1/4 pints) meat or vegetable stock
1 tsp finely chopped fresh rosemary
4–5 sage leaves, finely chopped

Bring the stock to the boil. Taste and adjust the salt and then gently drop in the gnocchi. When the stock comes back to the boil, regulate the heat so that it will keep a low but steady simmer. Do not let the stock boil vigorously, or the gnocchi will break up. Let them simmer for 20 minutes and then take them out with a slotted spoon and put them on a board lined with kitchen paper to drain. (Keep the stock for a soup, it is even tastier than it was before you started the dish.)

Heat the oven to 200°C (400°F) mark 6.

Transfer the gnocchi to a buttered ovenproof dish that is large enough for the gnocchi to fit more or less in a single layer.

Heat the rest of the butter with the rosemary and the sage in a small pan until the butter turns a deep gold. Remove and discard the herbs, pour the butter over the gnocchi and sprinkle with a little of the remaining cheese. Put the dish in the oven for a few minutes and then serve, with the rest of the cheese on the side.

preparation
You can prepare the gnocchi in advance and then heat them in the oven, covered in foil, for 20 minutes or so. These gnocchi are also very good dressed with a tomato sauce, as is done in Trentino.

When you serve these gnocchi with meat, make them larger – the size of a mandarin orange. They look better and it also takes less time.

bread cake
torta di pane

The bread puddings made from stale bread in Italy are quite different from the English equivalent. The Italian version is like a cake, unmoulded and served cold. There are as many different versions as there are regions of Italy, and a few more.

You can use bits of chocolate, or almonds and other nuts, in place of the candied peel – in fact you can vary it as you like, according to what you have in your store cupboard. You could also use less cream and more milk, or vice versa, to suit your taste, your diet or your health worries. I think my recipe is a reasonable compromise.

One of my secrets is to keep a small jar of sultanas steeped in rum ready for use; being already soaked, and in rum rather than in water, they come in very handy. Alternatively, you can soak them in marc or in brandy, and simply add them with the spirit to your pudding.

Heat the oven to 190°C (375°F) mark 5.

Cut the bread roughly and toast it in the oven for 5 minutes and then put in a bowl.

Bring the milk, butter and cream to the boil and pour over the bread. Beat well and leave to cool.

Meanwhile soak the sultanas in the rum for 15 minutes.

When the bread and creamy milk mixture is cool, beat it with a fork until soft and mushy. Add the sugar, sultanas and rum, lemon rind, spices, candied peel and pine nuts and mix very well.

Lightly beat the egg yolks and add to the bread mixture. Whip the egg whites until they form stiff peaks, but are not dry, and fold them gently into the mixture.

Line a buttered 18 cm (7 inch) cake tin with parchment paper, butter the paper and spoon the mixture into it. Bake for about 1 hour, turn the oven down to 150°C (300°F) mark 2 and bake for a further 20 minutes, or until a skewer inserted into the middle of the cake comes out dry.

Serves 8
150 g (5 oz) one- or two-day-old, good-quality white bread with the crust removed
200 ml (7 fl oz) full-fat milk
75 g (2 1/2 oz) unsalted butter
300 ml (1/2 pint) single cream
45 g (1 1/2 oz) sultanas
3 tbsp rum
120 g (4 oz) caster sugar
grated rind of 1 organic lemon
pinch of ground clove
1/2 tsp ground cinnamon
pinch of ground ginger
pinch of powdered saffron
30 g (1 oz) candied peel, chopped
30 g (1 oz) pine nuts
3 free-range eggs, separated
icing sugar

Allow to cool in the tin and then unmould and peel off the paper.
Before serving, sprinkle lavishly with icing sugar.

preparation
This cake is better made a day in advance, to allow all the flavours to
blend together.

dried breadcrumbs

In every Italian fridge there will be a jar of dried breadcrumbs, an
essential ingredient in many dishes. Breadcrumbs are used to thicken
sauces, as in salsa verde, to scatter on gratin dishes to form a thin
crust, and sprinkled into buttered tins to prevent cakes from sticking.
They are also added to most stuffed dishes, while in southern Italy they
are sometimes used instead of grated cheese in pasta dishes.

Dried breadcrumbs should be made with good-quality white bread
which is coarse in texture. White bread is best because breadcrumbs
should be tasteless as they are used as a background to other
ingredients. To make the breadcrumbs, break the bread into small
pieces and toast them in the oven. The pieces are then processed until
they become crumbs. The breadcrumbs should be stored in the fridge
in an airtight container, but they should not be kept for longer than two
months. I always make a lot of breadcrumbs, fill one jar and put the
rest in another jar in the freezer, where they will keep for several
months.

soup with breadcrumbs, cream, egg yolks and parmesan
zuppa di pangrattato

This soup is derived from a recipe in Cucina Teorica-Pratica *by Ippolito Cavalcanti, Duke of Buonvicino, which was published in 1837. This book is one of the two most authoritative works on Neapolitan cooking, the other being* Il Cuoco Galante *by Vincenzo Corrrado. In his book, Cavalcanti presents 25 menus for each of four basic ingredients: fish and seafood, eggs and vegetables. The menus emphasise the harmony so important to a well-balanced meal. The soup I have chosen, which is included in his egg section, can be made, as Cavalcanti suggests, with chicken or fish stock.*

Cut the bread into small cubes. Heat the butter and the oil in a frying pan until very hot. Add the bread and fry until golden. Transfer with a slotted spoon to kitchen paper to drain.

Bring the stock to the boil. Add the dried breadcrumbs, stirring constantly and simmer for 5 minutes.

Meanwhile beat the egg yolks lightly with a fork. Add the cream, lemon juice, Parmesan and plenty of pepper and continue beating until well blended. Draw the soup off the heat and beat in the egg and cream mixture. Taste and add salt if necessary.

Ladle the soup into heated bowls, sprinkle with the parsley and serve at once, with the fried bread cubes handed round in a bowl.

Serves 6

4 slices of good-quality white bread, 1 cm (1/2 inch) thick with the crust removed

45 g (1 1/2 oz) unsalted butter

1 tbsp oil

1.35 litres (2 1/4 pints) fish stock (page 486) or chicken stock (page 485)

5 tbsp dried white breadcrumbs

3 free-range egg yolks

120 ml (4 fl oz) double cream

3 tbsp lemon juice

45 g (1 1/2 oz) freshly grated Parmesan

sea salt and freshly ground pepper

4 tbsp chopped flat-leaf parsley

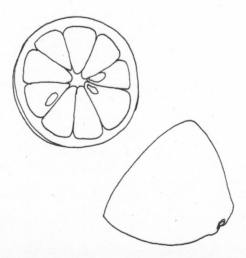

Chick-peas and other pulses were everyday food in Roman times. Horace, in one of his Odes, talks of going home to his supper of lasagne and chick-peas – *ciceri* in Latin. Indeed, one of Cicero's ancestors is said to have acquired the name because he had a wart on his nose that looked like a chick-pea. In the Middle Ages pulses were valued highly enough to be accepted as currency in the payment of taxes or alimony. By the Renaissance, however, pulses had fallen out of favour. In 1589 a doctor from Bologna, Baldassare Pisanelli, wrote that beans were 'food for peasants, not suitable for refined people'. Worst of all, lentils 'are harmful to melancholy people, make one have horrible dreams, fatten the blood in such a way that it cannot run in the veins . . . induce leprosy, cancer and other melancholy infirmities'.

All this reads very strangely nowadays, when pulses are considered among the healthiest of foods, and their popularity is so widespread. It is a well-deserved popularity, as they are quite delicious whether on their own, in combination with many other ingredients or mixed together in salads dressed with olive oil and generously flavoured with herbs.

The pulses that feature most often in Italian cooking are various varieties of the common bean, broad beans, lentils and chick-peas. The common bean (*Phaseolus vulgaris*), which reached Italy from the New World, quickly became a great favourite. It began to be successfully cultivated in Veneto early in the sixteenth century. It is said that Charles V gave a sack of these beans to Pope Clement VII, who in turn presented them to one Piero Valeriano, a tutor at the court of the Medici. Valeriano distributed the beans among the country people of Lamon, not far from his native Belluno, and when they planted some of these foreign beans an excellent crop resulted. Thus were born the *fagioli di Lamon*, which are large, with a very tender skin and a full flavour.

Different varieties were successfully developed from the *fagioli di Lamon*, of which the *borlotti* are perhaps the most popular. It is in northern Italian recipes that *borlotti* have come into their own, while Tuscany has given us the best ways to use the white *cannellini*. These include the *ribollita*, which is a soup based on *cannellini* and *cavolo nero*, and the *fagioli all'uccelletto* (dried beans with garlic, sage and oil). Just as remarkable are the various versions of *pasta e fagioli* from Veneto.

The motherland of broad beans is Puglia, where they are staple fare all year round. There, broad beans are mostly eaten dried, as in the excellent dish we had when we visited a farmhouse near Cisternino in Puglia. The first thing we noticed when Maria, the farmer's wife, showed us around was that, although there was only one very small sitting room totally dedicated to a leather suite and a massive television set, there were no less than three kitchens – 'one for everyday use, one for making pasta and the third for visitors,' Maria explained. It was fairly late in the evening as we sat in the visitors' kitchen drinking the strong local wine, but nonetheless a large bowl full of a purée of dried beans was placed in the middle of the table. Called *'ncapriata*, it was a soft creamy mixture of puréed dried broad beans and boiled turnip tops, flavoured with garlic and generously dressed with thick local oil. Even after a good dinner, this simple dish was memorable. I have made it here in Britain, using turnip tops or the long *cicoria* sold in Greek shops. Dried broad beans are sold in healthfood stores and Greek and Turkish shops, often already peeled.

The lentils of Italy are the brown variety, which keep their shape when cooked. The best ones are from Castelluccio, a town in Umbria. They are small and dark brown, with a full, sweet flavour, and they cook in only 20 minutes. When I ate them in Spoleto for the first time I wondered what Esau would have sold, had Jacob given him a dish of these lentils instead of the yellow Egyptian ones. Certainly much more than his birthright!

Chick-peas, like broad beans, are more popular in the South, where they are cooked very simply and are often mixed with pasta. Perhaps their popularity is due to their reputation as an aphrodisiac; they are one of the few peasant foods for which this claim is made.

how to choose and prepare pulses

The most important thing when buying pulses is to go to a supplier who has a quick turnover. In theory all dried pulses must be eaten within 12 months of being harvested – from one summer to the next – otherwise they stay hard however long you soak them, and they lose their flavour.

Lentils can be cooked without being soaked, a great advantage if, like me, you never plan a family meal in advance. Chick-peas and dried broad beans, on the other hand, need long soaking, sometimes as long as 24 hours, but certainly overnight. I soak chick-peas in the following way, which softens even the hardest skin. Cover the chick-peas with cold water. Make a thin paste with 1 teaspoon of bicarbonate of soda, 1 tablespoon of flour and 1 tablespooon of salt. Stir this mixture into the chick-peas and leave overnight. When they are ready, drain and rinse them, and cook them in unsalted water. Do not lift the lid of the saucepan for the first 1–1 1/2 hours, or the chick-peas may harden. Chick-peas sometimes take as long as 4 hours to cook, much longer than any other pulse.

When, as often happens, I have forgotten to put my beans in to soak for the recommended 6–8 hours, I fall back on the excellent method of boiling them for 2–3 minutes, draining and rinsing them and then cooking them in fresh water until soft: 1–1 1/2 hours is usually all they need. This method also makes the beans more digestible.

Cook pulses in an earthenware pot if possible. Add flavouring vegetables and herbs to the pot, but do not add salt until the very end of the cooking, about 10 minutes before they are ready. Harold McGee, in his *On Food and Cooking*, suggests cooking pulses in a small quantity of water, since 'the less cooking water, the fewer carbohydrates are leached out . . . So give the seeds enough water both to soak up *and* cook in, but don't drown them.'

Tinned pulses are a great shortcut and they can be bought everywhere. They are quite good but, whenever you can, I advise you to use dried ones because they have a far deeper flavour. And at the end of the cooking you are left with a most delicious stock to use to make soups.

red radicchio with borlotti beans
trevisana coi borlotti

Serves 4–5
**Two 400g (14 oz) tins
of *borlotti* beans
2 tbsp extra virgin
olive oil
1 clove of garlic,
chopped
sea salt and pepper
1 tbsp lemon juice or
vinegar (optional)
1 head of red
radicchio**

*While there is a strong contrast in the texture of these two ingredients,
their flavours blend beautifully. The beans are first heated so that they
absorb some of the oil more readily.*

Drain the *borlotti* beans from the tins. Rinse and heat them very gently
with a couple of tablespoons of water until hot. Drain and transfer the
beans to a bowl and leave them to cool. For the dressing, mix the
garlic and the oil and season with salt and pepper to taste. You can
add a tablespoon of lemon juice or wine vinegar if you wish.

Pile the *borlotti* within a circle of radicchio leaves and dribble the garlic
dressing all over the salad.

bean and pasta soup with radicchio
pasta e fagioli alla contadina

Serves 8
**450 g (1 lb) dried
borlotti beans
2 floury potatoes,
cut into large
chunks
2.25 litres (4 pints)
vegetable stock or
water with bouillon
powder
sea salt
1 head of red
radicchio, about
200 g (7 oz)
150 ml (1/4 pint)
extra virgin
olive oil**

continued over >>

After years of eating various versions of pasta e fagioli, *I recently
came across an excellent recipe in the Trattoria Veneta in Milan,
where peasant dishes from Veneto are served to the sophisticated
Milanese. The* pasta e fagioli *was decorated with leaves of red
radicchio, over which was laid half a hard-boiled egg. I was surprised
by both. The owner told me that the* soffritto *(fried mixture) in the
soup was based on radicchio, hence the decoration, while the egg
was 'for nourishment'. After all, it was a peasant soup which would
have been the only course for the contadini of Veneto. He also told
me to mash the egg into the soup and mix it up. So I tasted, and
once again I was pleasantly surprised, this time by a slightly tart
flavour. 'Aceto', the owner said. 'Aceto?' I queried. 'Eh sì, signora' —
vinegar to counteract the fattiness of the lard with which the
soffritto was traditionally made, and it makes the beans more
digestible. Now the lard has been replaced by olive oil for health
and diet reasons.*

Soak the beans overnight in cold water, and then rinse and drain them and put them in a stockpot, preferably earthenware, with the potatoes. Cover with the stock or water to which you have added some vegetable bouillon powder, such as Marigold Swiss Vegetable Bouillon powder. Bring very slowly to the boil with the lid tightly on. Dried beans will take at least 1 hour to cook.

When the beans are soft, purée about two-thirds of the beans and the potato in a food mill or a food processor and return the purée to the pot. Taste, add salt and bring the soup back to the boil.

Remove 8 of the larger outside leaves from the radicchio head and wash them. Set aside. Cut the rest of the radicchio into small strips, and wash and dry them.

Put about two-thirds of the oil, the celery, onion, parsley and shredded radicchio in a frying pan, add a pinch of salt and sauté over a low heat until the vegetables are soft, about 10 minutes. Add to the soup together with the vinegar and cook for 15 minutes. Season with a good grinding of pepper.

Add the pasta to the soup. If the soup is too thick, add a little hot water before adding the pasta, but remember that this type of soup should be quite thick.

When the pasta is just done, draw off the heat, mix in half the cheese and allow the soup to stand for 5 minutes before serving it. Pasta in this kind of soup does not need to be *al dente*. Ladle the soup into soup bowls and pour over the remaining oil. Float the reserved radicchio leaves on the soup and lay half a hard-boiled egg over each leaf. Serve with the remaining Parmesan separately in a bowl.

preparation
The soup, without the pasta, is best prepared 1 or 2 days in advance and refrigerated. It also freezes very well. The pasta must be added just before serving.

1 celery stalk with its leaves, finely chopped
1 small onion, finely chopped
3 tbsp chopped flat-leaf parsley
4 tbsp good red wine vinegar
freshly ground black pepper
225 g (8 oz) small tubular pasta, such as *ditalini*
90 g (3 oz) freshly grated Parmesan
4 hard-boiled eggs, shelled and cut in half

prawn and bean salad
i ricchi e i poveri

Serves 6
450 g (1 lb) dried
   cannellini beans, or
   4 x 400 g (14 oz)
   tins *cannellini*
   beans
2 onions, cut in half
2 bay leaves
120 ml(3 1/2 fl oz)
   extra virgin olive oil
450 g (1 lb) shrimps
   or prawns,
   preferably raw
1 tbsp wine vinegar
4 tbsp lemon juice
good pinch of
   cayenne pepper
sea salt
6 tbsp chopped flat-
   leaf parsley
1 garlic clove,
   chopped

The name of this recipe, i ricchi e i poveri, *means the rich and the poor, and it is easy to see why. It is a recent development from the tunny fish and bean salad, and was created by Tuscan restaurateurs who, though not afraid to alter old recipes, like to keep within their cuisine's tradition of simplicity. The dish is better made with raw prawns, which are slowly becoming more easily available.*

If you are using dried *cannellini*, put them in a bowl and cover with cold water. Leave overnight. Drain and rinse them and put them in a stockpot (earthenware is best) with the onions and the bay leaves. Do not add salt, as it may make the beans burst. Cover with water by about 5 cm (2 inches) and cook at a slow and steady simmer until done. I cannot give you an exact time because it depends on the quality of the *cannellini* and how long they have been in storage, but it should take no longer thant 1 1/2 hours. Drain them (you can keep the liquid for a soup for another occasion) and fish out and discard the onions and the bay leaves.

If you are using tinned *cannellini*, drain them into a colander and rinse them.

Transfer the beans to a large bowl, toss with half the oil and, only if you are using dried *cannellini*, season with 2 teaspoons of salt. (The tinned ones are already salted.)

Now prepare the seafood. When I use tiny shrimps, which are usually sold already cooked, I remove only the heads, leaving the carapace on. The carapace has a lot of flavour and, in the small specimens, can be chewed quite easily. You can, of course, peel them if you prefer. The prawns, however, must be shelled.

If you use raw prawns, which are of course better, put them in a saucepan, cover with cold water and add 1 tablespoon of salt and 1 tablespoon of wine vinegar. Bring to the boil and cook until a white foam forms on the surface. Drain the prawns and shell them while they are still hot. Raw prawns are usually large, so I suggest you cut them into small pieces.

Place the seafood in a second bowl and toss with the lemon juice.

Half an hour before serving, mix the shrimps or prawns gently into the beans.

Bring a saucepan of water to the boil, place the bowl over it, cover the bowl with a lid and heat the beans and seafood in this form of bain-marie. When the mixture is warm, dress with the remaining oil, season with the cayenne pepper and with salt if necessary and sprinkle with the chopped parsley and the garlic. Serve the salad while it is still warm.

chick-peas and rocket
ceci e rucola

I love the look of this salad, with the many-pointed green leaves of the rocket mixed in with the roundness of the chick-peas. I have used tinned chick-peas for this dish and they were perfectly all right, although I missed the fuller flavour of the dried ones. If you want to use dried chick-peas, see the instructions for soaking them on page 89. This is my lazy husband's favourite dish when he is alone: he opens a tin from the larder and collects the rocket from the garden. Easy, nourishing and really excellent.

The same recipe is good using lentils instead of chick-peas.

Drain the chick-peas and rinse quickly under cold water. Now, if you have time, squeeze the skin off the chick-peas one by one. This is much easier than it sounds, and quite quick, and it makes a big improvement to the final dish. Apart from avoiding pieces of skin between the teeth, it allows the oil to penetrate the chick-peas much better.

Heat half the oil and the garlic in a sauté pan. Add the chick-peas and heat until hot. Turn off the heat and leave the chick-peas to cool.

Remove the coarser stalks from the rocket and wash and dry the leaves.

Transfer the chick-peas to a salad bowl and add the rocket. Dress with the remaining oil, with salt to taste and plenty of pepper.

Serves 4
2 x 400 g (14 oz)
   tins chick-peas
5 tbsp extra virgin
   olive oil
1–2 garlic cloves,
   peeled and chopped
100 g (3 1/2 oz)
   rocket
sea salt and pepper

pasta and chick-peas
pasta asciutta e ceci

Serves 4
**150 g (5 oz) dried
  chick-peas
1 tbsp flour
1 tsp bicarbonate of
  soda
1 tsp sea salt
1 onion, cut in half
1 bay leaf
350 g (12 oz) small
  tubular pasta, such
  as *gnocchetti sardi*
  or shells
3 rosemary sprigs
2 garlic cloves,
  peeled
1 chilli, seeded
6 tbsp olive oil
225 g (8 oz) ripe
  tomatoes, skinned**

For this recipe I do recommend you use dried chick-peas – not tinned ones. You need some of the liquid for the best results.

Put the dried chick-peas in a bowl and cover with cold water. In a small bowl mix the flour, bicarbonate of soda and salt and add enough water to form a paste. Add this mixture to the chick-peas and leave for at least 8 hours to soften the skin.

The next day, drain and rinse the chick-peas and put them in a heavy pot. An earthenware pot of the sort you can put directly on the heat is the best for cooking pulses. Cover with water to come about 2.5 cm (1 inch) above the chick-peas, add the onion and the bay leaf, and cook, covered, at a gentle simmer until they are tender. This can take up to 3 hours, according to how long the chick-peas have been in store. Check that they stay covered with water. If necessary, add boiling water. Do not add salt to the pan until the chick-peas are nearly done; salt added at the beginning of the cooking will harden them. Do not lift the lid off the pan for the first hour or so; this would cool the water and toughen the skins.

When the peas are cooked allow them to cool a little in the liquid.

Now, if you have time, you should remove the skins from the chick-peas. The skin comes away very easily, but it is a lengthy job. However, the chick-peas are much better when skinned. The flavour of the *soffritto* – fried mixture – can penetrate the pulp of the chick-peas, and also you won't get unpleasant bits of papery skin between your teeth.

Cook the pasta in plenty of boiling salted water.

While the pasta is cooking chop the rosemary needles, the garlic and the chilli and put them into a large sauté pan with 4 tablespoons of the oil. I use a large, shallow earthenware (again!) dish. Sauté for a minute or so.

Cut the tomatoes in half, squeeze out and discard the seeds and the water and chop the flesh coarsely. Add to the rosemary and garlic *soffritto* and sauté for a couple of minutes. Add the chick-peas, scooping them out with a slotted spoon in such a way that a little of the liquid goes into the pan with them. Sauté for 5 minutes or so, coating the beans in the *soffritto*.

Drain the pasta when *al dente* and transfer quickly to the pan. Add the rest of the oil and stir-fry for about a minute. Serve immediately from the pan.

preparation
The chick-peas can be cooked up to 2 days in advance and refrigerated. They can also be frozen.

stewed lentils
lenticchie in umido

Vinegar is added to lentils to make them more easily digestible; I find cider vinegar more suitable here because it is sweeter.

Check that the lentils do not contain any stones or grit and then rinse and drain them.

Put the oil and the onion in an earthenware pot or a heavy-bottomed saucepan and sauté on medium heat until the onion is soft.

Add the sage to the onion, stir and then add the lentils. Stir until the lentils are well coated with oil and then add enough boiling stock to cover the lentils. Bring the liquid to the boil, turn down the heat, cover the pan and simmer for about 30–40 minutes. The cooking time varies depending on the variety of the lentils and also on how long they have been in store. During the cooking add a little hot water or stock if necessary, so that the lentils will not cook dry. Halfway through the cooking, stir in the vinegar and continue cooking until the lentils are tender. By the time they are cooked they should have absorbed nearly all the liquid.

Add salt and pepper to taste, mix well and serve at once.

preparation
Lentils are better done a day in advance. They can also be frozen.

Serves 6–8
450 g (1 lb) green lentils, such as Puy or Castelluccio
5 tbsp olive oil
1 onion, finely chopped
1.5–1.75 litres (2 1/2–3 pints) meat or vegetable stock
a dozen fresh sage leaves, chopped
2 tbsp cider vinegar
sea salt and freshly ground black pepper

The Italians' love of fish is reflected in every fishmonger's shop up and down the country. An amazing assortment of fish, nestling amongst crushed ice, is arrranged with neat precision on scrubbed Carrara marble. These shops are a joy to look at, a temple of cleanliness dedicated to the gifts of the waters. I often find myself staring at the display in some fishmonger's in Milan, only to have one of the assistants come up and ask what I would like. 'Oh, nothing,' I say, 'I was just admiring your fish.'

In the front row are the anchovies and sardines in their shiny silver-blue livery. Although these used to be fish for the poor, they are now exhibited with pride, since, alas, they are rare in the Mediterranean, their numbers having been decimated in the interests of the canners. Behind the blue fish are the mussels, clams, sea urchins, *canestrelli* – small scallops and date-shells, all tight shut waiting to finish their days in a soup, in a sauce for pasta or in a salad. Next to them are the large and small crustaceans, crawling sleepily over each other in a last attempt to survive. The delicious *moleche* – soft crabs from the Venetian lagoon – look naked and vulnerable next to the grey *cicale* – small flat lobsters. Cuttlefish, octopus and squid come in all sizes from the tiny *moscardini* no longer than 8 cm (3 inches) to big monsters who stare at you with their vacant deep blue eyes. The larger fish, the wild sea bass, daurade and turbot are displayed at the back of the shop for the mink-clad buyers who can afford to serve them at the dinner party they are giving that evening.

Unfortunately all too few fishmongers in Britain can offer such a profusion or such quality. Although there has recently been a great improvement in the choice of fish available, what is often still lacking is fish that is really fresh. Fresh fish straight from the sea has no trace of 'fishy' smell: it smells only of the sea. When you are in the shop, look at the fish's body; it should be bright and lively. Large fish last longer than small fish; sole, turbot or sea bass, for instance, do not go off as quickly as, say, sardines, mackerel or herring.

One last piece of advice: when you want fillets of small fish such as sole, plaice or whiting, buy the whole fish and have it filleted. It is usually fresher than the fillets, and the heads and bones you take home will make an excellent fish stock.

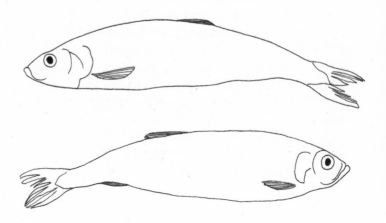

a light fish soup
zuppetta di pesce

In keeping with the fashion for lighter dishes, this zuppa di pesce *has often replaced the heavy* cacciucco, brodetto *and* burrida *of former days. It is a fresh, light* zuppa, *quite delicious and full of traditional Italian flavours. It is also less demanding to make than the heavier fish soups. Another advantage is that it does not depend so much on local fish, which means that it can be made with the more restricted selection of fish available in Britain.*

The fish head is quite necessary to give the soup flavour and body. If at all possible, buy uncooked prawns. If the prawns are frozen, defrost them completely before using them.

First clean the mussels, following the instructions on page 129, but do not cook them.

Shell the prawns and de-vein them if necessary. Wipe and skin the monkfish and cut into bite-sized pieces.

Heat half the oil in a pot, preferably earthenware, with the garlic, half the parsley and the chilli. Sauté until the garlic begins to change colour and then add the chopped tomatoes and the head of the fish. Splash with the wine and, as soon as it has nearly all evaporated, add about 900 ml (1 1/2 pints) of boiling water. Season with salt and cook for about 20 minutes.

Add the monkfish and the mussels and cook for 3 minutes. Add the prawns and cook for a further 2 minutes.

Lift the fish head out of the liquid and discard it (I add the cheeks to the soup). Dress the soup with the rest of the oil and the rest of the parsley. Taste and check the seasoning.

Put 2 slices of toasted *ciabatta* into each soup bowl and ladle the soup over it.

Serves 4
225 g (8 oz) mussels
450 g (1 lb) prawns
450 g (1 lb) monkfish
4 tbsp extra virgin olive oil
2 garlic cloves, cut into thick slices
2 tbsp chopped flat-leaf parsley
1 dried chilli
4 fresh plum tomatoes, peeled and seeded, or tinned plum tomatoes, coarsely chopped
1 fish head – cod or hake or other large white fish (but not salmon)
120 ml (4 fl oz) dry white wine
sea salt
toasted *ciabatta*

monkfish morsels with lentil purée
bocconcini di coda di rospo alla puré di lenticchie

Serves 8
1.35 kg (3 lb) monkfish
6 sage leaves
2 rosemary sprigs, about 10 cm (4 inches) long
1 garlic clove
3 tbsp olive oil
120 ml (4 fl oz) dry white wine
4 ripe tomatoes, skinned, seeded and chopped
sea salt and freshly ground pepper
4 tbsp chopped flat-leaf parsley

For the lentil purée
400 g (14 oz) lentils, Puy or Castelluccio
8 garlic cloves, washed but unpeeled
1/2 onion, stuck with 1 clove
2 bay leaves
2 tbsp wine vinegar
5 tbsp extra virgin olive oil
sea salt and pepper

I derived this recipe from an old one we used to make in my Milanese home: lentils and salt cod. Fish and lentils have complementary flavours which are very pleasing.

First prepare the lentil purée. Look through the lentils and pick out any tiny stones or pieces of grit. Rinse them and put them in a saucepan – ideally it should be an earthenware pot. Add all the other ingredients except the oil, salt and pepper, and add enough water to cover the lentils by about 2.5 cm (1 inch). Bring to the boil, turn down the heat so that the water simmers gently and cook until the lentils are very tender. How long this will take depends on the quality of the lentils and on the length of time they have been in storage. But they should be ready in about half an hour. Drain, reserving the liquid. Remove and discard the bay leaves and the garlic skins and the onion and clove and purée the lentils either through a food mill or in a food processor. Mix in enough of the lentil cooking liquid for the purée to be quite soft. Transfer to a clean saucepan and add the oil, salt and plenty of pepper. Taste, check the seasonings and keep warm over a low heat while you prepare the fish.

Trim all the grey skin and the membrane from the fish. (If left on they will cause the fish to shrink.) Cut the monkfish into 2.5 cm (1 inch) morsels and pat dry with kitchen paper.

Chop the herbs and the garlic and put into a large non-stick pan with the oil. Sauté for 1 minute and then add the fish and cook over moderate heat for about 3 minutes, shaking the pan frequently. Splash with the wine and let it bubble away for a minute or so while turning the fish over once or twice. Add the tomatoes and cook for 2 minutes. Season with salt and plenty of pepper to taste.

To serve, spoon the lentil purée around the outside of a heated dish and place the fish in the middle of the lentil ring. Sprinkle the parsley over the fish and serve at once.

preparation
The lentil purée can be made up to 3 days in advance and refrigerated, tightly covered. It can also be frozen.

monkfish and mussels in a tomato and saffron sauce
coda di rospo e cozze in salsa gialla

I had this very good dish at the home of one of our Venetian friends. It was a pleasant change from the usual grilled coda di rospo *one so often eats in restaurants in Venice.*

Clean and cook the mussels following the instructions on page 129. Remove and throw away the shells and put the mussels in a bowl. Strain the liquid into a small bowl though a sieve lined with muslin. Add the saffron to the liquid and stir well. Put aside.

Remove the dark skin from the monkfish, if still on, and remove the thin transparent skin, as this would cause the fish to shrink during the cooking. Wash and dry the fish, and cut into small chunks.

Put the tomatoes in a small saucepan and cook over a low heat for 10 minutes, stirring frequently, until they have become mushy.

Sauté the shallots or onion gently in the butter and oil until soft. Add the garlic, the chilli and about 2 tablespoons of the parsley and sauté for a further minute or so. Press the *soffritto* down against the bottom of the pan with a spoon to release the shallot liquid.

Add the fish and sauté for 3 minutes, turning it over and over. Splash with the wine and let it bubble away until there is only a little left.

Add the tomatoes and the saffron and mussel liquid, season with salt and pepper and continue cooking until the fish is done. This will take from 7–10 minutes depending on how big the pieces are. If there is too much liquid, remove the fish to a heated dish and reduce the liquid until it becomes rich and tasty. Add the mussels. Turn off the heat immediately as the mussels do not need to cook, only to heat up. Taste and check the seasoning. Transfer to the heated dish, sprinkle with the remaining parsley and serve with some boiled rice dressed with olive oil. No other accompaniment is needed, only a salad afterwards.

Serves 4
450 g (1 lb) mussels
1/4 tsp powdered saffron or saffron strands
800 g (1 3/4 lb) monkfish
225 g (8 oz) tomatoes, peeled and seeded and coarsely chopped or tinned plum tomatoes without their juice
2 shallots or 1/2 onion, finely chopped
15 g (1/2 oz) unsalted butter
3 tbsp olive oil
2 garlic cloves, peeled and chopped
1/2 small dried chilli, seeded and crushed
a bunch of flat-leaf parsley, chopped
100 ml (3 1/2 fl oz) dry white wine
sea salt and pepper

monkfish and tagliolini in a tomato sauce
coda di rospo e tagliolini in salsa

Serves 3–4
tagliolini made with
  200 g (7 oz) Italian
  00 flour and 2 free-
  range eggs or
  250 g (9 oz) dried
  egg **tagliolini** or
  tagliatelle
450 g (1 lb) monkfish
1 garlic clove, peeled
1 dried chilli, seeded
a bunch of flat-leaf
  parsley
100 ml (3 1/2 fl oz)
  extra virgin olive oil
sea salt and pepper
450 g (1 lb) ripe
  tomatoes, peeled

The ideal pasta for this dish is home-made tagliolini. *It is a simple dish that can be prepared with many different kinds of fish: monkfish, haddock, hake, cod or halibut, but not with blue fish such as herring which are too strong and oily. The cooking of the fish would vary, but the basic method will be the same. You can also serve the fish with boiled potatoes or boiled rice instead of* tagliolini.

First make the pasta dough as directed on page 27. Roll it out up to the last but one notch on the machine, or as thin as you can if you are rolling by hand.

Allow the pasta to dry and then put it through the narrow grooves of the cutting rollers of the machine, or, if you are cutting the pasta by hand, cut to a width of about 3–5 mm (1/8–1/4 inch)

Skin the fish fillets and cut into bite-sized chunks, removing any bones. Dry with kitchen paper.

Chop the garlic, chilli and parsley together and, in a non-stick pan, sauté in half the oil until you can smell the garlic. Add the fish, salt and pepper, cover the pan and cook for 10 minutes. Keep an eye on the fish, and turn it over once during the cooking.

While the fish is cooking, cut the tomatoes in half, squeeze out and discard the seeds and some of the water and cut the flesh into cubes. Add them to the fish and continue cooking for 5 minutes.

Meanwhile cook the *tagliolini* in salted water. Drain and return them to the cooking pot and dress immediately with the remaining oil.

Put the fish with all the sauce in the centre of a round dish and surround it with the pasta.

sole with artichoke purée
sogliole ai carciofi

This is a recipe I owe to Rita Stancescu, a Venetian friend no longer alive, alas, who was an excellent cook and who gave us many remarkable meals when we had a flat in Venice. The flat was near the Ca' d'Oro and whenever possible I started the day by visiting my two favourite places. First I went to the church of San Crisostomo, near Rialto, to revive my spirits with the perfect harmony of its architecture and with the beauty of the painting of the three saints by Sebastiano del Piombo. Then I retraced my steps and took the gondola ferry from Santa Sofia across the Canal Grande to shop at the Rialto market. Waiting for the ferry, or standing somewhat precariously in it, I chatted to the Venetians, who are the greatest chatterboxes in the whole of Italy.

At the market my first port of call was Sprizza, the cheese shop, for ricotta, mozzarella and the best *crescenza* ever. Then I walked in wonder up and down those amazing fish stalls seething with glistening fish, sometimes asking questions of the fishmongers and always comparing quality and prices. My expedition ended among the vegetable stalls, in the open space along the canal. We used to spend most Easters in Venice, just the right time for the *primizie* – the season's new vegetables – prominent among which were the local artichokes. The Venetians call them *canarini*, meaning little canaries, because of the yellowish colour of their tender leaves; in fact the *canarini* are so young and tender that you can eat them all when they are raw.

The combination of artichoke and fish is a very old one, and very good it is too. What differentiates Rita's recipe from the usual ones is that the artichokes are puréed, and it is this that makes the recipe suitable for the large, tougher Breton artichokes that we get in Britain.

Get your fishmonger to fillet the fish for you, rather than buying prepared fillets. The fish that is already filleted is often yesterday's (at best) so that you cannot see the part that gives its age away, the head.

Prepare the artichokes as directed on page 240. Cut the artichokes in half, scoop out and discard the fuzzy choke and then cut into thin vertical slices. Put the slices in a bowl of acidulated water. Remove and discard the tough outer layer of the stalks, cut the soft inside into rings and add to the bowl.

Serves 4

3 globe artichokes
3 tbsp olive oil
1 garlic clove, peeled and very finely chopped
a bunch of chopped flat-leaf parsley
a small bunch of chervil
a pinch of grated nutmeg
salt and pepper
30 g (9 oz) unsalted butter
3 Dover soles, filleted
150 ml (1/4 pint) double cream
4 tbsp freshly grated Parmesan

Heat the oil with the garlic and herbs in a sauté pan for about 1 minute. Add the artichoke slices and the stalk rings. Pour in about 100 ml (3 1/2 fl oz) hot water and add the nutmeg, and salt and pepper to taste. Cover the pan tightly and cook for about 45 minutes at the gentlest simmer – I use a flame disperser. Stir every now and then and add a couple of tablespoons of hot water whenever the artichokes seem too dry.

Preheat the oven to 200°C (400°F) mark 6.

Purée the artichokes and all the cooking juices through a food mill – quite hard work, but essential. A food processor does not do the job nearly as well, because it does not get rid of any remaining woody parts of the artichokes. But you can first whiz the artichokes in the food processor and then mill them – less hard work. Return the purée to the washed-out pan.

Choose a shallow ovenproof dish just large enough for the fillets to lie in a single layer. Grease the dish with half the butter. Sprinkle the fish with salt and pepper on both sides, place it in the dish in a single layer and dot with the rest of the butter. Cover tightly with foil and bake in the oven for about 10 minutes.

While the fish is cooking, heat the artichoke purée and mix in the cream and the cheese. Taste and check the seasoning.

Spoon the purée over the fish, cover with the piece of foil and return to the oven for a further 5 minutes. Allow the dish to cool for a few minutes out of the oven before bringing it to the table.

preparation
You can prepare the artichoke purée well in advance and chill it for up to 3 days, or freeze it.

apulian fish pie
tiella di pesce di claudia

This fish pie is an adaptation of an Apulian fish pie made by Claudia Wolfers, a young friend who is a good and enterprising cook. In a clever way she has partly anglicised my tiella by adding smoked haddock. The smoked haddock must be Finnan, which is now sold by most fishmongers. Do not attempt to make the dish with other self-styled smoked haddock, which sometimes is not even haddock, nor indeed smoked, having been dyed that dreadful bright yellow and given a smoke flavour artificially.

It is a perfect party dish to give to a gathering of friends.

Clean the mussels as directed on page 129.

Put the wine, 4 of the garlic cloves and the lemons in a large sauté pan. Bring to the boil and boil for 2 minutes. Add about half the mussels, cover the pan with a lid and leave them to steam open. Shake the pan every now and then, to turn the mussels over. When they are open, draw the pan off the heat.

Remove the mussels from their shells and put them in a bowl. Do this over the pan so that you collect the juices. Discard the shells.

Now put the remaining mussels into the pan and do the same again.

Strain the mussel liquor through a sieve lined with muslin into a bowl. Set aside.

Heat the milk, add the smoked haddock and cook for 2–3 minutes. Remove the fish from the milk, skin it and cut into pieces. Skin the fresh haddock fillets and cut into pieces.

Peel the potatoes and cut them into wafer-thin slices. A food processor with the fine blade disc is invaluable for the job. Put the potatoes in a bowl of cold water and rinse them as if you were washing them, to get rid of some of the starch. Drain them, dry them very thoroughly and put them in a bowl. Toss with 2 tablespoons of the oil and season with salt and pepper.

Heat the oven to 200°C (400°F) mark 6.

Serves 10

1.8 kg (4 lb) mussels
300 ml (1/2 pint) dry white wine
10 garlic cloves, peeled and bruised
2 organic lemons, cut into segments
300 ml (1/2 pint) skimmed milk
450 g (1 lb) smoked Finnan haddock
1 kg (2 lb) fresh haddock fillets
1.8 kg (4 lb) waxy potatoes
300 ml (1/2 pint) olive oil
sea salt and pepper
1 kg (2 lb) ripe tomatoes
6 tbsp chopped parsley
2 dried chillies, seeded and crumbled
225 g (8 oz) mature pecorino, grated
10 fennel seeds, pounded to coarse powder

Blanch the tomatoes and peel them. Cut them in half and squeeze out and discard some of the seeds and juice by pressing each half gently between your forefinger and thumb. Cut the flesh into slices.

Mix together in a bowl the parsley, chillies, pecorino and fennel seeds. Slice the remaining garlic cloves and add to the mixture with some salt to taste.

Grease a large lasagne dish or a shallow oven dish with a little oil. Cover the bottom with half the potatoes. Now make a layer with half the tomatoes. Sprinkle with one third of the herb and cheese mixture and place the smoked fish, the fresh haddock and the mussels on top. Sprinkle with half the remaining herb and cheese mixture and pour over half the remaining olive oil and half the mussel liquor. Cover with the remaining potatoes, then with the remaining tomatoes. Sprinkle with the remaining herb mixture and dribble the rest of the olive oil and the mussel liquor all over.

Cover the dish with a sheet of foil and place in the oven. After 20 minutes remove the foil and continue cooking until the potatoes are tender, about 40 minutes in all. Leave out of the oven for 5 minutes for the flavours to blend before serving.

preparation
The *tiella* is better made the day it is to be eaten, although the fish can be prepared up to 1 day in advance and refrigerated in a covered container.

red mullet

Red mullet is one of the best Mediterranean fish and one that, in Italy, has been highly prized since Roman times. It is usually cooked quite simply, often lightly flavoured with tomatoes and herbs, fennel being one of the most usual. Red mullet are easily available in Britain now.

red mullet with prosciutto and rosemary
triglie alla marchigiana

It seems odd, as in this recipe, to have prosciutto in a fish dish; it did indeed seem so to me when I first had these triglie. But the oddity turns out to be one of the most successful couplings of ingredients, and in fact the combination makes this dish one of the greatest of the cooking of Le Marche region. The link between the fish and the prosciutto is the rosemary.

Ask the fishmonger to scale and clean the fish, but to leave the liver inside as it is one of the best parts of a red mullet.

Heat the oven to 190°C (375°F) mark 5.

Wash the fish and dry them thoroughly inside and out. Lay them on a dish. Mix together the lemon juice and 2 tablespoons of the oil. Add salt and pepper and dribble a little of the mixture into the cavity of each fish. Brush the rest of the lemon and oil mixture all over the fish and leave to marinate for 2 hours.

Brush an oven dish with a little of the remaining oil.

Mix together the rosemary, garlic, breadcrumbs, a little salt and a generous amount of pepper. Coat the fish with the mixture, pressing the crumbs into it with your hands. Wrap a slice of prosciutto round

Serves 4
4 red mullet, cleaned but with the heads on
juice of 1 organic lemon
6 tbsp extra virgin olive oil
sea salt and freshly ground black pepper
2 tbsp chopped rosemary
1 garlic clove, peeled and chopped
6 tbsp dried breadcrumbs
4 large slices of prosciutto, not too thinly cut
2 organic lemons for garnish

each fish and lay the fish in the prepared dish. Dribble the remaining oil over and bake for 15–20 minutes, basting the fish twice during the cooking. Serve with the lemons cut into wedges.

red mullet en papillote with tomato, flavoured with garlic, ginger and basil
triglie al cartoccio

Serves 4
4 red mullet, about 250 g (9 oz) each
4 small tomatoes, ripe but firm, peeled
generous handful of fresh basil leaves
1 garlic clove, peeled
1 cm (1/2 inch) fresh ginger root, peeled
4 tbsp extra virgin olive oil
sea salt and freshly ground black pepper

Being so pretty and so tasty, red mullet is particularly suited to cooking al cartoccio. I have always liked to cook fish in this way, the main advantage being that the flavour of the fish is sealed in, plus the fact that there is no saucepan to wash up. In Italy this method of cooking has been used for centuries, and it is now a favourite with both hostesses and restaurateurs.

You can cook many things al cartoccio. My favourite is fish, but meat, too, is good done this way. Try pork fillets with mushrooms, a few dried porcini and a little vermouth. One warning: make sure you add the right amount of flavourings and seasonings. The food, once wrapped, stays that way until it reaches the table. When you cook fish al cartoccio you must be sure that it is fresh, because, with its juices sealed in the paper parcels, the flavour becomes concentrated.

In this recipe I add an exotic touch to the characteristic Mediterranean ingredients – a little chopped ginger which, as the Chinese have taught us, goes so well with fish and garlic. You can use foil instead of greaseproof paper, although personally I prefer to do it in the traditional way, with paper.

Ask the fishmonger to scale and clean the fish properly, but to make only a short slit underneath rather than a cut from the anal aperture to the head, a gash that ruins the look of the fish. Also ask him to leave the liver in, the *bonne bouche* of any red mullet lover. Naturally, head and tail must be left on, too. When you are at home check that the fish is properly scaled. Cut off the fins, and remove the gills if they are still there, since they can give off a bitter taste. Cut off a little of the tail, preserving its original shape, and wash the fish thoroughly. Leave it on a slanting board to drain and then dry it.

Heat the oven to 200°C (400°F) mark 6. Do not put the fish in the oven until you are sure it has reached the right temperature.

Cut the tomatoes in half, squeeze out and discard the seeds and the juice, cut the flesh into small cubes and put in a small bowl. Chop the basil leaves, garlic and ginger and add to the bowl with the oil. Mix everything together.

Cut 4 squares of greaseproof paper large enough to wrap around the fish and to fold together at the top and sides. Brush with a little oil.

Sprinkle the fish with salt and pepper inside and out. For each fish put a little of the tomato mixture on the square of paper, lay the fish over it and cover with another knob of the mixture. Now twist the paper over in tiny pleats all around the fish and seal well. Put the parcels in an oven tin. Cook in the hot oven for 15 minutes. For larger fish cook for longer.

Place the parcels on individual plates and open by cutting off the folded edges. Bring the plates to the table and let your guests eat from the paper dishes.

salmon carpaccio
carpaccio di salmone

Serves 8
**1 kg (2 lb) wild
salmon fillets or
salmon trout fillets
5 tbsp extra virgin
olive oil
6 tbsp lemon juice
sea salt and pepper
225 ml (8 fl oz)
single cream
cayenne pepper to
taste
1 fennel bulb**

The name Carpaccio is now used to describe any dish that features raw meat or raw fish. As is usually the case in gastronomy, there is no patent to protect the name or recipe from changes, embellishments or plagiarism. The original Carpaccio, made with raw fillet of beef, was created by Giuseppe Cipriani at Harry's Bar for his customer the Countess Nani Mocenigo. Some later versions that have sprung up in the last decade share nothing but the name with the original. In this recipe of mine, although there is fish instead of meat, the fish is finely sliced like the beef in the original Carpaccio. The other similarity is that a salmon Carpaccio like this one can certainly be as good as its famous progenitor. All it calls for is wild salmon, good extra virgin olive oil, lemon juice and the right length of time for the marinade.

If you are using salmon fillets cut them across into thin strips, but if you are using salmon trout fillets leave them whole.

Place the fish on a dish and dress with the olive oil, 2 tablespoons of the lemon juice, salt and pepper. Cover the dish with clingfilm and leave to marinate for 3–4 hours in the refrigerator.

Put the cream in a bowl and beat in 2 tablespoons of lemon juice, salt and cayenne pepper to taste. Add more lemon juice according to your taste.

About 1 hour before serving, transfer the fish, but not the juice at the bottom of the dish, on to individual plates and dribble over the cream mixture. Do not refrigerate any more, as Carpaccio is better eaten at room temperature.

Remove the stalks and any bruised part of the fennel. Keep any feathery top the fennel may have. Cut the fennel bulb into quarters lengthwise and then across into very thin strips. Wash, drain and dry the fennel and the feathery top.

Sprinkle the fennel strips and feathery top over the Carpaccio and serve.

steamed fish with a herb sauce
pesce in bianco con salsina alle erbe aromatiche

In this recipe I feel it is the fresh herb sauce that gives the dish its distinctive flavour. A pesce in bianco is a boiled or steamed fish. I prefer steaming, and this is the way I steam a single fish such as a sea bass, a wild salmon trout, a turbot or a large Dover sole of at least 1 kg (2 lb), which will serve 4 people. The fish keeps all its flavour and the cooking liquid is added to the herb sauce that accompanies the fish. The herb sauce is lighter and healthier than the usual mayonnaise. It is particularly good with salmon.

Put the dry white wine, and an equal quantity of water, in a fish kettle. Add the onion, carrot and celery stick, all cut in pieces, 1 or 2 garlic cloves, the bay leaves and 1 sprig each of parsley, rosemary and sage. Bring to the boil.

Cover the steamer rack with lettuce leaves (I use the green outside leaves that are too old for a salad). Season the fish inside and out, lay it on top of the lettuce leaves and cook for 5 minutes. Draw off the heat and let it cool in the kettle.

While the fish is cooling, put in a food processor the bunch of parsley leaves, the thyme, marjoram and fennel or dill and the basil. Process, pulsating the machine until the herbs are coarsely chopped. Scoop out the herbs and put them in a small bowl with the extra virgin olive oil, dried chillies and garlic cloves and leave to infuse.

When the fish is cold transfer it carefully to an oval dish and remove the skin if necessary. Strain the cooking juices and add to the bowl with the herbs mixture. Remove and discard the garlic and the chillies and add 2 tablespoons of lemon juice, and salt. Mix well, taste and check the seasonings. Serve with the fish surrounded by some steamed potatoes, which can be hot or cold.

preparation
If you do not have a fish kettle you can use a large oval pan with a tight-fitting lid or a deep roasting pan with a domed lid. Wrap the fish with the lettuce leaves and then loosely in foil, but without leaving any opening, put it in the pan with the wine, water and the flavouring vegetables and cook for 15–20 minutes.

Serves 4
1 whole salmon, trout or turbot, or Dover sole – about 1kg (2 lb)
150 ml (1/4 pint) dry white wine
1 onion
1 carrot
1 celery stick
1–2 garlic cloves
2 bay leaves
1 sprig each of parsley, rosemary and sage
lettuce leaves
sea salt and pepper

For the herb sauce
bunch of parsley leaves
1 tbsp each of thyme, marjoram and fennel or dill
12 basil leaves
4 tbsp extra virgin olive oil
2 dried chillies
2 garlic cloves
2 tbsp lemon juice

baked sea bream with tomatoes and basil
dentice al forno

Serves 8
**2 large sea bream
weighing about
1.35 kg (3 lb) each
sea salt and pepper
6 garlic cloves,
peeled and bruised
bunch of parsley,
chopped
6 tbsp olive oil
150 ml (1/4 pint) dry
white wine
8 ripe tomatoes,
peeled, seeded and
cubed
2 dried chillies
2 dozen fresh basil
leaves, torn into
small pieces
2 tsp anchovy purée**

Dentice *(dentex) is hardly ever found in Britain. But you can use a
daurade or a sea bream. This recipe is very easy, yet perfect for a
dinner party.*

Heat the oven to 200°C (400°F) mark 6.

Wash the fish and check that the fishmonger has removed all the
scales and the gills. Dry the fish thoroughly and season with salt and
pepper inside and out. Place 1 garlic clove and half a tablespoon of
parsley into each cavity.

Brush an ovenproof dish with 1 tablespoon of the oil and place the fish
in it. Pour over the wine and 3 tablespoons of the remaining oil and
place the dish in the oven. Bake for 25 minutes, basting occasionally.
The fish is ready when the eye bulges out and the flesh parts easily
from the bone. Keep warm while you prepare the sauce.

Put the rest of the oil, the tomato, chillies, basil, anchovy purée and the
remaining garlic cloves in a frying pan and cook for 5 minutes.

When the fish is ready, spoon a few tablespoons of the cooking juices
into the sauce and add salt to taste. Remove the garlic and the chilli
and pour the sauce into a heated bowl. When you serve the fish, spoon
a little of the cooking juices over each portion and hand round the
sauce separately.

preparation
I am afraid this is the sort of dish that must be cooked shortly before
eating. You can keep the fish warm, covered with foil, in the oven with
the heat turned off. The sauce can also be kept warm, or it can easily
be reheated.

sea bass stuffed with scallops, shrimps and black olives
branzino farcito coi frutti di mare

In Britain wild sea bass is easily available in spring and in the summer, when a certain number swim up to our southern shores. The wild fish is the king of fish for the Italians and the French, who love its firm flesh, free of bone, and its delicate flavour. There are also farmed sea bass on the market nowadays, but they are certainly not as good.

Sea bass is usually grilled, boiled or roasted as in this recipe. Here I have boned the fish before stuffing it, which makes it more attractive to serve and more agreeable to eat.

If your fishmonger has not been amenable enough to bone the fish for you, this is how you should proceed. With a boning knife, extend the slit in the fish's belly all the way from the head to the tail. Using your finger and a small knife, prise loose the rib bones that are embedded in the upper belly of the fish. Then proceed down the belly and loosen all the backbone, scraping any flesh off it. Now bend the head of the fish backwards sharply to snap it off from the backbone. If it does not snap, cut it with poultry scissors. Do the same at the tail end. Check that all the scales have been properly removed. Wash the fish and let it drain while you prepare the stuffing.

Peel the shrimps over a bowl to collect the juices. If large, cut the bodies into small pieces and put them in the bowl. Wash and dry the scallops, cut them into pieces and add to the bowl.

Cut the black olives into strips and add to the bowl together with the chopped parsley, the capers and the brandy. Add 2 tablespoons of the oil, some salt and a generous grinding of pepper. Mix very thoroughly, and leave to infuse for about 1 hour.

Heat the oven to 200°C (400°F) mark 6.

Grease a large sheet of foil with 1 tablespoon of the oil. Place the foil on a baking tray or roasting tin long enough to hold the fish without bending it.

Dry the fish and lay it open like a book, skin side down, on the foil. Season both sides with salt and pepper and then pile the stuffing on one half of the open fish. Close the fish and sew it down the belly. Loosely wrap the fish up by twisting over the edge of the foil all round,

Serves 6
1 sea bass weighing about 1.8 kg (4 lb)
120 g (4 oz) shrimps
4 scallops
10 black olives, stoned
2 tbsp chopped flat-leaf parsley
2 tbsp capers, rinsed and dried
2 tbsp brandy
6 tbsp extra virgin olive oil
sea salt and pepper

making sure that the corners are tightly sealed too. Place in the oven and bake for 40 minutes.

Remove from the oven and allow to stand in the sealed foil for 10 minutes or so. Transfer the fish, still in the foil, to a large oval dish and bring to the table. Cut round the twisted edges of the foil. Cut the fish across into slices and serve, spooning some of the cooking juices over the fish.

preparation
The fish can be stuffed, sewn and wrapped for baking up to 1 hour in advance.

john dory fillets with broccoli sauce
filetti di san pietro in salsa di broccoli

Serves 6
**60 g (2 oz) unsalted
butter**
**2 shallots, finely
chopped**
sea salt and pepper
**600 g (1 1/4 lb)
broccoli**
**225 ml (8 fl oz) fish
stock (page 486)**
**1 kg (2 lb) John Dory
fillets**
**100 ml (3 1/2 fl oz)
dry white wine**
4 tbsp double cream

I had this dish years ago at the Ristorante Dante in Bologna. I still remember my surprise at being offered such an unlikely combination as fish and broccoli in a restaurant in Bologna, where dishes outside the traditional range of local cooking are viewed with suspicion. Here a fish is combined with a broccoli purée made mellow with cream.

The fish is the very fine but rather ugly John Dory, a fish with a very large head which, with the backbone, accounts for two-thirds of its weight. It has two black marks on each side, these being responsible for its name in both Italian and French – San Pietro and Saint Pierre. These marks, the legend says, are the fingerprints of Saint Peter who, taking pity on it after it was caught, threw the fish back into the sea. If I ever caught a John Dory I fear I would not throw it back. I find it one of the best fish, with its firm white flesh, suitable for cooking in most ways from the simplest to the most elaborate.

As accompaniment, a few buttered new potatoes would be very welcome, although not necessary, and afterwards a green salad is all you need.

Heat the oven to 190°C (375°F) mark 5.

Put half the butter in a sauté pan. Add the shallots and a little salt and sauté for 5–7 minutes until soft.

Remove the tough outside layer of the broccoli stalks. Wash the broccoli thoroughly, cut them into small pieces and add to the shallots with a cupful of the fish stock. Cook until quite tender, not just *al dente*, adding a small ladleful of the broth whenever the broccoli are cooking with no liquid. They will take about 20 minutes. Season with salt and pepper to taste.

While the broccoli are cooking, butter an oven dish with the remaining butter and lay the fish fillets in it. Season with salt and pepper, pour over the wine and then cover the dish with foil and bake for 10 minutes.

When the broccoli are done, put them with all the cooking juices in the food processor and purée them. Spoon the purée into a clean saucepan and add the cream. Bring slowly to the boil and cook over a very low heat for 5 minutes, stirring frequently. Taste and check the seasoning. Keep the sauce warm.

Transfer the fish fillets on to individual heated plates, pour over the cooking juices and spoon a couple of tablespoons of the purée around each fillet.

preparation
The broccoli sauce can be prepared a few hours in advance and refrigerated, tightly covered with clingfilm, but the fish must be cooked at the last minute.

fish fillets with potato scales
filetti di pesce con le scaglie di patate

Serves 6
**6 waxy potatoes,
medium size
6 brill or sole fillets
of about 200 g
(7 oz) each
sea salt and pepper
90 g (3 oz) unsalted
butter
3 tbsp chopped dill**

I cannot remember how this fish dish came into my repertoire. I can only say that each time I make it I get the same enthusiastic reaction from my guests. This is one of the few dishes which I always place directly on my guests' plates, as it is rather difficult to handle. I find it enough of a worry to transfer the fish once, from the cooking dish to the plate, without inflicting this worry on my friends, with the attendant risk of the fish finishing up on their laps. It is easy to do in the kitchen with 2 fish-slices and no one watching.

I have found brill the best fish for this recipe, because of its size and the firmness of its flesh. Dover sole is good too. Both fish give firm, thick fillets and their flavour is quite delicious, so that they lend themselves to simple treatment as in this recipe, where the only flavouring is melted butter and dill. Try to buy whole fish, and ask the fishmonger to fillet them. Bring home the heads, bones and skin for making a fish stock. Serve a good green salad after, not with the fish.

Wash the potatoes and boil them in their skins for 10 minutes. Peel them as soon as you can handle them and set aside to cool.

Skin the fillets if necessary and wash and dry them with kitchen paper. Sprinkle with salt and pepper and lay them in an oven dish, preferably metal, greased with 15 g (1/2 oz) of the butter.

Heat the oven to 200°C (400°F) mark 6.

When the potatoes are cold (they slice better when cold), cut them into very thin slices.

Sprinkle the dill over each fillet. Cover each fillet with the potatoes, laying them down like the scales of the fish. Sprinkle with salt and pepper. Melt the remaining butter and pour it over the potatoes, using a brush to cover all the gaps and corners.

Bake for 15 minutes, basting two or three times, until the potatoes are tender.

Pass the dish under a very hot grill to brown the surface of the potatoes. Place the fillets on individual heated plates and spoon over the cooking juices. Serve at once, handing round a bowl of steamed courgettes or mange-tout, lightly dressed with butter.

preparation
The dish can be prepared, but not baked, up to 1 hour in advance, but no more.

baked fish steaks
trance di nasello al forno

I prefer to use hake for this dish, because the steaks are usually just the right size. But cod, a fish of the same family, can be used too.

Wash the fish steaks and dry thoroughly with kitchen paper. Close them up neatly and tie them round with string, so that they will keep a nice shape during the cooking.

Put the shallots, garlic, olive oil, bay leaves, oregano or marjoram and salt and pepper in an oven dish large enough to contain the fish in a single layer. Coat the fish in the mixture on both sides and leave to marinate for 1 hour, turning the steaks over once or twice.

Heat the oven to 180°C (350°F) mark 4.

Place the dish in the oven and bake for about 20 minutes, turning the steaks over gently halfway through the cooking.

When the fish is done, remove and discard the shallot, garlic and bay leaves. Dribble with the lemon juice and sprinkle with the parsley. Cut off the string around and serve at once.

Serves 6
6 fish steaks, about 2.5 cm (1 inch) thick
3 shallots, chopped in half
3 garlic cloves, bruised
6 tbsp extra virgin olive oil
4 bay leaves
2 tbsp fresh oregano or marjoram
sea salt and pepper
juice of 1 organic lemon
4 tbsp chopped flat-leaf parsley

fish timbale
timballo di pesce

Serves 6
1 onion
1 celery stick
1 bay leaf
a few parsley stalks,
   fennel and thyme
   (or other herbs,
   depending on the
   season)
sea salt
300 ml (1/2 pint) dry
   white wine
a few peppercorns
700 g (1 1/2 lb)
   assorted white fish
   – see recipe
lasagne made with 2
   free-range eggs,
   200 g (7 oz) Italian
   00 flour, a pinch of
   salt and 1 tsp olive
   oil (see page 27) or
   250 g (9 oz) dried
   lasagne
béchamel sauce
   made with 300 ml
   (1/2 pint) fish stock
   and 300 ml (1/2
   pint) full-fat milk,
   60 g (2 oz)
   unsalted butter and
   60 g (2 oz) Italian
   00 flour
2 free-range eggs
45 g (1 1/2 oz)
   freshly grated
   Parmesan
30 g (1 oz) unsalted
   butter

For the sauce
4 tbsp olive oil
2 garlic cloves,
   peeled and bruised

continued over >>

This dish is not to be attempted by a beginner, yet it is not too difficult for anyone who likes to try something a bit more enterprising.

The dish is so good that you should spare the time to make your own lasagne. The fish I use vary according to which are the freshest I can find. A halibut steak, a piece of hake, a tail of haddock are all suitable, as indeed are turbot and sea bass. Buy some fish with their heads on – lemon sole, for instance – to give more flavour. Try to buy three different kinds of fish.

Put the onion, celery, herbs and salt in a large pan, add a generous litre (2 pints) of cold water and bring back to the boil. Simmer, covered, for 10 minutes, add the wine and the peppercorns and continue to simmer for 20 minutes or so. The court-bouillon is now ready.

Add all the fish to the pan and bring back to the boil. Turn off the heat and let the fish cook in the liquid.

Now make the pasta following the instructions on page 27. Roll out the dough as thin as you can, if you are doing it by hand, or put it through the last but one notch of the hand-cranked machine.

Cut the pasta strips into 20 cm (8 inch) lengths, leaving them the width they are when they come out of the machine – about 10 cm (4 inches).

The best saucepan to use for cooking lasagne is a large deep one. Fill it with 4 litres (7 pints) of water and bring to the boil.

Meanwhile place a large bowl of cold water next to the pan, and lay two clean tea-towels on the work surface.

When the water is boiling, add 1 tablespoon of cooking salt and 1 tablespoon of oil and slide in 3 or 4 strips of pasta. Cook until just soft and then retrieve the strips (I use 2 fish-slices) and plunge them in the bowl of cold water. Give each strip a gentle rub, as you would a delicate piece of fabric, and lay it on the tea-towel. Repeat with the remaining strips, 3 or 4 at a time. Lay the strips so that they do not touch, otherwise they will stick together. When you have cooked, 'washed' and spread out all the strips, pat them dry with kitchen paper.

Lift out the fish and strain the liquid. Measure 300 ml (1/2 pint) of the liquid, add the same amount of milk and make a thickish béchamel as directed on page 489, using the milk and fish liquor mixture in place of the milk.

While the béchamel is cooking, remove the head, bones and every bit of skin from the fish. Put the fish in a food processor and, while the machine is working, add the eggs one at a time. Transfer to a bowl and add the béchamel and the Parmesan. Mix very well and check the seasoning.

Grease a 1 litre (2 pint) metal loaf-tin with half the butter. Line the mould with pasta strips, overlapping them as little as possible. Leave about 5 cm (2 inches) hanging over the edge all round. (It is easier to cut the strips with scissors than with a knife.) Spread about 3 or 4 tablespoons of the fish and béchamel mixture and then cover with a strip of pasta, cutting it to the right size if necessary. Continue alternating these 2 layers, finishing with the fish mixture. Fold the hanging-over pasta over the last layer of fish and place the last strip of pasta over the top, tucking it in all round the edges.

Melt the remaining butter, brush it all over the top and cover with a piece of foil. This dish is now ready to be finished off in the oven. It is cooked in a bain-marie in a preheated oven (200°C/400°F/mark 6). The timing varies; if the dish was cold it will need about 1 hour, while if you have just made it, 30 minutes will do. However, it will not spoil if you leave it in the oven for a little longer.

To make the sauce, heat the oil with the garlic and the chilli in a very heavy saucepan. When the garlic begins to give off its characteristic aroma, remove and discard it. Remove and discard the chilli as well.

Add the tomato purée to the sizzling oil and cook, stirring constantly, for 1 minute. I find that the rather unpleasant concentrated taste of the purée disappears more quickly if the purée is cooked by itself to begin with. Now add the wine slowly and bring to the boil. Let the sauce simmer very gently for 15 minutes.

Meanwhile put aside a few of the best prawns for the garnish. Peel the others. Put the heads and carapaces on a piece of muslin. Make a little bag with them and place in a mortar. Crush the bag with the pestle so as to break the heads and release all the succulent juices. Squeeze the

1 dried chilli
2 tbsp tomato purée
120 ml (4 fl oz) dry white wine
sea salt and freshly ground black pepper
300 ml (1/2 pint) double cream
300 g (10 oz) prawns

bag over the pan; the reddish-brown juice that will come out gives the prawn sauce a more marked flavour. This is very necessary with the prawns that are usually to be found on the market, i.e. cooked prawns that have also often been frozen. Mix well, then add the cream, the peeled prawns and salt and pepper to taste. Cook slowly until the sauce begins to boil. Simmer for a couple of minutes and then transfer to a food processor. Process until smooth and homogeneous. Return to the pan and keep warm in a bain-marie.

When the *timballo* is ready, run a palette knife round the edges to release it from the tin, then place an oval dish over it. Turn the dish upside-down to unmould and lift the tin away. Spoon some of the sauce around the *timballo* and pour the rest of the sauce into a bowl or a sauce-boat. Remove the carapaces from the prawns you have set aside, but leave the heads on; they are much prettier to garnish this glorious dish.

preparation

You can prepare the whole dish in advance, even the day before, and chill it. I expect you can even freeze it, although personally I find that frozen pasta becomes heavier in taste. If you do freeze it, bring it back to room temperature before heating it in the oven.

sardines

The zoological name of this fish, *Sardina pilchardus*, underlines the fact that sardines are young pilchards. Sardines should be small: no longer than 12 cm (5 inches). They swim in large shoals and in Italian waters are mostly caught in the seas off southern Italy and Sicily. The firms devoted to preserving them in salt or oil are also situated principally in the south and in Sicily. The livelihood of many villages used to depend on a good catch, as to a minor extent it still does. In the famous novel *I Malavoglia*, Giovanni Verga describes the cheerful activity in the village of Acitrezza in eastern Sicily in the summer of 1863, when the catch of sardines and anchovies had been particularly good. Everyone in the village was busy putting them in barrels (which was how they used to be preserved): they knew the sale of the fish would provide enough money to buy their provisions for the winter when fishing would be very poor.

Fresh sardines are utterly delicious as long as they really are fresh. They should have a firm, stiff body glistening with steely blue reflections, and bright clear eyes. In a play of Goldoni's called *Le Donne de casa soa*, Siora Angiola is sending her servant to buy some sardines. She tells him that he must help himself to the fish that are on top, the best and the fattest. 'When they are tired, their heads are red,' she says, which is indeed the case, since a large red spot appears under the eye, and the eyes themselves become totally bloodshot.

Many sardines sold in Britain would fit Siora Angiola's description. If this is the case, leave them and buy pilchards, or, if you can find them, sprats, which are of the same family. I have used sprats to make most of my sardine recipes and always been quite happy with the result.

Many recipes for sardines come from the south of Italy, and of these the best known and most worth looking out for are *sarde a beccaficu* and *pasta con le sarde*. The dish *sarde a beccaficu* takes its name from its appearance. The boned sardines are rolled up flat and set in the dish with their tails in the air, making them look like little *beccafichi* – warblers – pecking at the dish. *Pasta con le sarde* is so delicious that rather than be without it through lack of fresh sardines, I make it with herrings. It combines *maccheroni* with sardines, pine nuts and sultanas.

sardines in a sweet-and-sour sauce
sarde in saor

Serves 4
**700 g (1 1/2 lb) fresh
sardines, cleaned**
75 g (2 1/2 oz) flour
sea salt
**vegetable oil for
frying**
30 g (1 oz) sultanas
2 tbsp olive oil
**225 g (8 oz) onions,
thinly sliced**
2 tsp sugar
**120 ml (4 fl oz) dry
white wine**
**120 ml (4 fl oz) good
wine vinegar**
2 tbsp lemon juice
4 bay leaves
**12 black
peppercorns, lightly
bruised**
**1/8 tsp ground
cinnamon**
**1/8 tsp ground
coriander**

This is an ancient recipe from Veneto that was prepared for the sailors to take on their voyages. The amount of onion in the saor – the sauce – was supposed to protect the men from scurvy.

I have made this dish quite successfully with sprats and with herrings, both of which are usually much fresher in the shops or on the stalls than sardines. Fillets of sole or plaice can also be prepared in this way. They all make a most appetising first course.

Wash and dry the sardines thoroughly.

Spread the flour on a board and season with salt.

Heat the vegetable oil in a wok or a frying pan, and meanwhile coat the sardines lightly in the flour.

When the oil is very hot but not smoking (test by frying a small piece of bread: it should brown in 50 seconds) slide in the sardines, a few at a time, and fry gently for about 2 minutes on each side until a golden crust has formed. With a fish-slice transfer the fish to a side dish lined with kitchen paper.

Soak the sultanas in a little warm water.

Heat the olive oil and the onions in another frying pan, or use the same pan as for the fish once you have poured the cooled frying oil into a bottle or thrown it away. (Do not use the same frying oil more than twice. With repeated heating, any oil acquires an unpleasant taste and becomes highly indigestible.) Cook the onions gently and add a
pinch of salt and the sugar, stirring frequently. The onions should be golden by the end. Turn the heat up and pour in the wine, vinegar and lemon juice. Boil briskly until the liquid is reduced by half.

Lay the fish neatly on a dish: I use a rustic earthenware one. Spoon over the onion sauce and put the bay leaves on top.

Drain the sultanas and scatter them on top of the dish together with the spices. Cover the dish with clingfilm and leave for at least 24 hours.

preparation

The dish keeps well for 2 or 3 days in the fridge. Take the dish out of the fridge at least 2–3 hours before you want to eat it, so that it has time to reach room temperature.

tuna

'*Tonno* is a fish of exceptional proportions,' said Platina, the fifteenth-century writer in his *De honesta voluptate et valetudine*. It can in fact be as long as 2 metres (6 1/2 feet). It swims at amazing speed, its beautiful dark blue body looking like a torpedo flashing through the water. Tuna migrate towards the shore, and even up the mouths of rivers, to spawn early in the summer. Their migratory movements, however, are something of a mystery. The late Alan Davidson, in his invaluable *Mediterranean Seafood*, suggests that they 'might be mainly governed by water temperatures and by the movements of other fish on which the tunny feed'.

It is when the tuna are on the move to spawn that the Sicilian *mattanza del tonno* – the slaughter of the tuna – takes place. The *mattanza* has always been a ritualistic occasion much enjoyed by the Sicilian fishermen. Apparently the method of catching and killing the fish was learnt from the Phoenicians, and it has changed very little since then. Patrick Brydone, in one of his letters from Sicily written in 1770, describes how this was (and, for the benefit of the tourists, still is) done. 'These fish do not make their appearance in the Sicilian seas till towards the latter end of May; at which time the *tonnaros*, as they call them, are prepared for their reception. This is a kind of aquatic castle, formed, at great expense, of strong nets, fastened to the bottom of the sea by anchors and heavy leaden weights. These *tonnaros* are erected in the passages amongst the rocks and islands that are most frequented by the tunny fish. They take care to shut up with nets the entry into these passages, all but one little opening, which is called the outward gate of the *tonnaro*.' Brydone then describes how the fish are driven from the 'hall' to the 'antechamber' by the fishermen making a noise on the surface of the water, their escape being cut off by a net that is let down to shut them in. After the *anticamera* comes the '*Camera della Morte*, the Chamber of Death: this is composed of stronger nets and heavier anchors than the other. As soon as they have collected a sufficient number, the tunny fish are driven from all the other apartments into the chamber of death; when the slaughter begins. The fishermen, and often the gentlemen too, armed with a kind of spear or harpoon, attack the poor defenceless animals on all sides; which now, giving themselves up to despair, dash about with great force and agility, throwing the water over all the boats; and tearing the nets to pieces, they often knock out their brains against the rocks or anchors, and sometimes even against the boats of their enemies.'

The flesh of the tuna is rather dense and dry, and I find that it is improved by being marinated in a mixture of vinegar and oil. However I think tuna is an excellent fish, and it is now easily available; sometimes even caught in British water.

Tuna has been popular since Roman times. Apicius wrote recipes in which the tuna is boiled – a favourite cooking method of the Romans for both fish and meat – and then dressed with a sweet-and-sour sauce containing oil and garum. The combination of tuna with a sweet-and-sour sauce is still a favourite, together with the classic Mediterranean method of cooking it with tomatoes, as in the recipe given here.

A very important use of tuna is its preservation in olive oil or brine. In the old days it used to be preserved covered with olive oil in barrels, *tonno sott'olio*, the best part being the tender, juicy belly of the fish, called *ventresca*. You can buy tins of *ventresca* in some specialist delicatessens in Italy, as well as tuna preserved in barrels and sold by weight. Preserved tuna is used quite extensively in Italian cooking; rolls are made with it, vegetables are stuffed with it – as in the recipe for onion on page 215 – and it is used in many pasta sauces.

Possibly the best known dish made with tuna is the Tuscan *insalata di tonno e fagioli* – bean and tuna fish salad – which is found on the menus of most Italian restaurants outside Italy. The basic recipe is very simple, the principal ingredients being tuna, *cannellini* beans, usually tinned, and onions. I add a few touches which make it prettier and better. I use dried *cannellini*, which are better than the tinned ones, so that first I have to soak and cook them. I use red onions, which are sweeter than white ones or spring onions, and I marinate them in lemon juice for about 2 hours. I spoon the beans over a bed of red radicchio, which adds a touch of colour, a slightly bitter edge and a crunchy texture. The flaked tuna comes next and the red onion is scattered on top. The dressing is the best olive oil, lots of black pepper and a little salt.

tuna baked with tomatoes, capers, black olives and chilli
tonno alla calabrese

Try to buy steaks from the belly of the fish, which is more delicate in taste and less dry. If the steaks are too large, cut them in half.

Remove the tough skin from the fish, if it is still on, and rub salt and pepper into both sides of the steaks. Lay the steaks in an ovenproof dish and pour over half the oil and all the vinegar. Place a bay leaf on each steak and leave to marinate for 1 hour. Remember to turn them over once.

Heat the oven to 200°C (400°F) mark 6.

Blanch and skin the tomatoes. Cut them in half and squeeze out and discard the seeds, then chop the flesh roughly and spread on the steaks. Sprinkle with the breadcrumbs, scatter with the capers and the olives and add the chillies. Dribble with the remaining oil. Cover the tin with foil and bake until the fish is cooked through; this will take 15–20 minutes, depending on the thickness of the steaks.

Transfer the fish to a heated dish and remove and discard the bay leaves. Add salt and pepper to the cooking liquid if necessary, then spoon it over the fish. Garnish with the basil and serve.

Serves 4

- 4 fresh tuna steaks, about 1 cm (1/2 inch) thick
- sea salt and pepper
- 4 tbsp extra virgin olive oil
- 2 tbsp wine vinegar
- 4 bay leaves
- 4 fresh ripe tomatoes
- 2 tbsp dried breadcrumbs
- 3 tbsp capers, rinsed and dried
- 12 sweet black olives
- 2 dried chillies, chopped
- a dozen fresh basil leaves, roughly torn

tunny fish roll
il polpettone di tonno della mamma

Serves 4 to 6

400 g (14 oz) tinned tuna, drained

3 whole free-range eggs plus 1 yolk

2 hard-boiled eggs, coarsely chopped

100 g (3 1/2 oz) freshly grated Parmesan

2 pinches of grated nutmeg

sea salt and freshly ground black pepper

200 ml (7 fl oz) wine vinegar

200 ml (7 fl oz) dry white wine

10–12 sprigs flat-leaf parsley

2 small onions, sliced

3 tbsp olive oil

1 tsp lemon juice

black olives, lemon slices and capers to garnish

This is the way my mother used to make her tuna fish roll, quite different from the more common roll made with mashed potatoes. I know the addition of Parmesan seems odd, but don't be put off by it. It is a very good dish served as an antipasto, a second course in the summer or for a buffet. Buy the best tuna, not skipjack tuna.

Flake and mash the tuna in a bowl. Add the eggs, hard-boiled eggs, Parmesan, nutmeg and plenty of pepper. Taste and check the salt. Mix thoroughly.

Moisten a piece of muslin under cold water, wring it out until just damp, and lay it out double on the work surface. Place the tuna mixture on the cloth and roll it into a log shape, about 8 cm (3 inches) in diameter. Pat it all over to eliminate air pockets and then wrap the muslin around it and tie both ends with string.

Place the roll with the vinegar, wine, parsley, onions and a little salt in an oval casserole into which the roll will just fit. Add enough water to cover the roll by about 1 cm (1/2 inch). Cover the casserole and bring to the boil. Cook, over a very low heat, for 45 minutes.

Remove the tuna roll from the casserole and place it between two plates. Put a weight on top and leave to cool for at least 2 hours.

When the roll is cold, unwrap it carefully and cut into 1 cm (1/2 inch) slices. Arrange the slices, very slightly overlapping, on a dish. Mix together the olive oil and lemon juice and spoon over the slices 2 hours before serving. Garnish with black olives, lemon slices and capers. Serve with mayonnaise or with the Egg and Cream sauce that follows, which is lighter.

preparation
The *polpettone* can be made and cooked up to 2 days in advance and kept, wrapped, in the refrigerator. Slice it when chilled and then bring back to room temperature and dress with the oil and lemon.

egg and cream sauce
salsina all'uovo

This sauce is good with stewed or boiled fish, with vegetables or with poached chicken.

Whisk the egg yolks in a bowl. Add the mustard powder, salt and pepper and lemon juice and put the bowl over a saucepan half full of simmering water.

Add the oil slowly while whisking constantly, and continue whisking until the sauce thickens. Be careful not to let it boil or the egg will curdle. Draw off the heat and beat in the cream. Return to the bain-marie and cook for a further couple of minutes.

Transfer the bowl to a basin of cold water and leave to cool.

preparation
The sauce can be prepared up to 1 day in advance and refrigerated. Remove from the fridge at least 2 hours before you use it to coat the tunny fish roll.

5 free-range egg
yolks
1 tsp English
mustard powder
sea salt and pepper
5 tbsp lemon juice
6 tbsp extra virgin
olive oil
120 ml (4 fl oz)
double cream

prawns in a piquant tomato sauce
gamberi imperiali in salsa all'abruzzese

Fishmongers now sell raw prawns. They are often frozen tiger prawn tails from the East. You can also find raw fresh prawns, usually with the head still on, called either langoustines or king prawns. They are ideal for this recipe, an old one from Abruzzo. The fish flavour of the prawns is emphasised by a touch of anchovy purée, and enveloped in the classic Mediterranean ambience of tomato and garlic. To this, chilli is added, the characteristic spice of Abruzzo cooking. The secret for success with this dish is that the prawns and the tomatoes should cook for a very short time, so that their original fresh flavour comes through intact.

Rinse the prawns, shell and de-vein them.

Serves 6
25–30 king prawns
4 garlic cloves,
peeled and finely
chopped
1 large bunch of flat-
leaf parsley
1 or 2 dried chillies,
according to taste,
seeded
6 tbsp extra virgin
olive oil

continued over >>

2 tsp anchovy purée
450 g (1 lb) fresh
  ripe tomatoes,
  peeled, seeded and
  very coarsely
  chopped
120 ml (4 fl oz) dry
  white wine
sea salt and freshly
  ground black
  pepper

Chop the garlic, parsley and chillies either by hand or in a food processor.

Put the oil in a large sauté pan (I use a round earthenware pan) and add the parsley mixture. Sauté for 1 minute over a low heat, stirring very frequently, and mix in the anchovy purée. Add the prawns and the tomatoes. Turn them over once or twice in the pan and then splash with the wine and cook for 5 minutes. Season with salt and black pepper if you like. If you have a nice-looking sauté pan, serve directly from it.

preparation
You can prepare the prawns and the parsley mixture in advance. You can even make the *soffritto* (the fried mixture) beforehand, but you must cook the prawns just before serving.

fish stock
brodo di pesce

See page 486 in The Essentials section.

Many years ago, long before the days of 'food for free', I went on holiday with my family in north Cornwall. When we got down to the beach, two things struck me: that the rocks towering over the beach at low tide were covered with lovely mussels, and that nobody was collecting them. We soon set to, and back in our rented cottage we began the long but happy process of soaking and scrubbing them. We had them with spaghetti and in salads, we made soup out of them and we stuffed them. Why no one else took advantage of the God-given bounty was always a mystery to me.

The most popular Italian molluscs are mussels and clams, both available here in Britain. The best Italian clams are *vongole veraci – palourdes* – which you can order from any reputable fishmonger. The *vongola comune* – golden carpet shell – is also found in British waters. It is smaller and less sweet than the *vongola verace*, but it can be used for soups or with spaghetti. Mussels are becoming more and more popular in Britain, and there are now plenty of them around: French, Dutch, British and even huge New Zealand ones during the summer months.

To clean mussels or *vongole,* put them in a basin of cold water. Leave the clams in the water for some time so that they disgorge any sand in the shell. Scrub the molluscs hard with a stiff brush. Some clams and farm mussels are quite clean, while other mussels are often covered with barnacles, though these are easy to knock off. Also tug off the beards. Wash thoroughly in several changes of cold water if necessary. Drain and throw away any mollusc that remains open when tapped on a hard surface; it is dead and must not be eaten. When I cook them in order to open them, my secret is to put 8 or 10 garlic cloves and 1 or 2 lemons cut into quarters at the bottom of large pan. The lemons help to destroy any bacteria in the molluscs, and the liquor left at the bottom of the pan after the molluscs have opened becomes more tasty. Discard any mollusc which remains tight shut after heating.

risotto with mussels
risotto coi peoci

Serves 4
1.35 kg (3 lb)
  mussels
200 ml (7 fl oz) dry
  white wine
6 tbsp olive oil
3 shallots or 1
  medium onion, very
  finely chopped
sea salt
1 litre (1 3/4 pints)
  light fish stock
  (page 486) or
  vegetable stock
  (page 487)
1 celery stalk, with
  the leaves if
  possible
1 garlic clove
300 g Arborio, or
  other Italian risotto
  rice
4 tbsp chopped flat-
  leaf parsley
black pepper

When we had a flat in Venice, I used to go every morning on a pilgrimage by gondola-ferry across the Canal Grande from Ca' d'Oro to the Rialto market. The Rialto market is a sight that should not be missed by anyone visiting Venice. It stretches along a few calli *(alleys) and* campielli *(squares), around the bridge and along the Canal Grande. For the tourists there are stalls selling lace and tablecloths, and others selling bags, wallets and purses, but for the Venetians there are stalls piled high with the choicest fruits and the greatest selection of vegetables you have ever seen, as well as fish stalls with crawling crustaceans and slender silvery fish, so many different species and kinds that you can spend the morning in a study of ichthyology. But then, standing there, entranced by the sheer abundance and variety of it all, I would be reminded by the jostlings of more down-to-earth Venetian housewives that I had a lunch to cater for.*

After searching for whatever looked best, I would finish up, as often as not, giving in to my longing for seafood, and would return home with bags of molluscs for lunch and dinner. In the tradition of the local cuisine, rice would be the natural accompaniment to the seafood.

Clean the mussels following the instructions on page 129.

Put the wine in a large sauté or frying pan, add the mussels and cover the pan. Cook over a high heat until the mussels are open, which will take only 3 or 4 minutes. Shake the pan every now and then.

As soon as the mussels are open, remove the meat from the shells and discard the shells. Do not force the mussels open or the muscle around them will break and they will lose their shape and look messy. Strain the cooking liquid through a sieve lined with muslin, pouring it slowly and gently so that most of the sand and debris is left at the bottom of the pan.

Pour the oil into a wide heavy saucepan, add the shallots or onion and a pinch of salt, and sauté until they are soft and just beginning to colour.

Heat the stock to simmering point and keep it just simmering all through the cooking.

While the shallots are cooking, chop the celery and garlic together and then add to the pan. Sauté for a further minute or so.

Now add the rice and, as we say in Italian, *tostatelo* – 'toast' it in the oil, turning it over and over for a couple of minutes. Pour over the mussel liquid and stir well. When the liquid has been absorbed add the rest of the stock, one ladleful at a time. Stir very frequently. When the rice is done, draw the pan off the heat, stir in the mussels and the parsley, and season with salt, if necessary, and with plenty of black pepper. Transfer to a heated dish and serve immediately.

preparation

The mussels can be cleaned and opened up to 1 day in advance. They must be kept in the refrigerator. The risotto should be made just before serving. However, you can half cook the risotto, up to the point when you have added the first ladleful of stock. Bring to the boil, stir, and turn off the heat. Cover the pan tightly. The risotto can now be left until you want to finish the dish. When you come back to it you will find the risotto already half cooked, having absorbed all the stock. Stir in a knob of butter and continue cooking, gradually adding the remaining stock. The risotto will not be quite so perfectly cooked, but on the other hand you won't have to be banished to the kitchen by yourself for so long, and resent the making ot it.

spaghetti with clams
vermicelli alle vongole in bianco

Serves 3-4

1 kg (2 lb) *vongole* or mussels

4 tbsp dry white wine

350 g (12 oz) spaghetti or spaghettini

5 tbsp olive oil

3 garlic cloves, peeled and finely chopped

3 tbsp chopped flat-leaf parsley

grated rind of half an organic lemon

1 dried chilli, crumbled

sea salt and freshly ground black pepper

The sauce in this recipe is the pasta dressing that used to be made by Neapolitan fishermen on board their boats. Unlike the usual clam sauce, it does not contain tomatoes and as a result the taste of the molluscs comes through in a way that is fresher and more fragrant. Vongole can be ordered from any good fishmonger. You can use cockles, but they do not have the same sweetness. If you use cockles, you must leave them in cold water for at least 2 hours to get rid of the sand inside the shell. Mussels, too, are excellent served in this way with spaghetti.

Prepare the vongole or mussels following the instructions on page 129.

Put the wine in a large frying or sauté pan, add the cleaned molluscs and cook, covered, over lively heat, until they are open. Shake the pan frequently.

Remove the meat from the shells and discard the shells.

Strain the mollusc liquor through a sieve lined with muslin or kitchen paper into a small saucepan. Reduce it over high heat until only about half remains.

Bring a large saucepan of salted water to the boil. Drop the pasta into the water and cook until it is done.

While the pasta is cooking, put the oil, garlic, half the parsley, lemon rind and the chilli in a large sauté pan and sauté over a medium heat until the garlic begins to colour.

Drain the pasta and add to the sauce in the pan.

Mix in the *vongole* and their liquid and stir-fry for 1 minute, lifting up the pasta and the sauce as you stir. Remember that the molluscs should only heat up, not cook. Season with pepper, and salt if necessary.

Serve immediately straight from the pan.

tagliatelle with mussels and leeks
tagliatelle con cozze e porri

*Mussels and leeks make an unusual but successful marriage, the pasta
being the foil for the two flavours.*

*In the old days I would have hesitated to write a recipe containing
mussels for 8 people. Who would have stood at the kitchen sink for
hours on end to clean 2 kg (4 lb) of dirty, sandy, barnacled and
bearded mussels? Nowadays the mussels we buy are usually farmed.
The farms are on rafts or ropes, and as a result the mussels are pretty
clean when they reach our sinks.*

If you are making your own tagliatelle do this first, following my
instructions on page 27.

To clean the mussels turn to page 129 for the instructions.

You should cook this quantity of mussels in 2 batches. Use a large
sauté pan with a tight-fitting lid, so that the mussels can spread out
properly. Pour the wine into the pan and add the first batch of mussels.
Cover and cook over high heat until the mussels open. Shake the pan
frequently.

Remove the mussels from the shells as soon as they open, but do not
force them open or they will break. Discard the shells and cook the
second batch of mussels. Now filter the liquid at the bottom of the pan
into a saucepan through a sieve lined with muslin. Reduce the liquid
over a high heat until about 300 ml (1/2 pint) is left. Set aside.

The next step is to prepare the leeks. Trim them, cutting away the
roots and about 5–7cm (2–4 inches) from the top, depending how
fresh they are. Cut all the white part of the leeks, and the tender green
part, into thin rounds. Wash very thoroughly, removing any grit stuck
between the leaves. Drain.

Put about three-quarters of the butter in a very large sauté or frying
pan. Heat until the butter has melted and then add the leeks and cook,
turning them over in the butter, for 5 minutes. Cover the leeks with a

Serves 8
tagliatelle made with
  6 eggs and 500 g
  (1 lb 2 oz) Italian
  00 flour, or 500 g
  (1 lb 2 oz) dried
  tagliatelle
1.8 kg (4 lb) mussels
300 ml (1/2 pint) dry
  white wine
1 kg (2 lb) leeks (buy
  small ones if you
  can; they are
  younger and
  therefore sweeter)
100 g (3 1/2 oz)
  unsalted butter
sea salt and freshly
  ground black pepper
300 ml (1/2 pint)
  double cream

sheet of buttered greaseproof paper, put the lid on the pan and cook very gently for about 45 minutes, until the leeks become a purée. Keep a watch on the cooking and add a couple of tablespoons of the filtered mussel liquid whenever the leeks are too dry. Add the mussels and the rest of the mussel liquid. Taste and add salt and a generous amount of pepper.

Now you can cook the pasta, keeping in mind that fresh pasta takes less time to cook than dried pasta. While the pasta is cooking, heat the cream in a small saucepan. When the pasta is *al dente*, drain, but do not overdrain, reserving a cupful of the pasta water. Transfer the pasta immediately to a heated bowl.

Add the remaining butter, the hot cream and the lovely sauce. Toss thoroughly and, if the dish appears too dry, add a few tablespoons of the reserved pasta water. Serve immediately.

preparation
The leeks can be cooked up to 1 day in advance and refrigerated. The mussels could also be cleaned and opened 1 day in advance. Put them in a bowl with the strained liquid, cover with clingfilm and refrigerate.

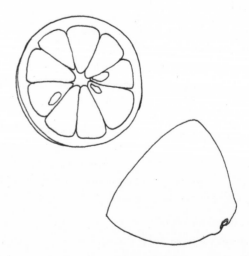

the cephalopods

This small group of aquatic creatures comprises cuttlefish, squid and octopus, none of them very attractive except when presented in the pot. But their taste is so delicious that you are unlikely to be put off by their looks. Like all fish, they should be fresh not frozen, although frozen have the advantage that their flesh is relaxed, making them cook more quickly. But they are less tasty. If you are at the seaside and lucky enough to have the chance of buying some squid or cuttlefish, or an octopus, that have just been caught, you must leave them in the fridge for about 2 days to relax their flesh before you cook them. Italians love to eat these strange-looking fish and have created many recipes around them

squid

This is the cephalopod that is most easily available in Britain. You can buy large or small fresh squid, or small squid from the Mediterranean that are usually frozen. You can even buy them packed in plastic bags and ready to cook. As I don't like frozen fish, I buy locally caught squid – they are tastier.

I cut the big squid into strips and stew them, or I boil them and use them in a seafood salad. I like to stuff the smaller ones in any one of a number of different ways. Basically the stuffing is made with the sautéed, chopped tentacles, parsley and garlic, plus breadcrumbs or rice to give body. Tomato may go in the stuffing or in the cooking liquid with the wine. You may find it fun to experiment with different stuffings.

It is not easy to cook squid – or the other cephalopods – properly. They should either be boiled or grilled, all very briefly, deep fried or stewed at length over a very low heat. In Italy the small *calamaretti* are fried, usually as part of a dish of *fritto misto di mare*. They are tiny, no longer than 5 cm (2 inches), and are lightly coated in flour and fried in hot oil. They are utterly delicious. Larger squid can be deep fried too, but they must first be cut into rings.

how to clean squid

Squid are quick and easy to clean. Hold the sac in one hand and with the other pull off the tentacles. As you do this the contents of the sac will come out too. Cut the tentacles above the eyes and squeeze out the small bony beak in the centre of the tentacles. Peel off the mottled skin, holding the sac under running water. Feel inside the sac and remove the transparent backbone and any bits left inside. Rinse the sac and the tentacles thoroughly under running water. Place into a colander to drain. The squid are now ready. Dry them thoroughly with kitchen paper before you cook them.

spaghetti with squid stew
spaghetti coi calamari

Serves 4
700 g (1 1/2 lb) squid
5 tbsp olive oil
1 medium onion, very finely chopped
sea salt
2 garlic cloves, peeled and finely chopped
2 tbsp finely chopped flat-leaf parsley
1 or 2 small dried chillies, seeded and chopped
400 g (14 oz) tinned plum tomatoes
150 ml (1/4 pint) dry white wine
freshly ground black pepper
300 g (10 oz) spaghetti

You can prepare this fish stew entirely in advance and keep it in the refrigerator for up to 2 days. I prefer to use local squid; they are large and take longer to cook, but they are tastier than the small calamari from the Mediterranean, which are usually frozen.

First clean the squid as directed above.

Put 4 tablespoons of the oil, the onion and the salt in a heavy-based saucepan and cook, covered, over gentle heat for about 5 minutes, stirring frequently. Salt added at this stage releases the onion's moisture and thus helps it to cook without browning.

Stir in the garlic, the parsley and the chilli and continue cooking for a further minute. Turn the heat up to medium and add the tomatoes. Cook for 10 minutes at a lively simmer, then pour in the wine and boil for 5 minutes.

While the sauce is cooking, cut the squid bodies and flaps in narrow strips and the tentacles into bite-sized pieces. Add them to the sauce with a generous grinding of pepper. Reduce the heat to minimum and cook, uncovered, until the squid are tender when pricked with a fork. (The length of the cooking depends entirely on the size of the squid.) You might have to add a couple of tablespoons of hot water if the sauce gets too dry, although it should be quite dense by the end of the cooking and not at all watery.

When the fish is ready, drop the spaghetti into salted boiling water and cook until *al dente*. Drain and turn the pasta into a deep heated dish. Toss with the rest of the oil and a few tablespoons of the sauce. Toss well and then spoon the rest of the sauce with the squid over the pasta.

stuffed squid
calamari ripieni

This recipe combines 2 of the pillars of Italian fish cookery, calamari *and preserved tuna. The recipe was created by Francesco Leonardi, a gifted Neapolitan chef of the eighteenth century who finished his successful career by becoming chef to Catherine the Great. But he became homesick, as all southern Italians do, and went back to Naples, and there he wrote his* Apicio moderno, *a vast book of 3,000 recipes, arranged more as an encyclopaedia than as a cookery book. In it, he often adapted foreign ideas and recipes to his Italian taste.*

Serve these squid at room temperature; they are much nicer than when they are hot.

Prepare the *calamari* according to the instructions on page 136. Remove the triangular flap from the body. Leave the sacs whole and cut the tentacles and the flaps into small bites.

Put the shallots and 2 tablespoons of the oil in a sauté or frying pan, add a little salt and sauté very gently for 10 minutes until the shallot is

Serves 4
- 1 kg (2 lb) *calamari*, with bodies about 10–12 cm (4–5 inches) long
- 2 shallots or 1 small onion, very finely chopped
- 5 tbsp olive oil
- sea salt
- 1 garlic clove, peeled and finely chopped
- 2 tbsp chopped flat-leaf parsley
- 1 dried chilli, seeded and crumbled
- 1 salted anchovy, washed and chopped or

continued over >>

**2 anchovy fillets,
chopped**
**60 g (2 oz) good-
quality white bread,
crust removed**
**5 tbsp dry white
wine**
**120 g (4 oz) tuna,
packed in olive oil
or natural brine**
**freshly ground black
pepper**

soft. Add the garlic, parsley and chilli and sauté for a further 2 minutes, stirring frequently. Add the cut-up tentacles and flaps and the anchovy to the frying pan and sauté gently until the liquid runs out of the tentacles.

Heat the oven to 160°C (320°F) mark 3.

Crumble the bread by hand or in a food processor and add to the pan. Fry on a slightly higher heat for 3–4 minutes, stirring very frequently and letting the bread absorb the liquid. Splash with 2 tablespoons of the wine and cook for a further 5 minutes. Remove from the heat.

Flake the tuna and chop it finely. Mix it into the breadcrumb mixture and add salt and pepper to taste. Mix everything together very thoroughly.

Fill the sacs with the stuffing, leaving about a quarter of the sac empty. This is because the squid shrinks during the cooking, and if the sacs are too full they will crack or burst open. Close the opening of each with a toothpick.

Grease an ovenproof dish with 1 tablespoon of the remaining oil and lay the *calamari* close to each other in a single layer on the bottom of the dish. Heat the remaining wine, boil for 30 seconds, and pour it over with the rest of the oil. Cover tightly with foil and cook in the oven for 1 hour. Baste occasionally during the cooking and turn the squid over two or three times.

When the squid feel very tender when pricked with a fork, they are done. If the juices are too thin, pour them into a small saucepan and reduce over a high heat until tasty and syrupy. Taste and adjust the seasonings. When the squid have cooled a little, remove the toothpicks and carve the sacs into rounds. Serve with the sauce spooned around them.

octopus

These slightly sinister creatures are now sold in some fishmongers' shops and stalls in Britain. They are usually frozen, or have been frozen, but I find that octopus is one of the few sea creatures that retains most of its flavour even after freezing. Freezing also has the advantage of softening them. There are two kinds of octopus; the best, the *polpo verace* or true octopus, has two rows of suckers on each of its 8 tentacles. The other kind, called *moscardino*, or *sinisco* in Naples, is tougher and less sweet. However the small *moscardini* of the Ligurian sea are excellent simply fried or stewed with ceps in tomato sauce, flavoured with the aromatic local basil.

In Italy, along the quays around the Mediterranean, you can often see fishermen banging a large octopus on the ground to relax its flesh and make it tender. In the shops, octopus are usually sold ready to cook. Octopus are stewed in earthenware pots, often with tomatoes, sometimes with wine. The cooking must be very slow and lengthy or the flesh will harden. My favourite way to eat fresh octopus is boiled – if possible in sea water – and dressed with the best olive oil.

stewed octopus
polpo in umido

The simplicity of this dish adds to its attractiveness. If the octopus is too big, and if your fishmonger is obliging enough, ask him to cut off the amount you need.

I like to serve this octopus with polenta, which is very unorthodox since it involves matching a Neapolitan dish with a northern accompaniment. Boiled new potatoes are good, too, or boiled rice.

Put the octopus in a basin of cold water and leave it there for about half an hour to get rid of the sand from the suckers. Examine the suckers and squeeze out any remaining sand. Beat the thick part of the tentacles with a mallet or a meat pounder. Drain thoroughly.

Serves 4–5
1.3 kg (3 lb) octopus
6 tbsp olive oil
3 ripe tomatoes, peeled and coarsely chopped
a lovely bunch of flat-leaf parsley
4 garlic cloves, peeled
pepper
sea salt

Choose an earthenware pot, as this will keep the liquid simmering at a very low heat. Put the oil, the tomatoes, half the parsley and 3 garlic cloves in the pot and lay the octopus on top. Season with lots of pepper, but do not add any salt at this stage as the octopus may be salty enough. Bring to the simmer and then cover the pot with foil and with a tight-fitting lid. Turn the heat down and let the octopus bubble away until tender – about 1 1/2 hours. When done, the prongs of a fork should easily penetrate the thicker part of the tentacles.

Chop the remaining clove of garlic and add to the pan with the rest of the parsley. Mix well, taste and add salt if necessary.

Lift the octopus out of the pot, cut it into pieces and transfer to a side dish. Keep it warm in a very low oven with the door ajar.

In cooking, the octopus will have released a lot of liquid, which you must now reduce fiercely. When it is rich and syrupy, return the octopus to the pot and serve.

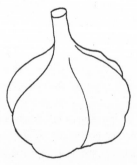

meat and poultry

Somehow one does not connect Italian food with meat and chicken. And yet there are many excellent original recipes and the repertoire is far vaster than the English one. The reason cannot be because these ingredients are not of the same outstanding quality as the fish or the vegetables.

Just think of the beef of Tuscany, the Chianina breed, or of Piedmont, the Fusone breed. Think also of the veal of the Po valley, of which Simon Hopkinson writes in his excellent book *Roast Chicken and Other Stories*, 'it is their (the Italians') number one meat.' Then there are the chickens of the Val d'Arno, comparable to the Poulets de Bresse, the superb pork of the Cinta breed from Siena, the Sardinian piglets, the wild boars of southern Tuscany, the guinea-fowl and the ducks of Treviso and Mantova, the *abbacchio* – baby lamb – of Rome, the kids and squabs of Le Marche and Umbria or the venison of Val d'Aosta . . . all animals and birds reared according to ancient traditions and cooked with the love and creativity that is the hallmark of Italian cooking.

You may have had some *porchetta* in the markets of central Italy or a chicken roasted there on the spit. This is food very simply cooked, superb just because the basic ingredients are superb. Sadly enough it is often in restaurants that the meat and poultry dishes are not of the same calibre as the antipasti or the first courses. And this might be the reason why meat is often considered second best.

In this chapter I give many recipes for meat and poultry, and they are my usual mixture of traditional, modern and family.

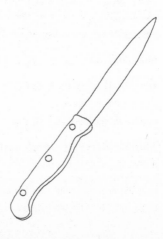

the authentic milanese ossobuco
ossobuco alla milanese

Serves 4
4 ossobuchi
2 tbsp olive oil
flour for dusting
sea salt
45 g (1 1/2 oz)
  unsalted butter
1 small onion, finely
  chopped
1/2 celery stick,
  finely chopped
150 ml (1/4 pint) dry
  white wine
300 ml (1/2 pint)
  meat stock
pepper

For the gremolada
grated rind of 1
  organic lemon
1 garlic clove, peeled
  and very finely
  chopped
2 tbsp chopped flat-
  leaf parsley

Two important characteristics distinguish a Milanese ossobuco from other versions of this dish. Firstly it is flavoured with lemon rind, which is incorporated in a sauce called a gremolada, and secondly it is cooked in bianco, without tomato. To some extent the one explains the other, since the flavour of the gremolada would be swamped by a tomato-based sauce. Another good reason for excluding tomatoes is that ossobuco alla milanese is eaten with risotto alla milanese, and this delicate saffron-flavoured risotto could not survive alongside an ossobuco with a strong tomato flavour. As a loyal Milanese who strives to defend our highly sophisticated cuisine from the intrusion of foreign flavour, I can do no better than quote from the great nineteenth-century writer, Artusi: 'This is a dish that should be left to the Milanese, since it is a speciality of the Lombard cuisine.'

When you eat ossobuco, don't forget to scoop out the marrow inside the bone. Nowadays, alas, very few households have that irreplaceable tool of days gone by, the marrow spoon, but an effective, if less gracious, substitute is the handle of a coffee spoon. All too often I see people in restaurants leaving the marrow in the bone, which seems such a waste of the best titbit.

Ossobuchi *should be cut from the middle of the shin where the bone is surrounded by meat. They should be about (1 3/4 inches) thick.*

Tie the *ossobuchi* around and across as you would a parcel. Choose a heavy sauté pan, with a tight-fitting lid, large enough to hold the *ossobuchi* in a single layer. Heat the oil, and meanwhile lightly coat the *ossobuchi* with some flour in which you have mixed a teaspoon of salt.

Brown the *ossobuchi* on both sides and then remove to a side dish.

Add 30 g (1 oz) of the butter to the sauté pan together with the onion and the celery. Sprinkle with a little salt, which will help the onion to release its moisture so that it gets soft without browning.

When the vegetables are soft, return the meat, and the juice that will have come out, to the pan.

Heat the wine and pour over the meat. Turn the heat up and reduce the liquid by half, while scraping the bottom of the pan with a metal spoon.

Heat the stock in the pan you used to heat the wine and pour about three-quarters over the *ossobuchi*. Turn the heat down to very low and cover the pan. Cook for about 1 1/2–2 hours, until the meat has begun to come away from the bone. Carefully turn the *ossobuchi* every 20 minutes or so, taking care not to damage the marrow in the bones. If necessary, add more stock during the cooking. If, by the time the meat is cooked, the sauce is too thin, remove the meat from the pan and reduce the liquid by boiling briskly.

Transfer the *ossobuchi* to a heated serving dish and remove the string. Keep warm in a cool oven.

Cut the remaining butter into 3 or 4 pieces and add gradually to the sauce. As soon as the butter is melted, draw off the heat, as the sauce should not boil. This addition of the butter will give the sauce a glossy shine and a delicate taste.

Mix the ingredients for the *gremolada* together and stir into the sauce. Spoon the sauce over the *ossobuchi* and serve at once.

preparation
You can prepare the dish in advance up to the point where you transfer the *ossobuchi* to the serving dish, and then reheat it.

costoletta e cotoletta

One of the main functions of breadcrumbs is to give that delicious outside coating to food that is fried in butter. This method of cooking is typical of Lombardy, where butter plays such an important part. The best known dish of this kind is *costoletta alla milanese*, which consists of a veal chop, lightly pounded, coated in eggs, breaded and fried in butter. It is a mouth-watering dish, though not so easy to make perfectly as you might think. The outside crust must be beautifully golden, with no black specks of burnt crumbs, while the veal inside must be cooked *à point*, i.e. no longer pink but still succulent. *Cotolette*, escalopes of veal cooked in the same way, are easier to make. The escalopes, being sliced thin, need very little cooking, and there is thus less danger of burning the crust. Both *costolette* and *cotolette* can also be eaten cold, when they make excellent picnic food.

I still remember the grand picnics we used to have every summer before the war, on our way to Forte dei Marmi in Tuscany for our seaside holidays. We went with our cousins, a caravan of three cars loaded with children, nannies, trunks, suitcases and dogs. The road over the Apennines was long and twisting (no Parma-La Spezia motorway then) and it took the whole day to get there. This was partly because we stopped high up on the Cisa pass to have our elaborate picnic lunch. White tablecloths were spread out on the emerald green pasture, the hampers came out of the vast car boots and the food boxes were opened. I was the youngest of the cousins and I had to fight to get my *costoletta*, my favourite food, so delicious, and so perfect to eat with its bone serving as a handle. The grown-ups often had *cotolette* instead, which they ate with a touch of mayonnaise. (French dishes and customs had become part of the Lombard cuisine during the nineteenth century.)

Pork, chicken or turkey breast, liver, brains and sweetbreads can be cooked *a cotoletta* – breaded and fried – as, of course, can fish steaks or fish fillets. Slices of aubergine are delicious prepared in this way. Meat *cotolette* can also form part of more elaborate dishes. You can put a slice of Gruyère over each *cotoletta*, place them in an ovenproof dish, spoon over some béchamel and bake them in the oven for 10-15 minutes. Another way to serve *cotolette* is to place a slice of mozzarella over the meat, cover with a spoonful of tomato sauce, sprinkle with a little oregano and then bake them until the cheese has melted. Breaded pork steaks can be served in *saor*, with the same sauce that is poured over sardines in the recipe on page 122.

veal chops cooked the milanese way
costolette alla milanese

This is by far the best way to prepare veal chops. It is not easy, but if you buy the right meat, and follow the method carefully, you will be amply rewarded by the result.

First you need a good and reliable butcher. When you buy veal chops for this dish, check that the meat is very pale pink and the fat milky white. Ask the butcher to pound the chops to a thickness of 1 cm (1/2 inch) and to knock off the corner where the rib joins the backbone, and to trim off the tail end of the chop. (You can use these trimmings for stock or for a ragù.)

I fry my costolette, and any other breaded food, by putting them with the butter in a cold pan which is only then put on the heat, a secret I learnt from the gastronome and author Livio Cerini di Castegnate in his book Il Cuoco Gentiluomo. In this way the butter does not become dark, and the chops cook through while remaining golden on the outside.

Beat the eggs lightly in a soup plate with a little salt.

Spread out the breadcrumbs in a dish.

Dip the chops in the egg, coating both sides, then let the excess egg fall back into the plate.

Then coat the chops with the crumbs, pressing them into the meat with your hands.

Choose a large, heavy frying pan into which the chops will fit easily in a single layer. Grease the bottom of the pan with the oil and then put little knobs of butter here and there. Only use about three-quarters of the butter. Lay the chops in the buttered pan and only then put the pan on a low to moderate heat. Move the chops around all the time while they are cooking to prevent them sticking. Cook for about 4 minutes on one side, then turn them over and fry the other side. Add the rest of the butter in small pieces, placing them here and there between the chops. Continue cooking gently and moving the chops around for a further 3 minutes. The timing depends on the thickness of the chop. The meat should be cooked through to the bone, but still moist and succulent.

When done, transfer the chops to a heated dish, pour over the sizzling butter and serve at once.

Serves 4
2 free-range eggs
sea salt
4 veal rib chops
about 150 g (5 oz) dried white breadcrumbs
1 tbsp olive oil
60 g (2 oz) unsalted butter

veal with lemon and cream
vitello al limone

Serves 6
1.5 kg (3 3/4 lb) veal joint in a single piece, tied in a neat roll
2 large organic lemons
sea salt and pepper
1 sprig of rosemary
6 fresh sage leaves
2 sprigs of thyme
1 small bunch of parsley
a handful of celery leaves
1 garlic clove, peeled
100 g (3 1/4 oz) unsalted butter
300 ml (1/2 pint) double cream

This is the sort of dish that can only be made if you can get hold of a good piece of veal. Ask your butcher for a joint suitable for roasting, such as top rump or sirloin.

Put the veal in a bowl and squeeze the juice of 1 lemon over it. Season with salt and pepper and marinate for about 2 hours. Chop all the herbs, the celery leaves and the garlic, and put in an oval casserole which will hold the piece of meat rather snugly. Add the butter and sauté the herbs for 1 minute.

Dry the veal thoroughly and add to the casserole. Sauté gently on all sides; the meat should just lose its raw colour.

While the veal is sautéing, peel the other lemon to the quick and slice the flesh very thinly. Tuck the slices under the meat. Heat the cream and pour it over the meat. Sprinkle with salt and pepper. Cover the casserole, putting the lid slightly askew – this will intensify the flavour of the sauce by letting the vapours evaporate. Cook for 1 1/2–2 hours, turning the veal over from time to time.

When the veal is cooked – the timing depends on the cut of the veal and the thickness of the joint, but it must be tender right through when pricked with a fork – taste and check the seasonings of the sauce. If it seems a little watery, remove the veal to a carving board and cover loosely with foil. Reduce the sauce by boiling it fast until rich and fully flavoured.

Let the veal rest for 5 minutes before carving it into 1 cm (1/2 inch) slices. An electric carving knife is a great help when carving a braised joint like this. Lay the slices, slightly overlapping, on a heated dish. Spoon some of the sauce over it and serve the rest separately in a sauce-boat.

preparation
The dish can be prepared up to 2 days in advance and refrigerated. It can also be frozen, but it must be thawed before reheating. Carve it before reheating it in the casserole.

cold roast veal with herbs
arrosto freddo alle erbe

This is a very easy dish. It is a normal roast, served with a sauce that adds a distinctive touch and makes it a suitable dish for a summer dinner party.

There are two things I should mention. Firstly, the sauce must be made with fresh herbs, and secondly, the choice of the right piece of veal is essential to the success of the dish. I find that the best joint to use is a rolled-up shoulder or breast of veal. These cuts contain some fat, which is necessary when roasting meat such as veal that tends to be dry. The marinating, too, helps to keep the meat moist during the cooking.

The fact that the meat is carved cold prevents it from falling apart, as can all too easily happen when a rolled-up joint is carved hot. The weight of the joint given here is for a shoulder or breast of veal already boned.

Ask your butcher to bone the veal and give you the bone. Ask him also to trim the sinews and any excess fat from the veal and to roll it and tie it up neatly.

Put the meat in a pot, add the ingredients for the marinade and leave for 24 hours. The pot should be left, covered, in a cool place, preferably not in the refrigerator. If you do not have a larder, a garden shed is ideal, as long as it isn't one of those rare British phenomena, a hot and sunny summer's day. (Although, I must add, a far more common kind of summer's day — sultry and humid without any sun — is even worse for keeping food.) If you have to put the meat in the fridge, cover it loosely and take it out at least 2 hours before cooking.

Heat the oven to 180°C (350°F) mark 4.

Heat 2 tablespoons of the oil in a heavy-bottomed roasting tin or in a frying pan, and brown the meat all over. Now transfer the meat to a roasting tin, if you are not already using one, and put the bones around it. Pour over 3 or 4 tablespoons of the marinade, sprinkle with a little salt and some pepper and cook in the preheated oven for about 1 1/4 hours. Baste every so often and add a further couple of tablespoons of the wine marinade whenever the meat gets too dry.

When the veal is tender, remove it from the tin on to a plate. Remove and discard the bones. Skim off most of the fat floating on the surface

Serves 6

1.2 kg (2 1/2 lb) boned shoulder of veal (see recipe)
6 tbsp olive oil
sea salt and freshly ground black pepper
4 tbsp chopped herbs: thyme, marjoram, parsley, rosemary, sage and 2 mint leaves

For the marinade
500 ml (16 fl oz) good dry white wine
sea salt
5 or 6 peppercorns, bruised
1 bay leaf
1 garlic clove, bruised

of the cooking juices and then deglaze with a couple of tablespoons of cold water. Boil rapidly for a minute or two and strain into a bowl.

About an hour before you want to serve the meat, put the chopped herbs into a bowl and gradually add the remaining oil, while beating with a fork to thicken the sauce. Remove any fat floating on top of the cooking juices and add 3 tablespoons to the herbs mixture. Taste and adjust the seasonings. You may like to add a little more of the juices, but remember that their strong flavour should not overpower the fresh taste of the herbs: it should only be a foil to them.

Carve the veal in thin slices and arrange them on a large dish. Coat the slices with the sauce and leave, covered with clingfilm, to absorb the flavour.

veal in a tuna sauce
vitello tonnato alla milanese

Serves 8
**1 joint of veal,
such as rump or
sirloin, about
1.5 kg (3 3/4 lb)**
1 carrot
1 celery stick
**1 medium onion,
stuck with 2 cloves**
1 bay leaf
a few parsley stalks
sea salt
**6 peppercorns,
bruised**
**150 ml (1/4 pint) dry
white wine**

continued over >>

Vitello tonnato is a very elegant summer dish – it is the dish most northern Italian hostesses would serve at a supper party. In the old days it was the traditional dish served on 15 August, Ferragosto, the feast of the Assumption of the Virgin. My recipe comes from my mother, and every time I make it I remember the occasion when her *vitel tonné* (as it was called in Milanese dialect) finished on the dining-room floor. It was at a lunch party at the beginning of the war, and my mother had managed to find the right joint of veal, a triumph at that time when meat was getting scarce. The beautiful dish was brought in by Augusta, our maid, who was a real exhibitionist when waiting at table. She loved to dress up with frilly apron, crest and white gloves, and would make her entry into the dining-room as if she was on stage, carrying large dishes poised delicately on one hand, and taking tiny elegant steps with her short fat legs. She tripped over the carpet, and the next thing I remember is the beige sticky mess on the floor. It was a family lunch with some aunts and uncles, and I remember my Aunt Esther getting up, scooping up the meat and saying, in Milanese dialect, '*Ma l'è tropo bun e mi me lo magni istess*' ('But it's too good and I'm going to eat it just the same'). Augusta, by now in tears, was asked to collect the debris, clean off the sauce and tell cook to reconstruct the dish with the left-over sauce. The *vitel tonné* reappeared a few minutes later, beautifully decorated with lemon butterflies and cornichon fans, just as it had been before.

My mother's recipe is the traditional recipe from Milan, where the sauce is made with cream instead of mayonnaise; the version with mayonnaise being from Piedmont.

Because it is difficult to find the right cut of veal, I have often used loin of pork or chicken instead, cooking it whole in the same way and cutting it into pieces when cold. But what you really need is good tuna, not skipjack. Buy Italian or Spanish tuna preserved in olive oil or brine, available in specialist shops and good delicatessens.

Ask the butcher to tie the joint in a neat shape. Put it in a casserole with the carrot, celery, onion, bay leaf, parsley stalks, a little salt and the peppercorns. Pour in the wine and half the stock and bring slowly to the boil. Cover the pan tightly and cook for about 1 1/2 hours until the meat is tender. Draw off the heat and leave to cool in the pan.

When the veal is cold, cut it into 1 cm (1/2 inch) slices and lay them, slighly overlapping, on a serving dish.

Remove the bay leaf and the parsley stalks from the cooking juices. Purée all the cooking juices and the vegetables in a food processor. Transfer the purée to a bowl.

Put the tuna and the anchovies in the food processor. Add a few tablespoons of the remaining stock and process for 1 minute or so. Scrape the bits down from the side of the bowl and add a few tablespoons of the purée, the cream and the sugar. Process again, while gradually adding the lemon juice and the olive oil. You might not need to add all the lemon juice, or you might want a little more. Taste a few times and correct the sauce to your liking, adding salt if necessary and a good grinding of pepper. The sauce should have the consistency of single

300 ml (1/2 pint) chicken stock
225 g (8 oz) tuna, packed in olive oil
6 anchovy fillets
6 tbsp double cream
1 tsp caster sugar
juice of 1 organic lemon
4 tbsp extra virgin olive oil
2 tbsp fresh tarragon

For the garnish
1 organic lemon
a few cornichons

cream. If necessary add more stock. Coat the veal slices with a few tablespoons of the sauce. Cover with clingfilm and refrigerate.

When you are ready to serve the veal, spoon over a little more sauce and transfer the rest of the sauce to a bowl, to be handed round separately. Coarsely chop or cut the tarragon and scatter over the veal. Garnish with the lemon and the cornichons, if you wish, and serve with a bowl of cold rice dressed with some extra virgin olive oil.

preparation
The dish is best made a day or even 2 days in advance.

roast leg of lamb with small onions
cosciotto di agnello arrosto con le cipolline

Serves 8–10
**30 g (1 oz) pancetta
or unsmoked
streaky bacon
3 garlic cloves, peeled
2.25–2.7 kg (5–6 lb)
leg of lamb
300 ml (1/2 pint)
good, but light,
Italian red wine
450 g (1 lb) small
white onions
1 tsp sugar
juice of 1 organic
lemon
juice of 2 oranges
sea salt and pepper**

continued over >>

I have chosen this recipe from a lovely old book that I found in my mother's bookcase. I have to confess that the book is no longer there, having mysteriously transferred itself to my collection. The book, published in 1863, is called Il Cuoco Milanese *and its subtitle says it is 'An indispensable cooking manual for families of every class'. Perhaps 'indispensable' is an overstatement, but the book is full of good recipes.*

The lamb should be cooked for 3 hours according to the recipe, but we are now used to meat that tends to be on the undercooked side, so I cut the time to 2 hours. This will give you a cooked roast, not a pink one, which is better for this kind of slow roasting with wine and onions. You can always shorten the timing if you like your lamb pink. The meat juices are sharpened by the juices of the lemon and oranges. Choose oranges that are not too sweet, such as blood oranges from Sicily.

Chop and mix the pancetta and the garlic. Make a few deep slits in the lamb along the grain of the meat and push little pellets of the mixture into the slits.

Rub the lamb with salt, place it in a roasting tin and pour over the olive oil. Add the herbs and peppercorns and leave to marinate for 24 hours. The dish should be kept in a cold place, but not in the refrigerator. Unless the weather is hot and sultry you can keep it, covered, in the kitchen.

Heat the oven to 180°C (350°F) mark 4.

Pour the wine over the lamb and place in the oven. Baste the meat every 30 minutes or so.

Put the onions in a pan, cover with cold water and bring to the boil, then drain them. This will make them easier to peel and help spare your tears. Remove the outside skin and any dangling roots, but do not remove any layer of onion or cut into the root: this is what keeps them whole during the cooking.

About 1 hour after you put the lamb in the oven, add the onions. Put the tin back in the oven and continue cooking until the meat is to your liking. A joint of this size will need about 2 hours, because when cooked in this way the lamb should be well cooked, not pink.

Remove the leg from the tin and set aside to rest while you prepare the sauce. Any large joint should be left to rest for at least 10 minutes before carving, for the juices to penetrate the meat.

Lift the onions with a slotted spoon and put them into a heated dish or bowl.

Strain the cooking juices into a clean saucepan. Skim off as much fat as you possibly can – a boring job but quite necessary for a delicate gravy. Heat the cooking juices and add the sugar and the juice of the lemon and the oranges. Taste and adjust the seasonings. When the sauce is simmering, add the butter in little pieces and let it dissolve, while swirling the pan. Transfer to a heated sauce-boat. Now you are ready to carve the joint at the table and hand round the onions, the sauce and any other vegetables.

30 g (1 oz) unsalted butter

For the marinade
1/2 tbsp coarse sea salt
4 tbsp olive oil
fresh herbs, e.g. 1 sprig of parsley, a few celery leaves, 1 sprig of rosemary, 2 or 3 sage leaves, 2 sprigs of thyme, 1 sprig of marjoram
6 peppercorns, bruised

roast leg of lamb with a saffron and balsamic vinegar sauce

agnello arrosto alla moda del rinascimento

Serves 8
2–2.25 kg
(4 1/2–5 lb) leg
of lamb
4 or 5 garlic cloves
2 tbsp mixed fresh
herbs (rosemary,
sage, thyme,
marjoram, parsley,
lovage or celery
leaves)
sea salt and pepper
75 g (2 1/2 oz)
pancetta or
unsmoked streaky
bacon, in a single
slice
2 tbsp olive oil
450 ml (3/4 pint)
dark meat stock
1/4 tsp saffron
powder or saffron
strands
4 tbsp balsamic
vinegar
1 free-range egg yolk
30 g (1 oz) unsalted
butter

*This roast lamb is an interesting and excellent dish which I have
adapted from a recipe in Maestro Martino's* Libro de Arte Coquinaria,
*published in 1450. Maestro Martino was the chef to the Patriarch of
Aquileia, a town near Venice. Little is known about the man, but
fortunately his manuscript was incorporated in full in the book* De
Honesta Voluptate et Valetudine *by Platina, first published in Latin in
1475, which became well known throughout continental Europe.*

*In those days, spices were used with great liberality. They came from
the Middle East via one of Italy's maritime republics and were sold at
very high prices; their use was thus a sign of wealth. Saffron was
especially popular because of its golden colour. In this dish the colour
does not come through the rich brown of the gravy, but the slight
metallic and highly aromatic taste of the spice certainly does.*

*If you have a butcher who knows his job, ask him to saw off the bone
at the extremity of the shin, just above the knuckle joint. The section of
pelvic bone can then be removed, making the carving much easier.
Also ask your butcher to remove any excess surface fat.*

*The cooking time is a question of personal taste, but for this dish 15
minutes per 450 g (1 lb) is enough.*

Heat the oven to 220°C (425°F) mark 7.

Chop the garlic and herbs and add salt and pepper. Cut the pancetta
into strips, coat with the herb mixture and lard the lamb joint with the
coated strips. Rub the joint with the oil and any left-over mixture of
garlic and herbs and place it on a rack.

Heat the stock. If you are using saffron strands, pound them in a
mortar. (You will find this easier to do if you sprinkle a pinch of
granulated sugar in with the saffron.) Dissolve the saffron in half the
stock, then beat in half the balsamic vinegar and the egg yolk. Add a
little salt and pepper and pour the mixture into a roasting tin. Place in
the oven. Place the meat on its rack above, so that the juices from the
meat drip into the tin.

Cook for 15 minutes and then turn down the heat to 190°C (375°F)
mark 5 and cook until the meat is done. (If you like the meat pink,

allow about 1 1/2 hours from the time you put it into the oven.) Baste the joint with the sauce in the tin every 20 minutes or so. Remove the meat from the oven and leave it in a warm place for 15–20 minutes.

Meanwhile make the sauce. Strain the contents of the roasting tin into a saucepan and add the remaining stock. Bring to the boil and add the rest of the balsamic vinegar and then the butter little by little, swirling the pan until completely dissolved. Taste and check the seasonings. Pour into a heated sauce-boat. Carve the meat into fairly thick slices and hand round the sauce.

meat and potato pie
tiella di carne e patate

An Italian meat pie usually has a topping of sliced potatoes, not mashed potatoes like the English equivalent.

If you have a friendly butcher, ask him to remove all the fat and gristle from the beef and pork and to cut the meat into 1.5 cm (3/4 inch) cubes. Otherwise you need to do this yourself.

Put the oil, a third of the butter and the onion in a heavy sauté pan (ideally it should be a large earthenware pot). Sprinkle with the sugar and 1 teaspoon of salt and sauté gently until the onion is soft.

Meanwhile chop the celery, carrots, garlic, thyme, sage and rosemary together either by hand or in a food processor. When the onion is cooked, add the vegetable mixture, nutmeg, pepper and oregano to the pan and cook for 10 minutes, stirring frequently. Stir in the tomato purée, cook for 1 minute and then add the meat. Cook until the meat has lost its raw colour, turning it over frequently. Splash with the wine and cook for 10 minutes. Mix in the milk and bring to the boil. Cook

Serves 10
1.35 kg (3 lb)
  braising steak
450 g (1 lb) pork
  steak
9 tbsp olive oil
120 g (4 oz) unsalted
  butter
1 Spanish onion,
  finely chopped
1 tbsp sugar
sea salt
3 celery stalks
2 carrots
4 garlic cloves
2 tbsp thyme
6 sage leaves
2 tbsp rosemary
  leaves
1/4 tsp grated
  nutmeg

continued over >>

pepper
1 tbsp dried oregano
6 tbsp tomato purée
300 ml (1/2 pint) red wine
180 ml (6 fl oz) full-fat milk
2 kg (4 1/2 lb) waxy potatoes
120 g (4 oz) freshly grated Parmesan
1 large bunch of flat-leaf parsley, chopped

over a very gentle heat until the meat is tender, about 40 minutes. If there is too much liquid by the end of the cooking, turn the heat up and boil rapidly to reduce the juice, which should be rich and full of flavour. Taste and check the seasoning.

While the meat is cooking, peel the potatoes and cut them into wafer-thin slices. A food processor with the fine blade disc is invaluable for what is otherwise a lengthy job. Put the potatoes in a bowl of cold water and rub the slices together to get rid of some of the starch. Drain and turn the potatoes on to a tea-towel. Dry them thoroughly.

Heat the oven to 200°C (400°F) mark 6.

Butter a large lasagne dish or a shallow oven dish into which the meat should spread to a thickness of about 2.5–4 cm (1–1 1/2 inches). Use 2 dishes if you do not have one large enough.

Melt the remaining butter in a small pan.

Spread the potatoes over the bottom of the dish, season with salt and pepper and pour over a little of the melted butter. Cover with the meat and sprinkle with half the cheese. Spread the remaining potatoes neatly over the meat and top with the remaining cheese. Spoon the remaining melted butter all over, cover with foil and place the dish in the preheated oven.

Cook for 20 minutes and then remove the foil and continue cooking until the potatoes are done, about 35 minutes. Allow the dish to stand for 5 minutes out of the oven before serving, so that all the flavours can blend. Sprinkle the top of the pie with the chopped parsley and bring to the table.

hand of pork braised in water with herbs and garlic
arrosto di maiale all'acqua

This might seem a dull way to cook a joint of pork, but I can heartily recommend it. All you need is some plump young garlic, a lovely bunch of fresh herbs and a top-quality piece of pork, plus patience at the end when adding the stock very gradually to brown the meat. Ask the butcher for the bones and the rind.

Remove the meat from the refrigerator 2 hours in advance. (All meat should be cooked at room temperature.)

Heat the oven to 170°C (325°F) mark 3.

Put the meat, bones, sage, rosemary, garlic, peppercorns and salt in an oval casserole. Add a piece of the rind (the rest can be frozen to add to vegetable or bean soups). Pour over enough water to just cover the joint. Place a tight lid on the casserole and bring slowly to the boil. Place a sheet of foil over the meat, re-cover with the lid and put the casserole in the oven. Cook for about 2 1/2–3 hours until the meat is very tender when pierced with a fork. Turn the joint over 2 or 3 times during the cooking. Transfer the joint to a large plate and strain the stock into a bowl.

Put about 120 ml (4 fl oz) of the stock into the washed-out casserole, bring to the boil and add the meat. Let the stock evaporate over a very lively heat, while turning the meat over and over. When there is hardly any liquid left, add another 120 ml (4 fl oz) of the stock and let it bubble away in the same manner. Continue adding stock and bubbling it away while turning the meat, until you have about 200 ml (7 fl oz) of the stock left in the bowl.

Transfer the meat, which by now should be dark brown all over, to a carving board. Deglaze the cooking residue with the wine. Boil for 2 minutes and then add the rest of the stock and reduce, still over a high heat. When the juices have reduced to about half their original volume, add the butter, a little at a time, while stirring gently. Taste and adjust the seasoning.

Carve the meat into 1 cm (1/2 inch) slices and lay them on a heated dish. Spoon over a little of the gravy and serve the rest in a sauce-boat.

Serves 6
1.35–1.5 kg
(3–3 1/4 lb)
rindless hand of
pork, boned and
tied in a roll
2 fresh sage leaves
3 fresh rosemary
sprigs, about 12 cm
(5 inches) long
10 garlic cloves,
peeled
5 or 6 peppercorns,
lightly bruised
sea salt
120 ml (4 fl oz) dry
white wine
freshly ground black
pepper
30 g (1 oz) unsalted
butter

preparation

The browning of the meat takes longer than you might think – about 20 minutes. You can prepare the dish half an hour in advance, and then keep the meat covered in foil, in a low oven. Remove the meat from the oven at least 10 minutes before carving; this relaxes the meat and allows the juices to penetrate the inside of the joint.

loin of pork braised in milk
maiale al latte

Serves 8
1.5 kg (3 1/4 lb) loin of pork, boned and rindless but with a thin layer of fat still on
4 tbsp vegetable oil
4 cloves, bruised
pinch of ground cinnamon
sprig of rosemary
3 garlic cloves, peeled and bruised
rock salt and freshly ground black pepper
6–7 peppercorns, bruised
1 bay leaf
30 g (1 oz) unsalted butter
450 ml (3/4 pint) full-fat milk

This is a traditional dish from central Italy. I marinate the meat because I find that pork these days is often dry, and sometimes tasteless. My mother, who used to come to England regularly for many years, would say, equally regularly, 'Ma pensare, che il maiale era squisito in Inghilterra anni fa' ('To think that pork used to be so good in England years ago'). I live in hope that the trend will change so that we can once again have good pork like those good old days! Perhaps the trend for organic meat, available in some butchers and supermarkets, will provide the answer. In the meantime, marinating is the solution.

After marinating, my pork is braised in milk, which at the end of the cooking turns into a thick, rich sauce studded with golden nuggets. With it I serve a potato purée, not too thin this time, to mop up the juices.

Tie the joint in several places, if the butcher has not done it for you.

Put the meat in a bowl and add 2 tablespoons of the oil, the cloves, cinnamon, rosemary, garlic, 1 teaspoon of rock salt, the peppercorns and the bay leaf. Coat the pork all over in the marinade, cover the bowl with a lid of some sort and marinate for about 8 hours. Do not put the bowl in the refrigerator unless the weather is very hot. Turn the meat over in the marinade whenever you remember.

Heat the butter and the rest of the oil in a heavy casserole into which the pork will fit snugly. When the butter foam begins to subside, add the dried joint and brown well on all sides to a rich golden colour.

Heat the milk to boiling point and pour slowly over the meat. Sprinkle with salt and ground pepper, place the lid over the pan slightly askew, and cook for about 3 hours at a steady low simmer. Turn the meat over and baste every 20 minutes or so. By the end of the cooking the meat should be very tender and the sauce should be a rich dark golden colour, and quite thick. If it is too thin by the time the meat is done, remove the meat to a side dish and boil the sauce briskly without the lid on until it darkens and thickens.

Transfer the meat to a carrying board and leave to cool for a few minutes.

Meanwhile skim off as much fat as you can from the surface of the sauce, add 2 tablespoons of hot water and boil over high heat for about 2 minutes, while scraping the bottom of the pan with a metal spoon. Taste and adjust the seasonings.

Remove the string and carve the pork into 1 cm (1/2 inch) slices. Arrange the slices on a heated dish and spoon the sauce over the slices, or spoon over only a little of the sauce and serve the rest separately in a warm sauce-boat.

preparation

The meat can be cooked up to 3 days in advance and kept, covered, in the refrigerator. It can also be frozen. Thaw completely before reheating. Carve the meat and cover with the sauce when still cold and then reheat very gently, covered, in a moderate oven for 15 minutes.

mixed boiled meats
bollito misto

Serves 10–12
**1 large onion, stuck
with 1 clove
2 celery sticks, cut
into chunks
1 leek, cut into
chunks
2 carrots, cut into
chunks
1 kg (2 lb) beef flank
or brisket
3 fresh ripe
tomatoes, cut in
half
5–6 peppercorns
lightly crushed
a few parsley stalks
sea salt
450 g (1 lb) shoulder
of veal, boned, or 2
large *ossobuchi*
1/2 a fresh free-
range or organic
chicken, preferably
a boiling hen
1 *cotechino*, about
450 g (1 lb)**

Bollito misto is the ideal dish when you have a lot of people to feed, since at its best it contains many different kinds of meat. *Bollito misto* is made in all northern Italian regions; if you go there, do keep a look-out for a restaurant that serves it – a sure sign of a top-class establishment. A trolley with many compartments will be wheeled to your table and from it you can choose a thick slice of beef, a small chunk of veal, a leg of chicken, a slice or two of *cotechino* (see page 178) and one of tongue, plus a few boiled vegetables. All the meats are immersed in steaming stock, giving off a rich and intense aroma that holds promise of the delights to come.

I was brought up on *bollito misto*. It appeared on the table of our home in Milan every Monday, so that there was stock in the kitchen for most of the week. When I came to live in England meat was still scarce (it was rationed until 1954, nine years after the end of the war) and cuts suitable for *bollito misto* were unobtainable. But slowly things improved and my mind turned to one of my favourite dishes. At first my husband, with the English 'boiled beef and carrots' in mind was dubious about this dish of which I spoke with such enthusiasm. But soon, as more and more of the right cuts became available my *bollito* began to be accepted with pleasure, until eventually *bollito misto* became a family favourite.

Bollito misto is a convivial dish which must be offered in generous quantities, accompanied by at least 2 sauces and the delicious *mostarda di frutta*. There are quite a few *mostarde* on the market, but the most popular and easily available kind is *mostarda di Cremona*. Also called *mostarda di frutta*, it consists of various fruits, previously candied and then preserved in a thick syrup of white wine and honey highly spiced with mustard. Truth to tell, I am quite happy to do without the other sauces and have only *mostarda*, but as it is not to everyone's taste I am including recipes for the three best sauces to go with *bollito misto*: green sauce, honey, walnut and pine nut sauce, and red sauce. The honey sauce is quite delicious, by the way.

My recipe for *bollito misto* is for 10–12 people, but you can of course scale it down, by leaving out the *cotechino*, for instance. When I do *bollito* for the family, I cook only a piece of flank or brisket and one or two *ossobuchi*. The trimmings are the same, although I would do only

one sauce, or just put my best olive oil on the table, plus the jar of
mostarda di Cremona, and let everybody get on with it. *Bollito misto* is
always accompanied by boiled vegetables.

Put the onion, celery, leek and carrots in a saucepan, cover with cold
water and bring to the boil. Add the beef and bring back to the boil.
Lower the heat – the stock should just be simmering. Remove the
scum that comes to the surface during the first few minutes of
cooking. Add the tomatoes, peppercorns, parsley and some salt. Cover
the pan and simmer for 1 1/2 hours.

Add the veal and simmer for a further hour. Put in the chicken and cook
for 1–1 1/2 hours, depending on whether it is a roaster or a boiler. If you
are using a precooked *cotechino*, follow the manufacturer's instructions.
If the *cotechino* is uncooked, follow my instructions given in the recipe
for *cotechino allo zabaione* on page 179.

When you serve the *bollito*, lift one piece of meat at a time out of the
stock and carve only as much as you need to go round for the first
helping. Keep the rest in the stock, as this prevents the meat from
getting dry. If you have also cooked the *cotechino*, transfer it to the
stockpot with all the other meats.

Put the carved meat on a large heated platter and bring it to the table,
with dishes of boiled potatoes, boiled carrots, boiled onions and any
other seasonal roots all cooked separately, and little bowls of sauces
such as the honey, walnut and pine nut sauce on page 382, the green
sauce on page 427, or the red sauce on page 206.

preparation

You can cook the *bollito misto* 1 day in advance, but do not put in the
chicken. Bring the *bollito* back to the boil and add the chicken about
1–1 1/2 hours before serving.

sweetbreads glazed with marsala
animelle al marsala

Serves 2
**225 g (8 oz) lamb
sweetbreads**
**2 tsp lemon juice or
wine vinegar**
**45 g (1 1/2 oz)
unsalted butter**
3 fresh sage leaves
2 tbsp white flour
sea salt
**6 tbsp Marsala or
sweet sherry**
**freshly ground black
pepper**

*Sweetbreads are a most delicious and delicate luxury. They also have
the prettiest name of any food, both in English and Italian, thus making
them the ideal dish for a romantic supper. Animelle, a delightful
sounding word, means little souls.*

*For this recipe I prefer to use lamb's sweetbreads, which are easier to
buy than calf's sweetbreads. They are the thymus gland of a young
animal, which shrivels up in adulthood. Because they are so delicate
they are best cooked very simply, as in this recipe. The sweetbreads,
sautéed in butter, are then cooked in Marsala until they become glazed
and succulent. The cooking is quick, about 10 minutes; the preparation
is tiresome, but it can be done well in advance.*

Place the sweetbreads in a bowl and cover with cold water. Leave to
soak for at least 1 hour, to purge them of their blood. Drain and rinse
them. Put them in a saucepan, add water to cover and add the lemon
juice or vinegar. Bring to the boil and simmer gently for 2–3 minutes,
until the sweetbreads have become white and firm. Drain them and
rinse under cold water.

As soon as they are cool enough to handle, remove any tubes or bits of
hardened blood. Put them between 2 plates with a weight on top and leave
for at least 3 hours, or overnight, in the refrigerator. When it is time to cook
them, divide them into nuggets and dry thoroughly with kitchen paper.

Heat the butter with the sage in a sauté pan in which the sweetbreads
will fit in a single layer.

Put the flour and 1/2 a teaspoon of salt in a plastic bag, add the
sweetbreads and shake the bag to coat them with the flour. Turn the
bag upside-down over a sieve and shake the sieve to remove the
excess flour. When the butter foam is beginning to subside, throw in
the floured nuggets and sauté quickly until brown. Splash with the
Marsala and continue cooking for 6–7 minutes until they are dark and
glazed. Season with salt and pepper. Taste and check the juices for
seasoning; they should be rich and syrupy.

preparation
The sweetbreads can be blanched and placed under a weight up to 1
day in advance, and refrigerated.

guinea-fowl cooked in champagne
faraona allo spumante

Guinea-fowl is a wonderful bird, but you must get a good one from a reliable supplier. I have never been disappointed with French guinea-fowl while sometimes the English birds have let me down. Guinea-fowl should have a taste of gaminess and the meat should not be just pale – it should be just a little dark and then it is perfect.

In this recipe the birds are cooked in champagne, which certainly does not need to be a Brut – it can even be a sparkling white wine, such as Prosecco.

Heat the butter and the shallot in a heavy sauté pan or oval casserole that will be large enough to accommodate loosely all the pieces of guinea-fowl. Add a pinch of salt and sauté until the shallot is soft. Set aside.

Cut each guinea-fowl into eight pieces: two wings, two drumsticks, two thighs and two pieces from each breast. Cut off the pinions and keep them with the backs to be used for stock on another occasion. Remove any feathers and wipe the joints all over with kitchen paper.

Put the vegetable oil in a frying pan and turn the heat to medium high. Spread the flour on a board and lightly dredge the guinea-fowl pieces in the flour. Shake off the excess flour and, when the oil is hot but not smoking, slip in as many pieces as will fit loosely into the pan. Fry until a fine gold crust has formed and then turn the pieces over and fry the underside. When the pieces are done on all sides, transfer them to the pan or casserole containing the shallot. Season with salt and pepper and fry another batch, if necessary.

When all the pieces are done, place the pan or casserole over a medium heat. Turn the pieces over once and after about 2 minutes pour over the champagne very slowly. Bring to the boil, turn the heat down to very low and cover the pan. Cook for about 40 minutes, turning the guinea-fowl pieces over every now and then. When the thighs feel tender when pricked with a fork, transfer all the pieces to a heated serving dish and cover with foil to keep warm in a warm oven.

Serves 6–8
90 g (3 oz) unsalted butter
4 shallots, very finely chopped
sea salt and pepper
2 guinea-fowl
6 tbsp vegetable oil
9 tbsp flour
450 ml (3/4 pint) champagne
120 ml (4 fl oz) double cream

Turn the heat up and deglaze the pan with a couple of tablespoons of hot water. Scrape the bottom of the pan with a metal spoon to release any bits, while reducing the cooking juices by a third. Turn the heat down to low and stir in the cream. Mix thoroughly, taste and adjust the seasoning. Bring slowly to the boil. When the cream has thinned down, the sauce is ready. Spoon a little of the sauce over the birds and pour the rest into a heated sauce-boat to hand round separately.

preparation
The birds can be cooked up to 3 days in advance and refrigerated. Reheat very slowly and make the sauce just before serving.

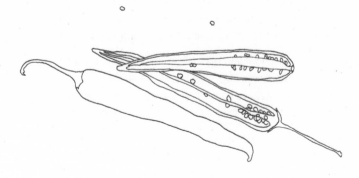

roast guinea-fowl with lemon juice and garlic
faraona arrosto al limone

Serves 6–8
**2 guinea-fowl,
  weighing about
  700 g (1 1/2 lb)
  each**

continued over >>

The Sicilian origins of this recipe can be seen in the liberal use of that island's most plentiful fruit, the lemon. It is certainly one of the most delicious ways I know to prepare a guinea-fowl.

The guinea-fowl is roasted in foil, and then it is jointed and lightly sautéed in olive oil, lemon juice and lots of garlic. The sharp taste of the lemon is counterbalanced by the richness of the oil and the piquancy of the garlic. The result is a beautifully clean and fragrant taste.

Heat the oven to 200°C (400°F) mark 6.

Singe the birds and wash them thoroughly in cold water, inside and out. Put them on a tilted board and allow to drain for about 10 minutes. Dry them well inside and out with kitchen paper.

Push the butter between the skin and the flesh of the breast and drumsticks of the birds. Make small incisions in the thighs of the bird and push small knobs of butter into the cuts. Rub a liberal amount of salt all over the guinea-fowl, pressing it into the flesh with your hands. Put some salt in the cavity and rub it in.

Wrap the guinea-fowls separately in buttered foil. Place the wrapped birds in a roasting tin and roast for 1 hour.

Remove the tin from the oven and cut open the foil. Allow to cool a little and then cut the guinea-fowl into small joints and collect all the juices in a bowl.

Heat the oil with the garlic cloves and then add the guinea-fowl joints. Fry them for 5 minutes on both sides. Splash with the lemon juice and add the lemon rind. Season with salt and lots of pepper and cook for a further 3 minutes, turning the joints over once or twice.

Transfer the joints to a serving dish and keep warm. Remove and discard the garlic.

Pour the cooking juices into the pan and bring to the boil. Cook briskly for about 1 minute and then taste and check the seasoning. Spoon the sauce all over the guinea-fowl joints.

This dish is excellent served with the joints surrounding a pile of *tagliolini* dressed with fresh unsalted butter and plenty of black pepper.

30 g (1 oz) unsalted butter
sea salt
5 tbsp olive oil
8 garlic cloves, peeled and bruised
150 ml (1/4 pint) lemon juice
grated rind of 1 organic lemon
freshly ground black pepper

pot-roast pheasant in a caper, prosciutto, vinegar and truffle sauce
fagiano alla cavalcanti

Serves 6
2 plump hen
 pheasants
a bunch of fresh
 herbs: sage,
 marjoram, parsley,
 rosemary
60 g (2 oz)
 unsmoked streaky
 bacon or pancetta
sea salt and pepper
30 g (1 oz) unsalted
 butter
1 onion
4 cloves
1 garlic clove
5 juniper berries,
 bruised
2 tbsp brandy
150 ml (1/4 pint)
 good dry white
 wine
150 ml (1/4 pint)
 good strong meat
 stock

For the sauce
120 g (4 oz)
 prosciutto
15 g (1/2 oz)
 unsalted butter
1tsp potato flour or
 arrowroot
150 ml (1/4 pint)
 good strong meat
 stock
2 tbsp capers
1 tbsp good red wine
 vinegar
1 tbsp truffle paste

This dish is something quite out of the ordinary. It is adapted from a recipe by one of my favourite cookery writers, Ippolito Cavalcanti, Duca di Buonvicino. You'll find quite a few recipes by Cavalcanti here and there in this book, since I find his *Cucina Teorico-Pratica*, published in 1847, an endless source of inspiration. I have to work hard to adapt the recipes because his quantities are erratic, sometimes extravagant for present-day palates, and are given in the measures used in Naples in the nineteenth century before the metric system was adopted. An example of the extravagance appears in the original recipe for this dish, where the amount of truffle to be added is 1 lb! Even though the truffles were probably not the much-esteemed white truffles of Alba, the *Tuber magnatum*, but only the more common and less flavoursome *Tuber aestivum*, the summer truffle, 1 lb seems somewhat excessive.

In my adaptation I have used truffle paste instead of real truffles. There are several brands of truffle paste, which can be found in the best delis and Italian shops. The cheaper brands contain porcini (ceps) as well as truffle purée, plus butter or oil. Better brands contain only truffle purée and butter or oil. There is also a new type of preserved truffle which I've been given in Italy but not yet seen elsewhere, in which the truffles, cut into pieces, are suspended in melted butter. This is quite delicious, since you can bite into the *cibus deorum*, or food of the gods, as Nero called them. Whatever you use, all these truffle derivatives make a remarkable difference to a dish, something you can verify by dressing some tagliatelle with truffle paste. And don't forget that you only need a very little.

Pheasant, these days, is so heavily farmed as to be closer in flavour to chicken than to the original bird of bygone days. Buy from a reputable shop; preferably buy an unplucked and undrawn bird, and ask the shopkeeper to hang it for the right length of time. How long that might be is the subject of some contention. Brillat-Savarin wrote that 'the desirable point is reached when the pheasant begins to decompose. Then its aroma develops and mingles with an oil that requires a little fermentation for its distillation, just as coffee requires roasting for its full development.' Without subscribing to Brillat-Savarin's instructions, or to those of Grimod de la Reynière, who suggested that 'a pheasant killed on Mardi Gras should be eaten on Easter Sunday' (that is, 40 days later!), I do find that all too often pheasants have an undistinguished taste because they are hardly hung at all. I prefer my pheasants hung for at least 2 weeks in cold weather, but, asking around, I have discovered that most people these days hang them for no longer than one week. It is a matter of personal preference. A hen bird is smaller than a cock, has a more tender flesh and is just perfect for 3 people.

I like to serve polenta with pheasant, either in the soft form or as grilled or fried slices. For a dinner party I always prefer grilled polenta. The polenta is made well in advance. It is cut and prepared in the grill pan and needs atttention only for the very short time it takes to grill. The recipe for polenta can be found on page 69.

For this dish the prosciutto need not be *prosciutto di Parma*. If you can, buy cheaper prosciutto, cut in two or three thick slices.

Remove any stubborn quills from the pheasants, then wipe them clean.

Process the herbs and the bacon or pancetta until the mixture is all pounded. If you do not have a food processor, chop very finely by hand. Season the birds with salt and pepper inside and out and push the bacon mixture into the cavities. Gently beat the breast-bones down with the palm of your hand to give a rounder appearance to the birds. Spread about half the butter all over the breasts.

Put the rest of the butter in a casserole, add the onion, cloves, garlic and juniper berries and sauté for 5–10 minutes. Add the pheasants and brown gently on all sides for a few minutes.

Heat the brandy and pour over the birds. Flame the brandy. Meanwhile heat the wine and half the stock and, when the flame from the brandy has died down, add to the pot. Season lightly, cover the pan and cook for about 1 hour, until the pheasants are cooked through and the juices run clear when you pierce the thighs with a knife.

To make the sauce, cut the prosciutto into neat matchsticks and sauté in the butter for 2 minutes. Dissolve the potato flour or the arrowroot in a little of the cold stock and then add to the saucepan with the rest of the stock. Rinse the capers and mix into the sauce, together with the vinegar and the truffle paste.

Cook for 15 minutes over a very low heat, stirring very frequently, then check the seasoning.

Cut the pheasants into neat joints (4 is ideal) and arrange on a heated dish surrounded by the grilled polenta (page 73). Keep warm. Spoon over some of the cooking juices and strain the remaining juices into the prosciutto and caper sauce. Pour the sauce into a sauce-boat.

preparation

The pheasants can be cooked and jointed up to 2 days in advance and refrigerated. Reheat in a low oven with all the cooking juices. Although pheasants freeze very well when uncooked, I don't recommend freezing the finished dish. The sauce can be made up to 1 hour before serving, and kept hot in a bain-marie.

pheasant with grapes
fagiano all'uva

Serves 3–4
225 g (8 oz) muscat grapes
3 tbsp Cognac or brandy
juice of 1/2 organic lemon
1 pheasant with its giblets
sea salt and pepper
60 g (2 oz) unsalted butter
120 ml (4 fl oz) good meat stock

For years I cooked pheasant *à la Milanaise*, i.e. *in cocotte* with a rich sauce of cream and spices. An excellent recipe, but one that makes a pheasant heavier than it would naturally be. Last year, however, I was introduced to an interesting new way to prepare pheasant. New to me, I should say, since it was in my cousins' home in Milan that I ate this delicious pheasant and they told me that the recipe came from the family's *ricettario* – recipe book – which had been kept by the grandmother who died during the war aged 85. An old Lombard recipe, therefore.

The combination of pheasant with grapes is a natural. After all, pheasants love grapes. I remember in Chianti, where we had a house for many years, the farmers used to shoo the pheasants away from the vines into the scrubland. But the pheasants were so domesticated that after a few minutes they were back among the vines, pecking at the grapes.

It is such a natural combination that Bartolomeo Stefani, chef to the Gonzaga in the second half of the seventeenth century, prepared a fantastic dish based on this theme for the banquet Ottavio Gonzaga gave in honour of Queen Christina of Sweden. The roast pheasant, covered with marzipan, was laid with its head on the edge of the dish, where 2 *putti* made of butter were sitting. One was holding the pheasant's head, while the other was putting grapes into its beak. But I must return to my nineteenth-century recipe.

The characteristic of this dish is a pronounced taste of grapes, sharpened by the cognac marinade. The pheasant, which finishes cooking jointed in the sauce, absorbs the grapey flavour.

I prefer a plump hen pheasant to a cock pheasant; it is tastier and more tender, but being smaller it is not really enough for 4 people. Two hens, if you or your butcher are willing to split the brace, make a perfect course for six.

Wash and dry the grapes and then peel them. A rather boring job, but quite easy if you buy ripe golden muscat grapes. Remove the seeds. (I have found that every cook has a special way of doing this. I remember that one of the most accomplished hostesses and cooks I know swore that the best tool, and the one that caused least damage to the grapes, was a hair-pin. 'Washed, of course,' she hastened to add. But I still prefer the point of a small knife.) Put the grapes in a bowl and sprinkle with 1 tablespoon of the Cognac or brandy and the lemon juice. Leave to marinate for 2 hours.

Heat the oven to 200°C (400°F) mark 6.

Cut the wing pinions off the pheasant. Wipe inside and out with kitchen paper and singe off any stubborn feather shafts. Put the liver, heart and gizzard inside the bird, together with a knob of butter and 2 pinches of salt. Truss the bird with string. Set aside half the butter and rub the remainder all over the bird. Sprinkle with salt.

Choose a roasting tin with a heavy base which you can put on direct heat. Lay the bird in the tin, breast side down. This will prevent the breast from becoming dry since the juices will flow downwards. Cook in the oven for 10 minutes and then turn the bird over and cook for a further 10–15 minutes, by which time the breast will be brown.

While the bird is cooking, melt the remaining butter in a small saucepan. Pour a little of the melted butter over the pheasant and sprinkle with a little of the Cognac or brandy at intervals during the cooking.

Remove the pheasant from the oven and cut into small joints. Don't worry if the pheasant is still bloody, as it is going to have a second cooking. Discard the liver, heart and gizzard.

Put the joints back into a cooler oven (180°C (350°F) mark 4) for 10 minutes, or until the pheasant is cooked to your taste, turning the joints over once during the cooking. Remove them from the tin, set aside and cover them.

Drain the grapes, reserving the marinade. Put the roasting tin on the heat and deglaze the cooking juices with the stock and the liquid from the marinade. Reduce over a high heat while scraping the pan with a metal spoon, until the gravy is rich and syrupy. Taste and check the seasonings.

Turn the heat down to low and return the pheasant to the tin.

Heat the remaining brandy in a ladle. Set fire to it and pour it, flaming, over the pheasant.

When the flames have died out transfer the pheasant to a warm serving dish, trying to return it to its orginal shape. Scatter the grapes on top and serve.

chicken with vinegar and herbs
pollo alla cacciatora

Vinegar is often used in cooking instead of wine, especially in central Italy, where wine is considered too rich for some kinds of stew. It is in fact a more lively, fresh way to cook a chicken or a rabbit, preferably a farm rabbit rather than a wild one.

Wipe the chicken joints all over with kitchen paper.

Chop together all the herbs, garlic and chilli to make a fine *battuto* – pounded mixture. The food processor, with the small bowl, makes a quick and good job of it. Scoop the *battuto* out of the bowl and put it into a frying pan large enough to hold all the joints in a single layer. Pour in the oil and sauté the *battuto* gently for a minute or two to release its aroma. After that scoop it up with a fish slice and put it aside.

Add the chicken joints to the pan, turn up the heat and fry them until brown. The joints must be nicely browned all over, which will take about 10 minutes. Be patient about doing this as it is very important to the final result.

Now splash with the vinegar and let it bubble away for a minute or so. Return the *battuto* to the pan and pour in about three-quarters of the stock. Season with salt and pepper. Cover the pan and turn the heat down. The chicken will be cooked in about 30 minutes. Turn the joints over once or twice during the cooking and add a little more stock if necessary. When done – test by pricking the fattest portion with the point of a knife – remove them to a heated dish and keep warm while you check the cooking juices.

If too liquid, reduce over a high heat until thicker and syrupy, if too dense, add a few teaspoons of stock; if too sharp, sweeten it with sugar. Now cut the butter up into small pieces and add bit by bit to the sauce. Let it melt, while swirling the pan around and then pour the sauce around the joints. Serve at once.

Serves 4
8 free-range or organic chicken drumsticks or thighs
sprigs of fresh rosemary, parsley, sage, thyme and bay leaf
2 garlic cloves
1 dried chilli
4 tbsp olive oil
100 ml (3 1/2 fl oz) red wine vinegar
150 ml (1/4 pint) chicken stock
sea salt and freshly ground black pepper
1 tsp sugar, if necessary
15 g (1/2 oz) unsalted butter

chicken with garlic
pollo all'aglio

Serves 4–6

1 fresh free-range or organic roasting chicken about 1.5 kg (3 1/2 lb)
4 tbsp olive oil
2 sprigs of fresh rosemary
sea salt and freshly ground black pepper
2 large garlic heads
150 ml (1/4 pint) dry white wine
45 g (1 1/2 oz) unsalted butter
1 French bread stick, cut into slices 1 cm (1/2 inch) thick
3 tbsp chopped flat-leaf parsley

My pollo *with garlic is light and fresh and quite garlicky, though not too much so. The garlic loses its strength through being cooked a long time in its skin, an unusual method in Italian cooking. It is then puréed and spread on bread, which is a perfect accompaniment to the chicken. For this recipe you can also use chicken thighs or drumsticks.*

Ask the butcher to cut the chicken into ten pieces: two wings, two drumsticks, two thighs, two pieces from each breast and two pieces from the back.

When you get home, remove and discard some of the loose fatty skin. Dry the chicken pieces with kitchen paper.

Heat the oil with the rosemary in a large sauté pan that can hold the chicken pieces in a single layer. When the oil is hot, slip in the pieces, skin side down, and sauté over a lively heat until brown. Turn the pieces over and brown the other side. Season with salt and pepper.

While the chicken is browning, remove the outer skin from the garlic heads, separate the cloves and add them unpeeled to the chicken. When the chicken pieces are nicely brown all over, splash with the wine and turn down the heat. Cook gently for 20 minutes, turning the pieces over two or three times during the cooking. Leave the pan uncovered so that the water that today's chickens often contain can evaporate. However, if the liquid has all dried up, add a couple of tablespoons of hot water.

When the chicken is done, fish out the garlic and reserve. Transfer the chicken to a heated platter and spoon over the cooking juices. Cover with foil and keep warm.

Heat the oven to 200°C (400°F) mark 6.

Peel the garlic cloves and purée them through a food mill, a chinois or in a food processor. Blend in the butter with a fork and spread the mixture on the bread. Place the bread on a baking tray and bake in the oven for 8 minutes.

Sprinkle the chicken with the parsley and serve, surrounded by the garlicky toasts.

chicken breasts in a seventeenth-century sweet-and-sour sauce
petti di cappone alla stefani

This recipe is based on one by Bartolomeo Stefani. I first had it at the restaurant Il Cigno in Mantova, where it has been recreated with great success. Stefani was chef to Ottavio Gonzaga, and his book L'Arte di Ben Cucinare was published in 1662. He was a great cook who had a flair for adapting traditional Mantovano country recipes to suit the table of his patron. He was also the first cook to discard the heavily spiced food of the Middle Ages and early Renaissance in favour of cooking with a lighter touch, flavoured with herbs and flowers. It was cooking of a brilliant inventiveness, and one that modern Italian chefs are keen to revive.

The original recipe is for capon breasts, capon being a tastier and less dry meat than chicken. As it is now illegal in Britain to caponise cocks, I decided to use large chicken breasts instead. It works very well as long as you buy fresh chicken from a good supplier.

Wipe the chicken breasts and remove any fat. Put them in a large sauté pan and cover with the stock and the wine. If you do not have a large enough pan for the chicken to lie in a single layer, use 2 pans, dividing the stock and wine accordingly. The pieces should fit closely together. Poach until the breasts are cooked through – about 30 minutes, depending on their size. Leave to cool in the liquid.

Prepare the sauce. Put the sugar and the wine in a small saucepan and bring very slowly to the boil. Simmer until the sugar has completely dissolved. Draw off the heat and add the sultanas and the lemon rind. Leave aside to cool and then strain over a bowl.

Add the balsamic vinegar, salt and pepper to the liquid in the bowl. Now pour in the oil gradually, whisking with a small wire whisk to form an emulsion. When you have added all the oil, mix in the sultana and lemon rind mixture. Taste and adjust seasoning.

About three hours before you want to serve the dish, lift the cold chicken breasts out of the stock and place them on a board. (Keep the stock for a soup; it's quite delicious.) Cut the chicken into thin slices, about 1 cm (1/2 inch) thick, and lay the slices on a very large dish, or preferably 2 smaller ones. Spoon the sauce over the chicken and cover the dish with clingfilm. Do not refrigerate, since the chicken is best at

Serves 10–12
10 free-range or organic chicken breasts, boned and skinned
1 litre (1 3/4 pints) light stock
300 ml (1/2 pint) dry white wine

For the sauce
4 tbsp soft brown sugar
100 ml (3 1/2 fl oz) dry white wine
75 g (2 1/2 oz) sultanas
grated rind of 2 organic lemons
4 tbsp balsamic vinegar
2 tsp sea salt
freshly ground black pepper
100 ml (3 1/2 fl oz) extra virgin olive oil

room temperature. Before serving, I put cold, steamed or boiled green beans and cauliflower florets alongside the chicken if I am using an oval dish, or in a mound in the middle if I am using a round dish.

preparation

The chicken breasts can be poached up to 2 days in advance and refrigerated, covered, in their liquid. The sauce can be prepared up to 1 week in advance and kept covered in the fridge.

duckling with lentils
anatra alla pavese

Serves 4

For the duckling
**1 fresh duckling,
weighing 2–2.25 kg
(4 1/2–5 lb)**
**3 shallots or
1 onion, very
finely chopped**
**handful of celery
leaves or 1 small
celery stick, very
finely chopped**
**2 tbsp *grappa* or
*marc***
sea salt
**150 ml (1/4 pint) dry
white wine**
**freshly ground black
pepper**
**1 tsp cornflour or
arrowroot**

continued over >>

Lentils are very successfully combined with duck in this recipe from Pavia, one of my favourite provincial cities in Italy. The lentils, partly cooked, are added to the seared duckling joints for a final braising. The lentils absorb some of the fat from the duck, thus becoming rich and tasty.

Prepare the duck. Wash it inside and out, put it on a slanting board and leave to drain for 10 minutes or longer. Cut into joints and pat dry with absorbent paper.

Put the back, the wings and the neck of the duck in a stockpot. Add all the other ingredients for the stock, cover with water and bring to the boil. Skim the scum, which rises at the beginning, off the surface. Turn the heat down very low – just enough for a bubble to break the surface of the liquid every now and then. Cook for 2 hours. Drain into a clean saucepan and reduce the stock until full of the flavour of the duck. Allow to cool and skim off the fat that floats to the surface. If you prepare the stock a day in advance, you can easily remove the fat from the cold stock.

To prepare the lentils put them in a sieve and rinse under cold water, picking out any small stones or bits of grit. Then put them in a saucepan, cover with cold water, add the oil, the onion, the celery and a little salt and bring slowly to the boil. Simmer gently in the covered pan until the lentils are just beginning to get soft. It is difficult to give an exact time since this depends on the quality and freshness of the lentils.

Choose a heavy sauté pan and lay the joints of the duck in it, skin side down. Cook until the fat runs out, about 10 minutes, moving the joints a little at the beginning to prevent the skin from sticking to the bottom of the pan. Transfer the joints to a casserole. Drain off most of the fat (keep it for roast or sautéed potatoes).

Add the very finely chopped shallot or onion, the celery and the salt to the pan and sauté until the vegetables are tender. Scoop them out and add to the casserole.

Pour the spirit over the duck and flame it. When the flame has died out, add the wine and about 120–150 ml (4–5 fl oz) of the duck stock. Bring to the boil and then add the lentils, having drained off any of their remaining liquid. Season with a little salt and a good deal of pepper. Cover the casserole and simmer gently until both the lentils and the duckling are tender, about 30–40 minutes. Mix the cornflour with a couple of tablespoons of the stock and stir into the saucepan. Let the liquid boil for a couple of minutes and then check the seasoning. Serve directly from the casserole or lay a bed of lentils and place the joints on top.

preparation

This dish can be prepared in advance and slowly reheated. Do not serve any other vegetables with it, just a fresh salad afterwards.

For the stock
1 onion, stuck with a clove
1 celery stick, with its green leaves if possible
2 bay leaves
4 parsley stalks
1 garlic clove
5 peppercorns, lightly bruised
1 tsp sea salt

For the lentils
200 g (7 oz) lentils, such as Puy or Castelluccio
1 tbsp olive oil
1 onion, cut in half
1 celery stick, cut into chunks
sea salt

rabbit with rosemary and tomato sauce
coniglio al rosmarino

Serves 4
**1.35–1.5 kg
(3–3 1/4 lb)
rabbit joints**
**1/2 organic lemon,
cut into wedges**
2 tbsp olive oil
**2 garlic cloves, finely
chopped**
**1 onion, roughly
chopped**
**150 ml (1/4 pint) dry
white wine**
**sea salt and freshly
ground black
pepper**

For the sauce
**2 or 3 shallots,
according to size,
or 1 onion, very
finely chopped**
**the needles from 3
sprigs of fresh
rosemary, 12 cm (5
inches) long, very
finely chopped**
3 tbsp olive oil
**450 g (1 lb)
tomatoes, skinned
and seeded, or a
400 g (14 oz) tin of
plum tomatoes,
drained**
**1/2–1 dried chilli,
according to taste,
seeded and very
finely chopped**
sea salt

Rabbit is now easily available everywhere. It is a white meat, less fat than chicken and therefore healthier, and it lends itself to being prepared in any number of different ways. The sauce in this recipe is really delicious, with the herby tomato taste everybody associates with traditional Italian cooking. It is a sauce often served in central Italy, where the recipe comes from.

Trim any gristle or fat from the rabbit joints, and rub with the lemon.

Heat the oil in a large, heavy sauté pan and brown the rabbit on all sides. Push it to the side of the pan and add the garlic and the onion. Cook over a low heat until the onion is soft, stirring frequently.

Heat the wine in a separate small saucepan.

Bring the rabbit back to the middle of the pan, turn the heat up and splash with the wine. Boil briskly for 1 minute or so to evaporate the alcohol and then season with salt and pepper. Cover the pan and cook for 20 minutes over a very low heat. Turn the rabbit over two or three times and, if necessary, add a little hot water during the cooking.

Meanwhile prepare the sauce. In a sauté pan, fry the shallots or the onion and the rosemary gently in the olive oil for 5 minutes. Chop the tomatoes coarsely and add to the pan with the chilli and salt to taste. Cook, uncovered, over low heat for 10 minutes. Adjust the seasonings.

Pour the sauce over the rabbit. Stir quickly, scraping the cooking juices and mixing them into the sauce, and continue cooking until the rabbit is done. Taste and check the seasoning. Transfer to a heated dish and serve.

preparation
The rabbit and the sauce can be prepared 1 day in advance and refrigerated. If necessary the dish can be frozen and, when thawed, very gently reheated.

rabbit with onion and vinegar
coniglio con le cipolle

You can use either imported domestic rabbit or wild English rabbit. I buy wild English rabbit when I can; it's tastier but it takes longer to cook – at least 2 1/2 hours, depending on its age. The best thing to do is to cook the rabbit in advance and reheat it before serving.

Slice the onions thinly. Put them in a heavy casserole with the oil, 2 teaspoons of salt and 6 tablespoons of the stock. Cover the casserole with the lid and cook for about 1 1/2 hours over a very low heat until the onions are reduced to a golden mush. Turn the heat up to moderate, mix in the sugar and cook for a further 15 minutes to caramelise the onion slightly. Stir frequently.

Heat the oven to 150°C (300°F) mark 2.

Wash and dry the rabbit pieces and add to the casserole. Check that there is enough liquid before adding them. If necessary add a couple of tablespoons of the stock. Turn the pieces of rabbit over a couple of times and then pour in the wine vinegar. Season with plenty of pepper and with 2 teaspoons of salt.

Cook for 5 minutes over moderate heat, then cover the casserole and place it in the oven. Cook until the rabbit is done, about 45 minutes. Stir in the balsamic vinegar and cook on top of the stove for a few minutes, turning the pieces over once or twice. Taste and check the seasoning. Serve from the casserole or transfer to a heated serving bowl.

preparation
The dish can be prepared up to 3 days in advance and refrigerated. Reheat in a moderate oven for 20 minutes.

Serves 8–10

1.8 kg (4 lb) onions, Spanish or white
120 ml (4 fl oz) olive oil
sea salt
150 ml (1/4 pint) meat stock, or 1/4 meat stock cube dissolved in 150 ml (1/4 pint) water
4 tbsp sugar
3 kg (6 3/4 lb) rabbit pieces on the bone
120 ml (4 fl oz) good red wine vinegar
freshly ground black pepper
4 tbsp balsamic vinegar

stewed venison with onions
cervo alla casalinga

Serves 6–8
1.5 kg (3 1/4 lb) venison
2 tbsp olive oil
75 g (2 1/2 oz) unsalted butter
1.35 kg (3 lb) Spanish onions, sliced
1 tbsp sugar
sea salt and pepper
300 ml (1/2 pint) strong meat stock
1/2 tsp ground cinnamon
1/2 tsp ground cloves
1/2 nutmeg, grated
300 ml (1/2 pint) dry white wine (if necessary)

For the marinade
600 ml (1 pint) dry white wine
2 tbsp olive oil
2 bay leaves
2 carrots
1 large onion
2 celery sticks
2 garlic cloves, peeled and bruised
10 juniper berries, bruised
1 tsp black peppercorns, bruised

You might think the amount of onions overpowering, but when it is cooked very slowly for a long time, as it is here, it becomes a golden brown, slightly caramelised mush, which absorbs and at the same time tones down the gameyness of the meat.

Cut the venison into small slices or large strips about 1 cm (1/2 inch) thick. I find that this type of meat becomes less dry and woody if cut into thin strips rather than chunks or cubes. Put the meat in a bowl and add all the ingredients for the marinade. Cover and leave in a cool place overnight. Except in the summer there is no need to refrigerate the meat for this short length of time, and in fact leaving it at room temperature will help to make the meat more tender.

Next day, heat the oil and butter in a casserole, add the sliced onion, and cook slowly until it softens. Sprinkle with the sugar and turn the heat up. The onion will caramelise slightly and take on a lovely golden brown colour. Season with salt and pepper and add the meat stock and the spices. Cover the casserole and cook over very gentle heat for about 30 minutes, stirring occasionally.

Heat the oven to 150°C (300°F) mark 2.

Remove the meat from the marinade and dry with kitchen paper. Strain the marinade and discard the vegetables.

Transfer about half the onion from the casserole to a side plate. Lay the venison over the remaining onion in the casserole, season with salt and pepper and cover with the onion previously transferred to the side plate. Heat the marinade and add to the casserole. Add more heated white wine if necessary so that the meat is just covered. Cook in the oven for about 1 1/2–2 hours until the venison is very tender.

preparation
The meat can be marinated up to 3 days in advance, in which case it must be refrigerated. The dish can be prepared up to 2 days in advance and refrigerated. If necessary skim the fat from the surface of the stew before reheating.

prosciutto, salame and all that

I may be accused of being chauvinistic, but I am sure Italy produces a greater variety of delectable foods from the pig than any other country. The products that are used in these recipes are, of course, limited to the ones that can easily be bought in Britain, but if you visit any *salumeria* – delicatessen – in Italy you will be confronted by a manifest tribute to the pig. Wreaths and chains of small and medium sausages, salami of all shapes and sizes, soft *cotechini* and manly *zamponi*, large brown prosciutti, fat pink mortadelle . . . they all hang from the ceiling like stalactites. And seductively displayed under the glass counter in front of you, giving off an appetising smell, are the same products, cut open so as to tempt you even more. It is a sight that testifies to the creativity of the Italians in culinary matters and their love of all the products of the pig.

Through the many centuries of privation and poverty suffered by the mass of Italian people, the pig has often been the only provider of meat, the only source of food worthy of some country celebration. Something is made out of every part of the pig. As they say in Emilia: *Il maiale è come la musica di Verdi, non c'è niente da buttar via* – a pig is like the music of Verdi, there is nothing to be thrown away. Another proverb, from the nineteenth century, says: *Se si ammazza il maiale, viene Carnevale* – when the pig is slaughtered, it's Carnival time. So, indeed, it is.

Of all the dishes that are made on the day of the *maialatura* – the slaughtering of the pig – the *ciccioli* are the best. *Ciccioli* are pieces of the crackling that has been melted down in huge copper pans to make lard. They are a speciality of Emilia Romagna, although they are made all over central Italy. I remember during the war, when we were evacuated to the countryside near Reggio Emilia, the screams of our poor friend the pig which woke us up at dawn. They were forgotten by the evening when an orgy of *ciccioli* and bread took place in the kitchen of the nearby farm. *Ciccioli* are made industrially now, and sold in vacuum packs. I bought some when I was in Modena recently, but any hopes I had of rediscovering the remembered experience were sadly disappointed. They were nothing like the sizzling *ciccioli* taken straight from the copper pan.

a dish of cured meats
un piatto di affettato

This is not a recipe: it is just to tell you how best to present a mixture of the best cured meats. A plate of *affettato* is lovely to look at in its shades of pink and red, and one of the most appetising dishes when you are hungry. It always appears at a buffet lunch in Italy, and is often a classic antipasto in a northern Italian home. Nowadays it is also a quick *secondo* for the working mother.

You need five or six different kinds of cured meat and a large oval or round dish. The traditional meats are: *prosciutto crudo*, ham, mortadella, *coppa* and 2 kinds of *salame*, a sweet one from the North, such as Milano or Varzi, and a peppery, garlicky one from the South. Buy about 100 g (3 1/2 oz) of each meat. *Affettato* needs to be abundant. Roll the prosciutto, make little waves with the *coppa* and lay the heavier cuts flat.

In Milanese homes, sometimes curls of butter are dotted around the dish and the *affettato* is served by itself with plenty of white bread. That is one of the few occasions when butter is served during a meal.

cotechino

A *cotechino* is a large sausage, about 20–25 cm (8–10 inches) long and 8 cm (3 inches) in circumference, weighing around half a kilo (1 lb). It is an ancient type of sausage, probably of Lombard origin, but made in Emilia Romagna as well as in Lombardy. When I recently visited a small *salumificio* – sausage and salami factory – in Missaglia, north of Milan, I was very interested to see that they still make a *cotechino* which I have not come across since my childhood, the *vaniglia*. It is a *cotechino* flavoured with vanilla instead of the more classic cinnamon, a flavouring that must have been due to a whim of fashion, since by the time vanilla reached Italy from Central America *cotechino* had long been a staple food.

Cotechino is made with lean and fat pork meat, and with a fair amount of *coteca* – rind – hence its name. The ground-up mixture is seasoned with salt and pepper, flavoured with spices and then pushed into natural pig casing. In a traditional *cotechino* only the rind is minced, the meat being pounded in a special mortar. After two or three months of ageing the *cotechino* is ready to be eaten. A good *cotechino* is sweet and tender with a creamy texture that literally melts in your mouth.

Fresh *cotechino*, which can be bought in Italy, is a better product than the precooked one found in Britain. However, the advantage of the precooked *cotechino* is that it only takes 20 minutes to cook, against the 3 hours needed to cook a fresh one.

how to serve cotechino

The most usual way to serve *cotechino* is boiled, with lentils or mashed potatoes – a perfect winter dish. It is the dish I always serve on New Year's Day, with plenty of stewed lentils. Lentils are supposed to bring wealth all through the year, each lentil representing a golden coin according to the old superstition. We all love it; hot, nourishing and very Italian.

cotechino with zabaglione
cotechino allo zabaione

Please don't shy away from the idea of serving zabaglione as a sauce for the cotechino. *It is not my invention – I wish it were – but a traditional combination from Modena, a city that offers some of the best food in Italy. It is a perfect match. In Modena they also eat* zampone, *the traditional pig's trotter stuffed with pork meat, with* zabaglione. *The zabaglione contains a little less sugar than when eaten as a sweet.*

Serves 6
**2 *cotechini*, about
500 g (1 lb 2 oz)
each
4 free-range egg
yolks
4 tbsp sugar
150 ml (1/4 pint)
Marsala**

If you have bought *cotechini* which are *precotto* (partly cooked), follow the manufacturer's instructions.

If your *cotechini* are raw, soak them in cold water for a few hours. Prick the *cotechini* with a thin needle in a few places, wrap with muslin, and tie each end with a piece of string. Put them in a saucepan and cover with water. Bring to the boil and cook gently for 2 1/2 hours. Turn the heat off while you prepare the zabaglione.

Using a balloon whisk, beat the egg yolks with the sugar until creamy. Place in a double boiler or over a saucepan of just simmering water and gradually add the Marsala while beating constantly. When the custard thickens, remove from the heat. Transfer to a warm bowl and keep warm in a bain-marie until you bring it to the table. Be very careful that the water in the bain-marie is not too hot, or the zabaglione will scramble.

Carve the *cotechini* into 1 cm (1/2 inch) slices and place them, slightly overlapping, on an oval dish. You can cover the dish with foil and keep warm until you bring it to the table.

preparation
Cotechino is one of those marvellous foods that does not need any preparation. The zabaglione takes such a short time to prepare that there is no point in making it beforehand, with the risk of it curdling or of serving it too cold. Do it just before you sit at table, and keep it warm.

pancetta

Pancetta comes from the *pancia* – belly – of the pig. It is in fact the same cut of meat as bacon, but its taste is different because it is cured in a different way. Streaky bacon can be used instead of pancetta, but if you want *il sapore Italiano genuino* – the authentic Italian flavour – you should keep some pancetta in your fridge.

Pancetta is mainly used as part of a *soffritto* (see page 488) and is essential in some dishes, such as *bucatini alla carbonara*, a Bolognese *ragù*, and a Venetian *pasta e fagioli* – bean and pasta soup. Pancetta is also used, cut into chunks and skewered with liver, meat or vegetables. A new idea is to skewer cubes of pancetta with chunks of monkfish, which has been marinated in olive oil, lemon juice and garlic, and cook the skewers on a barbecue. My favourite *spiedini* – kebabs – are of pancetta, *luganega* (see page 190) and a little piece of veal interspersed with small sage leaves.

There are two kinds of pancetta, *pancetta stesa* and *pancetta arrotolata*. *Pancetta stesa* is the belly left flat in its natural shape, like bacon, and it is mostly used in cooking. *Pancetta arrotolata* – rolled pancetta – is made with a belly which contains a high proportion of lean meat, and it is flavoured with cloves and peppercorns. It is eaten as it is, at the table, or in a bread roll, and, if the pancetta is good, it is delicious. Some types of pancetta are smoked, especially those from Alto Adige, Valle d'Aosta and Friuli, regions on the frontiers of Italy and thus more affected by the foreign preference for smoked food.

In supermarkets, pancetta is sold cut into cubes, ready for a *soffrito*.

prosciutto

There is an old adage from Parma that runs: *Grasso e magro non del tutto, ecco il pregio del prosciutto*. It means that the prosciutto must have the right balance of fat and lean meat. The *prosciutto di Parma* – Parma ham – and that of San Daniele in Friuli are the best *prosciutti crudi* – raw hams. Other *prosciutti crudi* are made in Modena, Reggio Emilia and in every country farm in central Italy. These last are less delicate in flavour, leaner, redder in colour and often more salty, and for these reasons they make the most appetising *panini* – filled rolls.

Prosciutto is the hind thigh of a pig. The first process it undergoes is salting, which is done by the *maestri salatori*. The prosciutti are then hung, and the long curing process, which lasts from 12–18 months, begins. It is supervised by other specialists who, every so often, insert a long stick right through to the bone and then take it out and smell it. Their sense of smell must be as keen as that of a Master of Wine, since the smell tells them all they need to know about the condition and readiness of the prosciutto. The high risk of wastage, as well as the long curing time, justifies its high price.

I recently visited a prosciutto factory in Langhirano, south of Parma. Langhirano is a town dedicated to the making of prosciutto, because it is ideally situated in the valley of the Taro river, through which the breezes from the South-west blow to *cullare i prosciutti* – rock the prosciutti. In Langhirano and neighbouring places 7 million prosciutti are produced each year. Mr Gino Tanzi, the owner of the factory, took me round from one cold room to the next. In his huge, dark, storeroom 20,000 prosciutti hung from wooden posts. It was an impressive sight which, oddly enough, brought to my mind a long pergola supporting a vine loaded with huge bunches of red grapes. Mr Tanzi explained that some of the prosciutti we could see were not *di Parma*. They came from pigs reared in other regions, even abroad in Holland and Denmark; they are smaller pigs, fed on different food, which produce prosciutti that will never be granted the ducal crown of Parma, the stamp of the authentic local prosciutti. These second-quality prosciutti are often sold in vacuum packs, or used to fill sandwiches and rolls all over Italy, and abroad, I suspect.

The genuine *prosciutti di Parma* are large and thus they make lovely large slices which have just the right amount of fat. When it is good, prosciutto does not need the usual accompaniment of melon, although this is often served as a matter of course. Green figs, perfectly ripe and *con la goccia* – with the milky drop – are also often eaten with prosciutto. While these accompaniments serve to enhance the flavour of the prosciutto as a result of the contrast of flavours, prosciutto is also used to complement other foods. The famous *saltimbocca* would be a totally different dish without the slice of prosciutto within the rolled escalope of veal. Prosciutto fat is used as a base for the most delicate *soffritti*, and chopped prosciutto is added to many fillings for ravioli, *crespelle*, etc.

Prosciutto on the bone is tastier than prosciutto from which the bone has been removed. In Italy I always buy the part of the prosciutto that is closest to the bone; the fuller flavour more than makes up for the fact that the slices are smaller and less regular. Although you are unlikely to find a perfect prosciutto on the bone outside the best shops in northern Italy, it is well worth hunting down the good prosciutto that can be bought from the best stores in Britain.

peas and prosciutto braised in onion and butter
piselli al prosciutto in tegame

Here the prosciutto is used as a condiment for the peas. The marriage of peas and prosciutto is even older than that of pasta and tomatoes, and it's still one of the most successful. It originated in Rome or, at least, it is the Romans who have made it well known. There are many recipes based on this union and here is mine, which I am sure you will like.

The prosciutto for this recipe should have some fat on it, and it s hould not be too thinly sliced. The peas should come from small, plump, unblemished pods of a bright green colour; large peas are not suitable for this recipe. You can, of course, replace the fresh peas with 300 g (10 oz) of frozen petits pois; thaw them before you use them.

Serves 4
1 kg (2 lb) fresh peas
   (or frozen peas –
   see over)
6 spring onions
45 g (1 1/2 oz)
   unsalted butter
sea salt
1 tsp sugar
4 or 5 tbsp vegetable
   stock
75 g (2 1/2 oz)
   prosciutto
black pepper

Cook for only 5 minutes, adding only a couple of tablespoons of stock at the end.

Pod the fresh peas.

Slice the onions into tiny rings and sauté in half the butter for 1 minute. Sprinkle with a little salt and the sugar and add a couple of tablespoons of the stock. Cover the pan and continue cooking until the onion is soft.

Add the peas, another couple of tablespoons of the stock and the pepper. Cook, covered and over a very low heat, for 15 minutes or so, until the peas are tender. Add a little more stock if necessary.

Cut the prosciutto into short matchsticks and add to the pan with the remaining butter and a generous grinding of black pepper. Cook for a couple of minutes, stirring frequently. Check the seasonings and serve.

ham in an onion and vermouth sauce
prosciutto cotto in salsa di cipolla

Serves 4
**350–400 g
(12–14 oz) onion
60 g (2 oz) unsalted
butter
sea salt
1 tsp sugar
120 ml (4 fl oz) dry
vermouth
1 tbsp flour
pinch of ground
cloves, if available
300ml (1/2 pint)
meat or vegetable
stock**

continued over >>

I find that the Christmas ham can outlast its welcome. It is delicious at first, hot, then cold with turkey once or twice, but after that something must be done. One good answer is to heat it up in this sauce. Left-over tongue, fresh or pickled, responds well to the same treatment.

Slice the onion thinly and heat it with the butter in a sauté pan. Sprinkle with a pinch of salt and the sugar. Add 4 tbsp of water. Put the lid firmly on the pan and let the onion cook over the gentlest heat for at least 45 minutes. Stir every now and then. Remove the lid, turn the heat up and cook the onion until it becomes coloured and almost like a purée.

Meanwhile carve the ham and cut the slices up fairly small.

Splash the onion with the vermouth. Boil until half the vermouth has evaporated.

Blend in the flour and the ground clove and cook for 1 minute, stirring constantly. Add the stock and bring to the boil. Continue stirring and cooking for 5 minutes over a very low heat. Taste and add salt, if necessary, and plenty of pepper.

freshly ground black pepper
500 g (1 lb 2 oz) cooked ham

Add the slices of ham and heat gently for a further 5 minutes or so. The dish is now ready.

prosciutto with rocket
prosciutto con la rucola

Next time you decide to serve prosciutto for your first course at a dinner party, buy some rocket to go with it instead of a melon. The piquancy of the rocket and the sweetness of the prosciutto di Parma *is as good a combination of flavours as it is of colours.*

Serves 4
100 g (3 1/2 oz) rocket
3 tbsp extra virgin olive oil
1 tbsp fresh lemon juice
sea salt and pepper
200 g (7 oz) prosciutto

Clean and wash the rocket. Dry very thoroughly and put in a bowl to dress. Add the oil, the lemon juice and salt and pepper to taste. Toss very well.

Place the slices of prosciutto either on individual plates or on a dish, and put the rocket on the side, around or in the middle, whichever you think looks prettiest.

bresaola with rocket
la bresaola con la rucola

Serves 6
225 g (8 oz) rocket
5 tbsp extra virgin
olive oil
1 1/2 tbsp lemon
juice
sea salt and pepper
300-350 g (10–12 oz)
bresaola

Bresaola is raw fillet of beef that has been cured in salt and air-dried for 2–4 months. It is a speciality of Valtellina, an Alpine valley in Lombardy. It has a flavour similar to prosciutto, though a little sharper. *Bresaola* is served thinly sliced and lightly dressed with olive oil and lemon juice. Or at least, this is the modern way to serve it. The old-fashioned way, still observed by the purists, is to eat *bresaola* as it is. Years ago the late food historian Massimo Alberini and his wife took me to the Ristorante Peck in Milan. He ordered *bresaola* and the maitre asked '*Cosi, al naturale?*' Alberini was shocked and replied '*E me lo demanda? Ma certamente.*' 'How could you ask me? Certainly.'

My mother was another purist as far as *bresaola* goes. At home in Milan we always had *bresaola* as it should be served, by itself with fresh bread. But the perfect *bresaola* one can buy in Milan is hard to come by anywhere else. The *bresaola* I buy in Britain is not of such exceptional quality, so a dribble of good olive oil improves it a lot. I sometimes add a bunch of rocket dressed with olive oil and lemon juice, and here is the recipe, if it can be called such. The slight peppery flavour of the rocket is a good foil to the meat. Buy *bresaola* – thinly sliced – the day you want to eat it, or it will become dark and leathery.

Pick and wash the rocket. Dry it very thoroughly and put it in a bowl. Dress with the oil, lemon juice and salt and pepper to taste. Toss well. Taste and add a little more lemon juice, if necessary.

Place the *bresaola* in the centre of a serving dish and surround it with the rocket. If you prefer to prepare individual plates, divide the rocket between the six plates and place the *bresaola* over it.

truffle-flavoured ham mousse
mousse di prosciutto cotto della signora gay

The Signora Gay of the ham mousse is the octogenarian mother of a great friend of mine in Milan. Ten years ago she moved to Milan from her native Turin to be nearer her daughter. But once a week she makes the 100-mile journey back to Turin to buy her poultry and meat, because, she says, 'La carne e i polli a Milano non sono buoni come a Torino.' ('Meat and chicken in Milan are not so good as in Turin.') This illustrates the high standard of Signora Gay's table, where the ingredients are her prime concern. And how right she is. Her cooking is light, but full of flavours, achieved through careful timing, absolute precision and great love, and not by the easy way out – that of adding cream and butter. The mousse is testimony to the lightness of her touch and the balance of the ingredients. This is a perfect dish for a buffet dinner.

First make the aspic jelly, a much easier job than you might think. All you need is some stock, thoroughly skimmed of fat and full of flavour, plus the ability to proceed with precision. Put the egg whites and the sherry in a saucepan and add the cold stock. Bring the liquid to the simmer while beating with a balloon whisk. Then stop beating, turn the heat down to minimum and leave for about 15 minutes. The stock should not boil but should just break some bubbles on the surface.

Now strain the stock very carefully through a sieve lined with a piece of muslin folded double. Taste and check for salt, remembering that food served cold needs more seasoning. If you have made the stock with all the right ingredients for an aspic jelly – beef, chicken carcass, pork rind and calf's foot or pig trotters (plus onion skin for the colour) – you may find that it does not need any added gelatine. To test it, put a tablespoon of stock on a saucer in the freezer for 10 minutes. If it sets, no gelatine is needed. If not, soften the leaves in cold water and then dissolve in the stock. Test again until you achieve the right consistency.

Pour enough jelly into a 1.25 litre (2 pint) loaf tin, to come about 2.5 cm (1 inch) up the side of the tin. Put the tin into the fridge for the jelly to set while you prepare the mousse.

Make the béchamel sauce in the usual way, but do not add any salt (see page 489). Cook very gently for 10 minutes or so, using the bain-marie method or a flame disperser. When ready, cool in a bowl of iced water.

Serves 10
a thick béchamel
  sauce made with
  15 g (1/2 oz)
  unsalted butter, 1
  tbsp flour and 150
  ml
  (1/4 pint) full-fat
  milk
325 g (11 oz) best
  ham
2–3 tsp truffle paste
120 ml (4 fl oz)
  whipping cream
pepper

For the aspic jelly
2 egg whites
4 tbsp dry sherry or
  dry Marsala
600 ml (1 pint) good
  meat stock
4 gelatine leaves, as
  necessary

Put the ham in the food processor and process until very finely chopped. Transfer to a bowl and mix in the truffle paste. Truffle paste varies from brand to brand. You might need 2 or 3 teaspoons. Just taste after you have added a little and add more if you want the truffle flavour to come through more positively. Add the béchamel as soon as it is cold, and lastly whip and add the cream. Season with a generous amount of pepper; salt should not be necessary.

Take a 600 ml (1 pint) loaf tin and press the mousse into it, taking care to eliminate any air pockets. Put the tin in the fridge to cool thoroughly. When the jelly in the first tin is set, slide a palette knife round the ham mousse. Turn the tin containing the mousse on to a plate and then turn into the larger tin with the aspic layer; the mousse should fall into the larger tin. Pour some of the jelly which is not set around the mousse, cover with clingfilm and refrigerate.

To unmould, immerse the tin in a bowl of hot water for 15–20 seconds and then turn it over on an oval dish. Keep in the fridge until the last minute and garnish the dish with sprigs of herbs, olives, cornichons, etc.

preparation
The whole dish can be prepared up to 3 days in advance and refrigerated.

salame

All salami are made from minced lean meat and pork fat, stuffed into a natural pig casing. The meat is usually pork, but there are a few salami, among which *salame Milano* is the best known, that also contain a small proportion of beef. The meat can be flavoured with garlic and chilli, as in most south Italian salami, or – in the best salami – with white wine. The meat and fat can be coarsely or finely ground, and the proportion of fat to meat varies according to the kind of *salame*. Most salami are cured for two or three months, although some of the better ones are aged for 12 months.

Salame should not be sliced too thinly. The rule is, the thinner the *salame*, the thicker the slice.

Salame is usually eaten by itself or as part of an *affettato* – a platter of mixed cured meats (see page 178). I prefer to eat *salame*, rather than prosciutto, with fresh figs. Sometimes a few slices of *salame* are added to a meat stuffing, to give a stronger flavour.

baked potato purée with salame and mozzarella
tortino di puré di patate

The salame *makes this a dish in its own right; it is perfect for a family supper.*

Wash the potatoes and boil them in their skins in plenty of lightly salted water. Drain and peel them as soon as they are cool enough to handle.

While the potatoes are cooking, heat the milk.

Purée the potatoes through a food mill fitted with a small-holes disc, or through a potato ricer. Do not use a food processor or blender, as these would make the potatoes gluey.

Heat the oven to 190°C (375°F) mark 5.

Add 45 g (1 1/2 oz) of the butter to the potato purée and beat hard until absorbed, then beat in the hot milk. The longer you beat a purée, the lighter it becomes.

Mix together in a bowl the egg, Parmesan, salt and pepper. Add to the potato purée and beat again. Now mix in the *salame* and the mozzarella.

Butter a soufflé dish and sprinkle with half the breadcrumbs. Shake off the excess crumbs.

Serves 4
700 g (1 1/2 lb)
  floury potatoes,
  such as King
  Edward
150 ml (1/4 pint)
  milk
60 g (2 oz) unsalted
  butter
1 free-range egg
4 tbsp freshly grated
  Parmesan
sea salt
freshly ground
  pepper, preferably
  white
200 g (7oz) *salame*,
  thickly sliced, cut
  into small cubes
200 g (7 oz)
  mozzarella, cut into
  small pieces
2 tbsp fine dry
  breadcrumbs

Spoon the potato mixture into the dish, sprinkle the top with the rest of the breadcrumbs and dot with the remaining butter.

Bake in the preheated oven for 20 minutes, until a golden crust has formed on top. If a crust has not formed, pass the dish under the grill for a few minutes. Allow to stand out of the oven for a few minutes before serving.

luganega

This mild sausage has ancient origins. Cicero and Varro mentioned it, and Apicius, in his *De re coquinaria*, explained how to make it: 'Crush pepper, cumin, savoury, rue, parsley, condiment, and laurel berries; mix with finely chopped fresh pork and pound well with broth. To this mixture, being rich, add whole pepper and nuts. When filling casings, push the meat through carefully. Hang the sausage up to smoke.' *Luganega* returned to fame during the Renaissance, as documented by the sixteenth-century writer, Teofilo Folengo, in his book *Baldus*. 'Different regions and towns send their best products to Paris for the Royal banquet, which follows the tournament held there by the King of France. Milan sends its golden cakes and its sausages, which compels the drunkard French to empty bottle after bottle.'

Milan, and all Lombardy, is still very famous for its *luganega*, and vies with Veneto for having the largest production and consumption. The *luganega* of Lombardy is reputedly the best, where the palm should be awarded to Monza, the suburb of Milan more famous for its car race than for its sausage. In Missaglia, north of Monza, I went to see a *salumficio* – sausage factory – that still makes *luganega* to order, adding grated Parmesan and moistening the mixture with dry white wine instead of water, in accordance with a traditional Lombard recipe.

Luganega is made from the fat and lean meat of a pig, preferably from the shoulder, seasoned with salt, pepper, cloves and cinnamon and pushed into a very long thin casing. It is also known as *salsiccia a metro* – sausage by the metre – because it used to be sold by length rather than by weight. It is sold fresh, and in Italy is to be seen in great lengths, coiled up like a Catherine-wheel. In Britain it is found in the best supermarkets and Italian delicatessens in vacuum packs.

Luganega, skinned and cut into small pieces, is an essential ingredient in many dishes, such as *ragù* and stuffings. It is also delicious by itself, split lengthwise and grilled, or stewed in a little water and then splashed in wine flavoured with sage. In a Milanese recipe 500 g (1 lb 7oz) of *luganega* cut into chunks is added to 500 g (1 lb 7 oz) of potatoes stewed in meat stock. It is added when the potatoes are half cooked. Some cooks prefer to blanch the *luganega*.

The Milanese have a little verse about their *luganega* which sums it all up.

> *Pan, vin e luganeghin*
> *L'é on mangia divin*

which might be translated:

> Bread, luganega and wine
> Make a meal that is divine.

risotto with luganega
riso e luganeghin

A classic Lombard dish which combines, in a perfect balance of flavours, two of the best local products, rice and luganega.

Choose a large deep saucepan. I use a round cast-iron casserole, but any heavy-based pan will do. Heat half the butter and the shallots or onion until the shallots are soft and just beginning to turn golden.

Heat the stock to simmering point.

Add the rice to the shallots and cook until the outside of the grains becomes translucent, stirring frequently. In Italian this is called 'toasting

Serves 3–4
75 g (2 1/2 oz) unsalted butter
2 shallots or 1/2 medium onion, very finely chopped
900 ml (1 1/2 pints) meat or chicken stock

continued over >>

300 g (10 oz) Arborio
or Carnaroli rice
300 ml (1/2 pint)
good red wine,
such as Barbera
350 g (12 oz)
luganega
sea salt and freshly
ground black
pepper
freshly grated
Parmesan for
serving

the rice', which gives the right idea of what is happening to it. Add half the wine and boil briskly until it has evaporated and then pour in a ladleful of simmering stock. Stir well and cook over a medium heat until the stock has been absorbed. Continue adding stock and cooking the rice until the risotto is done.

While the rice is cooking, blanch the *luganega* in boiling water. This will get rid of the excess fat. Drain and return the *luganega* to the saucepan. Cover with the remaining wine and simmer very gently with the lid firmly on for 7–8 minutes. Then transfer the sausage to a chopping board and stir the wine into the rice.

Cut the *luganega* into 2.5 cm (1 inch) pieces and mix into the rice a few minutes before it is cooked.

When the risotto is ready, turn the heat off and add the rest of the butter, cut into 2 or 3 small pieces. Cover the pan and leave for 1 minute. Stir well to make the rice creamy, adding salt and pepper to taste, and transfer to a heated dish. Serve immediately, handing the Parmesan round separately in a bowl.

baked macaroni with sausage and garlic
maccheroni gratinati con la luganega e l'aglio

Serves 12
2 heads of garlic,
peeled
1 kg (2 lb) *luganega*
or other coarse-
grained, pure pork
sausage, such as
Toulouse

continued over >>

Baked pasta dishes are ideal food for a party – they are also fashionable, nourishing and can be totally prepared in advance. It thus avoids those two hostess torments, the pre-prandial banishment to the kitchen and the nagging worry as to whether the dish will taste the way it should. Pasta is easy. To any Italian living abroad, pasta is also the food that, more than any other, brings back nostalgic memories of so many meals enjoyed over the years in so many places. A charming anecdote about Rossini 'the greatest composer among gourmets and the greatest gourmet among composers', illustrates how pasta can linger in the memory. *A man sat next to Rossini at a dinner party one day and said, 'You remember me, I'm sure, Maestro. I met you at that dinner given in your honour when there was a splendid macaroni pie'. Rossini thought for some time, then slowly shook his head. 'I certainly remember the macaroni pie', he said, 'but I'm afraid I don't remember you.'*

Thirty years ago I wrote a book, Portrait of Pasta, *to try and make this marvellous food better known and understood. As well as mouth-watering recipes it had hard facts on the non-fattening and health-giving properties of pasta. Since then I have written four other books on the same much-loved subject, but no matter how many pasta recipes I have to test, I am always pleased to test the results. I think I must be the original pastaholic.*

Put the peeled garlic cloves in a small saucepan and cover with about 300 ml (1/2 pint) of water. Bring the water to the boil, cover the pan tightly and cook very gently for about 1 hour. Check that there is always some water in the pan and add some boiling water if necessary. At the end there should be no more than 3 or 4 tablespoons of water left.

Purée the contents of the pan through a chinois or a food mill or in the food processor. Alternatively it is quite easy to mash them with a fork, which saves washing up.

While the garlic is boiling, skin the sausage, crumble it and put it into a non-stick frying pan with the oil. Chop the herbs and add to the sausage. Fry over a low heat until the fat runs out, then turn the heat up to medium and fry until the meat is lovely and brown, about 20 minutes. Remove the sausage meat from the pan with a slotted spoon, leaving the fat behind.

To make the béchamel sauce, heat the milk until it just begins to bubble at the edge. Meanwhile melt the butter in a heavy-based saucepan over a low heat. Blend in the flour, stirring vigorously. Now draw the pan off the heat and add the hot milk, a few tablespoons at a time. You must let the flour mixture absorb each addition thoroughly before going on to the next stage.

When all the milk has been absorbed, return the pan to the heat. Add salt to taste and bring to the boil. I recommend cooking the sauce for at least 10 minutes, setting the pan either in a bain-marie or over a flame

2 tbsp oil, vegetable, corn or olive
a dozen fresh sage leaves
sprig of fresh rosemary
a thin béchamel sauce made with 2.25 litres (4 pints) full-fat milk, 180 g (6 oz) unsalted butter, 150 g (5 oz) flour
sea salt and pepper
100 g (3 1/2 oz) Parmesan, grated
100 g (3 1/2 oz) Gruyère, grated
1/4 nutmeg, grated
45 g (1 1/2 oz) unsalted butter
1 kg (2 lb) penne, macaroni or any other large tubular pasta shape

disperser. Long, slow cooking makes the sauce more velvety and delicate. Mix in the garlic purée and the grated cheeses. Season with a lot of pepper and with the nutmeg. Taste and add more salt if necessary, bearing in mind that the sausage might well be on the salty side.

Generously butter a large oven dish or a lasagne tin.

Cook the pasta in plenty of boiling salted water. If you do not have a large enough saucepan, cook it in 2 batches. Always cook pasta in plenty of water. Drain it when still slightly undercooked and dress it immediately with about three-quarters of the béchamel and with the sausage meat. Turn it into the prepared dish. Spread the remaining béchamel all over the top and dot with butter.

Heat the oven to 200°C (400°F) mark 6 about three-quarters of an hour before you want to serve the dish. When the oven is hot, put the pasta dish into it and bake until heated through. To test if it is hot enough, insert a knife into the middle of the dish and feel the bits that stick to the blade. Let the dish stand for a few minutes outside the oven before bringing it to the table.

preparation
The whole dish can be prepared up to 1 day in advance, covered with clingfilm and refrigerated. It can also be frozen, although I find that freezing pasta alters its flavour slightly.

luganega and peppers in tomato sauce
luganega e peperoni in salsa

Serves 4
3 large yellow, red or orange peppers
500 g (1 lb 2 oz) luganega

continued over >>

If you cannot find luganega *you can use any coarse-grained Continental sausage made of 100 per cent pork, not too highly spiced or herbed.*

First roast the peppers in a preheated oven (240°C (475°F) mark 9) until you can see the skin coming away from the pulp – about 30 minutes. Put on a soup plate to cool.

While the peppers are cooling, cut the *luganega*, if it is in one long piece, into sausage lengths. Grill very gently so that it will cook without hardening or burning. I use a non-stick pan under the grill instead of the grill pan: the sausages are further from the heat and the pan is quickly washed out. Cooking the sausages separately gets rid of most of the unwanted fat.

Meanwhile heat the oil, the garlic and the parsley in a sauté pan that will be large enough to hold the sausages and the peppers. When the garlic begins to colour, add the tomatoes. Bring to the boil and then add the wine, sugar, salt and pepper. Stir well and cook over lively heat. Let the sauce boil nicely for 10 minutes or so.

By now the pepper should be cool enough to peel. Keep the same soup plate under them to collect more of the rich juice. Cut each pepper into quarters, peel them and then remove and discard all the seeds, the core and the ribs. Cut each quarter into half.

Cut the sausage into roughly 2.5 cm (1 inch) chunks and mix into the tomato sauce. Add the peppers and all the juice collected in the plate. Stir everything together, put a lid on the pan and cook for about 15 minutes to let the flavours blend. Check the seasoning.

2 tbsp olive oil
2 garlic cloves, peeled and chopped
a small bunch of parsley leaves, chopped
400 g (14 oz) tin chopped tomatoes
100 ml (3 1/2 fl oz) red wine
1 tsp sugar
sea salt and pepper

vegetables

'. . . a great mass of colours and vegetable freshness'. For me an excursion to the market is one of the highlights of my visits to Italy, and that vivid phrase from D. H. Lawrence's description of the market in Palermo exactly captures one's initial impression. When I am in Milan my weekly assignment is to go on Monday mornings to the market in Via Kramer, around the corner from my mother's house. It was the memory of this sight that brought waves of nostalgia when I first came to England in the early fifties. The vegetable scene here was a desert, and I felt the same as Giangiacomo Castelvetro had done, over three centuries earlier. Castelvetro lived for a long time, and died, in England, having taken refuge here when he incurred the wrath of the Inquisition through his leanings towards Protestantism. He wrote with longing about the artichokes, the sweet and tender peas, the lovely foliage of the beans that are grown on the balconies of Venice and through which can be glimpsed the beautiful ladies as they peer between the leaves. Things have improved greatly in the last two decades, and Castelvetro, if still here, could buy his fennel and artichokes anywhere in Britain, although he might well complain about their age and freshness.

Vegetables are treated with love and care by Italians. They are not just an accompaniment to meat or fish, simply to be boiled; they are dishes in their own right. Vegetables are stuffed and baked, they are stewed or sautéed or boiled and then *strascinati* – sautéed – or dressed with oil for a salad. Most delicious pies are filled with vegetables, and in the last decades chefs have created vegetable ravioli and many vegetable sauces for pasta.

little gem lettuces stuffed with pine nuts, sultanas, anchovies, capers and black olives
lattuga imbottita alla napoletana

Serves 4
8 Little Gems
4 tbsp dry white wine
2 tbsp extra virgin olive oil
1 garlic clove

For the stuffing
3 salted anchovies, boned and washed, or 6 anchovy fillets
milk
30 g (1 oz) sultanas
2 tbsp capers
30 g (1 oz) pine nuts
2 garlic cloves
100 g (3 1/2 oz) dried breadcrumbs
1 tbsp black olive purée (see page 418) or 12 black olives, stoned and chopped
4 tbsp extra virgin olive oil
freshly ground black pepper

First put the anchovy fillets in a saucer and cover with milk. The milk will sweeten the anchovies, making them more suitable for this dish. Leave for 15 minutes or so.

Put the sultanas and capers in a small bowl and cover with warm water. This is necessary to swell the sultanas and to rid the capers of excess vinegar or salt in which they have been preserved. Leave them for 10 minutes and then drain and dry thoroughly.

Blanch the lettuces in lightly salted boiling water for 3 minutes. Drain, reserving some of the water. Refresh under cold water, drain thoroughly, then gently squeeze out the liquid and dry with kitchen paper.

Put the pine nuts in a small cast-iron frying pan, or other heavy pan, and toast them for 2–3 minutes. This brings out their characteristic flavour.

Coarsely chop the pine nuts, sultanas, capers, anchovies and garlic and put in a bowl. Add the breadcrumbs and the olive purée, or chopped olives, and mix in with the oil. Season with pepper. You won't need to add any salt because of the saltiness of some of the ingredients.

Push the stuffing between the leaves of the Little Gems. Close the bunches up gently and lay them in a saucepan in which they will fit cosily. Add about 4 tbsp of the reserved water in which the Little Gems have cooked, the wine, olive oil and garlic. Cook over a low heat for 20 minutes, turning the Little Gems over once. Do this very gently, using 2 spoons.

Transfer the Little Gems on to a serving dish. Remove and discard the garlic. Taste the juice and check seasoning. If it is too watery, reduce by boiling fast until it is rich in flavour. Spoon over the Little Gems. Serve warm, not hot, or at room temperature.

tomato

Although it is hard to imagine Italian food without the tomato, Italian cooking had already reached great heights of sophistication, and was spreading its influence throughout Europe, 150 years before this fruit existed in Italy. The tomato, a native of Peru and Mexico, was brought to Europe by the returning Conquistadores and first reached Italy at the end of the sixteenth century. It was only in the late seventeenth century, however, that tomatoes began to gain popularity, and then only in southern Italy, where the best varieties were produced. As late as 1770 the Irish traveller Patrick Brydone, writing from Sicily, reported: 'They have likewise a variety of flowering shrubs; particularly one in great plenty which I do not recollect ever to have seen before. It bears a beautiful round fruit of a bright shining yellow. They call it *Il Pomo d'Oro* or golden apple.'

It was around that time that tomatoes began to appear in Italian kitchens. The earliest recipes for a tomato sauce for dressing pasta were written in Naples in the eighteenth century. Slowly through the nineteenth century, and then at a much faster pace through the twentieth, tomatoes became a common ingredient, often grafted on to traditional recipes such as the Milanese *ossobuco* or the Veronese *sopa coada*, a thick soup made with pigeon and vegetables.

'The word tomato now embraces the best and the worst of the vegetable kingdom': thus writes Jane Grigson in her admirable *Vegetable Book*. Without a doubt it is very difficult, in Britain, to buy good tomatoes. My advice is to buy the most expensive, since they are usually the best. I also think it is better to use tinned tomatoes rather than second-rate fresh ones which, being out of season, offer poor value for money. When you buy tinned tomatoes, shop around for a good brand, preferably of the San Marzano variety, and then stick to it. Tinned tomatoes are improved by adding a teaspoon of sugar and one of concentrated tomato purée when you cook them.

Tomatoes do not keep well for more than a few days. The refrigerator is really too cold for them, since the ideal temperature for storing tomatoes is 10°C; it is best, therefore, to buy no more than you can use within three or four days at most.

Being Italian, I peel tomatoes only when I am going to cook them. A good tomato with a thin, tender skin should not be peeled. Unfortunately the new breed of tomato has a tough skin tasting of grass, and they definitely need peeling. To peel tomatoes, pour boiling water over them and leave for up to 30 seconds, according to their ripeness. Then lift them out and drop them into a bowl of cold water. In Italy we remove all the seeds, but the tomatoes there contain much more pulp. If you remove all the seeds and the watery juice from the average tomato on sale in Britain you will have very little left! To remove only part of the seeds, cut the tomato in half and squeeze: enough seeds and juice will come out.

The best way to eat a good tomato is to cut it in slices or chunky wedges and dress it with extra virgin olive oil, salt and pepper. Oregano or basil and a touch of garlic add to the pleasure. Tomatoes can be stuffed in many ways. A good recipe is *pomodori ripieni di riso e olive nere* on page 418, where the tomatoes are stuffed with rice and black olives, but try them also filled with tuna and mayonnaise or filled with raw rice and then baked. The great nineteenth-century cookery writer Artusi suggests baking them, cut in half and dressed with a knob of butter, plenty of pepper and a little salt, to be served as an accompaniment to roast or grilled meats. One of my favourite dishes consists of plum tomatoes, peeled and cut in half and filled with extra virgin olive oil, a cube of Italian mozzarella and a leaf of basil. Before you dress them, leave them in the fridge with a sprinkling of salt on the inside, cut-side down on a board for half an hour, to drain a little.

Finally I should mention the use of tomatoes as a condiment. Even one ripe tomato, if it is good, adds flavour to meat or fish, as well as an attractive tinge of colour. And a soup is often improved by adding a chopped tomato to the basic *soffritto*.

tomato sauces

To make a good tomato sauce you can either cook the tomatoes for a very short time or let them bubble for at least 40 minutes. There is a reason for the wide variation in cooking time. Tomatoes only begin to release their acid liquid after they have cooked for about 10 minutes, and it takes half an hour of lively simmer to evaporate this liquid altogether. So if you have very tasty tomatoes with which you want to make a pasta sauce, make the fresh tomato sauce as described on page 204. For less good tomatoes, choose the recipe that calls for lengthy cooking, *la mia salsa*, on page 202.

Of all the dishes with which to start a meal in Italy, *pasta al pomodoro* is surely the most common. In millions of Italian families, when the children come home from school at lunchtime – few children eat at school – the mother *mette giù la pasta*, drops the pasta into a large pot of boiling water. The sauce is the usual sauce, called simply il *sugo* or *la salsa*, since the *di pomodoro* is understood.

Just as there are millions of families so there are millions of *sughi*. Some of the ones I have had in various homes have stuck in my mind particularly. One such is made by Micki di San Giuliano, a Sicilian friend. She puts about a dozen cloves of peeled garlic with the tomatoes and the oil, and nothing else. Then, when the sauce is eventually cooked, she takes all the garlic out. 'Eventually' is the key word: her sauce cooks slowly for an hour and a half. In Italy, tomato sauces are usually cooked for a long time – 35 minutes is the minimum, while an hour is usually regarded as the optimum cooking time. Admittedly there are a few kinds of *sughi* that are hardly cooked at all, but they are of a different generation; they are of recent birth and not part of the tradition of family cooking.

Here are three tomato sauces I have always made and two given to me by two of my children: *il sugo di Guy* and *il sugo di Julia*. Guy used not to be interested in food, even though I prepared it for him with great love and care. Up to his school days he was the most difficult eater any mother ever came across. He had perfected two special tricks. One was to keep little pellets of food tucked away somewhere in his mouth, pellets which we later found dotted around the house or in the garden. The second trick was to be able to regurgitate on the spot any food which I finally managed to make him swallow. I deserved it, I expect.

So for years Guy and good food were poles apart. Then, some years ago, he went to live in Pavia, in southern Lombardy, and it has been pleasant to see the change that has resulted from living in a country where food has a high priority. Guy has now developed an excellent palate; he loves to talk about food, to exchange recipes and even to cook for me. His tomato sauce is a northern Italian one, by which I mean that it is more complex than tomato sauces from the South, one of which is that made by his sister Julia.

Julia has always been a 'happy eater', and as such developed a discerning palate from the day she tasted her first solid meal. She now cooks very well, and when she went to be an au pair with some Neapolitan friends she came back with excellent recipes for vegetable torte, fish soups and, of course, pasta sauces.

I prefer Guy's sauce for large tubular pasta and for tagliatelle, while Julia's is certainly best for spaghetti. The oregano in Julia's sauce consists of the dried flowers of oregano plants, just as it does in southern Italy, where it is collected on the mountain slopes already dried on the plant. Oregano is the only herb sold and used dried in Italy; I cannot remember ever having heard of dried basil there. The unusual touch in this sauce lies in the fact that the basil is added at the beginning of the cooking. Julia was specifically told by her Neapolitan hostess that the basil flavour should not be all-pervading, as it would be if the basil were added at the end. It should just be an unidentifiable whiff.

Both recipes make enough sauce for about 450 g (1 lb) of pasta, equal to 4–5 helpings. Both sauces are better if puréed through a food mill, because the occasional tomato seeds and pieces of skin are not minced into the sauce as they would be in a food processor. However, if you have not got a food mill, use a food processor.

a basic tomato sauce
una salsa base – la mia salsa

This is a basic tomato sauce which I often make in large quantities when the tomatoes are good. I freeze the sauce in plastic pots of various sizes, the smallest coming in very handy for recipes that only call for a couple of tablespoons. I use it in meat and fish dishes, I add it to soups and I dress pasta with it, adding a couple of tablespoons of extra virgin olive oil or a good lump of butter when I reheat the sauce.

When added to a meat dish, the sauce must cook with the meat for a long time to allow the flavours to combine. This sauce is also perfect for a *ragù*, when it has to cook for even longer, as Eduardo de Filippo reminded us in a poem he wrote in his native Neapolitan dialect. It is called *O Rraù di Mamma* – Mama's *ragù* – and concerns the views of a newly married man on this subject, as expressed somewhat forcefully to his young wife. Loosely translated, what he says is, 'Only mamma made *ragù* the way I like it, and since the day we married we have kept on talking about it. I am not difficult, and it's not something to quarrel about. But do you really think that what you make is *ragù*? I eat it just for something to eat, but may I tell you something? This is just meat with tomato sauce.' What withering scorn!

The quantities given here make about 700 g (1 1/2 lb) of sauce.

Wash and cut into large pieces 1 kg (2 lb) of tomatoes. Put them in a heavy-based saucepan and add 1 celery stick, 1 medium onion and half a carrot, all cut into pieces, plus 2 or 3 garlic cloves, some parsley, 2 sage leaves, a sprig of thyme and some salt. I do not add the pepper at this stage. If the tomatoes are insipid I also mix in 1 teaspoon of concentrated tomato purée and 1 teaspoon of sugar. Bring the mixture to the boil and cook, uncovered, for 40–50 minutes, stirring frequently. Keep an eye on the sauce and do not let it catch: if necessary add a little vegetable stock or hot water. By the end of the cooking the sauce should be quite thick and all the liquid should have evaporated. Put the sauce through a food mill or a sieve; this, rather than a food processor, gives the sauce the best consistency. If you want to use a processor you will have to peel and seed the tomatoes before you put them in the pan. When puréed, add some milled pepper and check the salt.

uncooked tomato sauce for spaghetti or rice
sugo di pomodoro crudo

For 4 helpings of pasta
or rice
**700 g (1 1/2 lb) best
ripe tomatoes**
**4 tbsp extra virgin
olive oil**
**1 garlic clove, peeled
and very finely
sliced**
**a dozen fresh basil
leaves or a bunch
of flat-leaf parsley**
sea salt and pepper

*This is a classic recipe which, in Italy, is used to dress spaghetti or
spaghettini. I also like to dress boiled basmati rice with this sauce,
especially for a summer meal.*

Skin the tomatoes. Cut in half and squeeze out and discard some of
the seeds and juice. Cut the flesh into thin strips and put in the bowl in
which you are going to serve your spaghetti or rice. Add the oil, the
garlic and the basil leaves, coarsely torn into small pieces. If you are
using parsley, chop it, but not too fine, and add to the bowl. Season
with salt and pepper. Leave to marinate for at least an hour.

When the spaghetti or the rice is cooked, drain well and then toss
thoroughly in the sauce. I do not like Parmesan with this dish, but if
you do it should be served separately.

a quick and fresh-tasting tomato sauce
sugo fresco di pomodoro

For 4 helpings of pasta
or gnocchi
1 garlic clove
**1 small onion or 2
shallots**
1 tsp sugar
**2 tbsp vegetable
stock (see page
487)**
**700 g (1 1/2 lb) ripe
peeled tomatoes**
**sea salt and freshly
ground black
pepper**
**6 leaves of fresh
basil, torn**
**unsalted butter or
extra virgin olive oil**

Chop the garlic and onion or shallots together. Put them in a pan with
the sugar and the stock. Cover and cook very gently until the onion or
shallot is soft, by which time the stock will have more or less
evaporated. Stir every now and then.

Roughly chop the tomatoes. Add to the saucepan. Season with salt and
pepper and cook for 5 minutes, after the sauce has begun to boil.

Add the basil and mix in 30g (1 oz) of butter or 3 tablespoons of extra
virgin olive oil.

guy's tomato sauce
il sugo di guy

Chop the tomatoes coarsely. This is best done by cutting the tomatoes with kitchen scissors while still in the tin, having first poured a little of the liquid into a heavy-based saucepan. Put them in a saucepan, together with the tomato purée, sugar, onions, celery, olive oil, salt and pepper. Cook for 15 minutes or so, then purée the sauce through a food mill or a food processor.

Return the sauce to the pan and add the wine. Continue cooking for a further 40 minutes. Mix in the butter, taste and check the seasoning.

Cook 500 g (1 lb 2 oz) of penne or other large tubular pasta in plenty of fast-boiling salted water until *al dente*. Drain and dress immediately with the sauce. If you prefer, cook the pasta using the method described on page 15, which is less demanding as there is no need to stay in the kitchen.

preparation
The sauce can be made up to 4 days in advance and kept in the refrigerator. It can also be frozen.

For 5–6 helpings of pasta
800 g (1 3/4 lb) Italian tinned plum tomatoes
2 tsp tomato purée
1 tsp sugar
2 onions, chopped
2 celery sticks, chopped
5 tbsp extra virgin olive oil
sea salt and pepper
4 tbsp good red wine
30 g (1 oz) unsalted butter

julia's tomato sauce
il sugo di julia

Slice the onions coarsely and put them into a saucepan with a very heavy bottom. I use a shallow, round earthenware pot with a long handle, of the kind that can be put directly over the heat. Earthenware keeps the heat well and cooks evenly at the lowest heat.

Add the oil, the garlic and the oregano or basil. Chop the tomatoes coarsely and add to the pan with their juice. (The easy way to chop tinned tomatoes is to pour out some of the juice and then to cut the tomatoes through with a pair of kitchen scissors.) Season with sugar, salt and pepper and bring to the boil.

For 5–6 helpings of pasta
2 Spanish onions
6 tbsp extra virgin olive oil
3 garlic cloves, peeled
2 tbsp oregano, or a dozen fresh basil leaves

continued over >>

**800 g (1 3/4 lb)
Italian tinned plum
tomatoes
1 scant tsp sugar
sea salt and pepper**

Cook very gently for 1 hour, then purée the sauce through a food mill or a food processor. Taste and check the seasonings. The sauce is now ready to be spooned over 500 g (1 lb 2 oz) of spaghetti cooked *al dente*. Cook the pasta in plenty of salted boiling water in the usual way, or use the Agnesi method (see page 15) which allows you to leave the kitchen.

preparation

The sauce keeps very well in the refrigerator for up to 4 days, and freezes very well.

red sauce
salsa rossa

Makes about 225 ml (8
fl oz)
**3 tbsp olive oil
450 g (1 lb)
tomatoes, cut into
quarters
1 tsp tomato purée
2 onions, coarsely
chopped
1 carrot, coarsely
chopped
1 celery stick,
coarsely chopped
3 garlic cloves,
peeled
1 or 2 dried chillies,
according to taste,
seeded
1 clove
pinch of cinnamon
sea salt
1 tbsp red wine
vinegar**

Put half the oil and all the other ingredients except the vinegar in a saucepan with a very heavy bottom. I use an earthenware pot of the sort you can put directly on the heat. Cook over the gentlest heat for 1–1 1/2 hours, adding a little hot water if necessary.

Purée through a food mill or a sieve. If you use a food processor, you must skin the tomatoes before you cook them.

Return the purée to the pan and add the rest of the oil and the vinegar. Cook for a further 30 minutes, then taste and check seasoning. The sauce is now ready, but let it cool a little before you serve it. You can also serve it at room temperature.

preparation

This sauce can be prepared up to 3 days in advance, covered and refrigerated. It also freezes very well.

strips of *frittata* in tomato sauce
finte trippe

The odd name of this dish from Rome, 'fake tripe', is explained when you see the dish: the strips of flat omelette look like strips of tripe stewed in a tomato sauce. I love eggs, however they are cooked, and this is one of the best ways of cooking them I know.

Heat the butter and the oil in a saucepan. When the butter foam begins to subside, add the celery and the onion and cook very slowly for 5 minutes, stirring frequently. Add the tomatoes and the salt. Boil over a moderate heat for 30 minutes, stirring occasionally, then add the pepper and the basil. Mix well and check the seasoning. If the sauce becomes too thick, add a couple of tablespoons of hot water during the cooking.

Heat the oven to 200°C (400°F) mark 6.

While the sauce is cooking make the *frittata*. Lightly beat the eggs with the Parmesan, a little salt and a lot of milled black pepper.

Lightly butter a 25 x 30 cm (10 x 12 inch) baking tray. Sprinkle a little flour all over the buttered surface and then shake off excess flour. Pour the egg mixture into the tray and tilt the tray to spread the mixture evenly. Place the tray in the oven and bake until the *frittata* is set but still soft, about 8–10 minutes. You will, in fact, notice the smell of cooked egg when it is ready.

Gently ease the *frittata* from the tray with the help of a spatula. Turn the tray upside-down onto a wooden board and let the *frittata* fall onto it. Allow to cool a little and then loosely roll up the *frittata*, Swiss-roll fashion. Cut into strips 1 cm (1/2 inch) wide and mix gently into the sauce. Cook for 2–3 minutes to allow the *frittata* to soak up the flavour of the sauce.

Serves 3–4
15 g (1/2 oz) unsalted butter
2 tbsp olive oil
1/2 celery stick, very finely chopped
1/2 small onion, very finely chopped
400 g (14 oz) tinned plum tomatoes, roughly chopped
sea salt and pepper
6 leaves of fresh basil, torn into small pieces

For the *frittata*
6 free-range eggs
4 tbsp freshly grated Parmesan
sea salt and freshly ground black pepper

tomato soup
passato di pomodoro

Serves 6
4 shallots
**60 g (2 oz) unsalted
  butter**
1 small carrot
2 celery stalks
**1 kg (2 lb) ripe
  tomatoes**
**6 garlic cloves,
  unpeeled**
**15 g (1/2 oz) caster
  sugar**
sea salt and pepper
**600 ml (1 pint)
  vegetable stock**
3 tbsp rice flour
18 fresh basil leaves
**freshly grated
  Parmesan for
  serving**
croûtons (optional)

*This is a fresh and light tomato soup which needs good ripe tomatoes,
full of flavour.*

Chop the shallots and sauté them gently in the butter for 5 minutes.
Chop the carrot and the celery and add to the onion. Cook for a further
5 minutes or so.

Meanwhile cut the tomatoes into segments and add to the vegetable
soffritto together with the garlic, sugar, salt and pepper. Cook for 20
minutes then purée through a food mill. A food processor is not suitable
because the tomatoes and the garlic cloves are unpeeled. Add the stock
and simmer for a further 15 minutes. Add the rice flour in a thin stream
while beating the soup with a small wire whisk or a fork. Cook for 10
minutes over a very low heat. Taste and check the seasoning.

Pour the soup into 6 soup bowls. Garnish with the basil leaves and
serve at once. Serve the cheese separately. If you want the soup to be
more filling, hand round a bowl of croûtons.

preparation
This soup can be made up to 3 days in advance and refrigerate. It also
freezes well.

tomatoes with basil
pomodori al basilico

This is hardly a recipe but it is a nice way to eat tomatoes in the
summer. For 5–6 servings you need about a dozen ripe but firm
tomatoes of the best quality. Blanch them in boiling water for 15
seconds, then plunge them into a bowl of cold water. Skin them and
cut them in half. Squeeze out and discard some of the seeds and
water by pressing each half between your thumb and first finger.
Sprinkle some salt into each half and place, cut side down, on a
wooden board to drain. Leave for at least 1 hour.

Dry the tomatoes inside and out and put them on a large platter. Dribble 120 ml (4 fl oz) of your best olive oil all over them and season with a generous grinding of black pepper. Place 1 small basil leaf or a piece of a larger one on each tomato. Place a thin slice of garlic on top of the basil, so that people who do not like garlic can see it and leave it. Serve chilled.

potato and tomato pie
teglia di patate e pomodori

You can use left-over boiled or steamed potatoes for this very Mediterranean dish, which must be made with really good tomatoes.

For 4 people you need 6 or 7 medium-sized cooked potatoes and 450 g (1 lb) best ripe tomatoes. Slice the potatoes into 5mm (1/4 inch) rounds and put them in a well-oiled shallow ovenproof dish.

Chop a bunch of flat-leaf parsley, 1 garlic clove, 1 dried chilli, 1 tablespoon of rinsed and dried capers and about 6 stoned black olives. I use 1 tablespoon of olive purée, for which you'll find the recipe on page 418, instead of the olives. Put the chopped ingredients in a bowl and add 3 tablespoons of your best olive oil. Spread half this mixture over the potatoes.

Blanch and peel the tomatoes. Cut them in half, squeeze out and discard the seeds and then roughly slice or chop the flesh. Spread the tomato on top of the potatoes and then spoon over the rest of the parsley and capers mixture. Dribble a little oil all over the top and bake in a preheated hot oven (200°C (400°F) mark 6) for 30–40 minutes.

Serve warm, not straight from the oven.

pancakes layered with mozzarella and tomato sauce
tortino di crespelle pasticciate

Serves 4–6
For the *crespelle*
120 g (4 oz) flour
sea salt
2 free-range eggs
250 ml (9 fl oz) milk
30 g (1 oz) unsalted butter

For the tomato sauce
5 tbsp olive oil
30 g (1 oz) unsalted butter
1/2 small onion or 1 shallot, coarsely chopped
1 garlic clove, peeled and chopped
1/2 celery stick, coarsely chopped
1 small sprig of parsley
800 g (1 3/4 lb) tinned tomatoes with their juice
1 tsp tomato purée
1/2 tsp sugar
sea salt and freshly ground black pepper

béchamel sauce made with 30 g (1 oz) unsalted butter, 30 g (1 oz) flour and 300 ml (1/2 pint) full-fat milk

To assemble the dish
150 g (5 oz) mozzarella

continued over >>

Although this dish contains two of the ingredients most often used in peasant cooking – tomato and mozzarella – its presentation makes it very elegant. It looks like a cake made of baked lasagne, but the *crespelle* (pancakes) give the dish a fuller consistency and a more subtle taste. It is a stunning dish whether you serve it as a first course for a dinner party or for a light lunch followed by a green salad.

You can prepare the pancakes a day or two in advance and refrigerate them. They can also be frozen, interleaved with greaseproof or kitchen paper or clingfilm. Thaw before using. The tomato sauce, too, can be prepared well in advance. It keeps in the refrigerator for up to 3 days, or it can be frozen. The dish, however, must be assembled just before going into the oven or the pancakes will become too soft.

The *crespelle* can also be layered with a mixture of spinach, ricotta and béchamel or with ham, mushroom and béchamel. In fact, any filling you fancy is suitable as long as it is of the consistency of double cream. You can even turn it into a pudding by making a sweet filling of *crème patissière*, with poached pears, very finely sliced, and flaked almonds.

The quantities given here are for 4 hungry young people, or for 6 more normal appetites, when served as a first course. If you want to serve more people, it is better to make 2 shapes rather than to pile up too many *crespelle*.

Prepare the pancakes. Sieve the flour with a little salt into a bowl. Drop in the eggs and beat, while gradually adding the milk, until the surface of the batter is covered with bubbles. Alternatively, put all the ingredients in a blender or a food processor and blend until smooth. Let the batter stand for at least 30 minutes – it does not matter if you leave it for longer.

When you are ready to make the pancakes, melt half the butter and stir into the batter. Transfer the batter into a jug from which you will find it easier to pour.

Heat a cast-iron frying pan of 20 cm (8 inches) diameter across the bottom and add a small knob of the remaining butter. Swirl the butter around the pan to grease all the bottom.

When the pan is hot, turn the heat down to moderate. Stir the batter and pour enough batter to cover the bottom in a very thin layer, while tipping the pan quickly in all directions. Cook until pale gold, and then turn the pancake with a spatula and cook the other side, very briefly. Slide on to a plate or board. Remove the pan from the heat before you pour more batter or it will set before it can spread. You should be able to make about 8–10 pancakes, but you may have to add a tiny knob of butter every so often when the pan appears dry.

Prepare the tomato sauce. Put the oil, butter, onion or shallot, garlic, celery and parsley in a heavy saucepan and sauté gently until soft, about 10 minutes, stirring frequently.

Add the tomatoes, the tomato purée, sugar and salt. Bring to the boil while breaking up the tomatoes with a metal spoon. Cook, uncovered, at a steady low simmer for 1 hour. The sauce should be quite dense at the end, all the water having evaporated. If the sauce gets too thick, add a couple of tablespoons of hot water during the cooking. Purée the sauce through a food mill or in a food processor. Taste and check the salt.

Grate the mozzarella on the larger holes of a grater. Put it in a small bowl with a little salt and cover with milk. Leave for 30 minutes or so.

Make the béchamel (page 489) and mix thoroughly into the tomato sauce.

Heat the oven to 180°C (350°F) mark 4.

Use an ovenproof or round metal dish, if you have one. Otherwise use the base of a 20 cm (8 inch) flan or cake tin and lay it on a baking tray. Butter the dish generously.

Drain the mozzarella and squeeze out most of the milk.

Place 1 pancake over the dish and spread with a heaped tablespoon of sauce. Put a few small lumps of mozzarella here and there and sprinkle with a little Parmesan, basil and black pepper. Cover with a second pancake and repeat these layers until you have used up all the ingredients. The topping must be: tomato sauce, basil, Parmesan, pepper.

Melt the butter in a small saucepan and then pour it slowly over the mound, while making small deep incisions with a small knife, for the butter to seep through.

Cover the dish with foil or with a cake tin and place in the oven for about

full-fat milk
6 tbsp freshly grated
  Parmesan cheese
2 tbsp chopped fresh
  basil
freshly ground black
  pepper
15 g (1/2 oz)
  unsalted butter

15 minutes. Remove the foil and bake for a further 10 minutes. Allow the dish to stand out of the oven for about 5 minutes before serving. If you are using the metal base, slide the *tortino* on to a round dish and serve.

baked tomatoes
pomodori in teglia

Serves 6–8
10 ripe tomatoes
sea salt and pepper
5 tbsp extra virgin olive oil
4 tbsp chopped flat-leaf parsley
2 tbsp dried breadcrumbs

Wash and dry the tomatoes and cut them in half. Gently squeeze out and discard some of the seeds or fish them out with the point of a coffee spoon. If you have time, sprinkle the halves with salt and lay them on a board, cut side down, then leave them in the fridge for 1 hour or so. It does not matter if you leave them for longer.

Heat the oven to 190°C (375°F) mark 5.

Grease an oven dish, preferably metal, with some of the oil. Dry the inside of the tomatoes with kitchen paper and put them in the oven dish, cut side up.

Mix the parsley and the breadcrumbs together, season with salt and pepper and spoon a little of the mixture over each tomato half. Dribble with the rest of the oil and bake for 15–20 minutes, until just soft.

sun-dried tomatoes

In the old days sun-dried tomatoes were indeed sun-dried. They were split open, sprinkled with salt and laid on bamboo racks to dry in the hot sun. When the water of the tomatoes has evaporated they shrivel up and their flavour becomes very concentrated. Tomatoes are still dried like this, of course, but the majority of the sun-dried tomatoes on the market nowadays are dried in ovens. These dried tomatoes soaked in water and added to any suitable dish impart a strong tomato flavour.

Sun-dried tomatoes are available just dried or under oil. If you buy them dry, and I would advise you to do so, cover them with a mixture of boiling water and wine vinegar and leave them for about 1 hour. Drain them and lay them on a clean cloth. Pat them dry with kitchen paper and they are ready to be used. Alternatively, after soaking and drying them, you can put them in sterilised jars, layering them with chopped garlic, chilli and/or anchovy fillets and covering them with olive oil, ready to be used. Before you seal the jars, check that there is no air trapped between the layers, by sliding a palette knife down the side of the jar. Prepared in this way these tomatoes make a quick and delicious little antipasto added to some grilled peppers and/or hard-boiled eggs or used for a *bruschetta*. They are also the most appetising treat whenever you feel peckish while you are cooking.

There is also on the market now a wonderful product: *mi-cuit* tomatoes. These – as the name explains – are half-cooked. They do not need any soaking and have more tomato flavour than their sun-dried cousins. They make a very good *bruschetta* when there are no good fresh tomatoes on the market. If you use them for the following recipe you will need about 400 g (14 oz). Do not soak them, but add 2 tablespoons of balsamic vinegar to the dressing to give the right bite to the sauce.

thin spaghetti in a piquant tomato sauce
spaghettini eccitanti

Serves 12
250 g (9 oz) sun-dried tomatoes
250 ml (9 fl oz) red wine vinegar
250 ml (9 fl oz) extra virgin olive oil
4 or 5 dried chillies, according to taste, seeded and crumbled
10 garlic cloves, bruised
a dozen basil leaves
150 g (5 oz) black olives in brine
800 g (1 3/4 lb) spaghettini
sea salt

This is a recipe I had from a friend who prepared the dish for us when we arrived at her house in Lerici. The view from Grazia's house is breathtaking. It dominates the cosy little harbour littered with small boats to the west, while to the east it is dominated by the great expanse of the sea. On that balmy Mediterranean night the spaghetti seemed superb, although afterwards I was afraid that perhaps the secret of its success was the setting in which I had eaten it. But when, after a year, I decided to give it a try, I found to my delight that it was an excellent dish anywhere. However, it must be made with good olive oil and plain olives kept in brine, with no flavouring. It is an ideal pasta dish for a party. It is equally good hot or cold.

Put the sun-dried tomatoes in a bowl. Heat the vinegar with the same quantity of water and when just boiling pour it over the tomatoes. Leave to soak for 2–3 hours.

Drain the tomatoes, lay them on a wooden board and dry each one thoroughly. Cut them into thin strips and put them in a bowl large enough to hold the *spaghettini* later. Alternatively use 2 bowls, dividing all the ingredients between them. Add the oil, chillies, garlic and basil. Stone the olives, cut into strips and add to the bowl.

Cook the *spaghettini* in plenty of salted water. If you are serving them cold, drain them when they are even more *al dente* than you would like for eating them hot. Overcooked cold pasta is really unpleasant. Turn the pasta into the bowl or bowls and toss very thoroughly, lifting the strands up high so as to separate them. Leave to infuse for 2 hours or so, then fish out the garlic and discard.

If you are serving the pasta hot, prepare the dressing 2 hours in advance for the flavours to blend, and cook and add the pasta just before serving.

The tomatoes can be soaked and sliced up to 2 weeks in advance: they should be kept in a jar under olive oil. The olives, too, can be prepared in advance and kept under olive oil. You can use the preserving oil to dress the *spaghettini*.

onion cups stuffed with tuna, anchovies and capers
scodelle di cipolle ripiene

Of the many good ways to stuff onions, this is my favourite. This stuffing can also be used with large tomatoes, which are baked for 40 minutes or so. Another excellent stuffing for onions is to be found in the recipe for Little Gem lettuces on page 198. Buy best tuna, not skipjack.

Peel the onions and plunge them into boiling salted water. Cook for about 15 minutes, until the outer leaves are just soft, but still slightly crunchy. Drain and leave to cool.

Meanwhile drain the tuna and chop with the anchovy fillets, capers, chilli, oregano and garlic. Put the mixture in a bowl.

Soak the bread in the milk for 5 minutes. Then squeeze out the milk and break it up with a fork.

Heat the oven to 200°C (400°F) mark 6

When the onions are cool, cut them in half and put aside about 16 outer leaves. Chop the remaining leaves and sauté them in 2 tablespoons of the oil. Cook gently for 10 minutes, stirring frequently, and then mix in the bread soaked in milk. Continue cooking for a further 5 minutes to allow the flavour to penetrate the bread. Add this mixture to the bowl, pour over 1 tablespoon of the oil and mix thoroughly. Taste and adjust the seasoning. You will probably find that there is no need for salt, and that the chilli has imparted enough hotness to make pepper unnecessary also.

Place a smaller outside leaf inside a larger one to make 8–10 onion cups. Choose a shallow ovenproof dish (I use a small rectangular metal one) in which the onion cups will just fit and brush with 1 tablespoon of the oil.

Place the onion cups in the dish, sprinkle lightly with salt and pepper and fill them with the tuna mixture. Sprinkle with the dried breadcrumbs, pour over the remaining oil and bake on the top rack of the oven for about 20 minutes, or until a light golden crust has formed on top. If necessary, place under a hot grill for a few minutes to brown. Serve warm or at room temperature, neither piping hot from the oven nor freezing cold from the fridge. The flavours must be allowed to blend at the right temperature.

You can produce a most attractive first or second course by preparing two or three different stuffed vegetables and serving them together.

Serves 4
2–3 Spanish onions, about 450 g (1 lb)
200 g (7 oz) tuna preserved in brine or olive oil
4 anchovy fillets
1 tbsp capers, rinsed
1 small dried chilli, seeded
2 tsp dried oregano
1 garlic clove
2 slices of white bread without the crust: about 60 g (2 oz)
about 150 ml (1/4 pint) milk
5 tbsp extra virgin olive oil
sea salt and pepper
2 tbsp dried breadcrumbs

These onions, for instance, served with aubergines stuffed with *luganega*, pine nuts and sultanas (page 234), and with tomatoes stuffed with rice and black olives (page 418) would make a well-balanced combination.

onion *frittata*
frittata di cipolle

Serves 4
300 g (10 oz)
 Spanish onions or
 white onions
2 tbsp olive oil
sea salt
6 free-range eggs
4 tbsp freshly grated
 Parmesan
pepper
30 g (1 oz) unsalted
 butter

A frittata is an Italian omelette, but being flat is more like a thin Spanish tortilla or a Middle Eastern eggah than an omelette. It can be plain, dressed with Parmesan, or mixed with a variety of ingredients, of which the three here are examples. I find the frittata with tuna and peppers most appealing visually, and also gastronomically, provided it is made only with the best real tuna, tinned and packed in olive oil, rather than the cheap brands of skipjack tuna. When I was first given the recipe for this frittata by a great friend and a good cook, I was reminded of the mouth-watering description of such an omelette written by Brillat-Savarin in his The Philosopher in the Kitchen. The omelette was given to Madame Récamier by a curé she was visiting on a day of abstinence. He must have been delighted when the lovely Madame Récamier said, 'I have never seen such an appetising omelette on our worldly tables.' I hope your frittata will arouse such a comment.

Other good frittate are made with sautéed fennel, mushrooms and even cooked spaghetti. As you can see, frittate offer a great many ways of recycling leftovers. All frittate are good hot or cold, but not chilled.

Cut the onions into very thin slices and put them with the oil into a 20 cm (8 inch) non-stick frying pan. Add 1 teaspoon of salt to help the onion release its moisture, and cook very slowly until the onion has wilted. Stir frequently and add a couple of tablespoons of hot water if necessary. The onion should turn a lovely golden colour, but not get brown. Set aside to cool.

Break the eggs into a bowl and beat them lightly until well blended. Scoop the onion out of the pan, leaving behind the oil, and mix gently but thoroughly into the eggs. Stir in the Parmesan, a generous grinding of pepper and a sprinkling more of salt.

Wipe the frying pan clean with kitchen paper, add the butter and heat it until foaming. Pour the egg mixture into the pan, stirring it with a fork while pouring so that the onion will not sink to the bottom. Do not stir the mixture further, just turn the heat down to very low and leave it for 15 minutes. By the end of this time the eggs will have set and only the top surface will be runny.

There are two ways to cook the top. The method that gives a better result is to turn the *frittata* over by first freeing the sides with a spatula and then turning it over on to a round dish or lid. Slide the *frittata* back into the pan and brown the other side for no longer than 1 minute. The second method, which is easier but tends to harden the surface too much, is to pass the pan under the grill for 1 minute, just long enough to set the top. Transfer it to a dish or a wooden board lined with kitchen paper to absorb the extra fat.

courgette *frittata*
frittata di zucchine

Put the courgettes into a sink of cold water. Wash them thoroughly, dry them with kitchen paper and cut them into 1 cm (1/2 inch) cubes. If you have time, put the cubes in a colander, sprinkle with salt and leave for half an hour. This will release some liquid. Dry the courgettes and set aside.

Put the oil, garlic and parsley in a 20 cm (8 inch) non-stick frying pan. When the aroma of the garlic rises, add the courgettes and cook until lightly browned, about 10–14 minutes, stirring frequently.

Meanwhile lightly beat the eggs in a bowl until the yolks and the whites are properly blended. Season with salt and pepper, oregano and Parmesan.

Serves 4
**350 g (12 oz)
courgettes
sea salt
2 tbsp olive oil
2 garlic cloves,
peeled and finely
sliced
2 tbsp chopped
parsley**

continued over >>

6 free-range eggs
pepper
1 tbsp dried oregano
6 tbsp freshly grated
  Parmesan
30 g (1 oz) unsalted
  butter

When the courgettes are done, lift them out with a slotted spoon and transfer them to the bowl with the eggs. Now follow the instructions in the previous recipe, onion *frittata*, from the paragraph starting, 'Wipe the frying pan clean . . .' to the end.

peppers and tuna *frittata*
frittata di peperoni e tonno

Serves 4
2 sweet peppers,
  preferably of
  different colours
4 tbsp olive oil
1 Spanish onion, very
  thinly sliced
sea salt
5 free-range eggs
200 g (7 oz) tin of
  tuna, packed in
  olive oil or natural
  brine
12–15 sweet green
  olives, stoned and
  cut into narrow
  strips
freshly ground black
  pepper

Wash and dry the peppers. Cut in half, remove the core, seeds and ribs and cut into thin short strips.

Put 3 tablespoons of the oil in a pan, add the onion and the peppers and sprinkle with salt (this will help to release the liquid, and prevent the vegetables burning). Cover with a buttered paper and a tight-fitting lid. Leave to sweat until very soft – about 40 minutes. Keep a watch on the pan and add a couple of tablespoons of water whenever the vegetables are cooking dry.

Lightly beat the eggs and add the tuna, finely shredded, the olives and pepper to taste.

When the vegetable mixture is ready, leave it to cool a little and then add it to the egg mixture, scooping it out of the pan with a slotted spoon. Leave the cooking juices in the pan. Mix everything together very thoroughly.

Put the rest of the oil in a 20 cm (8 inch) non-stick frying pan. When the oil is hot, add the egg and vegetable mixture. Turn the heat to very low and cook until the underneath is set but the top is still runny – about 15 minutes.

Now follow the instructions on page 217 in the recipe for onion *frittata* from the paragraph starting, 'There are two ways . . .' to the end.

peppers

The first peppers to reach Europe in the wake of the returning
Conquistadores were much too fierce for the European palate. On 15
January 1493, Christopher Columbus wrote in his diary: 'In Haiti my
men found a lot of *aji* which the natives use as pepper, but which
merits a much higher value, as *aji* can be considered a dish in its own
right for anyone who can bear its very strong taste.' The popularity of
this berry spread far and wide, since peppers had become a favourite
in the Middle East and India within a hundred years of the discovery of
the New World. They took longer to establish themselves in Europe and
it is not clear exactly when they became popular in Italy.

I have not been able to find any mention of peppers in Italian cookery
books until 1847, when a recipe for stuffed peppers was written by
Ippolito Cavalcanti, Duca di Buonvicino, in his excellent book *Cucina
teorico-practica* published in Naples in that year. It is a simple recipe for
roast peppers with a classic Neapolitan stuffing of breadcrumbs, capers,
olives, oregano, anchovy fillets, parsley and garlic, a recipe still very
popular to this day. You will find the recipe for the stuffing in the recipe
for Little Gems on page 198. Nowadays peppers are recognised as one of
the most interesting and rewarding of vegetables, and most chefs have
directed their creativity towards them. And, although peppers only reached
Britain fairly recently, they are now very popular, and they cheer every
vegetable stall with their bright, pulsating colour.

buying peppers

Peppers should be smooth and shiny, without wrinkles. The heavier the
pepper, considering its size, the better it is, because it is meatier.
Colour is an indication of ripeness. Thus, when green peppers ripen,
they become red or yellow. I prefer those that are ripe and sweet,
although in some dishes it is right to include green peppers as well,
not only for the appearance of the dish but because it may need the
more pronounced capsicum flavour of the green berry.

how to peel peppers

To peel peppers you can either grill them, or char them over a direct flame (preferably using a wire mesh disc) as described below. You can also roast them in a very hot oven – 240°C (475°F) mark 9 – for about 30 minutes, but I find this method unsatisfactory because it cooks the actual flesh of the peppers too much.

grilled peppers
peperoni arrostiti

Serves 4
**4 beautiful red or
    yellow peppers**
**3 salted anchovies or
    6 anchovy fillets**
3 garlic cloves
**2 tbsp chopped flat-
    leaf parsley**
**1 small dried chilli,
    seeded**
**4 tbsp extra virgin
    olive oil**

When peppers are grilled and skinned their taste is quite different from that of raw or sautéed peppers. To my mind they are much nicer, and they are certainly more digestible. You can prepare a few kilos of peppers when they are in season and reasonably cheap, and keep them in the fridge in jars, well covered with olive oil, for two or three months. They will come in very useful as a first course on their own, or as an accompaniment to roast pork.

When I serve peppers on their own I like to dress them with the sauce given below, which is based on olive oil and garlic to which anchovy fillets and capers can be added. The sauce should be cooked for a couple of minutes so that the garlic and anchovy flavour combines well and becomes less pervasive. It is very important that the sauce should cook over a very low heat or the garlic will burn and the anchovy become bitter.

The ideal saucepan to use is a small earthenware pot of the kind that can be put directly on the heat. Earthenware has the property of distributing the heat all over the container and of retaining it for a ong time.

You can grill the peppers over charcoal, or over a direct flame using a wire mesh flame disperser. If you cook by electricity, use the grill. To start off choose heavy, meaty peppers. Put them on the flame or charcoal and grill them all over. As soon as the side in contact with the heat is charred, turn the pepper round until all the surface, including the top and the bottom, is charred. When all the skin is charred, take the pepper off the flame, otherwise the meat will begin to burn and you will be left with paper-thin peppers.

Leave the peppers to cool and then remove the skin; it will come off very easily as long as the peppers have been well grilled. (Although many cookery writers suggest that putting the peppers to cool in plastic bags makes them easier to peel, I find this totally unnecessary. When I was last in Milan I mentioned the idea to my mother's 'daily' who is from Puglia, and she laughed. As she pointed out, people have been peeling grilled peppers in southern Italy without difficulty since long before plastic bags existed. Another point is that I am none too happy about plastic coming into contact with hot food.) Cut the peppers in half, remove the stalk and seeds and then cut them lengthwise in strips. Put them on a dish.

If you are using salted anchovies, bone and wash them. Dry them with kitchen paper. Pound the anchovy fillets together with the garlic, parsley and chilli in a mortar, or chop very finely.

Put the oil and the anchovy mixture in a very heavy pot and heat very slowly while stirring and pounding the whole time until the mixture is mashed. Spoon over the peppers and leave to marinate for at least 4 hours. The longer you leave them, up to a week, the better they get. Serve plenty of bread with them.

bundles of monkfish and grilled peppers
fagottini di peperoni e coda di rospo

Serves 4
4 large peppers, red and/or yellow
sea salt and pepper
600 g (1 1/4 lb) monkfish
3 tbsp extra virgin olive oil
5 tbsp dry white wine
1 garlic clove, chopped
1 dried chilli, seeded and crumbled

The combination of fish and grilled peppers is most successful. This dish is as quick and easy to prepare as it is delicious; the only part that is a little slow is the grilling of the peppers.

Once when I was testing this recipe and had not made a first course, I put some steamed potatoes around the fish to help satisfy our hunger. They were perfect with the fish and, in fact, I've always served them since then.

Grill and peel the peppers as directed in the previous recipe. Set aside the smallest pepper and cut the other 3 into wide vertical strips: you need 8 of them. Remove the core, seeds and membrane. Sprinkle each strip with salt and pepper.

Heat the oven to 220°C (425°F) mark 7.

Remove both the dark skin, if still on, and the transparent skin from the fish and cut into 8 chunks. Sprinkle with salt and pepper. Wrap one of the strips of pepper round each piece of monkfish and lay the bundles in a well-oiled ovenproof dish. I use a small metal lasagne dish into which the bundles will fit snugly. Dribble 1 tablespoon of the oil all over and cover with foil. Place the dish in the oven and cook for 10 minutes.

Meanwhile prepare the sauce. Clean the remaining pepper and chop coarsely. Put it in a small saucepan with the wine, the garlic and the chilli.

When the fish is done, pour all the cooking juices into the small pan with the sauce. Turn the oven heat down to 160°C (325°F) mark 3 and put the fish back in the oven, but without the foil, for a further 10 minutes.

Cook the sauce gently for 10 minutes, stirring occasionally, and then mix in the remaining oil.

Place 2 bundles on each of 4 plates and spoon a little of the sauce round the bundles.

peppers filled with aubergines and croûtons
peperoni ripieni della zia renata

My aunt Renata, a Milanese, had all the characteristics I associate with good cooks. She was plump, cheerful and amusing, but temperamental. Her husband, *zio* Carlo, was a die-hard Neapolitan forced by circumstance to live in northern Italy. As a child, sitting in his house in drizzling grey Lombardy, I used to listen to his descriptions of the colourful vegetables ripened in the real sun, of the lively fish market at Pozzuoli where at least ten different kinds of clam could be had at any time, and of the abundance of food always ready for anyone who happened to drop in, a sure sign of the hospitality and warmth of the southerners.

These stuffed peppers were one of *zia* Renata's specialities, and they seem to represent a combination of her cooking skills with *zio* Carlo's fond memories of luscious sun-ripened vegetables. I was told later that the little croûtons were *zia* Renata's war-time addition to make the dish more nourishing and to use up any old crumbs of bread, but the addition was so successful that it became an integral part of the dish. The crisp squareness of the croûtons is a pleasant contrast to the soft roundness of the aubergine, both in shape and texture. The flavours, however, blend harmoniously, an essential requirement for most Italian dishes. Do remember to rinse the capers under cold water to get rid of the vinegar or the salt.

To save labour, I tried baking the peppers instead of grilling them, but it does not work as they become too floppy. The best method is to char them over charcoal, which gives them that special flavour. Failing that, put them directly over a flame or, if you cook with electricity, use a hot enough grill to burn the skin without softening the meat too much.

Peel the aubergines, cut them into 1 cm (1/2 inch) cubes and sweat with salt in a colander for at least half an hour.

Meanwhile char the peppers over a direct flame or using a very hot grill. Keep a watch on them and turn them over so that they blacken evenly.

While you are keeping an eye on the peppers, heat the vegetable oil and when very hot add the bread and fry until golden. Retrieve with a slotted spoon and transfer onto kitchen paper to drain.

When the peppers are cool enough to handle, peel them and cut them in half. Remove and discard the cores, seeds and ribs. Place in an oiled ovenproof dish.

Serves 6
700 g (1 1/2 lb) aubergines
sea salt
6 meaty peppers, red and yellow
vegetable oil for frying
4 slices good-quality white bread, 1 or 2 days old, cut into 1 cm (1/2 inch) cubes
6 tbsp extra virgin olive oil
1 garlic clove
1 dried chilli, seeded and crumbled
4 anchovy fillets
7 tbsp chopped flat-leaf parsley
2 tbsp capers, rinsed and dried
pepper
a dozen black olives for garnish (optional)

Heat the oven to 200°C (400°F) mark 6.

Rinse the aubergine cubes and dry them with kitchen paper. In a large sauté or frying pan heat 4 tablespoons of the olive oil and add the aubergine. Sauté until cooked, about 6 minutes, stirring frequently.

Chop the garlic, chilli and anchovy fillets and add to the aubergine with half the parsley. Cook for 1 minute or so. Draw off the heat and add the capers and the croûtons. Taste and adjust the seasoning.

Fill the peppers neatly with the aubergine mixture. Sprinkle with the remaining chopped parsley and dribble with the remaining olive oil. Bake for 10 minutes. Do not serve the dish straight from the oven; let it rest for half an hour or so, since stuffed vegetables are much nicer just warm. Scatter the olives in the dish before serving.

preparation
The peppers can be grilled up to 3 days in advance and refrigerated. The croûtons can be made up to 2 days in advance and refrigerated. They also freeze well. You can sauté the aubergine up to 2 days in advance and refrigerate it, but the peppers must be stuffed just before going into the oven or the croûtons will become soggy.

peppers in vinegar
peperoni all'aceto

Serves 6–8
2 Spanish onions
5 tbsp extra virgin
  olive oil
sea salt and pepper
8 meaty peppers, red,
  yellow and green
4 tbsp sugar
4 tbsp red wine
  vinegar

These peppers can be served as an antipasto or as an accompaniment to roast meat, chicken or boiled gammon.

Coarsely chop the onions and sauté slowly in the oil. Add 1 teaspoon of salt to release the moisture in the onion, thus preventing it from browning too quickly. Cover the pan and cook gently for 45 minutes, until the onion is very soft indeed. Add a couple of tablespoons of hot water if it begins to stick to the bottom of the pan.

Wash and dry the peppers, cut them in quarters and remove the seeds, cores and white ribs. Cut them into 1 cm (1/2 inch) strips.

Add the peppers to the onion and sauté for 5 minutes, stirring frequently. Turn the heat up a little, add the sugar and leave the mixture to caramelise for 10 minutes or so, stirring frequently. Pour over the vinegar, add salt and pepper and cover the pan tightly. Cook over a very low heat for a further hour, checking every now and then that the peppers do not burn. Add a couple of tablespoons of hot water whenever necessary. If, on the other hand, there is too much liquid at the end of the cooking, remove the peppers and boil fast to reduce until the juices are tasty and syrupy.

Serve warm or at room temperature, but neither piping hot nor straight from the fridge.

preparation
The dish can be prepared up to 8 days in advance, covered and refrigerated. It is actually better made 2 or 3 days in advance. It also freezes well.

meat terrine studded with roasted peppers
terrina coi peperoni

This terrine is just right for a summer buffet, and it looks particularly attractive. I find it is also a very useful standby for weekend lunches when you come in late from the garden and have to feed a hungry family in 10 minutes flat. It makes a change from a cold joint, and is more appetising. The terrine keeps very well in the fridge for three or four days wrapped in foil.

If you can, buy peppers of different colours, as this makes the sliced terrine more colourful. I prefer to buy a piece of braising steak and a pork steak and ask the butcher to remove all the fat and mince them for me.

Serves 8
3 meaty red, yellow and green peppers
450 g (1 lb) lean minced beef
225 g (8 oz) minced pork

continued over >>

**45 g (1 1/2 oz)
freshly grated
Parmesan cheese
2 free-range eggs,
lightly beaten
2 garlic cloves,
peeled and very
finely sliced
sea salt and pepper
1 tbsp extra virgin
olive oil**

Grill and peel the peppers as directed on page 220. When you have finished, cut the peppers into quarters and remove the core, seeds and ribs and then cut in 1 cm (1/2 inch) pieces.

Heat the oven to 190°C (375°F) mark 5.

Put the minced meats in a bowl, add the Parmesan, the eggs and the garlic. Mix well and then add the peppers, salt and a generous grinding of pepper. Remember that this dish is eaten cold, and cold food needs more seasoning. Mix again very thoroughly. I find this is best done with your hands, so that you can feel when the two kinds of meat have blended and the pepper pieces are equally distributed.

Brush a 1 litre (1 3/4 pint) metal loaf tin with the oil. Transfer the meat mixture into the tin and press down well with the palm of your hand, then bang the tin on the work surface to get rid of any remaining air bubbles. If the terrine has pockets of air trapped in it, it is likely to break when you slice it.

Cook in the oven for at least 1 hour. (You will find that the terrine has shrunk away from the sides of the tin.) Pour away the juice and allow to cool.

For a family lunch, slice the terrine at the table. If you want to be more formal prepare the dish in the kitchen, and garnish the sliced terrine with black olives, cornichons, lemon slices, etc.

Any salad goes well with this terrine, but I particularly like a potato salad, dressed with a thin lemony mayonnaise, and the salad of French beans and tomatoes in a wine dressing on page 274.

peppers and potatoes sautéed in oil
peperoni e patate in padella

*In this recipe from southern Italy, the peppers impart their characteristic
flavour and firm texture to a bowl of sautéed potatoes. It is particularly
good with a roast of pork, such as the Tuscan roast pork on page 450.*

Peel the potatoes and cut into thin slices. Wash and dry them
thoroughly. Keep them wrapped in a kitchen cloth to prevent from
getting brown while you prepare the peppers.

Wash the peppers and cut them into quarters. Remove and discard the
seeds, white ribs and cores and cut the pepper quarters into 2.5 cm (1
inch) cubes. Dry the pieces and set aside.

Chop the garlic, chilli and parsley together very finely.

Put half the oil in a heavy frying pan, add half the garlic, chilli and
parsley mixture and sauté over a medium heat for 30 seconds, stirring
constantly. Add the potatoes and continue cooking for about 5 minutes.
At this stage you should turn the potatoes over very frequently – use a
fork, as this breaks them up less than a spoon. Turn the heat down a
little and sauté until the potatoes are tender. Stir frequently and add a
couple of tablespoons of hot water whenever they stick too much to
the bottom of the pan.

While the potatoes are cooking, put the remaining oil, garlic, chilli and
parsley in another large frying pan. Sauté for 30 seconds and then mix
in the peppers. Cook over a medium heat until the peppers are cooked
but still just crunchy, which will take about 20 minutes. Stir and shake
the pan frequently during the cooking.

Add salt to the potatoes and the peppers, and mix well. Transfer both
the vegetables to a warm bowl and mix together thoroughly. Serve at
once.

Serves 4

**450 g (1 lb) waxy
potatoes**
**450 g (1 lb) yellow
and red peppers**
**2 garlic cloves,
peeled**
**1 dried chilli, or more
according to taste,
seeded**
**a lovely bunch of
fresh flat-leaf
parsley**
**120 ml (4 fl oz) extra
virgin olive oil**
sea salt

grilled peppers with anchovies, olives and capers in a rich vinegary sauce
peperoni alla siciliana

Serves 4
4 large peppers,
 about 700 g
 (1 1/2 lb)
1 medium onion,
 finely sliced
2 garlic cloves,
 chopped
3 tbsp extra virgin
 olive oil
sea salt and pepper
1/2 bouillon cube
2 tbsp *aceto
 balsamico*, or other
 best red wine
 vinegar mixed with
 1 tsp sugar
2 tbsp oregano
16 black olives,
 stoned and cut into
 strips
2 salted anchovies,
 rinsed and boned,
 or 4 anchovy fillets
1 1/2 tbsp capers,
 rinsed

If I had to name my favourite vegetable dish, this would certainly be one of the principal contenders. It is more like a relish than a vegetable dish, with all the flavours blending beautifully together during the lengthy cooking. In fact, I find the dish is even better if made a day in advance.

Grill and peel the peppers as described on page 220.

Cut the peppers into quarters, remove and discard the core, seeds and ribs and then cut the quarters into strips 2.5 cm (1 inch) wide.

Put the onion, garlic and oil in a sauté pan. Sprinkle with salt and add 2 tablespoons of water. Cook gently in a covered pan until the onion is so soft as to be like a purée. Uncover the pan and continue cooking until the onion turns gold. This will take about 40 minutes.

Add the peppers, the crumbled bouillon cube and the vinegar. Cook, uncovered, for half an hour, stirring occasionally. Add a couple of tablespoons of hot water if the peppers seem to become too dry.

Add all the other ingredients and continue cooking for a further 20 minutes or so, until all the flavours have blended into a rich sauce. You should keep the heat very low indeed for this final cooking, or the anchovies will acquire a bitter taste.

Serve warm or at room temperature.

aubergine

The aubergine – *melanzana* – is a first cousin of the tomato, with which it so often and so successfully is combined. But the aubergine grew in Italy long before the arrival of its American cousin. It reached Sicily from the east in the thirteenth century, and apparently grew wild there. The Sicilians did not eat them, however, fearing them to be poisonous. It was only during the famine that followed the Norman invasion at the turn of the millennium that they were driven to try them. The story goes that they first tested aubergines on their goats, who ate them and survived. But the doubts remained, and aubergines were even accused of causing madness. In the sixteenth century, in fact, the Italian word *melanzana* was thought to derive from the Latin *malum insanum*, meaning unhealthy apple.

When Artusi wrote his famous book *La scienza in cucina e l'arte di mangiar bene* in 1891 (it has been reprinted well over a hundred times) aubergines were only just beginning to be popular; in fact, as he wrote: 'Aubergines and fennel were hardly seen in the market in Florence 40 years ago.' They are now popular in all regions, although most of the preparations are from southern Italy. Aubergines grow best in the South, where the rainfall is very low and the temperature very high in the summer. These conditions produce berries with a pulp that is full of flavour, just as they do with tomatoes.

how to prepare aubergines

Aubergines can be large and bulbous, long and thin or small and round, and their colour can vary from deep purple to a creamy ivory. They all have the same taste. I do not salt aubergines now, because they do not have the bitter taste any more. I only salt them when I fry them because they then absorb less oil, or for some particular recipe. The salt is mixed in with the cubed or sliced aubergines, which are then put in a colander and weighed down with a heavy bowl or pan, or placed on a slanting wooden board. When you buy aubergines, choose ones that are firm and unblemished, with a smooth, glossy skin.

The recipes I have chosen show the versatility of this vegetable, and many more can be devised by the creative cook. Grilled aubergine slices are the healthier version of the old-fashioned, yet unsurpassably delicious, *melanzane fritte* – aubergines deep-fried in oil. I often cover my aubergine cubes, previously sautéed in olive oil, with a plain béchamel sauce (see page 489) flavoured with Parmesan and then bake the dish for about 10 minutes. This is a simple yet delicious recipe in which the taste of the aubergine is emphasised. Aubergines are also ideal for stuffing and baking in the traditional way. The stuffing is based on the pulp of the aubergine sautéed in oil, to which different elements are added.

lemon-flavoured aubergine
melanzane al limone

Serves 3–4 as an accompaniment
450 g (1 lb) aubergines
sea salt
vegetable stock – approximately 150 ml (1/4 pint)
1 tbsp lemon juice
rind of 1/2 an organic lemon
2 garlic cloves, peeled
1 tbsp oregano or chopped fresh marjoram
2 tbsp extra virgin olive oil
freshly ground black pepper

This is the lightest and freshest aubergine dish I know. Prepare the vegetable stock (see page 487) in advance or use a good vegetable bouillon powder.

Wash the aubergines and cut them into small cubes, without peeling them. The texture of the skin makes the cubes more pleasant to eat and it keeps them in a neat shape. Place the aubergine in a colander, sprinkle with salt and leave for no longer than 1 hour or it will become too soft. Squeeze out the juice and dry with kitchen paper.

Choose a medium-sized sauté pan or frying pan and heat 100 ml (3 1/2 fl oz) of the stock, the lemon juice, lemon rind, garlic and oregano or marjoram. Bring to the boil and simmer gently for 5 minutes. Add the aubergine and cook over a moderate heat, turning it over every now and then. You might have to add more stock during the cooking, which will take about 10 minutes. When the aubergine is ready there should be practically no liquid left.

Remove and discard the garlic and the lemon rind.

Transfer the aubergine and any cooking liquid to a bowl. Toss with the oil. Taste and add pepper and salt if necessary. You may like to add a little more lemon juice. The dish can be served warm or at room temperature. It can be made one day in advance, chilled if the weather is hot, but brought back to room temperature before serving.

aubergine sauce
sugo di melanzane

When I first tasted this sauce, at La Meridiana in London's Fulham Road, I was baffled. There seemed to be hints of several different flavours in it, suggesting many ingredients. Not so; the sauce is in fact made from aubergine and olive oil, and nothing else. It is the ideal dressing for meat ravioli, which is how it was served at La Meridiana, or for a lovely dish of home-made tagliatelle.

For 4 people you need a large aubergine and 4 tbsp of extra virgin olive oil. Prick the aubergine with a fork in a few places and grill it over charcoal, or over a direct flame using a wire-mesh disc, or under the grill. Turn it round until the skin is charred all over. When it is cool enough to handle, peel it and squeeze out as much of the bitter juice as you can.

Put the aubergine in a food processor and when the aubergine is puréed, with the processor still going, add the olive oil through the funnel. Do this very slowly, as you do for a mayonnaise. Season with salt and a really good amount of pepper. When the pasta is cooked, mix a couple of tablespoons of the pasta water into the sauce before you pour it over the pasta.

baked pasta and aubergine
pasticcio di pasta e melanzane in bianco

This excellent pasticcio *is another testimony to the aubergine's rare ability to blend with other flavours while retaining its own. Here, the aubergine, so often treated in a rustic and earthy manner, is combined with a delicate cheese-flavoured béchamel, a sauce usually connected with elegant dishes. The pasta shape I like best for this* pasticcio *is* ziti; *being thick and hollow they hold the béchamel, and they match the size of the aubergine. The only snag is that you have to break them into pieces. If you cannot find* ziti, *use* penne.

First make the béchamel sauce. Heat the milk with the bay leaves to boiling point and leave to infuse for about 30 minutes, if you can spare

Serves 6
700 g (1 1/2 lb)
  aubergines
sea salt
1 small dried chilli,
  seeded
2 garlic cloves
a bunch of parsley
5 tbsp olive oil
pepper
350 g (12 oz) *penne*
  or *ziti*

continued over >>

For the béchamel sauce
600 ml (1 pint) full-fat milk
2 bay leaves
60 g (2 oz) unsalted butter
30 g (1 oz) flour
sea salt and pepper
60 g (2 oz) Gruyère
60 g (2 oz) freshly grated Parmesan

the time. Melt the butter, add the flour and cook for 1 minute or so, stirring constantly. Bring the milk back to simmering and add a little at a time to the roux, having removed the pan from the heat. Beat hard to incorporate. When all the milk has been added return the pan to the heat, add salt and pepper to taste and bring to the boil. Set the pan on a flame disperser or in a bain-marie and continue cooking for 10 minutes or so. Remove and discard the bay leaves.

Wash and dry the aubergines. Cut them lengthwise in 1 1/2 cm (1/2 inch) slices, then into 1 1/2–2 cm (1/2–3/4 inch) strips and finally cut these strips into 4 cm (1 3/4 inches) length pieces.

Chop the chilli, garlic and parsley together and put in a frying pan with the oil. Fry gently for 1 minute and then add the aubergines. Sauté over a low heat for about 7–10 minutes until soft, turning them over frequently. Taste and adjust the seasonings. Turn off the heat and set aside.

Heat the oven to 200°C (400°F) mark 6.

If you are using *ziti*, break them into 4–5 cm (1 3/4–2 inches) pieces. Boil the pasta in plenty of salted boiling water. Drain when very *al dente* and transfer to the pan with the aubergines.

Sauté the pasta for 2–3 minutes, mixing it well with the aubergines.

Butter a shallow dish of the right size for the pasta to come about 5–8 cm (2–3 inches) up the sides. Turn the pasta and aubergine mixture into it.

Cut the cheeses in pieces and process or grate them. Add to the béchamel. Taste and check the seasonings. Pour the béchamel over the pasta and bake for 20 minutes until a light crust has formed at the top. Leave out of the oven for 5 minutes before serving, for the flavours to blend.

preparation
The dish can be prepared 1 day in advance and covered with clingfilm. It does not need to be refrigerated. Bake for a little longer in the oven until hot all through.

grilled aubergine with pizza topping
pizzette di melanzane

Here grilled slices of aubergine stand in for the bready base of a pizza. This is a cheerful and tasty first course or side dish. I prefer to top the aubergine slices with tomato sauce, of which I keep a supply in the fridge. But if you haven't any, and no time to make it, place a small spoonful of chopped fresh or tinned tomatoes or mi-cuit tomatoes, a little salt and a touch of garlic over each slice, and drizzle it with a teaspoonful of extra virgin olive oil.

Wash and dry the aubergines. Cut into slices no less than 1 cm (1/2 inch) thick. Sprinkle with salt and leave on a slanting board to drain for about 1 hour.

Heat the grill.

Dry the aubergine slices with kitchen paper. If too long, cut each slice across in half to make 2 square slices. Brush each slice with olive oil on both sides and place in the grill pan lined with an oiled piece of foil. Grill for about 3 minutes on each side until golden brown. You might have to turn the heat down to prevent the aubergine cooking too fast.

Meanwhile cut the mozzarellas into 1 cm (1/2 inch) slices.

Heat the oven to 200°C (400°F) mark 6

Transfer the foil with the aubergine slices onto a baking tray. Lay a slice of mozzarella over the aubergines and top with a dollop of tomato sauce (or a spoonful of chopped tomato and olive oil) and with some oregano. Sprinkle with lots of pepper and bake until the mozzarella has melted – about 5 minutes. Serve hot or at room temperature.

Serves 4
2 aubergines of about 350–400 g (12–14 oz) each
sea salt
olive oil
2 150 g (5 oz) Italian mozzarellas
250 ml (9 fl oz) basic tomato sauce made as directed on page 202
oregano
freshly ground black pepper

aubergines stuffed with luganega, pine nuts and sultanas
melanzane ripiene alla pugliese

Serves 4
2 aubergines,
  weighing
  300–400 g
  (10–12 oz) each
salt
30 g (1 oz) sultanas
4 tbsp extra virgin
  olive oil
1 large garlic clove,
  peeled and finely
  chopped
1/2 small onion or 1
  shallot, very finely
  chopped
1/2 celery stick,
  preferably with its
  leaves, very finely
  chopped
120 g (4 oz) spicy
  luganega or other
  coarse-grained pure
  pork Continental
  spicy sausage,
  skinned and
  crumbled
30 g (1 oz) soft white
  breadcrumbs
30 g (1 oz) pine nuts
30 g (1 oz) capers,
  rinsed and dried
1 free-range egg
1 tbsp oregano
2 tbsp freshly grated
  pecorino or
  Parmesan cheese
freshly ground black
  pepper
1 large ripe tomato,
  peeled

The stuffing in this recipe brings together an unusual combination of ingredients: sausage and sultanas. The piquancy of the spicy luganega sausage is subdued by the sweetness of the sultanas. The luganega is what distinguishes this recipe from others for stuffed aubergines.

Wash and dry the aubergines, cut them lengthwise and scoop out some of the flesh with the help of a sharp small knife and then with a small pointed teaspoon, leaving about 1 cm (1/2 inch) border all round. Be careful not to pierce the skin.

Chop the pulp of the aubergine coarsely and place in a colander. Sprinkle with salt, mix well and leave to drain for about 2 hours.

Sprinkle the inside of the aubergine shells with a little salt, place the shells upside-down on a board and leave to drain.

Put the sultanas in a bowl, cover with warm water and leave for about 20 minutes. Drain and dry them.

Put 2 tablespoons of the oil, the garlic, the onion and the celery in a frying pan and sauté over a low heat until soft, stirring frequently. Add the sausage and cook gently for 20 minutes.

Meanwhile, squeeze the liquid from the chopped pulp of the aubergines and dry thoroughly with absorbent paper. Add to the pan and fry gently for a few minutes, stirring frequently.

Preheat the oven to 190°C (375°F) mark 5.

Add the breadcrumbs to the mixture in the frying pan and after 2–3 minutes mix in the pine nuts. Cook for a further 30 seconds and then transfer to a bowl.

Add the capers, egg, oregano, cheese, pepper and sultanas to the mixture in the bowl and mix very thoroughly. Taste and adjust the salt.

Pat dry the inside of the aubergine shells and place, one next to the other, in an ovenproof dish, greased with 1 tablespoon of the remaining oil. Fill the aubergine shells with the mixture.

Cut the tomato into strips and place 2 or 3 strips on the top of each aubergine half. Pour over the rest of the oil in a thin stream. Cover the dish with foil and bake for 20 minutes. Remove the foil and bake for a further 20 minutes.

These aubergines are best eaten warm, about an hour after they come out of the oven. They make a lovely Mediterranean dish with other stuffed vegetables, such as onion cups stuffed with tuna, anchovies and capers on page 215 and Little Gem lettuces stuffed with pine nuts, sultanas, anchovies, capers and black olives on page 198.

aubergine cannelloni with tomato sauce
cannelloni di melanzane in salsa

A good vegetarian dish.

First make the tomato sauce on page 205 (Guy's tomato sauce).

Wash and dry the celery, leeks and courgettes and cut them into 5 cm (2 inches) julienne strips. Sauté the vegetables lightly in 3 tablespoons of the oil, beginning with the celery alone, as it takes a little longer to cook, then the courgettes and finally the leeks. Season with salt and pepper. Do not overcook the vegetables, but just cook enough to become tender. This takes about 6 minutes in all. Season well and set aside to cool.

Cut the Emmental into similar juliennes and mix into the vegetables. Mix together the breadcrumbs, herbs and garlic.

Wash and dry the aubergines, leaving the skin on. Cut them lengthwise into 5 mm (1/4 inch) thick slices. Brush each side with a light coating of olive oil. Cook quickly under or on a hot grill until soft, but not overcooked. Set aside.

Heat the oven to 200°C (400°F) mark 6.

Choose an ovenproof serving dish into which the aubergine cannelloni will fit snugly in a single layer. Spread half the well-seasoned tomato sauce

Serves 6
450 ml (3/4 pint) Guy's tomato sauce
200 g (7 oz) celery
200 g (7 oz) leeks, white part only
450 g (1 lb) courgettes
7 tbsp olive oil
sea salt and pepper
200 g (7 oz) Emmental
100 g (3 1/2 oz) fresh white breadcrumbs
2 tbsp chopped herbs: a mixture of rosemary, thyme, oregano, parsley

continued over >>

2 garlic cloves, finely chopped
2 aubergines, each weighing about 350– 400 g (12–14 oz)

over the bottom of the serving dish. Season each slice of aubergine with salt and pepper. Place a rounded tablespoon of the vegetable/cheese mixture in the middle of each slice and wrap the aubergine round the filling along the length of the slice. Place the cannelloni in the dish and sprinkle with the herbed breadcrumb mixture. Dribble over the remaining oil. Place in the preheated oven for 10–15 minutes, until the cheese begins to melt and the cannelloni are thoroughly heated.

Remove from the oven and let the dish rest for 5 minutes before serving, for the flavours to blend. Serve the bundles with the remaining tomato sauce.

preparation
The entire dish can be prepared 2 days in advance and refrigerated in the covered oven dish. Heat through just before serving.

baked aubergines with mozzarella and tomato sauce
parmigiana di melanzane

Serves 4–5
1 kg (2 lb) aubergines
sea salt
1 150 g (5 oz) Italian mozzarella cheese
5 tbsp olive oil
400 g (14 oz) tinned plum tomatoes without the juice, coarsely chopped
1 garlic clove, peeled and squashed

If you do not like fried food, you can grill the aubergine slices instead of frying them. However, provided that you salt the slices for at least 2 hours and keep the oil at the right temperature during the frying, the aubergine will hardly absorb any oil during the frying.

A tip I have learnt from Marcella Hazan, is to soak the mozzarella in oil. This improves the texture of the factory-made mozzarella available in Britain.

Wash and peel the aubergines and cut them lengthwise in slices about 5 mm (1/4 inch) thick. Sprinkle generously with salt, put in a colander and leave them to drain for 2 hours or longer. Rinse them under cold water and dry properly with kitchen paper.

Grate the mozzarella through the largest holes of a cheese grater, or cut into very small pieces. Put in a bowl, cover with 1 tablespoon of

continued over >>

the olive oil and leave to soak for 30 minutes or longer.

Heat the oven to 200°C (400°F) mark 6.

Put 1 tablespoon of the olive oil in a small saucepan together with the tomatoes, garlic and basil or oregano. Add the seasonings and cook at a lively simmer for 5 minutes. Purée the sauce through a sieve or a food mill or a food processor.

Pour enough vegetable oil in a frying pan to come 2.5 cm (1 inch) up the side of the pan. Heat the oil and when very hot (test it by immersing the corner of an aubergine slice: it should sizzle) put in as many aubergine slices as will fit in a single layer. Fry to a golden brown on both sides (this will take about 5 minutes) and then retrieve them with a slotted spoon and drain on kitchen paper. Repeat until all the aubergine is fried.

Smear the bottom of a shallow ovenproof dish with 1 tablespoon of the olive oil. Cover with a layer of aubergine, spread over a little tomato sauce and some mozzarella. Sprinkle with a lot of freshly milled pepper and with some Parmesan. Spread over a few slices of the hard-boiled egg and then cover with another layer of aubergine. Repeat these layers until all the ingredients are used up, finishing with a layer of aubergine. Pour over the remaining oil and bake in the preheated oven for about 30 minutes.

a few basil leaves, torn, or 1 tsp oregano
freshly ground black pepper
vegetable oil for frying
60 g (2 oz) freshly grated Parmesan
2 hard-boiled free-range eggs

grilled aubergine stuffed with tuna and anchovy fillets
rotoli di melanzana ripieni

This dish makes a delicious first course, with a most interesting combination of tastes and textures. The secret here is to use a light home-made lemon mayonnaise; a strong vinegary sauce would kill the characteristic aubergine flavour.

Wash and dry the aubergines. Cut them vertically into slices no thinner than 1 cm (1/2 inch) or they might crack and burn while grilling.

Serves 4
2 aubergines, about 350 g (12 oz) each
4 tbsp extra virgin olive oil

continued over >>

2 garlic cloves, peeled and squashed
sea salt and pepper
200 g (7 oz) best tuna, preserved in olive oil
2 anchovy fillets
1 tbsp capers, rinsed and dried
3 tbsp lemon mayonnaise, preferably home-made
tabasco

Put the olive oil in a soup plate and add the squashed garlic and a generous amount of pepper. Coat the aubergine slices with the oil and place on a grid.

Heat the grill and when hot place the grid under it. Cook the aubergine on both sides until tender, but not burnt. Keep a watch and turn down the heat if necessary. Allow to cool.

Meanwhile prepare the stuffing. Process the tuna with the anchovy fillets and the capers until smooth. Transfer to a bowl and add the mayonnaise gradually and a few drops of tabasco. You may not need to add all the mayonnaise; stop when you reach the consistency of a thick mousse. Taste and adjust the seasoning, and then spread some of the tuna mixture on each aubergine slice and roll it up Swiss-roll fashion.

preparation
You can prepare the stuffing and grill the aubergines in advance. Fill them just before you serve them.

artichokes

This thistle, *Cynara scolymus*, is the food that most vividly symbolises the civilised gastronomy of the Renaissance. There was, in that period, endless concern about novel and attractive things to eat, and the artichoke, with its peculiar shape and its many gradations of colour, was the ideal vegetable to serve – or to use as a centrepiece.

A native of Italy, the artichoke did not cross the Alps until Caterina de' Medici went to France. Indeed this is one of the few foods known to have been introduced at her behest, whereas most merely followed the general northerly spread of Italian culture. Caterina was a great glutton, and she had a particular weakness for artichoke hearts. At a banquet in 1575 she ate so many that she was taken ill. Her passion for this aristocratic thistle spread to the French court, so much so that Louis

XIII's doctor declared that no dinner could be considered complete that did not include at least one artichoke dish.

It was in Paris that Charles I of England and Henrietta Maria tasted their first artichoke. The Queen, who must have inherited a passion for artichokes from her mother, another Medici, grew artichokes in the garden of her country house at Wimbledon. I am sure she had more success than I did when I tried my hand at growing them in Barnes, not far away. I found that, through lack of sun, my artichokes became woody before they could develop fully. By way of compensation, I enjoyed the stalks of the side-shoots in creamy *risotti*.

In Italy there are two different kinds of artichoke, with and without thorns. Those without thorns are a smaller edition of the Breton variety found in this country. The prickly artichokes come from Liguria and Sardinia and are usually the ones we eat raw. No unpleasant fuzzy choke to deal with, only tender young leaves to dip in a pool of oil. Or they are cut into very thin wedges and served mixed with radicchio, a harmonious blend of flavours in a mix of contrasting colours. Roman artichokes are called by the charming name of *mammola* because of their purplish colour reminiscent of a *viola mammola* – a violet. In Venice the little artichokes are sometimes called *canarini* – little canaries – because of their pale yellow-green colour.

how to choose artichokes

It is easy; they should be green, showing no brown patches or tips. Ideally they should have leaves still attached to the stalk and the leaves should be silvery green and alive-looking.

how to prepare artichokes

Hold the artichoke in one hand and with the other break off the tough outer leaves. It is impossible to say how many layers of these tough leaves you will have to discard, since it depends on the quality, age and freshness of the artichoke. Next snap off the green part of each leaf by bending it back with a sharp movement. Continue snapping off the tough tops until you get to a central cone of paler leaves that are purplish-green only at the top. Then cut off about 1–2 cm (1/2–3/4 inch) of the top of the cone. Rub all the cut parts immediately with a half-lemon to prevent discoloration, and leave in a bowl of acidulated water. The artichokes are now ready for cooking.

Remember that the stalks, once you have removed the thick outer layer, are delicious in a soup or a risotto, or even cooked with the artichokes and eaten with them.

artichokes with a mint and parsley stuffing
carciofi alla romana

Serves 2–4, according
to size
4 young artichokes

For the cooking
1 garlic clove
2 or 3 parsley stalks
2 sprigs of mint
4 tbsp olive oil
sea salt and pepper

For the stuffing
**2 tbsp dried
breadcrumbs**
**1 or 2 garlic cloves,
peeled**

continued over >>

The touch that differentiates this classic Roman recipe from other recipes for stuffed artichokes is the addition of mint. The local mint – mentuccia romana – has very small leaves and a much sweeter taste than the mint we know in Britain. The sweet taste is, of course, partly due to the sun, yet the variety is definitely less pungent than the English mints. I grow mentuccia romana in my garden and I find it much sweeter than the apple mint or the spearmint growing next to it.

The advantage of this version of carciofi alla romana is that you can use the larger and tougher Breton artichokes, which are the ones most easily found in Britain. Eat them with your fingers as you would an artichoke vinaigrette, but don't forget the finger bowls or plenty of kitchen paper for your guests.

Prepare the artichokes following the instructions above.

Cut off the stalks evenly at the base. Remove the thick outer layer, keeping only the soft marrow inside.

Choose a sauté pan or a saucepan of the right size to hold the artichokes upright, very close together, so that they support each other. Add the stalks and all the ingredients for the cooking and enough water to come two-thirds of the way up the artichokes. Bring slowly to the boil and cover the pan with a piece of foil and a tight-fitting lid. Simmer over a very low heat for 10–15 minutes for the big artichokes or 5 minutes for the smaller ones.

While the artichokes are cooking, put the breadcrumbs and all the other ingredients for the stuffing in a bowl. Mix very thoroughly. Add enough of the flavourings to make the stuffing very tasty, otherwise the final result will be rather bland.

When the artichokes have cooled enough to be handled, open them up gently, like a rose, and pull out the prickly purple central leaves. Remove the fuzzy part of the chokes with a pointed teaspoon, being careful not to remove the delicious heart. You will find it easier to do this now, when the artichokes are partially cooked, rather than earlier. Season the artichokes lightly with salt and pepper.

Put the artichokes back in the pan and fill the centres with the stuffing. Cover with the foil and the lid and continue cooking until the artichokes are tender.

Transfer the artichokes to individual plates. Do not put them in the oven as they are best eaten at room temperature.

Strain the cooking juices into a clean saucepan ready to make the sauce. If they are too thin, reduce over a high heat until the juices are concentrated, then turn the heat down. Add the lemon juice and the butter a little at a time while you swirl the pan around. Do not let the sauce boil again. As soon as the butter has melted, spoon a little over the artichokes and put the remaining sauce in a sauce-boat to hand around.

large handful of parsley leaves
handful of mint leaves
1/4 tsp grated nutmeg
sea salt and freshly ground black pepper

For the sauce
2 tsp lemon juice
15 g (1/2 oz) unsalted butter

spinach

Baby spinach might be easier to deal with, but I find bunch spinach far tastier. I buy baby spinach when I want it raw in salad, but when I want to cook it, I prefer to have the bother of washing it and the pleasure of a better vegetable. Still, this is me – you do what you like.

lemon-flavoured spinach
spinaci all'agro

Serves 4
800 g (1 3/4 lb) bunch spinach or 500 g (1 lb 2 oz) baby spinach
sea salt
6 tbsp extra virgin olive oil
2 garlic cloves, peeled and bruised
the juice of 1 large organic lemon

If you are using bunch spinach cut off the roots and put it in a bowl of water, shake it around and leave for a few minutes for the earth to fall to the bottom. Scoop out the spinach and change the water two or more times, until no more earth settles on the bottom of the bowl. For baby spinach simply wash it in a sink.

Transfer the spinach to a saucepan with no water other than that which clings to the leaves. Add 1 teaspoon of salt, cover the pan, and cook over a high heat until the spinach is tender, turning it over frequently.

Now drain it and rinse under cold water. Drain again and squeeze out all the liquid with your hands. Cut the resulting mass into chunks.

Put the oil and garlic in a frying pan, add the spinach, and sauté it over a gentle heat for 10 minutes, stirring frequently. Do this on a low heat, since you only want to flavour the spinach with the oil, and to heat it. Remove the garlic, pour over half the lemon juice and toss thoroughly. Taste and adjust the seasoning, and add more lemon juice to your liking.

spinach tourte
scarpazzone lombardo

*This spinach tourte, an ancient recipe from Lombardy, incorporates
some sweet flavourings, which is something often done in the past.
Spinach tourtes can also be found in old English recipe books, and
here again spinach is combined with sultanas, biscuits and spices, plus
a small quantity of sugar added not so much to sweeten the food as to
enhance its flavour. A recipe by Patrick Lamb, a royal chef active in the
early eighteenth century, is very similar to this Italian one, as my friend
the food historian Michelle Berriedale-Johnson pointed out to me. Lamb
spread a similar mixture on toasted bread, which he then brushed with
white of egg and baked in the oven. These spinach toasts were
flavoured at the end with orange juice. I sometimes hand round a
warm tomato sauce (page 202), which gives a good combination of
taste and colour, but this is not essential.*

Put the bread in a bowl, cover with the milk and leave for half an hour
or so. Then break it up with a fork and beat to a paste.

Meanwhile, pick over the spinach; if you are using bunch spinach,
remove the roots, or if you are using leaf spinach remove the thicker part
of the stem. Wash in several changes of cold water until no more soil
settles on the bottom of the sink or basin. Bunch spinach has a much
better taste than the leaf variety, but it does need more careful washing.

Put the spinach in a saucepan with no more water than that which
clings to the leaves. Add 1 teaspoon of salt and cook, covered, until
tender. Drain in a colander and set aside. If you are using frozen
spinach, allow to thaw.

Heat the oven to 200°C (400°F) mark 6.

Put the sultanas in a bowl, cover with the orange juice and set aside.
Melt the butter in a saucepan, add the bread and milk mixture and
cook over a very low heat for 5 minutes, stirring constantly.

Squeeze all the water out of the spinach with your hands. Chop
coarsely by hand (a food processor would liquefy it) and add to the
bread mixture. Cook for a couple of minutes, stirring constantly, then
transfer to a bowl and allow to cool a little.

Beat the eggs lightly and mix thoroughly into the spinach mixture. Add the
sultanas and all the other ingredients. Taste and adjust the seasonings.

Serves 8
100 g (3 1/2 oz)
   good-quality stale
   white bread, crusts
   removed
450 ml (3/4 pint)
   full-fat milk
1.5 kg (3 1/4 lb)
   bunch spinach or
   young leaf spinach,
   or 600 g (1 1/4 lb)
   frozen leaf spinach
sea salt and pepper
45 g (1 1/2 oz)
   sultanas
juice of 1/2 an
   organic orange
150 g (5 oz) unsalted
   butter
5 free-range eggs
60 g (2 oz) digestive
   biscuits, crushed
45 g (1 1/2 oz) pine
   nuts
45 g (1 1/2 oz)
   almonds, blanched,
   peeled and chopped
2 tsp sugar
1 tsp fennel seeds,
   crushed
1/2 tsp ground
   cinnamon
1/2 tsp ground
   nutmeg
9 tbsp freshly grated
   Parmesan
butter and flour or
   dried breadcrumbs
   for the tin

Butter a 25 cm (10 inch) spring-clip cake tin. Line the bottom with greaseproof paper and butter the paper. Sprinkle with a little flour or breadcrumbs and then shake off the excess. Spoon the mixture into the tin and cover with foil.

Bake for 20 minutes, then remove the foil and bake for a further 25 minutes or so, turning down the heat to 180°C (350°F) mark 4. The *tourte* is ready when a toothpick inserted in the middle comes out dry. Allow to cool and then remove from the tin and serve at room temperature, set in a lovely round dish.

preparation
The *tourte* can be made totally up to 2 days in advance and refrigerated. I have never tried freezing it (I'm not keen on freezing dishes, because they lose their freshness), but I'm sure it could be done. If you freeze it, take it out of the freezer and leave in the kitchen for at least 6 hours in advance. Do not serve chilled.

carrots italian style
le carote di ada boni

Serves 8
1 kg (2 lb) carrots
60 g (2 oz) unsalted
   butter
sea salt and pepper
1 tsp sugar
2 tsp flour
350 ml (12 fl oz)
   stock, or 1 tsp
   Marigold Swiss
   Bouillon powder
   dissolved in the
   same amount of
   water

This is a recipe from the great classic, Il Talismano della Felicità, *by Ada Boni, and I think it is the best way to cook carrots.*

Scrape or peel the carrots. Wash them and cut them into 5 cm (2 inch) pieces. Cut each piece into quarters lengthwise and remove, if necessary, the inner hard core. Cut each quarter into matchstick-sized segments.

Melt the butter in a large sauté pan, add the carrots and sauté gently for 5 minutes. Season with salt, pepper and sugar and sprinkle with the flour. Stir well and cook for 1 minute. Add the stock, which should just cover the carrots. Bring to the boil and cover with a tight-fitting lid.

Turn the heat down and cook very gently for about 20 minutes, stirring every now and then. By the end the carrots should be soft. Taste and adjust the seasonings.

If there is still too much liquid when the carrots are ready, transfer them to a serving dish with a slotted spoon and reduce the cooking juices rapidly. Pour the juices over the carrots.

stewed vegetables
piatto rustico

A rustic dish from Umbria, which looks and tastes even better served in a hollowed-out round loaf.

Heat the oven to 160°C (325°F) mark 3.

Cut the aubergines, potatoes, courgettes and peppers into chunks of about 2.5 cm (1 inch).

Cut the peeled onions into thick slices and the garlic into small slices. Put all the vegetables into a casserole and add the tomatoes, half the olive oil, a teaspoon of salt, a generous grinding of pepper and the oregano. Cover the casserole with a lid and cook in the oven until the vegetables are tender, about 1 1/2 hours.

Remove from the oven and turn the heat up to 200°C (400°F) mark 6.

Cut the loaf of bread in half and make a container out of the bottom half by scooping out all the soft part. Brush the inside of the bread 'bowl' all over with the rest of the olive oil and put in the oven for about 8 minutes. Transfer the bread bowl to a round dish.

Taste the stewed vegetables and check the seasoning. Spoon them with their liquid into the bread bowl and serve at once.

preparation
The vegetables can be stewed up to 2 days in advance and refrigerated. The bread must be filled just before serving or it will become soggy.

Serves 4
150 g (5 oz) aubergines
225 g (8 oz) potatoes, peeled
180 g (6 oz) courgettes
180 g (6 oz) red peppers
200 g (7 oz) onions, peeled
1 or 2 garlic cloves, peeled
400 g (14 oz) tin Italian plum tomatoes
4 tbsp olive oil
sea salt
pepper
2 tsp dried oregano
round loaf of bread, 15–20 cm (6–8 inches) in diameter

stewed potatoes
patate in umido

Serves 4

700 g (1 1/2 lb) waxy potatoes
30 g (1 oz) unsalted butter
2 tbsp olive oil
60 g (2 oz) pancetta, chopped
1 onion, finely chopped
1 or 2 garlic cloves, finely chopped
1 tbsp fresh marjoram or 1/2 tbsp dried marjoram
1 tbsp tomato purée dissolved in 7 tbsp of hot stock or water
sea salt and freshly ground black pepper

Potatoes in Italy are hardly ever just boiled and served as an accompaniment to meat and fish, except with boiled meat or chicken, or boiled or roasted fish. They might indeed be served nature but they will be well doused with good olive oil. The potatoes in the following recipe are rich in flavour and can be an excellent dish in their own right.

Peel and wash the potatoes, and cut them into 2.5 cm (1 inch) cubes. Steam them for about 5 minutes.

While the potatoes are cooking, put the butter, oil and pancetta in a heavy saucepan and cook for 1 minute. Add the onion and the garlic and sauté gently for 5 minutes, stirring very frequently. Mix in the partly cooked potatoes, turning them over very gently but thoroughly to coat in the fat, and cook for 3–4 minutes.

Add the marjoram, the dissolved tomato purée and the seasoning. Stir well and cook, covered, until the potatoes are tender, turning them over often during the cooking. Use a fork to turn the potatoes, as this breaks them up less than a spoon, although some are bound to break a little. Taste to check the seasoning and serve them nice and hot.

carrot and potato timbales
sformatini di carote e patate

Serves 6

For the potato purée
700 g (1 1/2 lb) floury potatoes
150 ml (1/4 pint) full-fat milk
50 g (13/4 oz) unsalted butter

continued over >>

These little timbales are the sort of food that is currently appearing in so many fashionable restaurants everywhere. My sformatini *are made according to an old recipe from my mother's* ricettario *– recipe book. It is a recipe that uses béchamel, which nowadays is the Cinderella among sauces. I cannot understand why béchamel has been demoted; it is a wonderful sauce of many useful properties and excellent flavour. It can be a little tricky to get these* sformatini *to unmould neatly, but if you let the mixture cool slightly, they will unmould quite easily. In Italy* sformatini *are usually served without a* *sauce, but if you want to pass one round, I suggest the fontina and cream sauce on page 43.*

Wash the potatoes and cook them in their skins. Do not put any salt in the water, as it tends to break them up. At the same time, but in a different saucepan, cook the cleaned carrots in salted water. Drain the vegetables as soon as they are done. Peel the potatoes while still warm and purée them back into the saucepan through a food mill, fitted with the small-hole disc, or a potato ricer. Heat the potatoes slowly, while stirring constantly, to dry them. Meanwhile heat the milk and then add to the potatoes with the butter, Parmesan, salt and pepper and a generous grating of nutmeg. Beat hard until the purée is smooth. Beat in the egg and the yolk. Taste and check the seasonings.

Now prepare the carrot purée. Dry the carrots with kitchen paper and purée them through the food mill back into the saucepan in which they were cooked. Put the saucepan on the heat and dry the purée for a few minutes.

While the potatoes and the carrots are cooking make the béchamel. Heat the milk until just beginning to simmer. Meanwhile melt the butter in a heavy saucepan and stir in the flour. Cook for 1 minute and then draw the pan off the heat. Add the milk gradually, while beating vigorously to incorporate it. When all the milk has been absorbed, return the pan to the heat and bring to the boil. Add salt and cook over the gentlest heat for about 5 minutes, stirring frequently. Add the béchamel to the carrot purée and allow to cool before you add the egg and the egg yolk. Season with Parmesan, nutmeg and pepper and check the salt.

Heat the oven to 190°C (375°F) mark 5.

Grease the bottom of six 150 ml (1/4 pint) ramekins with some of the butter. Cut 6 discs out of parchment paper the size of the bottom of the ramekins and place them in the ramekins. Generously butter the paper and the sides of the ramekins. Sprinkle the ramekins all over with the dried breadcrumbs and shake off and reserve the excess crumbs.

Melt the remaining butter in a little saucepan.

3 tbsp freshly grated Parmesan
sea salt and pepper
grated nutmeg
1 free-range egg
1 free-range yolk

For the carrot purée
700 g (1 1/2 lb) carrots
sea salt
a thick béchamel made with 225 ml (8 fl oz) full-fat milk, 45 g (1 1/2 oz) unsalted butter, 50 g (1 3/4 oz) flour
1 free-range egg
1 free-range egg yolk
3 tbsp freshly grated Parmesan
grated nutmeg
pepper

To assemble
60 g (2 oz) unsalted butter
dried breadcrumbs

Half fill the ramekins with the carrot purée, levelling it with the back of a moistened metal spoon. Now spoon the potato purée over the carrot purée and smooth it with a wet spoon. Sprinkle with the remaining breadcrumbs and dribble with a little melted butter. Put the ramekins in a roasting tin. Pour enough boiling water into the tin to come two-thirds of the way up the side of the ramekins. Place the tin in the preheated oven and cook until set, i.e. until a toothpick inserted in the middle of the timbale comes out dry, about 25 minutes.

Remove from the oven and leave for 5 minutes. Run a small spatula round the side of the purée to loosen it from the ramekins and turn each ramekin quickly upside-down on to a plate. Shake the ramekins a little and lift them off. Remember to peel off the paper.

preparation
These *sformatini* can be prepared for the oven up to 1 day in advance, but they cannot be refrigerated because the flavour of the potatoes changes with chilling.

potatoes with parsley
patate trifolate

Serves 6–8
1.35 kg (3 lb) waxy potatoes
2 tbsp olive oil
60 g (2 oz) unsalted butter
4 tbsp chopped flat-leaved parsley
3 garlic cloves, bruised
sea salt and freshly ground black pepper

This is a very easy dish, a welcome change from the common or garden mash.

Peel the potatoes and rinse them. Cut them into small cubes of about 1.5 cm (3/4 inch) and dry them thoroughly.

Heat the oil and the butter with the parsley and the garlic in a large frying pan. When the butter foam begins to subside, remove the garlic and add the potatoes. Cook over a medium heat for about 8 minutes, turning them over and over until they are well coated and are just beginning to brown at the edges.

Turn the heat down to very low and add 120 ml (4 fl oz) of hot water. Mix well, cover the pan tightly with a lid and cook for about 30 minutes. Shake the pan and stir occasionally during the cooking. Use a fork to stir, as it is less likely to break the potatoes. If the potatoes get too dry add a little more hot water.

When the potatoes are tender, add salt and pepper to taste. It is better to add the salt at the end of the cooking, because it tends to make potatoes disintegrate. Mix well, taste and check the seasoning.

preparation

Potatoes should not be reheated. But if necessary you can cook them up to 1 hour in advance and keep them in the tightly covered pan. They will keep warm for quite a time. Before serving, heat them up over a high heat for 5 minutes, stirring very frequently.

grilled vegetables
verdure alla griglia

Serves 6
2 aubergines
sea salt
4 courgettes
150 ml (1/4 pint)
   extra virgin olive oil
pepper
225 g (8 oz) large
   mushrooms
4 peppers

For the sauce
30 g (1 oz) pine nuts
30 g (1 oz) basil
   leaves
4 garlic cloves, peeled
a small bunch of
   parsley
150 ml (3/4 pint)
   extra virgin olive oil
sea salt and pepper

These are my favourite grilled vegetables.

Wash and dry the aubergines. Cut them across into slices about 8 mm (1/3 inch) thick and put them in a colander. Sprinkle with salt.

Heat the grill and oil a grill pan or baking tray. To save time, fill the pan or tray with as many of the following vegetables as will fit, so that they cook together. You should follow the sequence given below, to allow for the different cooking times needed.

Wash and dry the courgettes, cut off the ends, and cut them lengthwise into 1 cm (1/2 inch) thick slices. If the slices are too long, cut them across in half. Put them in the grill pan, pour some drops of olive oil over them, sprinkle with salt and pepper and grill them on both sides.

Rinse the aubergines and pat them dry. Put them in the pan as soon as there is room. Pour some olive oil over them and season only with pepper, since you have already salted them. The aubergines will take only 4–5 minutes on each side. They should be tender when pricked with a fork. Undercooked aubergines are unpleasant, but overcooked ones tend to acquire a bitter taste.

Wipe the mushrooms and detach the stems, which you can use for another dish. Grill the mushroom caps, moistened with olive oil and seasoned with salt and pepper. The mushrooms are the quickest to cook.

I prefer to char the peppers directly over a flame, turning them over and over so that all the skin is charred. As soon as they have cooled down, peel them by wiping them with kitchen paper. Do not wash them under running water, as that will wash away the tasty juices. Cut them in half, remove and discard the core, seeds and ribs and cut the pepper halves into wide strips.

Now you can arrange all the vegetables in a dish or individual plates.

For the sauce, toast the pine nuts in a non-stick frying pan until just golden, shaking the pan very frequently. Put them in the food processor with the basil, garlic and parsley and process, pulsing until chopped very coarsely, while adding the oil through the funnel. Add salt and pepper, then check the seasoning. Spoon over the vegetables 1 hour or so before eating. If you do not have a food processor, pound the pine nuts, basil, garlic and parsley in a mortar moistened with 2 or 3 tablespoons of the oil. Add the remaining oil while beating with a small wire whisk or with a fork.

preparation
All the vegetables can be grilled up to 1 day in advance. Keep them, separated and covered, in the refrigerator. The sauce can be made up to 2 days in advance and chilled.

asparagus

A note about cooking asparagus. Lately, at a Guild of Food Writers lunch, I had to leave the asparagus because they were what I call raw. The inner part was still hard and the asparagus had had no time to develop its full flavour. This was no doubt due to the *al dente* mania which has infected Britain and the USA in the last few years. I am certainly not campaigning for the return of overcooked, tasteless, mushy vegetables such as used often to be served before the *al dente* craze. I am saying only that cooked vegetables should be properly cooked, i.e. cooked long enough for them to develop their full flavour, even at the expense of appearance. Harold McGee, the American food scientist, in his book *Curious Cook*, writes that flavour and colour evolve from two different chemical reactions. Chlorophyll breaks down quickly, but flavour compounds take time to develop. Asparagus, like green beans, releases its aroma as soon as it begins to be properly cooked. When asparagus is ready, the green tip should bend gracefully so that you have to lift your head up and open your mouth wide to receive it. It should not be like stiff green sticks. The correct cooking time depends entirely on its quality and age. I have had asparagus that cooked in 5 minutes and others that took 20 minutes. Just lift a spear out of the pan when you can smell the aroma, and taste it.

asparagus with fried eggs and parmesan
asparagi alla milanese

This is my favourite supper dish in June, when the first English asparagus appear on the market. It might be called 'asparagus with instant hollandaise'.

Italians prefer fat white asparagus, and some people maintain that those from Bassano del Grappa or from Greve del Piave in Veneto are the best. The Piedmontese, however, claim that their asparagus from Sàntena are even better. But, whatever the species, white, green, fat or lean, the asparagus must be fresh and young. You also need good cheese for this recipe, otherwise the cheese will kill the flavour of the asparagus instead of combining with it.

Serves 4
**1.35 kg (3 lb)
asparagus**
sea salt
**60 g (2 oz) unsalted
butter**
**4 tbsp freshly grated
Parmesan**
8 free-range eggs
**freshly ground black
pepper**

First scrape the ends of the asparagus stems and snap off or cut off the hard part. Wash thoroughly. Tie the asparagus in small bundles. Tie them in two places, at the top near the tips and at the bottom above the butts.

If you haven't got an asparagus boiler, use a tall narrow saucepan, half full of boiling water, or a large sauté pan. Remember to add salt to the water before you add the asparagus.

When the asparagus are cooked, lift the bundles out and place them on kitchen paper to drain properly before you transfer them and place them on 4 individual plates. Keep warm.

Melt three-quarters of the butter in a non-stick frying pan and pour it over the asparagus spears. Sprinkle with the Parmesan.

Melt the remaining butter in the same pan and break the eggs into the pan. When fried, slide 2 eggs on to each plate next to the asparagus tips. Grind some pepper over them and serve immediately, with plenty of crusty bread.

You can make the same dish with leeks, which, after all, the French call '*les asperges des pauvres*'.

peas

In Italy the vegetable that announces the arrival of spring is the pea. The spring peas are small and sweet in tender pods, which are themselves often used by thrifty housewives to make soups.

In Venice, in the old days, a purée of pea pods was added to *risi e bisi*, rice and peas, the dish served at the Doge's banquet every year on St Mark's day, 25 April. When we had a flat in Venice we spent many Easter holidays there, and I realised then why the pods were used as well as the peas. The peas that arrive at Rialto market from the islands in the lagoon are closer to mange-tout than to the garden peas sold in British shops. But, never mind, we cannot all move to Venice for the lovely peas.

In Britain peas arrive later, and when they are first on the market it is not too difficult to find small ones with shiny unblemished pods. Buy them, and welcome the spring with this easy dish of pasta in which the sweetness of the peas and of the cream is livened by the vermouth and the stock. Of course you can make this delicious dish at any time of the year using frozen peas, which, however, have a different flavour from the fresh ones.

linguine with peas and cream
linguine coi piselli alla panna

If you are using fresh peas, plunge them in a saucepan of boiling water and cook them for 5 minutes. Frozen peas do not need this blanching.

For the sauce, choose a large sauté or frying pan into which you can later transfer the drained pasta. Put the butter and shallots in the pan and sprinkle with the sugar and salt. Sauté the shallots until soft and then add the peas. Coat them in the butter for 1 minute, sprinkle with the flour and cook for a further minute, stirring the whole time. Stir in the vermouth, boil for 1 minute and then add the stock. Cover the pan and regulate the heat so that the liquid will simmer gently for the peas to cook. They must be tender, not just *al dente*. Stir in the cream, cook for a couple of minutes. Add pepper, taste and check the seasoning.

Meanwhile put a large saucepan of water on the heat and bring to the boil. Add 1 1/2 tablespoons of salt and when the water has come back to a roaring boil, slide in the *linguine*, pushing the bundle down gently as the part under water softens. Stir with a long fork, put the lid back on the pan until the water is boiling again, then remove the lid and cook at a steady boil until the *linguine* are done. Drain, but do not overdrain, and transfer immediately to the pan with the sauce. Stir-fry, using 2 forks, and stirring with a high movement so that all the pasta strands are well coated with the sauce.

Serves 6
450 g (1 lb) *linguine*
sea salt
**freshly grated
    Parmesan for
    serving**

For the sauce
**45 g (1 1/2 oz)
    unsalted
    butter**
**4 shallots, very finely
    chopped**
1 tsp sugar
1 tsp sea salt
**225 g (8 oz) fresh
    garden peas,
    podded weight, or
    frozen peas,
    thawed**
1 tbsp flour
**6 tbsp dry white
    vermouth**

continued over >>

120 ml (4 fl oz) meat
stock, or 1/4
bouillon cube
dissolved in the
same quantity of
water
150 ml (1/4 pint)
single cream
freshly ground white
pepper

Now, if your frying pan is a good-looking one, bring the pan directly to the table. The less pasta is transferred from one container to another, the better; it keeps hotter. But if you do not like to bring saucepans to the table, turn the pasta into a heated bowl and serve, handing round the Parmesan in a bowl.

fennel

'It is said that serpents are very fond of fennel, and that after feeding on this plant they do not get any older.' Thus wrote Bartolomeo Sacchi, known as Platina, in the fifteenth century, and after listing fennel's many therapeutic properties he wrote: 'it is therefore advisable to eat fennel, whether raw or cooked.' I love fennel, both the herb and the bulb, and as I eat it I cherish the hope that, like Platina's snakes, I may discover the secret of eternal middle age! I grow the herb in the garden with great ease, and I buy the bulbs whenever I see some that look fresh enough. Unfortunately the fennel you buy in Britain does not have as full a flavour as the fennel in Italy. I think Jane Grigson was right when she suggested in her *Vegetable Book* that the commercial variety grown in Italy for export is like some of the celery we import, 'beautiful but dumb'.

In the past fennel, sometimes with a little salt, was considered a very healthy food with which to finish a heavy meal. This habit has more or less disappeared, except for some places in Tuscany, where wedges of fennel are still placed on the table with apples and mandarins. But fennel is still eaten a great deal in Italy, as a vegetable or in salad; in fact, because of its versatility, it is the most popular of winter vegetables.

Fennel is one of the best ingredients for a Piedmontese *bagna caôda* – crudités dipped in a hot garlicky sauce – or for a Roman *pinzimonio* (see page 436). It is also excellent cooked. Try stewing it in milk and butter, or in a thin tomato sauce. A favourite of mine in winter is fennel baked with béchamel, Parmesan and nutmeg, while another is some pasta dressed with a creamy sauce of stewed fennel.

Fennel is best in the autumn and winter months. Try to buy it loose, rather than in plastic trays where the clingfilm prevents you from seeing whether it is fresh. When you buy fennel for eating raw, choose the round squat bulbs in preference to the flat, elongated ones. They are crisper and sweeter. For cooking, either variety is suitable. See that the bulbs have no brown or wilted patches and that the bottom is white.

When you prepare fennel, start by removing any brown or wilted parts. Then cut the fennel according to the recipe and wash thoroughly in cold water. For cooking you will need about three heads for four people, while if you are going to eat them raw two will be enough.

fennel mould
sformato di finocchio

'A *sformato*, a dish which figures largely in Italian home cooking but never in restaurants, is a cross between a soufflé and what we should call a pudding.' Thus wrote Elizabeth David in *Italian Food*, first published in 1954. And how right she was so many years ago, when nobody outside Italy, or even outside northern Italian families of a certain milieu, knew what a *sformato* was. In my home, *sformati* of different vegetables, often mixed in sections in the same mould, were the usual *entremets* at dinner parties. They replaced fish on *giorni di magro* – fast days – when a *sformato* would precede a sea bass or a daurade.

My impression is that nowadays *sformati* are rarely served at home; while, with slight modifications, they have become the most fashionable fare to be had in a restaurant, where they appear in individual portions and are called *sformatini* or *timballini* – timbales in Britain. One reason why a *sformato* is less often served at home is that the usual meal now consists of no more than three courses, and

Serves 6
**700 g (1 1/2 lb)
fennel bulbs**
**60 g (2 oz) unsalted
butter**
sea salt
**300 ml (1/2 pint) full-
fat milk**
30 g (1 oz) flour
**a generous grating of
nutmeg**
3 free-range eggs
**4 tbsp freshly grated
Parmesan cheese**
**freshly ground
pepper, preferably
white**
**3 tbsp dried
breadcrumbs**

the Italians like a *minestra* for the *primo* and meat or fish for the *secondo*.

A *sformato* makes a good supper dish or a perfect start to a dinner party. It looks most impressive when served, and it is less nerve-racking for the hostess than a soufflé, since it will not collapse. If you butter a mould very carefully and very generously, and sprinkle it all over with dried breadcrumbs, you will have no difficulty in unmoulding it.

A *sformato* can be made with French beans, with fresh or dried peas, with carrots, artichokes, spinach, aubergines, in fact with most vegetables that are cooked first and then chopped or puréed. In the past, eggs and béchamel were used for binding, but now cream is often used instead. A *sformato* can be served with various sauces, the most common being a tomato sauce, perfect with a *sformato* of French beans or of aubergines, and a *fonduta* (page 305), my favourite with spinach or with the fennel mould described below.

You can make individual *sformatini* by using darioles or ramekins. Unmould them on individual plates and surround them with a little of the chosen sauce. The recipe here is for a large *sformato*.

Cut away all the green tops of the fennel, also the stalks and any bruised or brown parts of the outside leaves. Reserve a handful of the green top. (Do not throw all the rest away, it will make a good soup for the family with the addition of a potato or two.)

Cut the fennel bulbs into vertical slices about 5 mm (1/4 inch) thick. Wash the slices, and the reserved fennel top and dry with kitchen paper.

Melt 30 g (1 oz) of the butter in a sauté pan. When the butter begins to foam, add the fennel and cook for 5 minutes. Add salt and half the milk. Cover the pan and cook very gently until the fennel is tender — about 20 minutes. Keep a watch on the fennel and add a little water if it becomes too dry.

Chop the fennel by hand or in the food processor to a very coarse purée. Transfer to a bowl.

Heat the oven to 190°C (375°F) mark 5.

Make a fairly thick béchamel sauce (see page 489) with the remaining butter, the flour and the rest of the milk. Flavour the béchamel with the grated nutmeg and then add to the fennel purée.

Beat the eggs together lightly with a fork and add to the fennel mixture together with the Parmesan and the pepper. Mix very thoroughly, then taste and adjust the seasoning.

Prepare the mould. Butter a ring-mould of 900 ml (1 1/2 pint) capacity very generously. If you are nervous about unmoulding the *sformato*, line the base of the ring with parchment paper and butter the paper. Sprinkle the mould with the breadcrumbs and then shake off the excess crumbs.

Spoon the mixture into the prepared mould. Place the mould in a baking tin and fill the tin with very hot water to come two-thirds of the way up the side of the mould. Place the tin in the preheated oven and cook for about 45 minutes, until a thin skewer or a toothpick inserted into the middle of the *sformato* comes out dry.

Allow to stand for 5 minutes. Loosen the sides of the *sformato* with a metal spatula and place a round dish over it. Turn the dish and the mould over, shake the mould lightly and lift it off. Remove the paper, if you were using it.

Fill the hole in the *sformato* with the sauce, and spoon a few tablespoons around it. Serve the rest of the sauce in a warm sauce-boat.

fennel stewed in stock
finocchi stufati

Serves 4
800 g (1 3/4 lb) fennel
60 g (2 oz) unsalted butter
vegetable or meat stock, about 200 ml (7 fl oz)
sea salt and pepper

The old-fashioned way of cooking vegetables in Italy is to stew them. This recipe will demonstrate how such slow cooking intensifies the flavour. The fennel become unbelievably tasty, although crunchy-vegetable freaks might not approve of their texture.

Trim the fennel, removing any brown parts as well as the stalks and the feathery tops. Cut the fennel lengthwise into quarters, then slice the quarters into wedges about 1 cm (1/2 inch) thick. Put in a colander and wash under a cold tap. Drain and dry thoroughly with kitchen paper.

Choose a sauté pan large enough to hold the raw fennel comfortably. Melt the butter and when it begins to become golden add the fennel and fry gently for about 10 minutes, turning them over and over to *insaporire* – make them tasty – on all sides.

Add enough stock to cover the bottom of the pan. Cover with a tight-fitting lid and cook over a very low heat for some 20 minutes, until the fennel are tender. You might have to add a little more stock during the cooking if the fennel gets too dry. By the time they are finished there should be just a little liquid left: the fennel should certainly not be swimming in it. It should be of a pale gold colour. Add salt and pepper to taste and serve.

fennel cooked in wine and flavoured with a pistachio, anchovy and vinegar sauce
finocchi del corrado

Serves 4
700 g (1 1/2 lb) fennel bulbs
300 ml (1/2 pint) dry white wine
2 bay leaves
piece of cinnamon stick, about 5 cm (2 inches)

continued over >>

I am at a loss to describe the taste of this superb dish which I adapted from an eighteenth-century recipe by Vincenzo Corrado, one of my favourite cookery writers. Corrado had the perfect touch when dealing with vegetables, to which he dedicated more of his writings than did any other writer of the past.

The dish leaves you delighted yet puzzled as to how such an unlikely combination of flavours could blend with such complete harmony. Those, at least, were my feelings when I first made the recipe.

Remove the bruised and brown parts of the fennel, as well as the stalks and the feathery tops. Cut the fennel into quarters, wash them and then cut them into very thin segments.

Put the wine, bay leaves, cinnamon, peppercorns and salt in a saucepan. Add the fennel and enough water to cover. Bring to the boil and cook, covered, at a steady simmer until the fennel is tender but still *al dente*. Drain and then put the fennel in a deep dish.

For the sauce, blanch the pistachios in boiling water for 20 seconds and then peel them. Put them in a mortar and add all the other ingredients except the lemon juice. Pound to a paste with a pestle, using a rotary motion, then taste and add enough lemon juice to achieve the desired amount of bite. You can use a food processor for this operation.

Spoon this little sauce over the fennel, cover with clingfilm and leave it in the fridge for at least 24 hours. Bring the dish back to room temperature before serving. You can garnish with a few sprigs of the feathery top.

8 peppercorns, bruised
sea salt

For the sauce
30 g (1 oz) pistachio nuts
2 anchovy fillets or 1 salted anchovy, rinsed and boned
1 tsp sugar
a generous grating of nutmeg
3 tbsp extra virgin olive oil
2 tsp white wine vinegar
grated rind and the juice of 1/2 an organic unwaxed lemon

roasted chicory with balsamic vinegar
cicoria belga all'aceto balsamico

The balsamic vinegar tempers and yet enhances the slight bitterness of the chicory with its complex sweetness.

Rinse and clean the salted anchovies under cold water or drain the oil from the anchovy fillets and pat them dry. Chop coarsely, put them in a small bowl and cover them with milk. This will remove the strong flavour.

Remove a thin slice from the root end of each chicory head and any brown edges from the outside leaves. Slice the heads in half along their length and rinse them under cold water. Lay them on a slanting board, cut side down, to drain for half an hour and then dry them with kitchen paper.

Serves 6
2 salted anchovies or 4 anchovy fillets
milk
8 fat, firm chicory heads of similar size
150 ml (1/4 pint) extra virgin olive oil
sea salt and pepper
2 tbsp pine nuts

continued over >>

4 tbsp balsamic vinegar
225 g (8 oz) endive (frisée)
3 free-range hard-boiled eggs

Heat the oven to 230°C (450°F) mark 8.

Grease an oven tray with a little of the oil. Lay the chicory halves, cut side up, on the tray, brush them with olive oil and season with salt and pepper. Bake for 10 minutes, until the inner core can be pierced with a fork. Transfer them to a dish.

Remove the anchovies from the milk and put them in a small frying pan with the remaining oil. Cook gently for 1 minute while mashing them with a fork. Keep the heat very low or the anchovies will acquire a bitter flavour. Stir in the pine nuts and the balsamic vinegar. Sauté for a further minute and then add salt, if necessary, and a good deal of pepper. Spoon three-quarters of the hot sauce over the chicory. Cover with clingfilm and set aside for 2 hours.

Wash the endive and dry it thoroughly.

Half an hour before you are ready to serve dinner, cut the endive into very thin strips. This is quite easy if you gather little bunches of the leaves and then shred them, the finer the better. Place the shredded endive on a serving dish, spoon over the remaining sauce, but do not mix the salad or you will spoil its appearance. Place the chicory halves neatly on the bed of endive and pour over all the juices from the dish where it has been sitting.

Cut the hard-boiled eggs in half and take out the yolks (you can use the whites in a salad on another occasion). Press the yolks through a sieve or through a food mill fitted with the small-hole disc. Do this directly over the dish so that the egg mimosa will stay airy and light.

preparation

The only thing that must be done at the last minute is the sieving of the egg yolks. The rest can be prepared up to 3 hours in advance. The chicory can be baked up to 1 day in advance and kept covered. It does not need refrigerating.

stewed broccoli
broccoli stufati

This is a dish I had recently at a friend's house in Milan. Her broccoli brought back nostalgic memories of all the vegetables cooked the way they used to be in Italy. Nowadays vegetables are often cooked in Britain for a very short time and served as they are, i.e. undressed. When cooked in my friend's way, the flavour of the broccoli is fully developed, with the result that – both in looks and in taste – they are a different dish from the broccoli spears we are used to today. Don't be put off by the quantity of garlic. Its flavour fades with the long cooking, and at the end the cloves themselves are removed.

For 4 people you will need 500 g (1 lb) of broccoli. Separate the stalks from the florets. Remove the outer layer of the toughest stalks, leaving only the sweet marrow, and cut the stalks into short pieces. Divide the florets into small buds. Wash the broccoli and blanch in salted boiling water for 3 minutes, then drain them thoroughly. Peel 10 cloves of garlic and thread toothpicks through them. (This will make it easier to remove the garlic at the end of the cooking.) Heat 3 tablespoons of extra virgin olive oil, with the garlic and a chilli, in a sauté pan. Remove and discard the chilli and add the broccoli. Turn them over and over for a couple of minutes and then cook them, covered, and very gently, for about 40 minutes, stirring every now and then with a fork. By the end they will be fairly mashed up, but they will taste delicious. Fish out the garlic and discard, or remove only half the cloves and leave the others, but remember to remove the toothpicks.

celery soup
passato di sedano

Italian vegetable soups traditionally consist of a mixture of seasonal vegetables that are cut into small pieces and cooked in stock or water, with some pasta or rice. When the vegetables are made into a purée, as in this soup, it is as a result of French influence. Yet this puréed soup is typically Italian in flavour, since it is rounded out by ricotta instead of cream. The ricotta gives the soup a lighter taste and a

Serves 8
1 1/2 medium heads of celery
75 g (2 1/2 oz) unsalted butter

continued over >>

2 tbsp olive oil

3 potatoes, cut into
small pieces

2 litres (3 1/2 pints)
meat or vegetable
stock

sea salt

4 slices of brown
bread, crust
removed, very
lightly toasted

225 g (8 oz) ricotta

freshly ground black
pepper

freshly grated
Parmesan for
serving

rougher texture, emphasised by the addition of the sautéed
breadcrumbs, here replacing the more formal croûtons.

Remove the strings and leaves from the celery sticks, wash thoroughly and cut into pieces. Keep the leaves for flavouring other dishes or for chopping into a salad.

Heat 30 g (1 oz) of the butter and 1 tablespoon of the oil, and when the butter begins to foam add the celery and the potatoes. Sauté very gently for 5 minutes, stirring frequently.

Meanwhile bring the stock to the boil and pour over the sautéed vegetables. Add salt to taste and simmer for 30 minutes.

While the soup is cooking make coarse breadcrumbs from the toasted bread. A food processor is ideal for the job.

In a small frying pan heat the rest of the butter and oil and, when very hot, mix in the breadcrumbs and fry until all the fat has been absorbed and the crumbs are darker in colour and crisp.

Purée the soup in a food processor or a blender and return to the pan. Bring the soup back to the boil. Draw off the heat. Break up the ricotta with a fork and add to the soup with the pepper. Mix well, taste and adjust the seasoning.

Ladle the soup into bowls and hand the fried breadcrumbs and the Parmesan round in separate bowls for everyone to help themselves.

leek and rice pie
la torta di porri

I can particularly recommend this pie. The original of this torta was made with courgettes and was given to me by a great friend in Genoa. When I arrived there I heard a thumping noise coming from the kitchen where I found my friend, a distinctly aristocratic lady, bent double bashing the bottom of the pie dish against the tiled floor. 'This is how the Ligurian peasants dislodge their vegetable pies,' she explained.

When I came back to London the local courgettes were not in season any more. So I tried making the pie with the young leeks that had just come into the shops, and it turned out to be just as delicious. But in the spring and summer when the young English courgettes are available, substitute them for the leeks, adding 1 white onion to the filling. The quantities and method are the same.

The leeks and rice become soft by soaking in the egg and oil mixture, with the result that, when cooked, the filling is moist yet firm. Although these vegetable pies are usually made with pasta frolla – shortcrust pastry – in Italy, I think filo pastry is the perfect container. It's also quicker, since you buy it already made!

First prepare the leeks. Cut away and discard all except the white part and the inside of the green part. Cut into very thin rounds, about 3 mm (1/8 inch). Wash thoroughly, removing all the earth. If the leeks are large and have a strong smell, meaning that they are rather old, leave them for about an hour in plenty of cold water to which you have added a couple of tablespoons of salt. Drain and put them in a bowl.

Lightly beat the eggs and add to the bowl with the rice, half the oil, 2 teaspoons of salt, plenty of pepper and the Parmesan. Mix very thoroughly (I use my hands). Set the bowl aside for a couple of hours, but toss again whenever you remember because the liquid sinks to the bottom and you want the leeks and rice mixture to have a fair share of it.

Heat the oven to 180°C (350°F) mark 4.

Oil a 25 cm (10 inch) spring-clip tin and lightly flour it. Shake away the excess flour. Pour the rest of the oil into a bowl. Carefully unfold the filo pastry leaves, one at a time, taking care to keep the other leaves covered; filo pastry dries out and cracks very easily. Lift out and lay 1 leaf over the bottom and up the sides of the prepared tin, allowing the ends to hang

Serves 8
700 g (1 1/2 lb) leeks
4 free-range eggs
150 g (5 oz) Italian risotto rice (e.g. Arborio)
200 ml (7 fl oz) extra virgin olive oil
sea salt and pepper
7 tbsp freshly grated Parmesan
225–250 g (8–9 oz) frozen filo pastry, thawed

down over the outside of the tin. Using a pastry brush, brush the leaf all over with a little of the oil and then cover with another leaf of filo pastry. Lay it across the previous one so that the sides of the tin are covered all round. Brush with oil and lay 2 more leaves in the same way.

Now fill the tin with the leek mixture. Fold the overhanging pieces of filo back over the top, one at a time, to make a lid. If the filo is not long enough, lay 4 more leaves over the top, brushing each sheet with oil. Cut them to fit inside the tin and fold the overlap over to form a ridge round the edge. Brush each one with oil before you place the next. If necessary cut some of the pieces with scissors and patch up any that need it so that the filling is evenly covered. Bake for 45–50 minutes.

Let the pie cool for 10 minutes and then remove the side of the tin and turn the pie over on to an oven tray. Remove the base of the tin. Put the pie back in the oven, upside-down, for 5 minutes to dry the bottom. Turn it out onto a lovely round dish ready to serve.

preparation
The pie is best served hot or warm. You can make it 1 day in advance and then reheat it in the oven for 15 minutes or so.

baked courgettes in tomato sauce
tortino di zucchine

Serves 4–6
700 g (1 1/2 lb) courgettes
30 g (1 oz) unsalted butter
4 tbsp olive oil
2 onions, finely sliced
sea salt

continued over >>

A tortino is a baked vegetable dish of any sort, usually baked without a pastry case. It is the sort of dish that I like: tasty, uncomplicated and with as many variations as you like to make. The crust here is made with a mixture of breadcrumbs and Parmesan; brown breadcrumbs are perfect in this dish.

Wash and dry the courgettes and then cut them into rounds 5 mm (1/4 inch) thick.

Heat the butter and half the oil in a medium-sized sauté pan and, as soon as the butter is melted, add the onions and a pinch of salt (this will make the onion wilt without browning). Sauté over a low heat until soft and then add the garlic and the parsley. Fry gently for 1 minute, stirring constantly.

Turn the heat up to medium and add the chopped tomatoes with their juice. Bring to the boil, turn the heat down to low and simmer for 10 minutes, stirring frequently.

Preheat the oven to 190°C (375°F) mark 5.

Mix in the courgettes and cook uncovered for about 10 minutes. They should be tender but still firm. The timing depends on the freshness and size of the courgettes. Stir every so often, using a fork rather than a spoon, as this is less likely to break them. Add salt, pepper and oregano and then check the seasoning.

Mix the breadcrumbs and the cheese in a bowl.

Grease a shallow ovenproof dish with a little of the remaining oil and then spoon the courgettes onto the dish and spread the breadcrumb mixture on top. Pour over the rest of the oil in a thin stream and bake for about 15 minutes, until the crumbs have formed a light crust. Allow the dish to stand for a few minutes out of the oven before serving.

2 garlic cloves, peeled and finely sliced
1 tbsp chopped flat-leaf parsley
225 g (8 oz) ripe tomatoes, peeled, seeded and coarsely chopped, or tinned plum tomatoes, coarsely chopped
freshly ground black pepper
1 tsp dried oregano
4 tbsp fresh soft brown breadcrumbs, very lightly toasted
4 tbsp freshly grated Parmesan

cauliflower and breadcrumbs with anchovies, capers and olives
cavolfiore strascinato con la mollica

Brown breadcrumbs are better than white for this tasty dish from southern Italy. I make my soft crumbs in a food processor, a very quick job. You can use broccoli instead of cauliflower, but the vegetable I like best prepared in this way is catalogna. *This is a kind of long green chicory which you can occasionally find in Britain in Greek shops, where it is called, simply, chicory. It has a slightly bitter flavour perfect for this dressing.*

Serves 4
1 cauliflower head, about 500 g (1 lb 2 oz)
sea salt

continued over >>

6 tbsp extra virgin olive oil

100 g (3 1/2 oz) soft breadcrumbs

3 salted anchovies, boned and washed, or 6 anchovy fillets

1 or 2 dried chillies, according to taste, seeded

2 garlic cloves, peeled

1 1/2 tbsp capers, rinsed and dried

12 black olives, stoned and cut into strips

Divide the cauliflower into small florets, cut the tender stalks into small pieces and wash carefully. Blanch in boiling salted water for 3 minutes and then drain and dry with kitchen paper.

Heat the oil and then add the breadcrumbs. Cook for 3 minutes, stirring to coat them with the oil.

Add the cauliflower, florets and stalks, and cook until tender but still crunchy, stirring very frequently. Use a fork rather than a spoon as this helps to keep the florets whole.

Meanwhile chop all the other ingredients except the olives, and then add them to the cauliflower and bread mixture. Add the olives and cook for a further minute or so. Stir well. Taste and add salt and pepper as necessary.

Serve this dish hot, warm or cold, but not chilled or piping hot.

vegetable stock
brodo vegetale

See page 487 in The Essentials section.

battuto e soffrito

See page 488 in The Essentials section.

roast potatoes
patate arrosto

See page 490 in The Essentials section.

In Italy all vegetables are likely to be served as salads. They may be raw, such as lettuces or endives, tomatoes, cucumbers, fennel, artichokes, etc., according to the season, or they may be boiled vegetables: French beans, potatoes, courgettes, spinach or cauliflower.

Whatever the salad may be, the traditional dressing is extra virgin olive oil, wine vinegar – or in some cases lemon juice – salt and sometimes pepper. Green salad is often dressed at the table, since the dressing must be added at the last minute, or the salad will 'cook', that is, lose its crispness. The dressing is an integral part of an Italian salad, not an addition.

It is difficult to state how much oil or vinegar is needed in a salad, since it depends on the salad itself, as well as on the fruitiness of the oil and the acidity and strength of the vinegar. French beans, for example, will need less oil than potatoes or lettuce, whereas cucumbers and beetroots require more vinegar or lemon juice. The only way to solve the problem is to taste and correct the seasonings before serving. As a rough guide, however, you will need 1 tablespoon of vinegar and 4 tablespoons of olive oil for a salad for 4 people, plus salt and pepper to taste.

green salad

The number of different kinds of green salad displayed in shops and supermarkets in Italy is proof of their popularity. At any time of the year there are at least ten varieties, all fresh and inviting. Traditionally, green salads are served on their own, although I have recently come across some successful combinations: red radicchio and thin wedges of raw artichoke, lamb's lettuce with grilled peppers and finely sliced *cicorino* – dandelion – with cubes of tomato and cucumber.

Green salad must be thoroughly washed and then well dried. Everybody has their own way of adding the dressing; mine is to put the vinegar into the salad spoon, add the salt to it and sprinkle over the salad, at the same time rapidly stirring the vinegar and salt in the spoon with the salad fork. I add the oil last. A grinding of pepper, and *ecco fatto* – it is done and ready to be mixed.

However you choose to dress your salad, it must be tossed many times after adding the seasonings. Some people swear that 36 times is the secret for a successful salad! It is said that you need 4 people to dress a salad: a generous man to pour the oil, a wise man to sprinkle the salt, a miser to add the vinegar and a patient soul to toss it.

green salad with herb dressing

See page 491 in The Essentials section.

red radicchio

This pretty salad is in the shops all year round to cheer our salad bowls with its mauvy red colour but, pretty though it is, this mass-produced radicchio lacks the delicious bitter flavour of the original varieties. What it has instead is its property of keeping crisp and fresh for days and, as a consequence, its ready availability.

The radicchio we see in Britain is the latest variety called *radicchio di Chioggia*; it was developed after the war around the town of Chioggia on the southernmost point of the Venetian lagoon. The other three varieties, *radicchio di Verona*, *radicchio di Treviso* and *radicchio di*

Castelfranco are hard to come by. The *radicchio di Verona* has spear-shaped leaves that grow in a bunch, similar to a small cos lettuce. Its flavour is very delicate and sweet. *Radicchio di Treviso*, a provincial city to the north of Venice, grows in small bunches, with lanceolate leaves and is, to my taste, the best.

The other radicchio comes originally from Castelfranco, also in Veneto, a lovely town and a place of pilgrimage for art lovers who go there to see the exquisite Madonna by Giorgione. This radicchio has round leaves and a slightly more bitter flavour than the other two varieties. Its appearance has been likened to that of an open rose, with a pale reddish colour veined with white streaks.

These varieties of radicchio are part of the traditional cooking of Veneto. *Radicchio di Treviso* is used because it has no trace of the bitterness that, released in cooking, would disturb the result. It is used in a traditional *risotto al radicchio*: the radicchio is added to a buttery *soffritto* at the beginning.

In modern cooking, a number of recipes have been created for radicchio: gnocchi, lasagne, sauces and even sweets, about the last of which I will spare you my comments.

grilled radicchio with parmesan
radicchio alla griglia col parmigiano

This simple recipe achieves a most successful combination of an old dish with a modern topping. It is ideal for a barbecue.

The radicchio should really be *radicchio di Treviso*, but you can happily use the *radicchio di Chioggia* found in Britain. For 4 people you will need 1 kg (2 lb) of radicchio, 5 tablespoons of extra virgin olive oil and 120 g (4 oz) of best *parmigiano-reggiano*.

Cut the radicchio heads into quarters and place them in the grill pan. Pour over some olive oil and season with salt and a lot of pepper. Cook on charcoal or under a preheated grill for 10 minutes and then transfer to a dish and cover with Parmesan flakes. Dribble a little more olive oil over the top. The cheese should just melt in contact with the hot radicchio. A perfect antipasto.

The grilled radicchio without the Parmesan on top is an excellent accompaniment to grilled meat.

celeriac, chicory and radicchio salad
insalata veronese

Serves 8
1 medium-sized celeriac
3 chicory heads
3 medium-sized radicchio heads

For the dressing
3 tbsp lemon juice
1 tsp English mustard powder
120 ml (4 fl oz) extra virgin olive oil
sea salt and pepper

This is an autumnal salad, full of colour and flavours.

First make the dressing. Put the lemon juice in a bowl and mix in the mustard. Add the oil in a very thin stream while beating with a fork to emulsify and then season to taste.

Peel the celeriac and cut into julienne strips. (This is easily done in a food processor with the julienne disc.) Toss with some of the dressing and put in a bowl. Cover with clingfilm and leave in the refrigerator for 2–3 hours.

Cut the chicory and the radicchio into 1 cm (1/2 inch) strips. Wash and dry thoroughly and toss with the remaining dressing. Put the celeriac in the middle of a serving dish and spoon the salad mixture around it.

courgette and tomato salad dressed with balsamic vinegar and flavoured with mint

insalata di zucchine e pomodori all'aceto balsamico e alla menta

A courgette and tomato salad is a natural. It is a delicious, classic dish, prepared in most Italian homes. By adding the balsamic vinegar and the mint, and by spending a little longer on the preparation, you can make it more interesting and more attractive. Serve plenty of good bread with it – a ciabatta is ideal.

Wash and scrub the courgettes thoroughly, but leave the ends on to prevent water getting inside. Cook them in boiling salted water until tender, but not soft. Take them out of the saucepan and refresh under cold water. Leave them to cool a little, dry them and cut off the ends. Cut the courgettes in half lengthwise and lay them neatly on a dish.

Mix together the oil, balsamic vinegar, pepper and salt and spoon over the courgettes, reserving 2 tablespoons of the dressing. Sprinkle the garlic slivers on top. Cover with clingfilm and set aside for about 1 hour.

Blanch and skin the tomatoes. Cut them in half and squeeze out and discard the seeds and some of the liquid. Cut each half into 1 cm (1/2 inch) cubes. Before serving, place the tomatoes over the courgettes, sprinkle lightly with salt and pepper and the mint, and spoon over the remaining dressing.

Serves 8
1 kg (2 lb) young courgettes
sea salt
6 tbsp extra virgin olive oil
3 tbsp balsamic vinegar
freshly ground black pepper
1 garlic clove, very thinly sliced
4 tomatoes, preferably plum tomatoes
3 tbsp chopped mint

green beans

On the subject of cooking green beans, I would like to insert a short parenthesis inspired by a pen and telephone friend from across the ocean, Corby Kummer of Boston. In the September 1990 issue of the magazine *The Atlantic* he wrote an article titled *An End to al Dente*, explaining why green beans, more than any other vegetable, must be well cooked, which does not mean overcooked. 'Green beans are immature beans in their casings, bred to be edible . . . All these casings contain lignin, a substance found in wood, hemp and linen, but in few other green vegetables. Boiling seems best at breaking down the lignin, better than braising, steaming or microwaving.' As I told Corby Kummer, I boil my beans until their particular smell rises. That is when I taste them; they may be ready or they may need a few more minutes.

green bean and tomato salad
insalata di fagiolini e pomodori

Serves 8–10
1 kg (2 lb) green beans
sea salt
7 tbsp extra virgin olive oil
450 g (1 lb) firm ripe tomatoes
6 garlic cloves, bruised
2 tbsp lemon juice
freshly ground black pepper
a dozen fresh basil leaves

Top and tail the beans. Wash well and cook uncovered in plenty of boiling salted water until *al dente*. I find the *al dente* point easy to catch, since the beans give off a characteristic smell when they are nearly cooked. Remember to add a good deal of salt to the water, as green beans are very insipid. Drain and refresh quickly under cold water. Blot with kitchen paper, heap them in the middle of a dish and dress with a third of the oil while they are still warm. Leave to cool.

While the beans are cooking, drop the tomatoes into the same saucepan. Count up to eight, then retrieve them with a slotted spoon and plunge them immediately into a bowl of cold water. Skin them and cut them into wedges or slices, discarding the seeds.

Put the rest of the oil, the garlic, lemon juice and plenty of pepper in a bowl and leave to infuse for at least 1 hour.

Lay the tomatoes all round the beans and season them with salt and pepper. Remove and discard the garlic from the little sauce and spoon the sauce over the beans and the tomatoes. Scatter the basil leaves over the salad.

preparation
The beans can be cooked up to 2 days in advance and refrigerated in a closed container. The tomatoes can be skinned and cut a few hours in advance, but they must be dressed at the last minute.

potatoes and green beans with pesto
patate e fagiolini al pesto

In Genoa pasta al pesto often contains potatoes and green beans. Here I eliminate the pasta and serve the potatoes and beans dressed with pesto as a warm salad. It is a very good and nourishing antipasto.

To make the pesto, put all the ingredients in the food processor and process at high speed until they are completely blended. Taste and check the seasonings.

Boil the potatoes in their skins. When ready, drain and peel them while still hot. Leave aside.

Top and tail the beans and wash them. Cook them in plenty of salted water until properly cooked, but not overcooked. (See my note about cooking green beans on page 271. When green beans are nearly ready they give off a characteristic smell.) Drain the beans and transfer them to a piece of kitchen paper to dry. Cut them into 2.5 cm (1 inch) pieces.

While the beans are cooking, cut the potatoes into 2 cm (3/4 inch) cubes, put them in a bowl and dress with olive oil.

Add the beans and toss. Spoon the pesto into the salad and toss thoroughly but gently. Serve warm.

preparation
You can cook the vegetables up to 2 hours in advance and dress them with the olive oil. Reheat them by placing the bowl, covered with a lid, over a saucepan of simmering water. It will take only 10 minutes to reheat. Mix thoroughly and then add the pesto. Pesto can be made in advance and frozen.

Serves 6–8
1 kg (2 lb) new potatoes, all the same size
700 g (1 1/2 lb) green beans
5 tbsp extra virgin olive oil
sea salt

For the pesto
60 g (2 oz) fresh basil leaves
2 garlic cloves, peeled
30 g (1 oz) pine nuts
salt and pepper
2 tbsp olive oil

french bean and tomato salad in a wine dressing
insalata di fagiolini al vino

Serves 4
450 g (1 lb) French
   beans
salt
2 tbsp good-quality
   dry white wine
3 tomatoes, peeled
6 strands of fresh
   chives

For the sauce
1/2 tsp Dijon mustard
1 tbsp dry white
   wine
1 tbsp lemon juice
3 tbsp extra virgin
   olive oil
sea salt
a few drops of
   tabasco

I came across this recipe in the book Dieta e fornelli *by Romana Bosco, a leading Italian cook, and Giorgio Calabrese, a dietician. The beans and tomatoes are dressed with wine, part of which is poured over the beans while they are still hot, which gives flavour to the beans and softens the taste of the wine.*

Top and tail the beans and then wash them thoroughly. Cook in plenty of boiling salted water. Drain as soon as they are ready – they should be still crunchy. You can literally smell when they are cooked, as the particular aroma of cooked beans begins to arise just at that moment. Splash them straight away with the wine.

To make the little sauce, put the mustard in a small bowl and dilute with the wine and the lemon juice. Add the oil gradually, beating hard and thoroughly with a fork to emulsify the sauce, then add salt and tabasco to taste.

Slice the tomatoes and place them in the centre of a dish, surrounding them with the beans. About half an hour before serving, spoon the sauce over the vegetables and then snip the chives all over the tomatoes. Serve at room temperature.

purslane

This annual, *portulaca oleracea*, has small fleshy leaves that grow in bunches. In looks it is similar to samphire, although not in taste. It has a much more pleasant flavour, mild yet with a touch of sourness reminiscent of young spinach. The pretty green leaves are succulent and very satisfying to the bite. Eat them in a tomato salad, as is done in southern Italy, or mixed with grilled and peeled peppers, as Jane Grigson suggests in her *Vegetable Book*.

In past centuries purslane was a popular vegetable both in Italy and in

England. Here it was usually pickled, while in Italy it was eaten raw in salad as it still is, this being the best way to appreciate its delicate flavour.

I recently came across, and immediately bought, some lovely bunches of purslane at the Greek shop, Adamou, in Chiswick High Road, London. Yan Kit So tells me that it is also sold in Chinese shops under the name of *yin choy*. Although not easy to buy, purslane grows very easily in the garden: I get the seeds from Jekka's Herb Farm (www.jekkasherbfarm.com).

purslane, spring onion and cucumber salad
l'insalata del bronzino

This salad is so delicious that it inspired the sixteenth-century painter Bronzino to write this little poem:

> Un'insalta di cipolla trita
> Colla porcellanetta e citrioli
> Vince ogni altro piacer di questa vita.
> *(A salad of chopped onion*
> *With purslane and cucumber*
> *Beats any other pleasure in life.)*

Serves 4
bunch of purslane
4 spring onions
1/2 cucumber
4 tbsp extra virgin olive oil
sea salt and freshly ground pepper
lemon juice to taste

Remove the leaves from the stalks of the purslane and discard the stalks. Wash the leaves in two or three changes of water and then drain and dry them well. Put them in a salad bowl.

Slice the white part of the spring onion into thin rings and add to the bowl.

Slice the cucumbers very thinly – I use a swivel-action peeler – and add to the salad.

Dress with the oil, salt and pepper and add lemon juice to your taste. Toss well and serve immediately.

salad of fennel, orange, chicory and olives
insalata di finocchio, cicoria belga e arance

Serves 6
2 medium-sized
   fennel bulbs,
   preferably the
   round bulbs which
   are sweeter than
   the long ones
2 large organic
   oranges
4 large chicory
   heads, or the white
   leaves of a batavia
   bunch
the juice of 1 1/2
   organic lemons
5 tbsp extra virgin
   olive oil
sea salt
2 dozen black olives

In Sicily there are two kinds of salad containing oranges. One is with onion and the other is the one given here. The salad used there is the heart of a young cos lettuce or of a bunch of batavia. I use chicory as well because it is on the market when fennel is at its best.

Remove the stalk, green foliage and any bruised or brown parts from the fennel bulbs. Cut the bulbs in half lengthwise, and then cut them across into thin slices. Wash the slices, drain and dry them thoroughly; then put them in a bowl.

Peel the oranges to the quick (i.e. removing all the pith) and slice the flesh across on a plate so as not to waste any of the juice. Cut the smaller slices in half and the larger slices into quarters. Add to the fennel in the bowl together with the juice collected on the plate.

Cut the chicory into rings or the batavia leaves into short pieces. Wash and dry thoroughly and then add to the bowl.

Beat the lemon juice and the olive oil together, add salt and pour over the prepared vegetables. Toss very well. Taste and adjust the salt. (Pepper is never added to this kind of salad in Sicily: its hotness would clash with the sweetness of the fennel and the orange.)

lamb's lettuce, rocket and fennel salad
insalata bianca e verde

Serves 6
225 g (8 oz) lamb's
   lettuce
120 g (4 oz) rocket
1 large fennel bulb,
   preferably of the

continued over >>

A salad of intense flavour which should be served on its own as an antipasto (this is not an Italian way) or as a palate cleanser after a meat dish and before a pudding.

Pick and wash the 2 salads. Dry them well and put them neatly on a dish. Remove and discard any brown patches on the outside of the fennel. If the fennel has some feathery green attached, cut it off, wash and dry it and add it to the green salads.

Cut the fennel bulb into quarters lengthwise, and then across into very thin strips no more than 5 mm (1/4 inch) thick. Wash and dry them and scatter them over the salad.

Trim and wash the spring onions. Cut the white part into thin rings and scatter them over the salad. Put the olives here and there on the dish.

Beat the soured cream, oil, lemon juice, sugar, salt and pepper to an emulsion and pour over the salad. Do this just before you bring it to the table or the green leaves will wilt.

round kind, which
is sweeter
5 spring onions, the
white part only
120 g (4 oz) green
olives in natural
brine, drained
4 tbsp soured cream
2 tbsp extra virgin
olive oil
juice of 1 organic
lemon
1 tsp caster sugar
sea salt and pepper

carrot, celeriac and orange salad
insalata di carote, sedano di verona e arance

Peel and grate the carrots through a mandolin or in a food processor fitted with a grater disc. Put in a bowl. Peel the celeriac, cut into chunks and discard, if necessary, the spongy flesh in the middle. Grate the celeriac and add it to the bowl.

Wash one of the oranges and dry it. Grate the rind of half the washed orange and squeeze the juice of the same orange. Pour half this orange juice and some of the lemon juice into a bowl and whisk in the mustard, the grated orange rind and salt and pepper to taste. Gradually add the olive oil while whisking constantly to emulsify the sauce. Taste and adjust the seasonings, adding more lemon or orange juice, according to your taste. Spoon over the carrot and celeriac mixture. Toss thoroughly and then pile the grated vegetables on to a dish.

Peel the remaining 2 oranges to the quick and slice them. Place the slices around the vegetables. Cover with clingfilm and leave for 30 minutes or so before you eat it.

Serves 6
450 g (1 lb) carrots
225 g (8 oz) celeriac
3 organic oranges
juice of 1 organic
lemon
1 tsp French mustard
sea salt and pepper
4 tbsp extra virgin
olive oil

a mixed salad of vegetables, grapefruit and prawns
l'insalata di luisetta

Serves 10
**750 g (1 1/2 lb)
prawns, preferably
raw
bunch of rocket
heart of 1 curly
endive
225 g (8 oz) green
beans, steamed or
boiled
hearts of 2 celery
heads
6 small tomatoes
2 pink grapefruit
225 g (8 oz) very
small young
courgettes
150 ml (1/4 pint)
extra virgin olive oil
5 tbsp raspberry
vinegar, if available,
or cider vinegar
sea salt and pepper**

A lovely antipasto or a buffet dish.

If you are using raw prawns, cook them in a vegetable stock made with water flavoured with 1 carrot, half an onion, 1 stick of celery, a bay leaf, 2 sprigs of parsley, fennel tops or dill, peppercorns and a little salt, adding a little olive oil and some white wine. They take only 2 minutes to cook.

Clean, trim and wash the rocket and the white heart of the endive. Cut into very fine strips and lay on a large oval dish. Cut the beans into 4 cm (1 3/4 inch) pieces, the celery into very thin strips and the tomatoes into thin segments and place them over the green salad.

Peel the grapefruit to the quick, remove the membrane between the segments and scatter the grapefruit flesh over the dish.

Wash and dry the courgettes and cut into thin rounds. Add to the dish.

Shell the prawns and de-vein if necessary. Keep about half a dozen of the best for garnish; cut the others into small pieces and put them here and there among the vegetables.

Beat the oil and vinegar together in a bowl with a fork, add salt and pepper and pour all over the salad. Garnish with the reserved prawns and serve at once.

preparation
All the vegetables can be prepared up to 4 hours beforehand, but they should be laid on the dish no longer than 1 hour in advance. The salad must be dressed just before serving.

toasted bread with vegetable salad
la panzanella a modo mio

Panzanella *is the traditional poor man's salad, based on bread. When we had a farmhouse in Chianti, it was our luncheon fare: a large earthenware pot full of* panzanella *was put on the scrubbed table under the fig tree, the air heavily scented with fig leaves and wild mint. The fig tree was next to the well which for years served as our fridge, until electricity was brought to the house. Dangling in the cool water, at the end of a rope, was a* fiasco *of Chianti, while a pull on another rope brought up a bucket containing a watermelon.* Panzanella, anguria e vino – *an ideal trio for the perfect lunch.*

Back in England, I couldn't find the pan sciocco – *unsalted country bread – needed for a good* panzanella. Panzanella *was forgotten until I came across Marcella Hazan's recipe, made with croutons. From that recipe I developed mine, in which the bread, moistened with olive oil, is toasted, not fried. This* panzanella *is very pretty to look at, especially if you serve it on a white dish, or on white plates, so as to set off the vivid greens and reds of the vegetables. It will remind you of Matisse's palette.*

At least an hour before you want to serve the *panzanella*, slice the onion into very thin rings, put the rings in a bowl and cover with cold water. Add a pinch of salt and leave to soak. (This is not necessary if you don't mind the strong flavour of raw onion.) Put the olive oil in a bowl, add the garlic and the chilli and leave to infuse for the same length of time.

Heat the oven to 200°C (400°F) mark 6.

Put the bread slices on a baking tray and brush them with a little of the olive oil. Place the tray in the preheated oven for about 8 minutes. When the bread is toasted, remove, and while it is cooling prepare the vegetables.

Wash the pepper, remove the core, seeds and ribs and cut in 3.5 cm (1 1/2 inch) cubes. Wash the tomatoes and cut into same-sized morsels, eliminating the seeds. Do the same to the peeled cucumber. Put everything in a bowl and add the basil.

Drain and dry the onion rings and add to the bowl.

Remove the garlic and the chilli from the oil.

Serves 6
1/2 red onion
sea salt
120 ml (4 fl oz) extra virgin olive oil
2 garlic cloves, bruised
1 chilli pepper
6 slices of best country bread, without the crust
1/2 yellow pepper
2 tomatoes, ripe but firm
1/2 cucumber, peeled
2 handfuls of basil leaves, torn into small pieces
1 tbsp capers
2 anchovy fillets
2 tbsp wine vinegar
freshly ground pepper

Chop the capers and the anchovy fillets and add to the oil together with the vinegar, pepper and salt. Mix well and pour this sauce on the vegetables. Stir thoroughly and then taste and adjust the seasoning.

Put a slice of bread on each plate and spoon some of the vegetable mixture over each slice. Serve at once.

chicory, radicchio and little gem salad with an anchovy and garlic sauce
le tre cicorie in bagna cauda

Serves 8
450 g (1 lb) chicory
450 g (1 lb) red radicchio
1 Little Gem lettuce
8 anchovy fillets
6 garlic cloves, peeled
2 dried chillies, seeded and crumbled
150 ml (1/4 pint) extra virgin olive oil
sea salt and pepper

If you are in or go to the country in the spring, pick a lot of dandelions and use them instead of Little Gem lettuce. They have the right degree of bitterness for this dish.

Finely shred the chicory, the radicchio and the dandelion or lettuce. Wash them in two or three changes of water and then drain and dry them. Put into a salad bowl.

Cut the anchovy fillets and the garlic in pieces and put them in a mortar with the chillies. Pound to a paste while gradually adding the olive oil. If you have not got a mortar, pound the ingredients in a bowl. Transfer, the sauce to a small saucepan or, better, to a small earthenware pot and cook over a very gentle heat for 2–3 minutes, while pounding the mixture against the side of the pan or pot.

Taste the sauce, add salt if necessary and pepper if you wish, and pour over the vegetables while still very hot. Toss and serve immediately with plenty of crusty bread.

cauliflower salad with anchovy and pine nut dressing
insalata di cavolfiore in salsa bianca

This recipe is for a cauliflower salad that I have adapted from a recipe by Vincenzo Corrado, a Neapolitan cookery writer of the eighteenth century. Cauliflower and anchovy have always been a successful combination of flavours. Here they are joined by the delicate resinous flavour of pine nuts, which also provide a contrast of texture.

Divide the cauliflowers into small florets. Wash the florets thoroughly and then cook them in plenty of salted water until tender. How long cauliflower should cook is entirely up to you. As an Italian, I like my vegetables properly cooked and not the way they are served today in so many places. What I mean by 'properly cooked' is that they should be tender when pricked with a fork, but not soft. It is at that stage, and only then, that vegetables begin to develop their full flavour.

Drain thoroughly and spread the florets out on kitchen paper. Pat them dry and transfer to a bowl or a dish. Toss them gently with 2 tablespoons of the oil while the cauliflower is still hot, so that it can absorb the oil better.

Roast the pine nuts for a couple of minutes in a non-stick pan to bring out the flavour. Clean and rinse the salted anchovies or drain the anchovy fillets from the oil. Put them in a mortar with the pine nuts. Pound the mixture with the vinegar, lemon juice, salt and pepper, using the pestle. Stir in the remaining oil with a fork to form an emulsion. The sauce can also be made in a good food processor.

Spoon the sauce over the cauliflower, cover with clingfilm and leave for 1 hour. Serve at room temperature with a sprinkling of chopped parsley for garnish, and plenty of good bread.

preparation
The cauliflower can be cooked, and the sauce prepared, up to 1 day in advance, but do not pour the sauce more than 1 hour before serving or the cauliflower will 'cook' in the sauce.

Serves 6–8
2 medium
  cauliflowers
100 ml (3 1/2 fl oz)
  extra virgin olive oil
120 g (4 oz) pine
  nuts
6 salted anchovies or
  12 anchovy fillets
2 tbsp white wine
  vinegar
2 tbsp lemon juice
sea salt and pepper
4 tbsp chopped
  parsley

282 amaretto, apple cake and artichokes

tomato, cucumber and pepper salad
insalata di pomodori, cetrioli e peperoni

Serves 6–8
2 large red onions
juice of 4 organic
  lemons
2 tsp sugar
1 large cucumber
sea salt
4 good tomatoes
4 large peppers, red
  and yellow
6 tbsp extra virgin
  olive oil
ground black pepper

I do not like raw onions. They are usually too overwhelming and can kill any other flavour. If you are like me you must start this very traditional Italian salad a day in advance. Otherwise, forget it.

Peel the onions and slice them very thinly. Put them in a bowl and add 6 tablespoons of the lemon juice and the sugar. Mix well, cover the bowl and leave overnight.

Peel the cucumber and slice it thinly. Put the slices in a bowl and sprinkle with salt. Leave for 1 hour.

Wash and dry the tomatoes, slice them thinly and put them in a salad bowl.

Wash and dry the peppers, cut them into quarters, remove the cores, ribs and seeds and cut the quarters across into 1 cm (1/2 inch) strips. Add to the bowl.

Squeeze the liquid out of the cucumber and add the slices to the bowl. Do the same with the onion.

Just before serving, toss with the olive oil and most of the remaining lemon juice and season with a generous amount of pepper and some salt if necessary. Taste and correct the seasonings, adding a little more lemon juice according to your taste.

beetroot, grapefruit and watercress salad
insalata agra di barbabietola

Serves 6
5 medium-sized
  beetroots, cooked
4 tbsp extra virgin
  olive oil
sea salt and pepper

continued over >>

Peel and slice the beetroots. Put them in a bowl and toss them with 2 tablespoons of the olive oil, a little salt and a lot of pepper. Pile them on a dish.

Peel the grapefruit, divide into segments and remove the thin transparent skin. Cut each segment in half and scatter over the beetroot, together with the white part of the spring onions, cut into thin rounds.

Wash and dry the watercress. Remove the long stalks but leave in nice short sprigs.

Surround the beetroot mound with the watercress. Dribble the remaining olive oil over the watercress and sprinkle with salt and pepper.

1 1/2 grapefruit
6 spring onions
2 bunches
    watercress

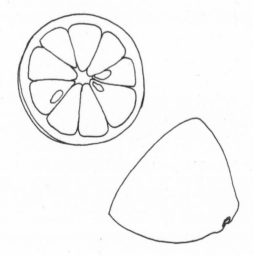

edible weeds

In my childhood the *prati* – open fields – outside Milan were only half an hour's bicycle ride from our house in the centre of the city. Many a happy Sunday was spent with a group of friends picking nettles, dandelions, rocket, purslane, wild beets, daisies and poppies. Then home with bulging baskets, whose contents were quickly made into delicious salads and lovely little bouquets for the table. I pick anything eatable. Here are a few recipes to show how I use them.

rocket

Rocket grows wild in southern Italy and has always been used a lot in the local cooking. In ancient Rome it used to appear on the tables of the gourmands and the gourmets, just as it does now. It was mainly used in sauces together with other herbs, or in a vegetable pie called *moretum*. This must have been a popular dish; it was even described in a poem written by Septimus Serenus, a contemporary of Virgil.

It is only in recent decades, however, that it has found favour with the foodies of the world. Strange to say, not a single recipe listing *rucola* appeared in Italian cookery books until the seventies. It only became known in Milan and Turin with the invasion of the southerners when, in the sixties, they came north to find work. They are very chauvinistic people where food is concerned. As with *provolone*, which they brought north and which afterwards began to be manufactured near Milan because of the demand from the new 'locals', rocket also began to be cultivated to satisfy the southerners' craving for their beloved leaves.

The cultivated variety of rocket is less pungent or tingly on the tongue than the wild species, and its taste had a more distinct resemblance to cabbage, rocket in fact being of the cabbage family. This cabbagey taste is rather overwhelming when the rocket becomes old. Rocket grows so easily that if you sow a little patch under your rose bushes you can have rocket from June to November.

rocket and tomato sauce
salsa di rucola e pomodoro

Makes enough sauce to
accompany 4 servings
30 g (1 oz) rocket
200 g (7 oz)
tomatoes, very firm
and not fully ripe
a sliver of peeled
garlic
1 small chilli, seeded
1 tbsp balsamic
vinegar
sea salt and pepper
5 tbsp extra virgin
olive oil

Towards the end of last autumn I found I still had a lot of rocket in my garden. So, rather than let the frost destroy this delicious and versatile salad, I collected it all and prepared this sauce (which freezes well) as well as making the soup on page 288 and the pasta dish on page 287.

I first had this rocket and tomato sauce many years ago at the Locanda dell'Angelo near Sarzana, in Liguria. In 1983 the owner and chef of that restaurant, Angelo Paracucchi, was invited by Gault et Millau to open a restaurant in Paris, the Carpaccio – surely the greatest accolade any foreigner could receive from the French. In his book Cucina creative all'italiana, *Angelo Paracucchi suggests this sauce as an accompaniment to boiled fish or meat. I also like it on hard-boiled eggs, but perhaps that's just because I like eggs, whether by themselves or dressed with a delicious sauce such as this.*

In this sauce the rocket loses some of its pungency through being combined with the raw tomato. Although the sauce is not a very pretty colour, its taste is most appealing, sweet and herby at the same time.

Wash the rocket and dry carefully in a kitchen cloth. Remove and discard the hard stalk of the older leaves. Put the rocket in a food processor.

Blanch and peel the tomatoes. Cut them into quarters and squeeze out and discard the seeds and the watery juice. Add the quarters to the rocket together with the garlic, chilli, vinegar and a little salt and pepper. Process for 15 seconds. Push the sauce down around the bowl and process until smooth and thick, while gradually adding the oil, as for mayonnaise.

pasta with rocket
pasta con la rucola

The Calabresi love to eat these two favourite foods together. Here is how they cook them.

The pasta is long maccheroni, also called *ziti*, broken into 4 cm (1 1/2 inch) lengths. While the pasta is boiling, the washed and dried *rucola* – you need about 200 g (7 oz) for 4 people – is stir-fried in 5 tbsp of the best extra virgin olive oil, with 2 sliced cloves of garlic and 1 or 2 chillies. A couple of tablespoons of the pasta water are added to the *rucola* and the drained cooked pasta is then transferred to the pan and fried with it for a minute or two. Some grated pecorino is put on the table to sprinkle on the pasta. Don't forget to remove the chilli before you serve.

If you find the rocket is too pungent for your taste, you should blanch it before frying it.

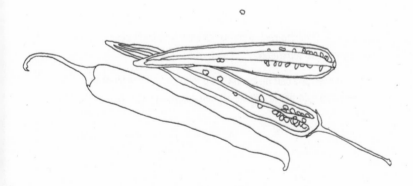

rocket and potato soup
minestra di rucola e patate

Serves 4
120 g (4 oz) rocket
handful of parsley
leaves
1 small dried chilli,
or more according
to taste
2 garlic cloves, or
more according to
taste
3 tbsp extra virgin
olive oil
225 g (8 oz) potatoes
1.5 litres (2 1/2
pints) vegetable
stock
sea salt and pepper
good-quality white
bread, toasted
grated pecorino

The grated cheese for this soup should be pecorino, which has the right pungency to match the rocket. If you cannot buy pecorino, use good freshly grated Parmesan.

Wash and dry the rocket and remove any thick stalks. Cut it roughly into strips.

Chop the parsley, chilli and garlic and put them in a heavy pot with 2 tbsp of the oil. I use an earthenware pot, so that the garlic won't get burnt. Sauté over a gentle heat until you begin to smell the garlic aroma.

Peel and cut the potatoes into about 1 cm (1/2 inch) cubes and add to the pot. Stir them in the *soffritto* until they are shiny and slightly translucent and then add the rocket. Stir and cook for 2–3 minutes.

Meanwhile heat the stock. (You should always heat any liquid before pouring it over potatoes, since a cold liquid will harden them.) Pour into the soup pot and stir, adding salt if necessary. Turn the heat down to minimum and let the soup simmer for 40 minutes or so. Taste and check the seasoning.

Put 1–2 slices of toasted bread into each soup bowl and ladle the soup over them. Pour the rest of the oil directly into each bowl and hand the grated cheese separately.

If you prefer, you can make the soup with pasta, instead of bread, by adding 120 g (4 oz) of *ditalini* 10 minutes before the soup is ready.

nettles

It seems a sad waste that these eminently edible weeds should hardly be eaten in a country where they grow in such profusion. In Jane Grigson's *Vegetable Book* there are only two recipes using nettles, both Irish. The only English person I know who has eaten nettles in abundance is our cousin Daniel Waley. The subject came up when we were staying with him and his wife in Sussex, and I was going around with gloves on even though it was a warm spring day, so that I could pick nettles. He told me that a purée of nettles used to replace cabbage at his preparatory school during the spring. This was before the war, and he wondered if the custom was simply a health fetish, or whether it was an unusual economy on the part of the headmaster. Whatever it was, the boys ate the nettle purée more for the fun of boasting about it than for the gastronomic pleasure involved.

During my childhood in Milan, nettles were eaten in various guises, the most usual being in a soup with rice, *riso e ortiche*. A similar dish is the *pasta con le ortiche* made in Puglia.

Nettles are good when young and bright green. Pick only the young shoots, when the sting is minimal, and pick a lot since, like spinach, they boil down to very little. Nettles are covered with stinging hairs which lose their sting when boiled. Wear gloves when picking and washing them. When you pick them you will be surprised by the smell they give off. It always reminds me of that milky-sweet Mediterranean scent of fig leaves, and this is indeed the flavour nettles have when young.

risotto with nettles
risotto alle ortiche

The sweet, delicate taste of nettles is just discernible in this moist creamy risotto. Pick a large bag of tender nettle shoots in April or early May. It will boil down as much as spinach does. Cooking removes their sting. The same recipe can be made with very young spinach or Italian spinach, but don't use the larger and older beet spinach as its taste is too coarse.

Pick the leaves and shoots of the nettles and discard the stalks. Wash in two or three changes of water. Put the nettles in a saucepan with 1

Serves 4
**500 g (1 lb 2 oz)
nettle shoots**
sea salt
**2 shallots or 1 small
onion, very finely
chopped**

continued over >>

60 g (2 oz) unsalted butter
1 litre (1 3/4 pints) vegetable stock or light meat stock
300 g (10 oz) Arborio rice
4 tbsp single cream
60 g (2 oz) freshly grated Parmesan

teaspoon of salt and boil over a high heat until cooked. You don't need to add any water; as with spinach, the water that comes from the leaves is enough. When cooked, drain, keeping the liquid. Set aside, keeping the nettles in a sieve placed over the bowl containing the nettle water.

Sauté the shallots or onion in half the butter, very gently, until soft.

Heat the stock to simmering point.

Squeeze all the liquid out of the nettles into the bowl. Chop the nettles coarsely and add to the shallots or onion. Sauté for a minute, stirring constantly, then add the rice and fry it until the outside of the grains becomes translucent.

Pour the nettle liquid into the simmering stock and add about 150 ml (1/4 pint) of the simmering stock to the rice. Mix well. The rice will soon absorb the stock. Then add another ladleful of stock and continue cooking and adding more stock until the rice is done. Stir frequently, but not all the time. The better the rice the longer it takes to cook: Arborio rice takes about 20 minutes from when it is put in the pan.

Draw the pan off the heat, add the cream, the rest of the butter and half the cheese. Leave it to rest for a couple of minutes and then stir vigorously to incorporate these final condiments; this makes the risotto *mantecato* – creamy – as any risotto should be. Transfer to a heated dish and serve at once, handing the remaining cheese round separately.

dandelions

In Italy one of the pleasures of early spring is a trip to the countryside to collect dandelions. It is quite usual to have a salad of dandelions, or to eat them cooked. I was amazed, therefore, when I first came to England to find that no one here gathers dandelions to eat, particularly so since the British are so knowledgeable about flowers and plants and are much more geared towards the countryside than the Italians.

I have recently discovered that this was not always so, for Eliza Acton, in her *Modern Cookery For Private Families*, first published in 1845, has a section headed 'TO DRESS DANDELIONS LIKE SPINACH, OR AS A SALAD (Very wholesome)'. The first part of it reads:

> This common weed of the fields and highways is an excellent vegetable, the young leaves forming an admirable adjunct to a salad, and much resembling endive when boiled and prepared in the same way, or in any of the modes directed for spinach. The slight bitterness of its flavour is to many persons very agreeable; and it is often served at well-appointed tables. It has also, we believe, the advantage of possessing valuable medicinal qualities.

Eliza Acton serves her blanched dandelions dressed with melted butter. I prefer them *strascinati* – literally, dragged – in a frying pan with 2 or 3 tablespoons of extra virgin olive oil, a clove of garlic and maybe a little chilli. You might like to remove both garlic and chilli before serving. You will need about 450 g (1 lb) for 2–3 people. Another way is to serve them at room temperature dressed with extra virgin olive oil, lemon juice, salt and pepper.

If you are going to cook your dandelions, it is best to pick very young leaves. This is because, as with any greens, the flavour is released in cooking. In the case of dandelions this means that their bitter flavour will be more noticeable when cooked than in a raw salad.

Dandelions are also excellent raw, and this is how I suggest you prepare them. Gather little bunches of the washed leaves, as many as will fit in your hand, and shred them very finely. The narrower the strips, the nicer the salad. Put them in a bowl, cover with cold water and add some salt. Leave for 1 hour or so. This removes some of the bitterness of the dandelion. About half an hour before serving, drain and dry the dandelion thoroughly and put in a salad bowl. Dress with 2 tablespoons of red wine vinegar, 3 tablespoons of extra virgin olive oil, salt and pepper to taste and, if you want, 1 teaspoon of Dijon mustard which goes well with dandelion. Toss well (36 times is the magic number!) and leave for 20 minutes *pour fatiguer* the salad, as the

French say, which I find improves its flavour. Add some sliced red onion on the top.

Eliza Acton gives many invaluable hints and tips, and I end with one of these: 'A very large portion of the leaves will be required for a dish, as they shrink exceedingly in the cooking.' I would add that they also shrink in the dressing of the salad.

wild mushrooms and truffles

Mushroom hunting is a solitary activity whose secrets you share only with the wind and the trees. I even jib at writing about how many good species of wild mushrooms I find during a day's outing around London. I have some Milanese friends who, not long ago, sent us a postcard from Scotland, where they had gone to see that country's many sights. A week later there arrived another card from the same place. They had discovered the treasure of the Scottish woods: wild mushrooms everywhere, and in great abundance. They were utterly amazed that no one else was in sight, no one either picking the mushrooms or preventing them from picking all they wanted.

When we had a house in Chianti, the *caccia* – hunt – for the fungi started just after the objectionable *caccia* of the birds, with its continuous salvoes of gunfire and flurry of birds and hares. I used to go up the Apennines with Remo, a local who, like me, preferred the silent hunt for mushrooms. He knew all the species which grew there, but we collected mainly porcini – ceps – or chanterelles, which are by far the best. Back in England I tried limiting my search to these two species, but soon enough I was collecting any edible mushrooms: *Russulas virescens,* puff balls (delicious raw with oil and lemon), *grisettes*, wood blewits, parasols, *Coprinus comatus* and all kinds of boletus. There simply weren't enough ceps and chanterelles.

Although not all fungi are worth cleaning and cooking, they are all worth the fun of picking, bringing home and identifying. There are only five lethal species, and once you are familiar enough with these to be sure of avoiding them the worst than can happen to you is a stomach upset. Buy a good book such as the *Collins Guide to Mushrooms and Toadstools* or *The Mushroom Book* by Thomas Lessoe, for which I wrote the recipes, published by Dorling Kindersley.

how to prepare mushrooms

Mushrooms should not be peeled and they should be washed as little
as possible. It is a fallacy to think that field mushrooms are only good
if they peel easily. I wipe mushrooms with damp kitchen paper and cut
away the base of the stalks and any blemished parts. The spongy
underside of the caps of ceps is good and should not be removed
unless soggy or wormy. All mushrooms should be sautéed quite briskly
in oil and/or butter until they have absorbed all the fat. The heat should
then be turned down and the mushrooms will then release their liquid.
Most wild mushrooms release more liquid than cultivated ones. This
liquid will evaporate with a brisk cooking, but you must be careful not
to overcook the mushrooms. Some mushrooms – the incomparable
chanterelles, for instance – are spoiled by prolonged cooking, while
others such as ceps should have a minimum of 15–20 minutes'
cooking to release their aroma.

dried porcini

These are available in Britain in many supermarkets and in all Italian
shops. Before you buy them, look into the packet if you can; the pieces
of dried ceps should be large and well formed, not small and crumbly.
Dried porcini are expensive, but even as little as 20 g (3/4 oz) gives the
dish more flavour than five times as many cultivated mushrooms. You
must reconstitute them before you use them by soaking in hot water
for at least 20 minutes or by pouring boiling water over them and
leaving them for 15 minutes or so. The liquid, filtered through a kitchen
paper, is usually added to the dish for extra flavour. If you add a few
dried porcini to some cultivated mushrooms for a stronger flavour,
sauté the porcini first for 5 minutes before you add the mushrooms.

mushrooms baked with anchovies, capers and breadcrumbs
funghi al forno

You can now find a few different species of cultivated mushrooms in the best supermarkets; for this dish you will need at least three, plus the dried porcini. I use some common cultivated field mushrooms, some chestnut mushrooms, which have a compact texture and a fuller flavour, and – my favourite – some oyster mushrooms. These, Pleorotus ostreatus, *are the fungi with a delicate taste that most resembles the taste of white truffles. You can also add some shiitake, although personally I find them too pricey for what they are. Alternatively you can use only cultivated field mushrooms, although the final taste would not be very rich, or, best of all, wild mushrooms.*

The dried porcini, on the other hand, although expensive, are worth every penny. You only need 30 g (1 oz), or even less, to make all the difference. They have a distinct fungus aroma without having the rather heady and overwhelming flavour of some wild species.

The breadcrumbs can be either white or brown. Both are suitable as long as they are made from good-quality bread.

Soak the dried porcini in a cupful of boiling water for 15 minutes or so. Lift them out gently and sift through to make sure there is no grit stuck to them. Cut up the larger pieces. Strain the liquid into a little pan through a sieve lined with damp kitchen paper. Add the porcini and cook very gently for 10 minutes to soften them. Transfer to a bowl.

Heat the oven to 190°C (375°F) mark 5.

Wipe the mushrooms with kitchen paper and then slice them. Add them to the bowl.

Chop the parsley, garlic, anchovies, chilli and capers, and put them in a small bowl. Add 5 tablespoons of the oil and season with salt and pepper to taste. Mix well and then spoon this little sauce over the mushrooms. Mix very thoroughly; your hands are the best tool for doing this.

Grease a shallow ovenproof dish with a little of the remaining oil. Pile the mushrooms into the dish. Sprinkle the breadcrumbs all over the top and dribble with the remaining oil.

Serves 4–6

30 g (1 oz) dried porcini
700 g (1 1/2 lb) mushrooms, a selection
a lovely bunch of fresh flat-leaf parsley
2 garlic cloves
4 anchovy fillets or 2 salted anchovies, boned and rinsed
1 dried chilli, seeded
2 tbsp capers, rinsed and dried
100 ml (3 1/2 fl oz) extra virgin olive oil
sea salt and pepper
60 g (2 oz) fresh breadcrumbs

Bake for about half an hour. The top will have formed a crust and the mushrooms will be just tender, but still keeping their shape. Serve the dish cool or tepid: it will be much nicer then, when all the flavours have blended.

Serve this dish as a first course – it is perfect.

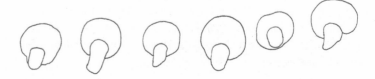

sautéed mushrooms with oregano and garlic
funghi al funghetto

Serves 6
**700 g (1 1/2 lb)
mixed mushrooms,
cultivated and wild**
4 garlic cloves
5 tbsp olive oil
sea salt
2 tbsp dried oregano
pepper

This is my adaptation of a original recipe that appears in the classic book La Cuciniera Genovese *by Giobatta and Giovanni Ratto, which is now, after a century, in its eighteenth edition.*

The mushrooms used in the original recipe are, of course, fresh porcini. As these are very difficult to find in Britain, I suggest you use a selection of what you can buy or what you can pick, if you know which ones to pick. Freshly picked mushrooms will give your dish a better flavour.

Clean the mushrooms by wiping them with kitchen paper. Slice them thinly.

Chop 2 of the garlic cloves very finely. Thread a wooden cocktail stick through the others so that you can find them easily and remove them at the end of the cooking. Or chop all the cloves if you like a strong garlicky flavour.

Put all the garlic and the oil in a large sauté pan. Add the mushrooms and salt and cook at a lively heat, stirring frequently, until all the liquid that comes out at the beginning has evaporated. Season with the oregano and with pepper.

Continue cooking for 15 minutes, taking care that the mushrooms do not stick to the bottom of the pan. If they do, add a couple of tablespoons of water and stir well. Fish out the garlic cloves and serve immediately.

preparation
Mushrooms should not be refrigerated because they lose their flavour. You can cook them up to 1 day in advance and reheat them, uncovered, over a low heat before serving.

truffles

Truffles – *tartufi* in Italian – are fungi, many species of which are found in northern and central Italy. The only three species that are of importance gastronomically are the *Tuber magnatum* – the white truffle or *tartufo d'Alba*; the *Tuber melanosporum* – black truffle or *tartufo di Norcia* (which the French call *truffe de Périgord*); and the *Tuber aestivum* or *scorzone*. This last, also known as *tartufo d'estate or maggengo*, is not on a par with the white or the black truffle, and it differs from them in that it matures in the summer. It has a delicate and quite pleasing flavour, but is rather bland and uninteresting. It is mostly used in pâtés, sausages, terrines, truffle paste, etc. In the context of this book, I am mainly concerned with the white truffle, which is found only in Italy.

Truffles have been known in Italy since the beginning of history. The Romans were passionate about them and studied them in great detail. Pliny, Martial and Juvenal wrote treatises about truffles, while Apicius collected recipes for them. Nero ate truffles in abundance, calling them *cibus deorum* – food of the gods. After the fall of the Roman empire, truffles were ignored even by the monks, who preserved so much of the Roman civilisation. It is said that they did so deliberately because they considered truffles to have aphrodisiac properties – hardly an encouragement to chaste living.

During the Renaissance, however, the truffle once again became king of the high table. The Emperor Charles V enjoyed truffles at the dinner prepared in his honour by Bartolomeo Scappi, chef to Cardinal Campeggi who was entertaining the Emperor. The truffles were stewed in bitter orange juice and also served simply raw in salad. In the eighteenth century, hunting parties were organised to search for *tartufi*. Dogs, rather than pigs, were used in Piedmont, and *tartufi* were found in amazing quantities. It was at that time that all the European royal houses were asking the House of Savoy for experienced men and trained dogs to search for truffles. In 1751 Carlo Emanuele III sent George II two *trifolai* and eight dogs to search for truffles in Windsor Park. Apparently truffles similar to the *tartufi d'Alba* were found in moderate quantities.

Black truffles, too, were much more common in the past than they are now. William Whetmore Story, an American who lived in Rome in the 1860s, gives a graphic description of the market in Piazza Navona. There were 'excellent truffles. They grow in great quantities in the country around Rome, and especially at Spoleto, and used to be very cheap before the French bought them up so largely for the Parisian markets.'

I am old enough to have enjoyed truffles in good quantities as a child. They were cheaper then. Before Mass on Sundays in the autumn months we used to go and buy truffles from the stalls under the arches in the Piazza del Duomo. I was allowed to carry the parcel, and during Mass I held it under my nose, the piquant aroma of truffles mixing deliciously with the heavy scent of the incense. A salad that used to be served in my home at lunch parties was made up as follows: one-third of a dish was covered with sliced *ovuli*, the choicest wild mushrooms, another third with Parmesan flakes and the remaining section with sliced *tartufi d'Alba* The three parts were dressed with olive oil, lemon juice, salt and pepper.

Truffles cannot be cultivated like other fungi. Pliny the Elder wrote *'nascuntur et seri non possunt'* – they grow but cannot be cultivated. And this is still so, despite endless researches into the matter. White truffles grow in symbiosis with poplars, willow, limes, hazel bushes, oaks and hornbeams, in places around 1,000 feet high where rains in August and September keep the soil moist. They are usually found only a few inches below the ground. They are roughly globular in shape and can weigh over 500g. These are the real diamonds, since their price per gram increases in direct proportion to their size. There is a closed season for collecting truffles which starts on a certain date in October and ends in December. Truffles keep only for a very short time, but they can be preserved by sterilisation or pounded into a paste and mixed with other ingredients.

I advise anyone who is interested in food to buy a truffle at least once in his/her lifetime, and handle it and absorb its aroma. To prepare a truffle you must brush it with a soft brush, gently but thoroughly, then rinse it quickly and dry it well. White truffles are added to a dish of tagliatelle that has been dressed only with butter and Parmesan. They are also shaved over a creamy risotto, a rich *fonduta piemontese* or a fresh *Carpaccio*. Black truffles mixed with anchovy fillets and garlic make a divine sauce for spaghetti, *spaghetti alla nursina*. They also change an everyday trout into a *haute cuisine* dish when used to stuff the fish.

There are now on the market jars of very good truffle paste and bottles of olive oil infused with truffle – of the two I prefer the paste, which is made of black truffles, porcini mushrooms and the usual flavourings – marvellous to add to a risotto or a creamy sauce for poultry or pasta.

tagliatelle with white truffles
tagliatelle all'albese

Serves 4
**75 g (2 1/2 oz)
unsalted butter
4 tbsp dry white
wine**
grated nutmeg
sea salt and freshly
ground black
pepper
**tagliatelle made with
300 g (10 oz)
Italian 00 flour and
3 free-range eggs
or 250 g (9 oz)
dried egg tagliatelle
60 g (2 oz) freshly
grated Parmesan
1 white truffle, about
60 g (2 oz), cleaned**

Melt the butter in a small saucepan and then pour in the wine. Boil briskly to reduce by about half and then turn the heat off. Season with salt and pepper.

Cook the tagliatelle in plenty of salted boiling water according to the manufacturer's instructions, or for a very few minutes if you made them yourself. Drain, reserving a cupful of the pasta water. Return immediately to the pan and dress with the butter and wine sauce and the Parmesan. Mix thoroughly and, if the pasta seems too dry, add a little of the reserved water. Spoon the tagliatelle onto 4 heated plates, and then slice the truffle over each mountain of pasta, using a truffle slicer or a small sharp knife.

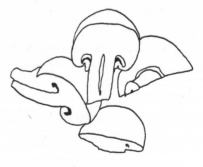

Across the length and breadth of Italy there are innumerable different pastures and methods of cheese-making, contributing to countless local dishes made with these various cheeses.

The origins of Italian cheese-making are ancient, and rooted in legend. In the *Odyssey*, Homer, who is thought to have lived between the seventh and sixth centuries BC, describes the arrival of Ulysses in Polyphemus' cave in Sicily in which 'there were baskets laden with cheeses'. After the Cyclops had returned with his herd of goats and ewes, 'he sat down to milk his ewes and bleating goats, which he did methodically, putting her young to each mother, as he finished. He then curdled half the white milk, gathered it all up and stored it in wicker baskets.'

By Roman times the craft of cheese-making was firmly established in Sicily, and Sicilian cheeses came to be well known all over the Empire. The Romans soon discovered that animal rennet could replace the natural curdling of the milk, and the Sicilians became expert in the dosage of the rennet. Even during the barbarian invasions, cheese-making remained an important activity, and it was eventually around the turn of the millennium that some of what are now traditional cheeses began to take shape.

The first farm known to have been mainly devoted to cheese-making appeared near Parma in the thirteenth century, and by the Cinquecento Italian cheeses had found a place on the tables of the nobility all over Europe. Cheese appears in most of the menus and dishes of the great chefs of the past. The common people, too, used cheeses to enrich their simple soups, to flavour their rissoles and to dress their plain buckwheat polenta. It was at the end of the nineteenth century that cheese production became an important industry. Some cheeses disappeared, others became the cheeses we know now.

The majority of today's well-known Italian cheeses are made in northern Italy. Most of them are used as table cheeses as well as in local dishes, either as *formaggi da grattugia* – grating cheeses, or as *formaggi da cucina* – cooking cheeses, according to their properties. Bel Paese, for instance, is a good melting cheese and can replace mozzarella. Some local *tome* – soft cheeses – are delicious for dressing polenta and gnocchi. In Sicily, *ricotta salata* – salted ricotta – is grated over a dish of pasta.

In what follows I am only writing about the most common Italian cheeses used in cooking that can be found in Britain: Gorgonzola, fontina, mozzarella, Parmesan, pecorino, mascarpone and ricotta.

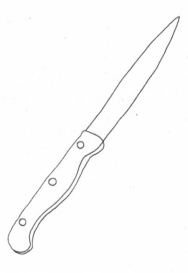

gorgonzola

Gorgonzola, the north Italian cheese par excellence, is one of the oldest of cheeses. It is thought to date from Roman times, and its association with the town of Gorgonzola was officially recognised in 1251. Gorgonzola used to be a country town to the east of Milan, but it is now part of the outer suburbs of that city. It was once, but is no longer, a stopping place for the cattle on their journey home in the autumn after spending the summer months on the high pastures of Valsassina. The cows were tired – *stracche* in Milanese dialect – from the long journey, and it was then that the various *Stracchini* cheeses were made, of which Gorgonzola is the most popular and the best known outside Italy.

The centre of its production is now in Novara, a province of Piedmont, where the *Consorzio Gorgonzola* is situated. All producers of Gorgonzola must belong to the consortium, which protects the use of the name. Each cheese is stamped on the crust with the identification number of the farm or factory of origin.

Gorgonzola is made from a hot and cold curd of cow's milk from two different milkings. These are put into round moulds of 25–30 cm (10–12 inches) diameter, and very thin metal needles are inserted into the cheese and then removed. The resulting tiny holes aerate the cheese, which encourages the formation of the mould. The ageing, of about 50 days, used to take place in caves in Valsassina and Val Brembana, two Alpine valleys north-east of Milan. Now only farm-produced Gorgonzola is aged in this way. The industrially produced cheese available outside Italy is aged in storerooms in which similar atmospheric conditions are reproduced.

At its best, Gorgonzola is creamy-coloured, with blue-green veins that become more marked towards the centre of the cheese. It has a fat content of about 45 per cent. Its pleasing, aromatic taste varies from mellow in the *Gorgonzola dolce*, such as *dolcelatte*, to piquant in the *Gorgonzola piccante*, an older type of cheese found only in the best delicatessens and the largest supermarkets. All experts agree as to the superiority of the latter. While it is admittedly more expensive, it is an outstanding cheese and one which the writer on the subject, James Aldridge, prefers to Roquefort or Stilton.

Gorgonzola is mainly a table cheese, although more recently it has started to be used in cooking, principally as the main ingredient in the many sauces for pasta or potato gnocchi.

gorgonzola sauce for gnocchi or home-made pasta
salsa al gorgonzola

For 4 helpings of gnocchi or pasta

60 g (2 oz) Gorgonzola
30 g (1 oz) unsalted butter
6 fresh sage leaves
1 garlic clove, peeled and sliced
120 ml (4 fl oz) double cream
freshly ground black pepper

I like to use this sauce to dress the choux pastry gnocchi on page 315.

Cut the Gorgonzola into small pieces

Heat the butter, sage and garlic in a small saucepan. When the butter has just melted, add the cheese, the cream and a good grinding of pepper. Cook, stirring the whole time, until the cheese has melted. Simmer for 1 minute. Taste and check if salt is needed: owing to the saltiness of the cheese it probably will not be. Remove and discard the sage before using the sauce.

fontina

Fontina is a semi-soft cheese made from cow's milk in large round shapes. It has a very characteristic flavour that is redolent of the wild herbs and flowers of the high pastures of Valle d'Aosta where the farm-made fontina is produced. There is also an industrially produced variety of fontina. Both kinds of this cheese have FONTINA VALDOSTANA stamped on the crust. Unfortunately fontina is very difficult to find in Britain. What you usually get here when you ask for fontina is the Danish fontal, which has similar melting properties but not such an aromatic flavour.

The origins of fontina are very old. It is known to have been made in the fifteenth century – the name fontina appears in a list of cheeses made in the Valle d'Aosta – and is thought to date back to Roman times. From the eighteenth century onwards *fontina* was considered important enough to be listed in various local documents and inventories.

There are many theories concerning the origin of the name. Some writers maintain that it comes from a mountain called Fonti near Aosta, while others see it as a derivative of *fondere* – to melt. This is in fact the most important property of fontina: it melts beautifully. For this reason the experts argue that fontina is not a table cheese, and should only be used as a condiment, traditionally for polenta and potato gnocchi, or to make *fonduta*, for which the recipe is given below.

Fontina is one of the best cooking cheeses. It melts gorgeously, imparting to the dish a delicious nutty-milky flavour.

piedmontese fondue
fonduta piemontese

Fontina cheese, the principal ingredient of this sauce, can be bought in Italian shops or specialist cheese shops. The other characteristic ingredient is white truffle. I use truffle paste, but the sauce is very good even without it. If you are lucky enough to have a white truffle, it should be added, thinly sliced, at the very end just before serving the sauce.

The sauce must be made at the last minute or the cheese becomes thick and gluey. It only takes 10 minutes if you put boiling water into the lower part of a double boiler or in a pan into which you can fit another metal container for the bain-marie. I add a little flour to stabilise the emulsion, as this sauce is rather tricky to make.

Fonduta piemontese is traditionally served with crostini – croûtons – *or with bread. I also like it with a stiff polenta or, as described at the end of this recipe, with a* riso in bianco – *boiled rice.*

About 6 hours before you want to serve the *fonduta*, cut the fontina into dice. Put in a bowl and add enough milk just to cover the cheese.

Put the butter in the top half of a double boiler, add the fontina with the milk and set on simmering water.

Beat the flour into the egg yolks and then add this mixture to the cheese and milk mixture, while beating constantly with a wire whisk. Continue cooking and stirring until the fontina has melted and the sauce is very

Serves 4
**300 g (10 oz) fontina
about 250 ml
(9 fl oz) milk
60 g (2 oz) unsalted
butter
1 tbsp flour
3 free-range egg
yolks
1 1/2 tbsp truffle
paste (optional)
freshly ground black
pepper**

smooth, creamy and shiny. Mix in the truffle paste and add the pepper. Salt is not necessary because the cheese gives enough saltiness to the sauce. Do not cook any longer or the cheese will become stringy.

Serve in a heated bowl, which should be earthenware so as to retain the heat and keep the fontina fluid.

rice in a mould

Cook about 350 g (12 oz) of long-grain rice until *al dente*. Drain and dress with a good knob of butter. Butter a ring-mould generously, and sprinkle with breadcrumbs. Shake off the excess crumbs and spoon the rice into the mould, pressing it down to avoid holes. Turn the mould over on to a round dish to remove the ring of rice and spoon the *fonduta* into the hole and around the rice. If you have not got a ring-mould you can easily shape the rice with a spoon.

mozzarella

The popularity of pizza has made this cheese well known the world over. Only a few people, however, have had the gastronomic experience of tasting the real mozzarella, made from just buffalo's milk. It is this that was first made in Campania and Latium from the milk of water buffaloes introduced to Italy in the sixteenth century. And it is in those regions that one can still come across the best thing.

Some years ago I visited a *caseificio* (cheese factory) near the ruins of the Greek city of Velia, which flourished in the fifth century BC at the same time as Paestum further north. Like Paestum, Velia was an important port from which the goods that had arrived overland from the legendary Sybaris on the Ionian coast were shipped to the western Mediterranean. Unlike Paestum, however, Velia today remains largely buried. It stands at the foot of the hills overlooking the peaceful and fertile countryside of the 'happy land', as the Romans later called Campania, a land that yields a wealth of pleasures besides the real mozzarella that I was looking for.

My *caseificio* was totally dedicated to the production of mozzarella, although in its little shop I bought good *provolone* and *caciocavallo* made nearby. The *casaro* – cheese maker – was standing next to a large vessel in which a mechanical paddle was churning round and round. The rennet had already been added and the so-called *pasta filata* – 'plastic curd' cheese – was in the process of being made. This is done by covering the crumbled curd with boiling water which forces all the whey out with the rotary movement of the paddle. The *casaro* has to watch carefully and add boiling water from time to time. When a thread is formed, the cheese is *mozzato* – cut away from the original lump (hence the name of the cheese) and put through an extruding machine. There three girls were breaking off pieces of *pasta filata* which they quickly shaped into smooth, glistening golf balls and threw into a basin nearby. These were the delicious *bufaline*.

There is also a mozzarella made from cow's milk, a cheaper and less good product, also called *Fior di Latte*.

Mozzarella can be eaten raw, by itself or with vegetables, tomatoes being the best. In Italy this combination is known as *insalata caprese*, a salad of mozzarella, tomatoes and basil. But because of its binding property the main use of mozzarella is in cooking. To keep the flavour of the mozzarella when it is cooked I follow Marcella Hazan's useful suggestion, which is to grate the mozzarella and mix it with a couple of tablespoons of olive oil an hour or two before using it. If the dish you are making is not based on olive oil, use milk instead. The other secret is to add only a limited amount of mozzarella to the dish, and to achieve the desired cheesy flavour by the addition of some Cheshire or Lancashire cheese, thus avoiding too much of the white rubbery substance. Do not lay thick slices of mozzarella on the top of a dish, such as pizza, that you are going to bake. Either grate the mozzarella, as suggested above, or cut it into small pieces or thin strips and scatter them around. Another way is to tuck the mozzarella in thin slices underneath the tomatoes or any other ingredient that goes in the dish.

fried sandwiches of mozzarella and salame
la mia mozzarella in carrozza

Serves 2–4 (see recipe)
200 g (7 oz) fresh mozzarella
about 100 ml (3 1/2 fl oz) milk
100 g (3 1/2 oz) flour
2 free-range eggs
sea salt and pepper
8 slices of good-quality white bread, about 1 cm (1/2 inch) thick
4–8 slices Italian salame, according to size, not too thinly cut
oil for frying

Mozzarella in carrozza *is one of the most delicious creations of the inventive Neapolitans. They slice their mozzarella, made from buffalo's milk, sandwich it between two slices of white bread and fry it. But, while the mozzarella sold in Britain melts in the same way as the mozzarella sold in Naples, it has far less flavour. For this reason I add a slice of good Italian* salame *to the sandwich. I buy a* salame felino, *which can be bought sliced, in vacuum packs, in the best supermarkets. It is excellent, and is a perfect size for this dish. Other good salame would do, but it should not be too spicy or the mild flavour of the cheese will not come through.*

The quantities in this recipe are enough for 4 people as a primo. *If you serve mozzarella in carrozza as a secondo the quantities are enough for 2 or 3, depending on their appetites.*

Cut the mozzarella horizontally into slices of the same thickness as the slices of bread.

Put the milk in one soup plate and the flour in another.

Break the eggs into a third plate, add salt and pepper and beat lightly.

Dip one side of each slice of bread very briefly into the milk. Season the mozzarella with pepper. Put 1 slice of mozzarella and 1 or 2 slices of *salame* (according to thickness) between the dry sides of the bread. Pin with 2 toothpicks at each end of the sandwich.

Put enough frying oil in a large frying pan for the sandwiches to be deep-fried. Heat until very hot but not smoking.

Meanwhile dust each sandwich lightly with flour and dip in the beaten eggs, coating both sides and letting the excess egg flow back into the plate.

Fry the sandwiches until golden and crisp and then turn them over and fry the other side. The mozzarella should just begin to melt. Drain in a dish lined with kitchen paper and serve immediately.

rissoles stuffed with mozzarella in a pizza sauce
polpettine alla pizzaiola

These are Mediterranean-tasting rissoles containing mozzarella and cooked in a tomato sauce. The mozzarella melts inside the rissoles and sometimes oozes out to mix with the tomato sauce. In Italy a sauce is called alla pizzaiola *when it contains only tomatoes and oregano. The mozzarella here is an integral part of the meat, not of the sauce.*

Buy the best mince or, better still, buy some lean braising steak and have it minced.

First prepare the tomato sauce. Sauté the onion in the 2 tbsp of oil, using a heavy frying pan or a sauté pan of about 20 cm (8 inches) diameter. (A large pan will make the water in the tomatoes evaporate faster, thus concentrating the flavour of the sauce.) Add a pinch of salt; this releases the moisture in the onion and prevents the onion from browning. Cook the onion until it becomes soft, stirring frequently.

Meanwhile finely chop the garlic and the celery together and add to the onion. Cook for a further minute or so and then add the tomato purée. Cook, stirring constantly, for 1 minute. Add the tomatoes and the sugar

Serves 4
60 g (2 oz) good-quality white bread
milk
1 free-range egg
sea salt and pepper
450 g (1 lb) lean minced beef
1 mozzarella, weighing 225 g (8 oz)
3 tbsp extra virgin olive oil

For the tomato sauce
2 tbsp extra virgin olive oil
1 onion, finely chopped
sea salt
1 garlic clove, peeled

continued over >>

1 celery stalk with
   its leaves
2 tsp tomato purée
400 g (14 oz) tinned
   plum tomatoes or
   550 g (1 1/4 lb)
   fresh ripe tomatoes,
   peeled and with the
   seeds removed
1 tsp sugar
black pepper
1 tbsp dried oregano

and plenty of pepper. Simmer for about 45 minutes until the sauce is thick and the oil has separated from the tomatoes.

While the sauce is cooking, remove the crust and soak the bread in a little milk for 5 minutes or so. Squeeze out and put in a bowl.

Beat the egg lightly, with salt and pepper. Put the meat in the bowl with the soaked bread and add the beaten egg. Mix very thoroughly; this is best done with your hands.

Divide the meat mixture into 8 portions. Make these into fairly flat, round shapes and pat them hard to release any pockets of air.

Cut the mozzarella into slices and cover 4 portions of the meat mixture with these slices, leaving a clean edge all round. Place the other 4 portions on top and press all round the edges to seal.

Heat the 3 tbsp of oil in a non-stick pan and fry the rissoles until a lovely dark crust has formed. Turn them over and fry the other side, then transfer to the pan with the sauce. Add a couple of tablespoons of hot water to the pan in which you fried the rissoles, boil very rapidly and then pour this juice into the tomato sauce. Sprinkle with the oregano. Cover the pan and cook for 20 minutes, so that the flavour of the meat, the mozzarella and the tomato blend together.

parmesan

The terminology of the various cheeses that in Britain and elsewhere are loosely known as Parmesan is much more precise in Italy. There are in fact four distinct cheeses of this kind, and their generic name is not Parmesan, but *grana*. They are all very hard cheeses with a grainy texture (*grano* means 'grain') but whereas abroad they are all likely to be called Parmesan, in Italy each of the four is called by its own name. These names describe each *grana* by its place of origin; thus from Lodi comes *grana lodigiano*, from Piacenza *grana piacentino* and from the

Po valley *grana padano* (from the river's Latin name Padus). The exception is the genuine Parmesan, the correct name for which is *parmigiano-reggiano*. These cheeses are all made the same way, the differences arising from the different forage on which the cows are fed, so that their milk differs from place to place. They are all made into the huge shapes you will have seen, on the crust of which is stamped very clearly the name of the *grana* in question.

I often buy *grana padano* in Pavia, one of the centres of its production, when I go there to visit my son, who is lucky enough to live in that charming city. It is an excellent cheese, used as a table cheese when young and in cooking when aged. In Pavia I can also find the very rare *grana lodigiano*, which I like as a table cheese; it is softer and more mellow than the other *grana* cheeses. Giacomo Casanova, who enjoyed good food, although perhaps better known for his other appetites, noted in his famous diaries that 'Lodi was renowned for its cheese, known all over Europe as Parmesan'.

Grana piacentino is a very old cheese and used to be well known throughout Europe, challenging the supremacy of its rival, *parmigiano-reggiano*. Many people through the ages have paid tribute to this cheese; one of the earliest, so the story has it, having been Hannibal. The cheese, in fact, is said to have been the cause of his defeat at Capua. On passing through Piacenza, Hannibal acquired a quantity of *grana piacentino* and then spent his days gorging himself on it instead of re-arming against the Romans. A nice story, even if a trifle hard to believe. What is certain is that *grana piacentino* is an excellent cheese.

Parmesan, like the other *grana* cheeses, is still produced in small factories, called *caselli*. When I was in Parma some years ago I was taken to visit one. We went to a *casello* outside Parma where the cheese maker, Signor Mariani, showed me around. The milk from the morning's and the previous evening's milkings is partly skimmed and then curdled with calf's rennet, after which it is scooped out into shapes of about 25–30 kg (60–70 lb) each. An impressive statistic is that each of these shapes accounts for about 450 litres (78 pints) of milk!

There are two cheeses in Britain that are called Parmesan – *parmigiano-reggiano* and *grana padano*.

The birthplace of *parmigiano-reggiano* lies in an area between Reggio Emilia and Parma that was once part of the Duchy of Parma. For this reason the cheese was originally called, simply, *parmigiano*. Then Reggio rightly claimed its share of the provenance and the name was changed to *parmigiano-reggiano*. *Parmigiano-reggiano* is made in strictly defined areas in the provinces of Reggio Emilia, Parma, Modena, Bologna and Mantova.

There are three grades of *parmigiano-reggiano*, named according to the length of time for which they have matured. The youngest Parmesan, the *nuovo*, which is good as a table cheese, may be up to one year old. *Parmigiano vecchio* has aged for between one and one and a half years, while the *stravecchio*, which is Parmesan at its best, has aged for two years or more.

Good *parmigiano-reggiano* is pale buff in colour with a crumbly texture and a rich yet mellow flavour. When you come across Parmesan in this perfect condition you should buy a large piece and then divide it into wedges of about 200 g (7 oz) each. Do this, not by cutting, but by pushing the point of a knife into it: the cheese will break apart following its natural structure. Wrap the wedges in foil, except one for immediate use, and put them in the freezer. Parmesan keeps its flavour quite well when frozen, the main effect of freezing being that, once thawed, it crumbles more easily. Wrap the reserved piece in a double thickness of muslin and place it in the vegetable drawer of the fridge. The muslin will allow the cheese to breathe and prevent the formation of mould on the outside for up to a month or so.

Parmesan is a very nourishing cheese: a 100 g (3 1/2 oz) portion has the same protein content as 200 g (7 oz) of beef and 300 g (10 oz) of fish. It also has a lower level of cholesterol and saturated fats than most other hard cheeses.

The origins of Parmesan are lost in the mists of time. We know that by the fourteenth century it was already considered an excellent cheese. Boccaccio, in the Decameron, when describing the pleasures of the *Paese di Bengodi* – the Village of Good Cheer – writes: 'And on a mountain all of grated cheese dwelt folk that did nought else but make macaroni and ravioli.' There can be little doubt that the cheese in question was *parmigiano-reggiano*, and it can be seen that the successful union of pasta and *parmigiano-reggiano* was already popular. *Parmigiano-reggiano* was also used a lot during the high Renaissance, when it was usually served at the end of the meal with truffles, fennel, cardoons, grapes and pears.

In Emilia, where this cheese often appears as a table cheese, *parmigiano-reggiano* with pears has remained a favourite end to a meal. Elsewhere, quite recently, the habit of serving the cheese with some fresh fruits or vegetables has started to come back into fashion.

The custom of handing round a piece of the best *parmigiano-reggiano* with the drinks has spread from Emilia Romagna to other regions. Recently I had the impression that a large *scheggia* – splinter – of golden Parmesan next to the bottle of Champagne or Prosecco is now *de rigueur* as a pre-prandial snack. It is also the best way to savour a good glass of Chianti, such as Cepparello or a Chianti Rufina. Furthermore, Parmesan is not appreciated only for its taste. Some afficionados love its smell, as Squire Trelawney of *Treasure Island* did. He used to keep a snuffbox full of grated Parmesan in his pocket, which he then brought to his nose with great relish.

Its table use notwithstanding, *parmigiano-reggiano* is mainly regarded as a grating cheese and, for its melting qualities, a good cooking cheese. Of all cheeses it is the one without which Italian cooking would not be really Italian. It is used a lot, though never indiscriminately, with pasta, soups and risotto. In Emilia and Romagna there are a few meat dishes that call for *parmigiano-reggiano* and even a dish made with sole, while in Lombardy, *parmigiano-reggiano* is added to vegetables sautéed in butter, to asparagus and to leeks (see the recipe on page 263). Most gratin dishes need *parmigiano-reggiano*, on which a word of warning. *Parmigiano-reggiano* sprinkled by itself on the top of gratin dishes will acquire a bitter taste when exposed, dry, to the heat. My secret for a better topping is to use only a couple of tablespoons of *parmigiano-reggiano* and to mix it with dried breadcrumbs. Put the rest of the cheese in the sauce or in between the layers of the other ingredients. Don't throw away the rind of your *parmigiano-reggiano*: scrape it thoroughly and add it to a minestrone, a pasta and bean soup or any other vegetable soup that needs lengthy cooking.

Grana padano is the other popular cheese of the *grana* ('grainy') family. It is made in the Po valley and I find it an excellent table cheese, although for cooking I would choose the real McCoy.

egg, parmesan and parsley dumplings in stock
minestra mariconda

Serves 4

200 g (7 oz) fresh white breadcrumbs, with crust removed

200 ml (7 fl oz) full-fat milk

120 g (4 oz) unsalted butter

2 free-range eggs

4 tbsp chopped flat-leaf parsley

60 g (2 oz) freshly grated Parmesan

1/2 a nutmeg, grated

sea salt and pepper

2 litres (3 1/2 pints) meat or chicken stock

Lombardy offers quite a number of delicate and attractive looking soups. These are based on properly made stock, richly yet delicately flavoured, with the right proportion of meat to bone (see the recipe on page 485). Minestra mariconda, one of these soups, contains little cheese-flavoured dumplings. I have adapted the recipe from a book, Il Cuoco Senza Pretense (The Unpretentious Cook), a collection of Lombard recipes published in 1834. The original recipe suggests using fish stock for fast days. What fascinates me in this book is that at the end of each recipe there is a list of costs for each ingredient, and the total. This soup, with quantities for at least 12 people, cost Lire 53, equal, today, to 2 1/2 pence!

Soak the breadcrumbs in the milk for 10 minutes or so, then squeeze the milk out very thoroughly. Heat the butter in a small frying pan, add the breadcrumbs and sauté for 10 minutes, until the mixture is very dry, like dry paste. Transfer to a bowl.

Add the eggs to the bowl and then add all the other ingredients except the stock. Mix thoroughly with a fork, cover the bowl with clingfilm and refrigerate for at least 2 hours.

Bring the stock slowly to the boil in a large saucepan. Taste and adjust the seasoning.

Pick up a small teaspoonful of the bread mixture and, with the back of another teaspoon, push it down into the broth. If the mixture is hard enough, you can make little pellets, the size of hazelnuts, with your hands. To prevent the dumplings breaking, keep the heat low so that the broth just simmers. Cook gently for 5 minutes and then ladle the soup into heated soup bowls. Serve with more Parmesan handed round separately.

preparation
You can prepare the dumpling mixture up to 1 day in advance and keep it covered in the fridge. Ideally the dumplings should be cooked shortly before serving, but I have successfully cooked them about 1 hour before and reheated the soup very slowly.

choux pastry gnocchi
gnocchi alla parigina

In spite of being of Parisian origin, as their name implies, these gnocchi are very popular in northern Italian homes, and possibly better known there than they are in Paris.

Gnocchi alla parigina are easier to make than potato gnocchi. You can dress them with Parmesan and melted butter flavoured with garlic and sage or with the Gorgonzola sauce (see page 304). They are also delicious with a very thin béchamel to which 3 tablespoons of grated Parmesan and grated Gruyère are added at the end.

Put the milk in a saucepan, add the butter and 1 teaspoon of salt and bring to the boil.

Take the pan off the heat and add the flour, all at once. Beat very hard with a wooden spoon until well blended and then return the pan to the heat and cook, over a low heat, beating the whole time. This will cook the flour, thus getting rid of the unpleasant taste of uncooked flour. Beat until the paste begins to make a sizzling noise – about 3 minutes – then draw off the heat.

Mix in the nutmeg and the cheese and allow to cool for about 5 minutes, beating very frequently.

Add one egg to the paste and beat until thoroughly incorporated. Do the same with all the other eggs, incorporating one egg at a time and beating quite hard after each addition. This paste needs a lot of beating

Serves 4
250 ml (9 fl oz) full-fat milk
100 g (3 1/2 oz) unsalted butter
sea salt
150 g (5 oz) Italian 00 flour, sifted
1/4 tsp grated nutmeg
2 tbsp freshly grated Parmesan cheese
4 free-range eggs
extra freshly grated Parmesan for serving

to aerate it. I use an electric beater for about 10 minutes. At the end the paste will be very glossy and smooth.

Preheat the oven to 180°C (350°F) mark 4.

Choose a large and wide saucepan or casserole of at least 3 litres (5 pints) capacity. Fill the pan with water and bring to the boil. Add 1 tbsp of salt.

Turn the heat down so that the water in the saucepan is only just simmering. Pick up small spoonfuls of the mixture and, with the heel of another teaspoon, slide them into the simmering water. Alternatively, pipe the mixture through a forcing bag fitted with a plain 1 cm (1/2 inch) nozzle, while cutting it into 2.5 cm (1 inch) lengths. Cook the gnocchi in 2 batches. They will soon come to the surface. Cook them for about 1 minute and then lift them with a slotted spoon and place them on a clean cloth to dry. Transfer them to a generously buttered ovenproof dish on which you have spread a couple of tablespoons of the sauce of your choice. Choose a large shallow dish so that the gnocchi can be spread out in a single layer.

When all the gnocchi are cooked, spoon over the remaining sauce and bake in the oven for about 15 minutes Allow to stand out of the oven for 3–4 minutes before serving with more Parmesan handed round.

preparation
The dish can be prepared in advance, and baked for about 25 minutes to allow the *gnocchi* to get hot all through.

Another excellent way to dress the gnocchi is with this cream mixture. First season the gnocchi with a couple of tablespoons of Parmesan. Then melt a knob of butter in a small saucepan and add 200 ml (7 fl oz) of double cream. Heat the cream mixture and then spoon it over the gnocchi. Bake for about 15 minutes in the preheated oven and serve with more Parmesan on the side.

pecorino cheese with raw broad beans
pecorino con le fave

This is hardly a recipe. It is the way Tuscans start their meal in April when the broad beans are still young and their skin is tender. In the autumn the same seasoned pecorino is served with pears, and that is at the end of a meal.

All you have to do is buy 450 g (1 lb) of pecorino, preferably seasoned and Tuscan, and 1.5 kg of young broad beans.

Cut the pecorino into wedges and put them on a dish. Put the unpodded broad beans in a bowl and let everybody get on with it. The drink must be red wine; a good Chianti Classico would be perfect.

mascarpone

When I was a child in Milan, a woman came to the house every Tuesday, selling ricotta and mascarpone. I can still see her, dressed in black with a black and white scarf around her head. On her arm she carried a flat basket packed with cheeses wrapped in muslin, ricotta at one end and mascarpone at the other. From her shoulder there hung a steelyard for weighing out the cheeses, which were placed on its large brass pan. How I looked forward to her Tuesday visits, and how I loved the smell and the whiteness and, best of all, the taste of those cheeses! I ate them as they should be eaten – as they are, just with a little sugar.

The author of a dictionary of the Milanese dialect written in 1839, Luigi Cherubini, endorses this. In the entry for mascarpone he wrote:

> A kind of milk product from cream that is boiled and treated, as soon as it comes to the boil, with a moderate dosage of vinegar or acetic acid. It is of the same consistency as butter and of a very white colour . . . It is usually eaten simply sweetened with sugar; gourmands, however, enjoy it even mixed with *rosolio* or rum, or dressed in many other ways. The word mascarpone apparently owes its origin to the Spanish expression *Mas cher bueno*.

Cherubini is usually very reliable on the etymology of Lombard words, but here, I think, he fails. I feel that the origin of the word suggested by the twentieth-century food historian Massimo Alberini, must be right; the word, he says, comes from *mascarpa*, a type of ricotta made in the province of Como and referred to in a document dated 1168.

Until recently mascarpone was little-known outside Lombardy and Piedmont. Mascarpone could only be made in the cold months, from November to February, and it had to be consumed within a few days. Now modern food technology has changed all that by means of the high-temperature process (UHT) that makes mascarpone a 'long-life' product. Mascarpone is now made all the year round and keeps several weeks, with the result that it is popular throughout Italy and is well known also abroad.

The mascarpone that you buy in tubs does not have the same taste as the fresh and highly perishable mascarpone that can still be bought in the best delicatessens in Milan. But long-life mascarpone is better than no mascarpone, and I am delighted that I can now buy it in my local supermarket.

Mascarpone is made from the very best milk, which comes from cows that have been fed on fresh or naturally dried forage, in which the aromas and flavours of the herbs and flowers have been preserved.

The recipes given here are my favourites. You can also mix mascarpone with other cheeses. Try mashing it with Roquefort or Gorgonzola, or add some grated Parmesan or pecorino to it for a delicious pre-prandial dip. Mascarpone is an excellent substitute for butter in any kind of butter-cream: with smoked salmon, tuna, caviar or truffles, or with green olives.

tagliatelle with mascarpone and egg yolks
tagliatelle al mascarpone

Serves 3–4
**tagliatelle made with
2 eggs and 200 g
(7 oz) Italian 00**

continued over >>

This is an old recipe from Pavia, a university city in southern Lombardy, brimming with artistic treasures and good food. It is the birthplace of several excellent traditional recipes which are based on local products such as mascarpone. Strangely enough, there is not the wealth of good local restaurants that one might expect, and it is for this reason that when I go to Pavia to see my son, who teaches at the University, I stop off at the market to buy the ingredients with which to cook a meal in his flat. I am known at the stall selling cheese and salumi, where the lady calls me la mamma del professore, since I go there to buy my prosciutto, salame and luganega to bring back to England, as well as the fresh mascarpone with which to make this dish for lunch. It is a heavenly dish, especially if you can spare the time to make your own tagliatelle. The sauce takes less time to make than the tagliatelle takes to cook.

If you are making your own tagliatelle, look up the instructions on page 27. Stop thinning out the sheets of pasta at the last but one notch.

Put the mascarpone, the butter, nutmeg and pepper in a serving bowl. Place the bowl in the oven and turn the heat on to very low.

In another bowl beat the egg yolks with half the Parmesan.

Drop the pasta into boiling salted water and cook in the usual way, remembering that if the tagliatelle are home-made and still soft they will take no longer than 2 minutes to cook.

Mix about 4 tablespoons of the pasta water into the mascarpone mixture.

Drain the tagliatelle as soon as they are ready, reserving some of the water in a small jug.

Transfer the tagliatelle to the bowl containing the mascarpone mixture, toss thoroughly and then add the egg yolk mixture. Mix again and check the seasoning. Grate a little more nutmeg on top and bring straight away to the table together with the little jug of reserved water. Hand round the remaining Parmesan separately.

The jug full of pasta water is a Neapolitan touch about which I was reminded recently by a friend. He told me that at the home of his Neapolitan grandmother the cooking water was always brought to the table in a little jug, which was made of earthenware to retain the heat. The hot water is for people who like their pasta more slippery. This sauce, and the ricotta, olive and Gruyère spread on page 420 are typical of the sauces that often need the addition of a little water. Another well-known sauce of this kind is carbonara.

---

flour or 250 g (9 oz) dried tagliatelle
200 g (7 oz) mascarpone
15 g (1/2 oz) unsalted butter
grated nutmeg
freshly grated black pepper
2 free-range egg yolks
60 g (2 oz) freshly grated Parmesan

mascarpone dressed with balsamic vinegar
mascarpone all'aceto balsamico

This new concoction is based on two of the most ancient ingredients in Italian cooking, mascarpone and *aceto balsamico*.

For each person you need 100 g (3 1/2 oz) of mascarpone, caster sugar to your liking – I add 1 1/4–1 1/2 teaspoons – and about 2 teaspoons of *aceto balsamico*. Try with 1 teaspoon of *aceto balsamico*, taste and then add a little more until you get the right balance between the sugar and the vinegar. That's all; so easy, yet so good, but use *aceto balsamico tradizionale*, if you can find it, because the common or garden *aceto balsamico* is not as good.

mascarpone with elderflower and rose geranium sauces
mascarpone alle due salsine

Serves 12
1 kg (2 lb) mascarpone

For the elderflower sauce
2 dozen elderflowers
150 ml (1/4 pint) dry white wine
caster sugar
the rind of 1 1/2 organic lemons, the yellow part only
1 tsp fennel seeds
4 peppercorns

For the rose geranium sauce
about half a dozen rose geranium leaves

continued over >>

Large parties are easier to cater for in the summer than in the winter – and here is a very easy pudding which must not, however, be underrated.

If picking your own, pick your elderflowers in full bloom from the south-facing side of the bush because they will be more scented.

The two sauces are very different from one another, yet each combines deliciously with the richness of the mascarpone. The geranium leaf sauce has a deeper, sweeter and darker flavour, reminiscent of Arabian nights, while the elderflower sauce – my favourite – is lighter and fresher. It seems to encapsulate the scent of the English countryside on a warm evening in June.

To make the elderflower sauce, put the elderflowers in a bowl, cover with boiling water, add the wine and leave to infuse for at least 6 hours. Strain the liquid. Measure the liquid and pour it into the saucepan with the sugar, the weight of which should be half the volume of the liquid; e.g. to 300 ml (1/2 pint) of liquid you should add 120 g (4 oz) of sugar. Add the lemon rind, fennel seeds and peppercorns and bring slowly to the boil, stirring constantly to dissolve the sugar. Simmer for 10 minutes, then strain the sauce into a jug. When cold, cover the jug and refrigerate.

To make the rose geranium sauce rinse the rose geranium leaves and crush them gently in your hands to release their aroma. Put them immediately into a bowl and cover with boiling water. Leave to infuse for 6 hours, then strain. Measure the liquid and pour it into a saucepan. Add half that amount of sugar, as for the elderflower sauce. Pour in the lemon juice, add the peppercorns, and bring slowly to the boil. Simmer gently for a few minutes. Taste and add more lemon juice if necessary, to give a slightly sharp edge. Strain into a jug and when cold, cover and refrigerate.

Spoon the mascarpone into a big glass bowl and let everybody serve themselves and pour over the sauces.

preparation
Both sauces can be made up to 1 week in advance and kept in the refrigerator.

caster sugar
juice of 1 organic lemon
4 peppercorns

mascarpone and coffee trifle
tiramisú

This is a pudding of recent birth for the ancient Italian tradition of cooking, yet it is extremely popular, perhaps even more so abroad than in Italy. I often prefer to make tiramisú *without the coffee or the chocolate, also substituting white rum or Grand Marnier for the brandy (see next recipe). I find it lighter and more pleasant, but this may be because I am not mad on chocolate. Of course it is then no longer a real* tiramisú, *which means 'pull-me-up'. Tiramisú is made with Italian sponge fingers – savoiardi – which are soft and absorb the coffee mixture.*

Mix together the coffee and the brandy.
Grate about a quarter of the chocolate and cut the rest into small pieces.

Beat the egg yolks with the sugar until very pale and forming soft peaks and then fold in the mascarpone, a tablespoon at a time.

Serves 6–8
120 ml (4 fl oz)
  strong espresso
  coffee or 1 1/2 tsp
  instant espresso
  coffee dissolved in
  the same quantity
  of water
3 tbsp brandy
100 g (3 1/2 oz)
  bitter chocolate
3 free-range eggs,
  separated
4 tbsp caster sugar

continued over >>

250 g (9 oz)
mascarpone
18 *savoiardi* biscuits
coffee beans for
decoration

Whisk the egg whites until stiff, then fold them into the mascarpone and egg yolk mixture.

Put a layer of biscuits on a pretty dish. Dip a pastry brush into the coffee and brandy mixture and soak the biscuits with it.

Spread about 4 tablespoons of the mascarpone cream over the biscuits and scatter with some pieces of chocolate. Cover with a layer of biscuits, soak with coffee and brandy and continue to make similar layers until you have used up all the ingredients. Finish with a layer of mascarpone cream. Place the pudding in the refrigerator for at least 6 hours.

Before serving, sprinkle with the reserved grated chocolate and decorate with coffee beans.

preparation

You can make *tiramisú* in a glass bowl. It looks stunning with the alternate layers of pale and dark brown seen through the glass, and the top speckled with the dark brown of the grated chocolate.

white mascarpone trifle: a summer tiramisú
il tiramisú di edda

Serves 6–8
small meringues,
made with 2 free-
range egg whites
and 120 g (4 oz)
caster sugar
2 free-range eggs,
separated
90 g (3 oz) caster
sugar
325 g (11 oz)
mascarpone
90 ml (3 fl oz) white
rum, such as
Bacardi

This is a lovely white tiramisú *which I prefer to the usual concoction, especially in summer.*

Heat the oven to 140°C (275°F) mark 1.

First make the meringues. Remember that the egg whites must be at room temperature before you start whipping them.

Line a baking tray with parchment paper.

Whisk the egg whites until firm. Sprinkle half the sugar across the surface and beat it in until the mixture looks glossy and smooth. Sprinkle another half of the remaining sugar over the surface and fold it in with a large metal spoon. Fold in the rest of the sugar.

Using 2 spoons or a forcing bag fitted with a large round nozzle, place small rounds of the mixture, well spaced, on the lined baking tray.

continued over >>

Dredge the surface of the meringues very slightly with extra sugar and bake until firm and a very light golden colour. Leave them in the switched-off oven until cold (at least 2 hours). Set aside 7 or 8 of the prettiest meringues and crumble the others.

Now make the trifle. Beat the egg yolks with the sugar until pale and mousse-like. Fold in the mascarpone gradually and then beat until it has been incorporated. Whisk only one of the egg whites until firm (discard the second egg white or keep for another recipe) and fold into the mascarpone cream.

Mix the rum and the milk in a soup plate. Dip the biscuits into the mixture just long enough for them to soften. Lay about 9 moistened biscuits in an oval dish. Spread over about one-third of the mascarpone cream. Sprinkle with the meringue crumbs. Dip another 9 biscuits into the rum and milk mixture and arrange them on top of the meringue crumbs. Spread over about half the remaining cream. Cover with clingfilm and refrigerate. Put the remaining cream in a closed container and refrigerate.

Before serving, smooth the remaining cream all over the pudding and decorate with the pretty meringues you have set aside.

preparation
Tiramisú, whether white or brown, should be made 1 day in advance and served chilled.

100 ml (3 1/2 fl oz)
full-fat milk
18 *savoiardi* biscuits

mascarpone ice-cream
gelato di mascarpone

This rich ice-cream is ideal to go with poached fruits, such as the plums baked in wine on page 345 or the cherries stewed in wine on page 346.

Beat the mascarpone with the icing sugar. Beat in the egg yolks and the *amaretto*. Mix thoroughly until well blended.

Spoon the mascarpone cream into the bowl in which you want to serve it, and cover with clingfilm. Freeze for at least 6 hours.

Remove from the freezer and put in the fridge about 1 hour before serving.

Serves 8
**400 g (14 oz)
mascarpone**
**120 g (4 oz) icing
sugar**
**3 free-range egg
yolks**
**4 tbsp *amaretto*
liqueur**

ricotta

Strictly speaking, ricotta is not a cheese but a by-product of cheese-making: it is made from the whey after it has been separated, by heating, from the curd. To make ricotta, the whey is heated again (*ricotta* means 'recooked') and the ricotta then forms on the surface.

Ricotta is a healthy food with a low fat content of 15–20 per cent. It can be made from the whey from cow's, ewe's or goat's milk. The two traditional ricottas are the *piemontese*, made with whey from cow's milk, and the *romana*, made with the whey from ewe's milk. *Ricotta piemontese*, also called *seiras*, is very creamy and is mainly eaten fresh with a little sugar and maybe a sprinkling of ground coffee or cinnamon. It is now a rare commodity which can only be found in the best delicatessens of northern Italy. If you are ever in Milan go to Peck, to Il Salumaio or to the less well known but equally excellent Salumeria Il Principe in Corso Venezia. As well as your pot of *ricotta piemontese* buy a pot of fresh mascarpone; eat both just as they are to enjoy their full flavour.

Ricotta romana is traditionally made with ewe's milk. When I was in Canino, a small market town near Viterbo, I went to see ricotta being made at a very small *caseificio* – cheese factory – nearby. It was the spring after Chernobyl and production had just started again the previous week. All cheese production had been stopped in Italy for about six weeks, and the owners of the co-operative, who were the six men who worked there, were facing heavy losses. Having just been allowed to start work again, the atmosphere was almost festive and the *casaro* – cheese maker – was only too pleased to show me the process.

He first showed me how pecorino is made; it is put into cylindrical moulds with perforated walls and placed on long stainless-steel counters to drain. It stays there for two or three months for fresh pecorino, longer for the more matured cheese and six or seven months for the grating cheese. Then the ricotta-making took place. The whey is heated up to 80°C, at which temperature small blobs form on the surface. These blobs are scooped out and put in a *cestello* – the traditional wicker basket – to drip-dry.

After seeing all this delicious cheese in the making I had no intention of leaving empty-handed, but it was equally clear that I couldn't buy the sort of quantity one would ask for in a shop. So I came away the proud owner of a pecorino of 10 kg (22 lb) as well as 2 kg (4 1/2 lb) of freshly made ricotta. I was worried about having to get through so much ricotta before it became stale, and the alternative of having to spend my holiday making ricotta stuffings and ricotta puddings didn't appeal to me at all. I need not have worried, however, since that ultra-fresh ricotta kept in perfect condition for five days, by which time we had consumed it all without difficulty. We ate it just like that, sometimes as a cheese with a little oil, salt and pepper, sometimes as a pudding with a sprinkling of sugar. It had a richer flavour than the usual ricotta, and no trace of the slight bitterness that is sometimes detectable in ricotta bought in Britain.

In Britain UHT ricotta is sold in any supermarket. It is all right – not marvellous – it is a cow's milk product quite suitable in cooking. In Italian delicatessens you can also find *ricotta salata*; it is ricotta that has been drained in small moulds, salted and dried in the sun. *Ricotta salata* is a typical product of Sicily and southern Italy where it is used, coarsely grated, on pasta dressed with a tomato sauce. It gives a milky flavour to the dish, as an alternative to Parmesan. But remember, if you use it, not to put salt in the tomato sauce, adding it, if needed, after you have mixed in the ricotta.

Ricotta is used extensively in Italian cooking. It is a very common ingredient in savoury stuffings and fillings and in vegetable pies, as well as in puddings and cakes. It also makes an excellent spread mixed with a strong cheese such as Gorgonzola.

ricotta ice-cream
gelato di ricotta

This is a recipe kindly given to me by Caroline Liddell and Robin Weir and is included in their book, Ices, published by New English Library. The authors write: 'Both the flavour and the texture are clearly ricotta,' and indeed they are. I have tried the recipe both with fresh ricotta and with long-life ricotta, and the ice-cream is delicious with either.

Serves 8
**400 ml (14 fl oz) full-
  fat milk
225 g (8 oz)
  granulated sugar**

continued over >>

3 free-range egg yolks
250 g (9 oz) ricotta
150 ml (1/4 pint) whipping cream, chilled
1 tbsp dark rum

First make the custard. Combine the milk and half the sugar in a medium-sized saucepan and bring to boiling point. Meanwhile in a medium-sized heatproof bowl combine the egg yolks with the remaining sugar and beat, preferably with a hand-held electric mixer, until the mixture is pale and thick enough to hold the shape when a ribbon of mix is trailed across the surface. Pour the hot milk in a thin stream on to the egg yolks and sugar, whisking steadily as the milk is added.

The bowl can now be placed over a pan of simmering water, or the custard can be returned to the saucepan which should then be put on top of a heat diffuser mat so that it is not in direct contact with the heat. Only if you have an accurate thermometer, and/or are confident that you will not overheat the sauce, should you put the saucepan over a gentle direct heat.

Use a small wooden spoon or spatula to stir the custard. Heated over water, the custard will not suffer as long as it is stirred frequently; it will take 25–30 minutes to thicken sufficiently, or to reach 85°C. Over direct heat the custard needs constant attention and will take 8–10 minutes. Without a thermometer to judge if the custard has thickened sufficiently, remove the spoon and tilt the back of it towards you. Look first at the way the sauce coats the spoon. If it forms only a thin film, try drawing a horizontal line across the back of the spoon. This should hold a clear shape. If not, continue cooking the custard until it coats the back of the spoon more thickly and holds a clear line. As soon as the custard has reached the right temperature and thickened sufficiently, remove the pan from the heat and plunge the base in a few inches of cold water.

Gradually beat in pieces of the crumbled ricotta and continue to beat vigorously until the custard is almost smooth. (Do not worry if a few small lumps remain; these will be broken down in the churning process.) When cold, remove, cover and chill in the fridge.

When ready, start the ice-cream machine. Stir the chilled cream and rum into the custard and then pour into the machine and churn until the mixture has frozen to a consistency firm enough to serve. Quickly scrape into plastic freezer boxes, cover with waxed paper and a lid. Allow about 25–30 minutes in the fridge to soften sufficiently to serve.

courgettes stuffed with ricotta and amaretti
zucchine ripiene alla mantovana

These courgettes are characteristic of the cooking of Mantua, where some aspects of the grande cucina *of the Gonzagas were incorporated into the local cooking, thus producing a very distinctive cuisine.*

The stuffing here contains sweet elements, and ricotta, which not only blend beautifully with the delicacy of the courgettes, but in fact enhance their flavour. There are many recipes for stuffed courgettes, but to my mind this is the most delicious. Buy amaretti di Saronno *if you can; they are less sweet than other brands.*

Wash the courgettes very thoroughly. Drop them whole in boiling salted water and cook for 2–3 minutes after the water has come back to the boil. Drain and dry them. Cut off both ends and cut in half lengthwise.

Scoop out the inside of the courgettes with a potato peeler or with a vegetable corer, being careful not to puncture the skin and reserving the pulp. Leave a 1 cm (1/2 inch) layer of pulp all around the shell. Sprinkle the inside of the shells lightly with salt and leave upside-down on a wooden board to drain off the excess water.

Meanwhile prepare the stuffing. Put half the butter and 1 tbsp of the oil in a sauté pan. Add the shallot and a little salt and sauté over a very low heat until soft but not at all brown. The salt helps the shallot to cook without browning, since it releases the moisture inside it.

Finely chop the courgette pulp and add to the shallot. Cook for 10 minutes, stirring very frequently and mashing the mixture with a wooden spoon.

Preheat the oven to 190°C (375°F) mark 5.

Combine the crumbled *amaretti*, the ricotta, thyme, nutmeg and the egg in a bowl. Add the courgette pulp mixture with all its cooking juices and work everything together. Add pepper, and salt if necessary.

Pat dry the courgette shells inside and out with kitchen paper.

Smear the bottom of a rectangular oven dish, preferably metal, with the remaining oil and lay the courgette shells in the dish, hollow side up.

Fill the shells with the stuffing. Sprinkle with some dried breadcrumbs and dot with the remaining butter.

Serves 4

- 4 medium-sized courgettes, about 15 cm (6 inches) long
- sea salt
- 30 g (1 oz) unsalted butter
- 2 tbsp olive oil
- 1 shallot, very finely chopped
- 3 *amaretti*, finely crumbled
- 150 g (5 oz) ricotta
- 2 tsp chopped fresh thyme or 1 tsp dried thyme
- pinch of grated nutmeg
- 1 free-range egg
- freshly ground black pepper
- dried breadcrumbs

Bake for about 35 minutes or until the courgette shells are tender and a light golden crust has formed on the top. If the top is still very pale, flash for a minute under a hot grill. Serve warm or at room temperature. The whole dish can be prepared and baked in advance and lightly reheated, if wished, in a medium oven for 5 minutes.

roulade stuffed with tomato sauce, anchovies and ricotta
rotolo di salsa di pomodoro con acciughe e ricotta

Serves 6–8
For the roulade
30 g (1 oz) unsalted butter
30 g (1 oz) plain flour
300 ml (1/2 pint) full-fat milk, or half milk, half single cream
75 g (2 1/2 oz) freshly grated Parmesan
5 free-range eggs, separated
sea salt and pepper
pinch of nutmeg
5 tbsp fine dried breadcrumbs

For the filling
1 medium onion, finely chopped
4 tbsp olive oil

continued over >>

In this dish fresh flavoured ricotta is used to counterbalance the tomato sauce which is spiced with anchovy fillets. The recipe was given to me by Betsy Newell, who runs a cookery school in her home in Kensington, London. Betsy is a very creative cook with a particular talent for combining elements from different cuisines. She is very familiar with Italian ingredients as a result of the time she spends in her beautiful farmhouse in Chianti, and here a French soufflé roulade is filled with a classic Italian tomato sauce. The result is mouth-watering.

Butter a 30 x 35cm (12 x 14 inch) Swiss-roll tin and line with bakewell paper.

Make a roux with the butter and the flour. Heat the milk or milk–cream mixture until just before it boils and whisk quickly into the roux. Bring to the boil and place the saucepan over a larger saucepan one-third full of hot water. Cook for 20 minutes, stirring occasionally. The water should just simmer. Keep a watch on it and add boiling water if necessary.

Meanwhile prepare the tomato sauce by slowly sautéing the finely chopped onion in the olive oil. When it is very soft and slightly coloured add the finely chopped garlic and continue to sauté for 1 more minute. Then add the tomatoes and cook slowly for about 30 minutes or more until they are well thickened and have slightly separated from the oil.

Lift the anchovy fillets out of the milk, chop them and stir into the tomato sauce. Season with a generous grinding of pepper. Taste and add salt.

Finely chop together the parsley and the spring onion and set aside.

Preheat the oven to 180°C (350°F) mark 4.

When the béchamel sauce has cooked, remove from the heat and stir in 45 g (1 1/2 oz) of the Parmesan. Then stir in the 5 egg yolks and the nutmeg. Taste for seasoning.

Beat the egg whites to the meringue stage, stiff but not dry, and fold into the béchamel and egg mixture. Spread carefully and evenly over the prepared tin and bake for 10–12 minutes, or until just firm.

Meanwhile lay a clean tea-towel on the table and sprinkle with the remaining Parmesan and the breadcrumbs.

When the soufflé is cooked, turn it over immediately on to the tea-towel, remove the bakewell paper and allow to cool.

When you are ready to assemble the roulade, crumble the ricotta over the cold soufflé, then spread the tomato sauce all over, leaving a 2.5 cm (1 inch) edge all round. Sprinkle the chopped parsley and spring onions evenly over the whole surface. Roll up carefully and place in the oven for 10 minutes or until heated through. Slice the roulade and serve at once on warm plates.

preparation
You can prepare the roulade and the sauce in advance and assemble it before you heat it in the oven.

1 or 2 garlic cloves, peeled and very finely chopped

400 g (14 oz) tin of Italian chopped tomatoes

4 anchovy fillets, soaked in milk for 30 minutes

sea salt and pepper

5 tbsp fresh flat-leaf parsley, finely chopped

4 or 5 spring onions, green part only, finely chopped

100 g (3 1/2 oz) ricotta

ricotta with mint
ricotta alla mentuccia

I am indebted to Massimo Alberini, the food historian, for having told me about this exceedingly pleasant way of eating a good fresh ricotta. If you manage to find ricotta made with ewe's milk, use it in this way.

The mint must be a sweet variety such as apple mint or Bowles mint.

For 4 people you will need 250–300 g (9–10 oz) of best ricotta. Leave the ricotta in the coldest part of the fridge for about 2 hours and then cut it into 2.5 cm (1 inch) thick slices. Lay the slices neatly on a dish and sprinkle with 2 tablespoons of demerara sugar. Put back in the fridge for a further hour. At the end the sugar will have partly dissolved and penetrated the surface of the ricotta.

Meanwhile chop a couple of handfuls of mint leaves. Scatter the mint over the ricotta slices before bringing to the table. Hand around more sugar, which I think is needed; it also gives a pleasant contrast of texture.

ricotta cake (or undressed sicilian cassata)
cassata siciliana nuda

Serves 8
4 hard-boiled free-
  range eggs
450 g (1 lb) ricotta
130 g (4 1/2 oz)
  caster sugar
1 tsp ground
  cinnamon
1 tbsp rose water
1 tbsp orange water
45 g (1 1/2 oz)
  angelica, chopped
120 g (4 oz) candied
  peel, chopped
3 candied cherries,
  chopped
2 tbsp pistachio nuts,
  shelled, peeled and
  chopped
grated rind of 1
  organic orange

continued over >>

The traditional Sicilian cassata *has an outer layer of Madeira cake covered with almond paste or sugar icing. Once when I was making this dish I didn't have time to make the Madeira cake. So when I served my version to a friend from northern Italy who is married to a dyed-in-the-wool Sicilian, I was delighted when she said 'Che bellezza – how lovely – it's* cassata, *but you don't have to munch through the boring outside layers before you get to the good part.'* Una cassata nuda – *a naked cassata – in fact.*

I also had to alter the usual cassata siciliana *recipe slightly in order to be able to turn the cake out. The result is, in fact, a hybrid, being part* cassata siciliana *and part Russian* pashka. *But it is a very successful hybrid.*

Buy the candied peel in large pieces, not the chopped-up kind. You can keep them, well sealed, in the freezer. The best rose water and orange water is sold in specialist Middle Eastern shops; neither is essential to the dish, but they give the right exotic flavour. The influence of Arabic cooking in Sicily is, after all, very important.

Shell the eggs and cut them in half. Scoop out the yolks, and set aside the whites for another meal (they are good added to any cooked vegetable salad). Purée the yolks through a food mill or a wire sieve into a large bowl.

Sieve the ricotta into the bowl in the same way.

Beat in the sugar, cinnamon, rose and orange water and then add the angelica, candied fruits, pistachios, grated zest and the liqueur. Mix very thoroughly.

Place the gelatine leaves in a dish and cover with cold water. Leave until soft and then squeeze them and dissolve them in the hot milk.

Butter a 20 cm (8 inch) spring-clip tin and line it with parchment paper.

Spoon a couple of tablespoons of the ricotta mixture into the gelatine and milk, mix very thoroughly and then transfer this mixture into the bowl with the rest of the ricotta mixture. Fold very thoroughly and at length.

Whip the cream until it forms very soft peaks and then fold it into the mixture, a few tablespoons at a time. When the mixture is beautifully blended, spoon it into the prepared tin. Cover with clingfilm and chill for at least 4 hours.

Remove the tin band and the paper from the side of the *cassata*. Place a large round dish over it and turn upside-down to unmould the cake. Remove the metal base and the paper. Serve chilled, and eat it within 2 days.

grated rind of 1 1/2 organic lemons
2 tbsp maraschino or Grand Marnier
4 gelatine leaves
4 tbsp full-fat milk, hot
200 ml (7 fl oz) whipping cream

sicilian cassata
cassata siciliana

This pudding is a pièce de resistance *of any dinner party. It is, to paraphrase the words of the song, 'lovely to look at, delightful to eat'. This is the authentic cassata siciliana, which has nothing to do with the ice-cream that has stolen its name.*

Make your own sponge cake or follow my recipe for fatless sponge on page 492, doubling the quantities. Buy fresh ricotta from a reputable

Serves 8
450 g (1 lb) ricotta
150 ml (1/4 pint) whipping cream

continued over >>

120 g (4 oz) caster
sugar
225 g (8 oz) candied
peel, chopped
1 tsp ground
cinnamon
75 g (2 1/2 oz) bitter
chocolate, chopped
30 g (1 oz) pistachio
nuts, blanched,
skinned and
chopped
120 ml (4 fl oz)
Marsala or rum
450 g sponge cake,
cut into 1 cm (1/2
inch) thick slices
225 g (8 oz) glacé
fruits

For the icing
375 g (13 oz) icing
sugar
2 tbsp water
1 tbsp lemon juice

shop with a quick turnover. Ask to taste it before you buy: ricotta should have no bitter flavour. Otherwise use the UHT ricotta now sold in pots in most supermarkets. I have added a little cream to the filling. This is not in the traditional recipe, but I feel that the ricotta available in Britain needs it.

Mix the ricotta thoroughly in a large bowl until smooth. Lightly whip the cream and fold into the ricotta with the sugar. Add the candied peel, cinnamon, chocolate, pistachios and half the Marsala or rum. Mix very thoroughly.

Line the base of a 20 cm (8 inch) spring-clip tin with parchment paper. Cover the base with slices of cake, plugging any holes with bits of cake. Moisten with some of the remaining Marsala or rum, using a pastry brush. Line the sides of the tin with the sliced cake and moisten with some more spirit. Spoon in the ricotta mixture, cover with a layer of sliced cake and moisten with the rest of the spirit. Cover with clingfilm and chill for at least 3 hours.

To make the icing, put 45 g (1 1/2 oz) of icing sugar and the water in a small heavy saucepan and bring slowly to the boil, stirring constantly. This stock syrup, as it is called, helps make the icing run evenly. Put the rest of the sugar in the top of a double-boiler, or into a saucepan that can fit inside a larger pan half full of simmering water. Add very gradually enough stock syrup to moisten and dilute to the consistency of double cream, working it well in with a wooden spoon. Add the lemon juice and continue cooking in the bain-marie until just warm.

Unmould the cake and slowly pour the icing on to the centre, letting it run all over the surface and down the sides.

Put the cake back in the refrigerator to allow the icing to set.

Just before serving, place the cake on a dish and decorate with the glacé fruits. Serve chilled.

If you have neither time nor inclination to make the icing, simply cover the cake with a lavish layer of sifted icing sugar just before serving and decorate with the glacé fruits.

preparation

Cassata must be made at least 8 hours before serving. If it is made with fresh ricotta it can be prepared up to 1 day in advance; if you are using UHT ricotta, you can make it up to 3 days in advance.

ricotta and almond cake with orange sauce
torta di ricotta e mandorle con la salsina di arancia

I am sure you must have eaten a ricotta pudding of one sort or another if you are at all keen on Italian cooking, as it is one of the most popular sweets with Italians. But I doubt if you have ever had one like this, where the ricotta absorbs the flavour of the almonds and the orange, one of the great duets in the culinary repertoire. The cake can be served as it is, when it is ideal with a cup of tea or with coffee and liqueur after dinner. But, when serving it at the end of a meal, I prefer to hand round this little orange sauce. Pouring cream is also good with it, especially if you flavour it with a couple of spoonfuls of Grand Marnier and sweeten it with icing sugar.

I prefer to buy unskinned almonds because they usually have more flavour. But you can of course buy the skinned ones and avoid the blanching and peeling.

Butter and line a 25 cm (8 inch) spring-clip tin with baking parchment.

Heat the oven to 180°C (350°F) mark 4.

Blanch the almonds (and bitter almonds, if used) for 30 seconds in boiling water. Peel them, dry them with kitchen paper and spread them out on an oven tray. Place the tray in the oven and leave it for about 10 minutes to bring out the flavour of the almonds. After that chop them in the food processor to a finely grained texture, though not so fine as ground almonds.

Serves 8
150 g (5 oz) almonds
3–4 drops pure almond essence, or 5 bitter almonds
450 g (1 lb) ricotta
150 g (5 oz) caster sugar
7 free-range eggs, separated
grated rind of 1 organic orange
3 tbsp Grand Marnier (optional)
75 g (2 1/2 oz) potato flour
icing sugar

For the orange sauce
3 large organic oranges
200 g (7 oz) granulated sugar
1/2 organic lemon

Push the ricotta through a food mill or a sieve into a bowl, add the sugar and beat hard until creamy and smooth. Mix in the almonds, the almond essence (if used) and the egg yolks, one by one, beating hard after each addition. Mix in the orange rind and the liqueur (if used).

Whisk the egg whites until stiff and fold into the ricotta mixture a little at a time, alternately with the potato flour. Use a metal spoon and a high movement to incorporate more air. Spoon the mixture into the prepared tin and bake for about 40 minutes or until set. A cocktail stick inserted into the middle of the cake should come out very lightly moist. Allow to cool in the tin and then remove onto a round dish. Sprinkle lavishly with icing sugar just before serving.

To make the orange sauce, wash and scrub the oranges thoroughly. Remove the rind, being very careful not to remove the pith while doing so. Cut the rind into julienne strips and put into a small saucepan. Cover with cold water, bring to the boil and cook until they are soft and slightly transparent. Drain.

Put the sugar and 4 tablespoons of water in the saucepan and bring very slowly to the boil. When the sugar has dissolved, add the juice of the oranges and of the half lemon. Stir in the strips of rind and simmer for a couple of minutes. Pour into a sauce-boat and serve cold.

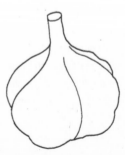

It is a delight to drive around some areas of Italy and enjoy the sight of fruit trees in beautiful straight lines either flowering or bearing fruit. Cherries, apricots, peaches, plums, apples and pears hang from loaded branches waiting to be gathered, inspected, put in boxes and sent all over Europe. Although so many different fruits grow in this orchard of Europe, other crops – some of them new – tend to be concentrated in particular areas. I was surprised to see plantations of persimmons growing near Nocera, to the south of Naples, a fruit that was rare before the war. The fashionable explosion of the kiwi has produced acres of land in Venezia Giulia and Puglia given up to the cultivation of this fruit – totally unknown in Italy until the seventies. Citrus fruits and almonds thrive best in the South, while the cultivation of raspberries, currants and other soft fruits takes place mainly in the North. Grapes, of course, are everywhere. 'Even the rocks were mantled with vines' was one of William Beckford's first impressions on arriving at Bolzano in the eighteenth century. Later on, in Venice, he loved to look out of his window on to the Grand Canal at dawn to see the barges carrying loads of grapes, peaches and melons to the Rialto market, a sight still to be enjoyed by today's early riser.

It was Beckford again who remarked that in Italy 'all meals finish with several dishes of fruit', and this, too, has not changed in two centuries. A meal nearly always ends with a bowl of seasonal fruit set in the middle of the table. It is only on special occasions that fruit is used to provide a different ending to the meal, usually as the flavouring for an ice-cream or sorbet or very occasionally poached to flavour savoury dishes. This was a practice much in use in the past and it is now being resuscitated by chefs who are turning to previous centuries for new ideas.

In what follows I have kept to the fruits that I connect particularly with Italy, fruits that I love for their taste and their looks and that are strongly redolent of the Mediterranean. There is one fruit, however, that I have not included even though it is one of my favourites – the fig. This is simply because I think figs should be eaten where they grow, preferably popping them straight from the tree into one's mouth, still warm from the sun. This, at any rate, is the best way to eat them, without any cream or anything else. The other acceptable thing to do with figs is to serve them with salame, *prosciutto* or *coppa*, or a mixture of all three.

peaches

The peach is a native of China, where its fruit and flowers were regarded as sacred. It reached Greece via Persia, thanks to Alexander the Great, hence the botanical name *Prunus persica*. The Romans introduced the peach tree throughout their empire, and peaches have been cultivated in Great Britain since that time. During the Renaissance, peaches, like all fruit, were often used in savoury dishes. And they were appreciated for their beauty as well as for their flavour, often forming part of the elaborate table decorations that were a feature of Renaissance banquets.

Peaches are the most beautiful and the most delicious of all fruits. The greatest delight among peaches are the small *pesche da vigna*, so called because, in the days before concrete posts, they grew on the trees that were used to support the vines. These small white peaches ripen late, at the same time as the grapes, and their flavour has been intensified by a full summer of hot sun. They are covered with a greyish-green down and their flesh is a pale vermilion all through to the stone. Another variety which has become comparatively rare is the white peach, so much more succulent than the usual yellow peach.

Some yellow peaches are better stewed, or macerated in wine or in lemon and orange juice and sugar, sometimes mixed with the last strawberries of the season. You can ripen them a little more by keeping them for a day or two on a sunny window-sill. Some people keep them in the fridge once they are ripe. I am against this because their flavour, instead of developing, is deadened. Nor do I like chilled fruit.

The nectarine is a variety of peach, but with a smooth skin rather than the downy skin of other peaches. In Italian it is called *pesca noce* – walnut peach – perhaps because of its shape.

To peel peaches and nectarines plunge them in boiling water for 20 seconds and then refresh them straight away in cold water.

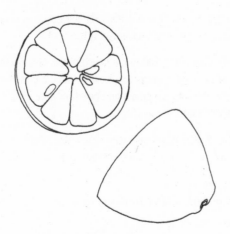

peach mould
budino alla pesca

I love the peach mould, but then I love peaches. I am not sure to what degree my love of peaches is tied up with memories of my Italian childhood, but, be that as it may, this delicious pudding is not here merely to assuage my nostalgia. It calls for peaches that are full of flavour, so buy white peaches if you can. They are usually more fragrant than yellow ones, but unfortunately they are rarer.

If the peaches are really ripe they should peel quite easily. Otherwise put them in a bowl and cover them with boiling water. Leave them for about 20 seconds and then refresh them under cold water. Peel them and cut them in half, removing the stones.

Serves 6
700 g (1 1/2 lb) ripe peaches, preferably white
150 g (5 oz) caster sugar
150 ml (1/4 pint) sweet white wine
4 gelatine leaves
juice of 1 organic lemon
200 ml (7 fl oz) double cream
225 g (8 oz) strawberries for garnish

Poach the peaches with the sugar in white wine until tender. Leave to cool and then purée them coarsely in a food mill set with a large-hole disc. Alternatively, you can mash them up with a fork, or whiz them in a food processor.

Soak the gelatine leaves in cold water until soft and then dissolve them in 2 tablespoons of the lemon juice over a low heat.

Partly whip the cream and add to the peach purée. Mix a couple of tablespoons of the cream and peach mixture into the dissolved gelatine and then spoon this into the cream and peach mixture. Fold in very thoroughly with a metal spoon.

Wet a 1.2 litre (2 pint) ring-mould with cold water. Spoon the peach mixture into the mould and chill for at least 4 hours.

Wash and dry the strawberries. Put them in a bowl and sprinkle with 1 tablespoon of sugar and the remaining lemon juice. Cover the bowl and chill.

To unmould, run a palette knife down the side of the mould. Put a round dish over the mould and turn the mould over. If the pudding does not drop, place a cloth soaked with hot water over the mould and give the mould a few sharp jerks. You should now be able to lift the mould off the pudding.

Put some strawberries in the middle of the ring and others around the dish for decoration.

preparation
The pudding can be prepared up to 1 day in advance and refrigerated. The strawberries must be prepared no longer than 2–3 hours in advance or they will 'cook' in the lemon juice.

meringued peaches
pesche in camicia

In this sweet, the poached peaches are in camicia, *dressed in a white shirt, the shirt being the meringue covering. When you eat them you break through the lemony, sugary meringue into the flowery flavour of the peaches. For meringues, remember to use egg whites at room temperature, not straight from the fridge.*

Peel the peaches. If they are rather hard, put them in boiling water for 20 seconds and then plunge them into a bowl of cold water.

Choose a large sauté pan in which the peaches can fit snugly.

Make a syrup with the granulated sugar, wine, lemon juice and 150 ml (1/4 pint) of water. Boil the syrup for about 3 minutes. Add the peaches and cook over a very low heat with the lid on until they are soft, about 10–15 minutes. Lift the peaches out of the juices and leave them to cool. Taste the juices and if necessary boil rapidly for a few minutes until rich and tasty. Pour the juices into a little jug. Chill the peaches for at least 2 hours.

About 1 hour before serving, heat the oven to 150°C (300°F) mark 2. Whip the egg whites until stiff. Add about one-third of the caster sugar and whip again. The mixture will become beautifully shiny. Now fold in the remaining sugar and the grated lemon rind, using a large metal spoon.

Line an oven tray with baking parchment. Roll each peach in the meringue and place on the tray. Patch up any spots of naked peach with a little meringue. Place the tray in the oven and bake until the meringue has set and is golden on top, about 15–20 minutes.

Transfer the peaches to individual plates and place a leaf of lemon balm or mint on each peach. Hand round the jug of peach syrup.

preparation
The peaches can be cooked up to 4 days in advance and chilled in a covered box. They can also be frozen. You cannot bake the peaches in the meringue covering too long in advance or the meringue will be made soggy by the peach juices. Leave the baking of the meringue until about an hour and a half before beginning the meal. Do not refrigerate the meringued peaches because the humidity in the fridge will spoil the meringue.

Serves 8
8 firm but ripe peaches, all of the same size
120 g (4 oz) granulated sugar
150 ml (1/4 pint) sweet white wine
juice of 1 organic lemon
lemon balm or mint leaves to garnish

For the meringue
2 egg whites
100 g (3 1/2 oz) caster sugar
grated rind of 1 organic lemon

peaches with raspberry sauce
pesche al sugo di lampone

Serves 8
**8 or 9 large yellow
peaches, ripe but
firm**
**7 tbsp dry white
wine**
4 tbsp caster sugar

For the sauce
**450 g (1 lb) fresh
raspberries**
**150 g (5 oz) icing
sugar, sifted**
**juice of 1 organic
lemon**
**4 young sweet
geranium leaves,
torn into small
pieces (optional)**

*Peaches come into season when raspberries are plentiful. This is a
good mix.*

Peel the peaches with a small sharp knife. If the skin does not come
away easily, plunge the peaches into boiling water for 30 seconds
and then straight into cold water. Cut the peaches into segments of
about 2 cm (3/4 inch) each. Lay the segments, overlapping, in a deep
dish.

Mix together the wine and the sugar and spoon over the peaches.
Cover with clingfilm and refrigerate for at least 2 hours.

Now make the sauce by simply blending together the raspberries,
icing sugar, lemon juice and the optional sweet geranium leaves in
the food processor or blender. Taste and add more sugar and/or
lemon juice according to taste. If you want a smooth sauce, strain it
through a fine sieve, pushing the purée with a spoon. I like it as it is,
with a coarser consistency. Transfer the sauce to a bowl, cover with
clingfilm and chill.

Just before serving, mask the peach segments with some sauce and
serve the rest of the sauce separately in a bowl.

preparation
The raspberry sauce can be prepared up to 2 days in advance and
kept in the fridge in an airtight container. It also freezes very well, but
do not leave it for longer than 2 months.

I prefer to prepare the peaches no longer than 4 hours in advance
because I do not like their appearance if they stay too long in the
wine.

pears stewed in red wine with liqueur-flavoured cream

pere alla crema del lario

This pudding has an intriguing name – Lario is another name for Lake Como, the lake that was a fashionable resort for the English upper class up to the Great War. They must have taught their local cook how to prepare syllabub and she, like any self-respecting cook, decided to add her personal touch. In this case it was the pears, which lighten the cream, and the flavouring of the cream to go with them.

Peel the pears, cut them in quarters and remove the cores. To prevent discoloration, drop them immediately into a bowl of cold water to which a few drops of lemon juice have been added.

Put half the sugar and the cinnamon in the wine and heat gently until the sugar has dissolved. Add the pears and cook until tender, about 10–15 minutes.

While the pears are cooling, mix the remaining sugar and the lemon rind and add the lemon juice and the liqueur. Stir until the sugar has dissolved. Whip the cream until it forms stiff peaks and then slowly fold the liqueur mixture into it.

Lift the pears out of the wine syrup (you can use the syrup to flavour a fruit salad) and place 2 quarters in each individual glass bowl. Spoon over the cream and chill for at least 1 hour.

preparation

The pears can be cooked up to 3 days in advance and refrigerated but the pudding must be finished no longer than 1 hour before serving.

Serves 4

2 ripe but firm pears
grated rind and juice of 1/2 organic lemon
165 g (5 1/2 oz) caster sugar
1 cinnamon stick, about 2.5 cm (1 inch) long
200 ml (7 fl oz) good red wine
2 tbsp Poire William eau-de-vie or Italian Grappa alla Pera
300 ml (1/2 pint) whipping cream

sharon fruits with lime juice
cachi al sugo di lime

Serves 8
a dozen Sharon fruits
4 limes
3 or 4 tbsp caster
sugar, according to
taste and the
sweetness of the
fruit

Sharon fruits, which were developed in the Sharon Valley in Israel, are one of the few fruits to have improved a lot in recent years. They are similar to Japanese persimmons but with the advantage that they can be eaten when still firm, as opposed to persimmons which are mouth-contorting if not perfectly ripe. Thus you can eat Sharon fruits, skin and all, as a salad, dressed with a light lemon and oil sauce, or as a dessert dressed with cream and/or yoghurt.

Wash the Sharon fruits very thoroughly and dry them well. Slice them as you would an orange and lay the slices, slightly overlapping, on a dish or on individual plates.

One hour before you want to eat them, squeeze the limes and pour the juice over the Sharon fruits. Sprinkle with the sugar and leave in the fridge, covered with clingfilm, until you want to serve them.

preparation
The fruits can be cut a few hours in advance and arranged on the serving dish. The dressing must be spooned over no more than 1 hour before serving or the Sharon fruits will macerate.

melon

'Three things in life are difficult: picking a good wife, choosing a good horse and buying a good melon.' Thus wrote Francesco Sforza, Duke of Milan, in the fifteenth century. And to buy a good melon is just as difficult in the twenty-first century. To look at a melon tells you nothing. If it has a scent that is a good sign, although there are some delicious melons with no smell at all until they are opened. A good melon should be heavy; when you buy a melon, take two equal-sized ones, put one in each hand and go for the heavier.

The melons of Italy are the *napoletano*, a yellowy-green melon, oval in cross-section, with bright orange pulp, and the well-known cantaloupe. In Italy, melons are usually eaten with prosciutto or with a lovely dish of cured meats (see page 178). It is probably the best marriage for a good melon and it is also the healthiest. Melons are very indigestible and 'should always be eaten at the beginning of the meal followed by a glass of good wine', wrote Platina in the fourteenth century. But I find that, when good and sweet, they also go well at the end of a meal, as in the following recipe.

melon in apple syrup
melone al sugo di mela

I had this dish at dinner with our friend Mary Trevelyan. Mary is a natural cook, almost as creative with her pots and pans as she is with her paintbrushes. She 'invented' this melon salad just before we arrived, and brought it to the table in one of her beautiful pottery bowls.

There is nothing Italian about the recipe except that, for me, good melons, full of flavour, bring back such strong memories of blue skies, hot sun and heady Mediterranean smells. It is also one of the finest ways to end a meal.

For 4 people you will need a fragrant ripe melon, or 2 smaller ones. Discard the skin and seeds and cut the melon into small cubes. Make a syrup with 300 ml (1/2 pint) of unsweetened apple juice and some sugar. The quantity of sugar needed depends on the sweetness of the melon, the sharpness of the apple juice and, of course, your personal taste. Heat the syrup until the sugar has dissolved. I add a little lemon juice to give the salad a slight edge.

Pour the syrup over the melon no more than 1 hour before serving; serve well chilled. You will love it.

plums in wine syrup with rosemary and spices
prugne sciroppate al rosmarino

Serves 6
300 ml (1/2 pint) good red wine
225 g (8 oz) caster sugar
1 sprig of fresh rosemary, about 15 cm (6 inches) long
1 strip of organic lemon rind, the yellow part only
2 cloves
1 cinnamon stick, about 5 cm (2 inches) long
4 peppercorns, bruised
1 kg (2 lb) plums, ripe but firm

Like several other dishes, zabaione *and* tarte Tatin *among them, these poached plums owe their origin to a mistake. Many years ago I had two saucepans on the stove, one with some plums that were gently stewing away, the other with some potatoes that were being briskly sautéed. The usual untimely and insistent ringing of the telephone took me out of the kitchen. I shouted to my little daughter to go and pick a sprig of rosemary from the garden and put it into the pan . . . but which pan I forgot to specify. Back in the kitchen after my chat on the phone, I found the rosemary in with the plums! To my surprise and relief, the plums were delicious, and since then I have always added fresh rosemary to poached plums.*

The rosemary is hardly detectable, yet it gives the juices of the fruit a delicious je ne sais quoi *which never fails to puzzle people. When you serve the dish, try asking your guests what has gone into it. You can bet for high stakes and you will win!*

Put the wine, sugar, 300 ml (1/2 pint) of water, the rosemary, lemon rind, cloves, cinnamon and peppercorns in a large sauté pan. Heat gently until the sugar has dissolved, stirring frequently with a wooden spoon.

Wash the plums and add to the pan. Cover with a tight-fitting lid and cook very gently until the plums are soft but still whole. Transfer the plums to a bowl with a slotted spoon.

Strain the syrup into a clean saucepan and boil very rapidly until it is thick and syrupy. Pour over the plums and, when cold, cover with clingfilm and refrigerate.

plums baked in wine
prugne al vino

In Italy plums, like all other fruit, are mainly eaten raw. But for that they must be ripe and of the best quality. If they don't come up to that, as is often the case, I prefer to cook them. The plums release more flavour through the heating and the wine enhances their flavour while adding a special note of its own.

This pudding consists of plums that are stewed in wine and then served hot with the ricotta or mascarpone ice-cream on pages 325 and 323 respectively. With the ice-cream, the pudding rises to a different plane and becomes an exquisite combination of flavours. The ice-cream melts in contact with the hot fruit, so that the plums float in a rich, velvety white sauce. This ice-cream has the further advantage that it can be made without an ice-cream machine. I prefer to bake the plums rather than stewing them in a pan because they keep their shape much better: they swell up during the cooking and look very round and smooth. To preserve this look you should catch them just before the skin bursts.

Heat the oven to 170°C (325°F) mark 3.

Wash the plums and put them in a shallow ovenproof dish large enough to contain them in a single layer.

In a saucepan heat the wine, sugar, peppercorns, bay leaves and cinnamon. It is difficult to give a right amount of sugar, but if the plums are ripe and good, this amount should be enough. When the wine is just boiling, pour it over the plums. Cover the dish with foil and tie the foil under the rim of the dish. Put the dish in the oven and bake for 20–30 minutes. Check after 20 minutes; the plums should be just soft, but whole, and beautifully plumped up. When they are ready, taste one plum and if not sweet enough add a little more sugar.

preparation
The plums can be cooked in advance and refrigerated for up to 5–6 days, or you can freeze them. Reheat in a moderate oven for 10 minutes just before serving.

Serves 8
1 kg (2 lb) red plums
300 ml (1/2 pint) dry
   white wine
200 g (7 oz) sugar
10 peppercorns
2 bay leaves
1/2 tsp ground
   cinnamon

cherries stewed in wine
ciliege cotte al vino

Serves 8
1 kg (2 lb) cherries
600 ml (1 pint) good
   red wine
325 g (11 oz)
   granulated sugar
1–2 tsp fennel seeds
1/2 tbsp peppercorns
2 bay leaves

I find cherries the most 'moreish' of all food. But they have to be good – sweet, yes, but with the right amount of acidity which makes all fruit different from a sweetie.

Cherries are also the prettiest of fruit. When I was a young girl I used to put a pair of cherries over my ears. I suppose I must have seen, or heard of girls in village fêtes dangling little bunches of cherries over their ears, not only for the look but also for daring young men to come and nibble the fruit.

Until a few years ago cherries had a season. The appearance of the first cherries in the shops signalled the beginning of summer. And the shops were full of them, in all colours from the pale orange and yellow Duracine to the deep bluey-red Duroni di Vignola – my favourites. With luck, you can still find some good cherries in the market. In that case, buy them and eat them as they are. If less good try to poach them as in the recipe below, a method that helps to bring out the evanescent flavour.

Wash the cherries and remove the stalks. Make a syrup with the wine and the sugar in a large heavy sauté pan. Boil gently for 3 minutes. Pound the fennel seeds and add to the syrup with the peppercorns and bay leaves. Now stir in the cherries and cook gently for 20 minutes.

Remove the cherries with a slotted spoon and put them in a glass bowl. Taste the syrup and, if necessary, boil fast to make it stronger and more full of flavour. Leave to cool and then pour over the cherries through a strainer. Cover with clingfilm and refrigerate.

morello cherry jam tart
crostata di conserva di amarena

Morello cherries are a variety of sour cherry, and they are mostly used in cooking and for making jams. They have a deep red colour and, when ripe, they are also delicious raw. In this recipe the morello cherry jam is used to fill a tart, a crostata in Italian, which is the only traditional pastry dish in the Italian cuisine.

To make the pastry, pile the flour on a work surface. Mix in the salt, sugar and lemon rind and rub in the butter. Add the egg yolks and work quickly to form a ball. If you prefer, make the pastry in a food processor. Wrap in foil and chill for at least 30 minutes.

Heat the oven to 200°C (400°F) mark 6.

Butter a 20 or 22 cm (8 or 9 inch) tart tin with a loose bottom and sprinkle with 1 tablespoon of flour. Shake off the excess flour.

Remove the dough from the fridge. Put aside about one-third and roll out the rest into a circle. Line the prepared tin with the circle of dough and press it down firmly into the angle between the base and the side. Sprinkle the ground almonds over the bottom.

Put the jam in a bowl and mix in the lemon juice. Spread the jam over the circle of dough. Roll out the reserved dough and cut several strips about 1 cm (1/2 inch) wide. Place these strips over the tart to form a lattice that goes right across the tart. Don't worry if you have to make one or two joins in the strips: once the tart is baked the joins won't show. Brush the pastry lattice with the egg yolk and milk glaze.

Bake in the preheated oven for about 10 minutes. Turn the heat down to 180°C (350°F) mark 4 and bake for a further 20 minutes until the pastry turns a lovely light golden brown. Remove from the tin and transfer to a wire rack to cool. In Italy, as indeed in France, tarts are served without cream.

preparation
Make the *crostata* on the day you want to eat it. The pastry can be made up to 2 days in advance and refrigerated, wrapped in foil. It also freezes well.

Serves 6–8
For the pastry
225 g (8 oz) Italian 00 flour
1/2 tsp sea salt
100 g (5 1/2 oz) granulated sugar
grated rind of 1/2 an organic lemon
120 g (4 oz) cold unsalted butter
2 free-range egg yolks

For the filling
4 tbsp ground almonds
350 g (12 oz) morello cherry or damson jam
juice of 1/2 an organic lemon
1 egg yolk and 2 tbsp of milk for glazing

oranges

When I was in an orange grove in Sicily some years ago it struck me how much less attractive a place it must have been before the Saracens invaded the island over 1,000 years ago. As I walked, the air in the groves was still, and heavy with the scent of the white blossom, while every now and then there was a tree still spangled with bright oranges hanging among the dark green leaves. For it was the Saracens who first brought the orange tree to Sicily; it was the *Citrus aurantium*, or bitter orange, grown for use as a flavouring rather than for eating as a fruit.

The orange soon became the symbol of riches, so much so that the Medici incorporated it in their coat of arms: the five golden balls are oranges. John MacPhee, in his book *Oranges*, describes a banquet given by the Archbishop of Milan in 1529: '. . . sixteen courses that included caviar and oranges fried with sugar and cinnamon, brill and sardines with slices of orange and lemon, oysters with pepper and oranges, lobsters with citrons, sturgeon in aspic covered with orange juice, fried sparrows with oranges, individual salads containing citrons into which the coat of arms of the diner had been carved, a soufflé of pine nuts and raisins covered with orange juice, and candied peel of citron and orange.'

Nowadays the bitter orange is not cultivated for culinary use – Italians do not make marmalade (a great failing). It is grown as a decorative tree or for the extraction of oil. If you are in Rome in the winter, go to the *Giardino degli Aranci*, the orange tree garden on the Avellino hill. You will enjoy an hour of utter peace while admiring Rome at your feet and gathering the windfall oranges for your marmalade.

The *Citrus sinensis*, the sweet orange, arrived much later. It was introduced to Europe, via India, by the Portuguese in the seventeenth century. It began to appear in eighteenth-century books under the name of *arancia del Portogallo* and continued to be referred to by that name as late as the nineteenth century. At first sweet oranges were used only for making drinks; these were very expensive, and only wealthy people could quench their thirst with a glass of orange juice. By the beginning of the nineteenth century, however, sweet oranges were widely grown in Sicily and southern Italy, and the orange became the popular fruit it is today.

how to buy and prepare oranges

Today oranges are the world's most widely cultivated fruit. There are a vast number of varieties, among which the Sicilian *tarocco* and *sanguinello* are the most highly regarded. These are certainly my favourites, sweet yet with just enough acidity to make your tongue tingle. Another favourite kind are the late Spanish blood oranges, small and juicy and brimming with the perfect orange flavour. You might find that your favourite variety is from Mexico, from Spain or from Jaffa, this last being one of the largest and best-looking oranges, although I find its flavour rather uninteresting.

The best oranges are thin-skinned, just soft to the touch, yet full and heavy – all characteristics that mean they are juicy. To get more juice out of an orange or a lemon, pour boiling water over it; it will also help if you roll it backwards and forwards on a hard surface, or you can microwave it for 30 seconds.

If you want to use the zest for puddings or marmalades you must buy organic oranges, or at least unwaxed.

Candied peel is easy enough to make and is so much nicer than any you can buy. It is a necessary ingredient in many traditional Italian sweets. *Cassata siciliana*, *zuccotto* from Florence, *panforte sienese*, *panettone* from Milan . . . none would be what it is without citron, orange and lemon peel cut into juicy pieces.

The white pith should be left on; it is deliciously bitter and it contains riboflavin, which is good for you. Remove the peel of the oranges (lemons and grapefruits are excellent too) in neat segments and plunge it into boiling water. Boil until tender. Drain and refresh, then boil again in fresh water for a further 15 minutes or so to get rid of all the bitterness. Make a syrup with sugar and half its quantity of water. Add the peel and simmer until all the syrup has been absorbed. Spread the peel on oiled trays, or trays lined with greaseproof paper, and dry in an airing cupboard or a very low oven, turning the pieces over every now and then. When the peel is properly dry, sprinkle it with caster sugar and store in an airtight jar

strawberries with orange
fragole all'arancia

Serves 6
2 large organic
  oranges
450 g (1 lb)
  strawberries
60 g (2 oz) caster
  sugar
juice of 1 organic
  lemon
5 tbsp sweet white
  wine, such as
  Moscato
sprigs of fresh mint
  or lemon balm to
  decorate

In this recipe the fragrance of the strawberries is intensified by the sharpness of the citrus fruits and the wine. With its clean fresh taste, this is the perfect finale to a meal when British strawberries are in season.

Peel the oranges to the quick and cut the flesh into thin slices. Put aside a few of the best slices for decoration, and cut the other slices in half, or quarters if very large. Put these slices in a glass bowl.

Rinse the strawberries very quickly under cold water and then dry them and hull them. Cut any large strawberries in two, or four, and add to the orange slices in the bowl.

Put the sugar and 120ml (4 fl oz) water in a small saucepan and heat slowly until the sugar has dissolved. Raise the heat and boil for 5 minutes. Draw off the heat and leave to cool.

Add the lemon juice and the wine to the syrup. Mix well and pour over the fruit. Cover the bowl with clingfilm and refrigerate for about 1 hour. Do not leave in the fridge for much longer than an hour or the strawberries will macerate too much. Place the reserved orange slices on the top before bringing the bowl to the table and decorate with the mint or lemon balm.

caramelised oranges
arance caramellate

Serves 8
10–12 thin-skinned
  organic oranges,
  seedless if possible
200 g (7 oz)
  granulated sugar
4 tbsp Grand Marnier
  or Cointreau

In the past, in an Italian restaurant, a familiar sight used to be oranges in a syrup covered with caramelised strips of rind. More recently they have gone out of fashion, which is a pity because they were good. This is my version of that dish, where the oranges are served already sliced and not whole.

Wash the oranges and dry thoroughly. Remove the zest of 3 of the oranges very thinly, leaving all the pith on the fruit. Cut 3 strips of skin from a fourth orange. Put all the oranges in the freezer to harden while you make the syrup.

Cut the zest from the 3 oranges into julienne strips about 2.5 cm (1 inch) long and put them in boiling water. Boil for 5 minutes to get rid of the bitter taste. Drain and refresh under cold water and set aside.

Put the sugar, the 3 orange strips and 150 ml (1/4 pint) of water in a small saucepan and cook over a low heat. When the syrup begins to boil, turn the heat up slightly and continue boiling until the syrup begins to turn pale gold at the edge of the pan. Now remove the orange strips and add the juliennes. Boil for 5 minutes, stirring constantly, until the juliennes become slightly transparent and syrupy-looking. Add the liqueur, stir and draw off the heat.

Take the oranges out of the freezer and peel carefully with a small sharp knife, removing every scrap of pith. Cut the oranges across into thin slices and put them in a glass bowl or deep dish. Do this over a plate so that you can collect the juice and pour it over the oranges at the end.

Spoon the syrup and the juliennes over the oranges and chill for at least 2 hours.

preparation
You can cut the oranges and make the syrup up to 1 day in advance, and keep, covered, in the fridge. Pour the syrup over the oranges no longer than 6 hours before serving them.

pineapple and oranges
ananas e arance

Serves 6
1 large ripe pineapple
6 large organic oranges
2 tbsp caster sugar

Peel the pineapple and slice thickly. Peel the oranges to the quick (i.e. removing all the pith as well) and slice the flesh. Remove any pips.

Put the pineapple slices on a large dish. I use a round dish so that everything is round. Cover each pineapple slice with a slice of orange and sprinkle with the sugar. Cover with clingfilm and refrigerate. Serve straight from the refrigerator.

preparation
You can prepare this dish about 6 hours in advance.

oranges and kiwi fruit
arance e kiwi

Serves 8
a dozen large organic oranges
8 kiwi fruit
caster sugar to taste

Cut both ends off the oranges and stand them on one end. Place each orange on a plate to collect the juice, remove the skin and white pith with a sharp knife by cutting off the skin downwards. Then slice the oranges horizontally.

Set aside the smaller slices for another occasion. Allowing 3–4 slices per person, lay the large central slices on a large round dish.

Peel the kiwi fruits and slice them across. Lay a slice of kiwi fruit on each orange slice, matching the sizes as much as you can.

Pour over the juice that has collected from the oranges and sprinkle with a little sugar if you wish. Cover the dish with clingfilm and refrigerate.

preparation
You can prepare this dish up to 6 hours in advance and keep refrigerated until required.

lemons

I feel totally lost when I discover I haven't got a single lemon in the larder. Like onions and garlic, lemons are an essential adjunct to my cooking, as they are for all Italians.

Lemons play a larger part in Italian cooking than any other fruit. Grated lemon rind is added to many meat dishes, to poultry and vegetable stuffings, to most cakes and biscuits, to fruit compôtes, custards and creams. The juice is used as a condiment in salads and in sweet and savoury sauces, and it is added to fish and meat dishes. One of the most succulent ways to cook a chicken is to rub it hard with lemon and then put another lemon, cut in half, perhaps with some garlic, into its cavity. And I always rub a rabbit with half a lemon before I cook it. When I heat mussels or clams to take them out of their shells, I put one or two lemons, cut in wedges, at the bottom of the pan: the lemon imparts flavour to the molluscs and also helps to kill any bacteria. Two recipes with lemons that have recently become fashionable are for tagliatelle and risotto. You will find the delightfully fresh recipe for risotto on page 56. The tagliatelle are easily made; they are dressed with a little sauce made with butter, cream and lemon juice.

I always splash raspberries, strawberries and all other soft fruit with lemon juice to emphasise their flavour, except when I feel extravagant and use *aceto balsamico*. The same effect of enhancing flavour is produced by adding a tablespoon or two of lemon juice to any fruit purée or juice prepared for ice-creams and water-ices. The lemon juice also helps to prevent crystals forming. Any fruit salad is improved by being splashed with lemon juice an hour or so before serving, while tropical fruits and pomegranates need it even more to compensate for the lack of flavour of the fruit you buy in Britain.

When you slice apples and pears, when you prepare globe or Jerusalem artichokes or cardoons, rub the cut parts with half a lemon to prevent them discolouring. Rub your hands too, to prevent them being blackened before you start preparing these or any other vegetables. Never throw away halves of lemon; keep them on the sink to whiten your hands, to strengthen your nails and to cleanse them of any unpleasant smell.

You will be able to squeeze more juice out of a lemon if, before you cut it in half, you pour boiling water over it and leave it for a couple of minutes.

It will also help to roll it backwards and forwards on the work surface to soften it, or to microwave it for 30 seconds. If, however, you only want a few drops of juice, do not cut the lemon in half, but pierce it with a toothpick in two or three places and squeeze. Enough juice will come out.

When you buy lemons choose the largest you can find. Go for the softer yet full ones with a smooth skin.

My final word is of warning about the use of the rind of most lemons available nowadays. Lemons, like all other citrus fruits, are heavily sprayed with fungicides and pesticides, which penetrate their skin. They are also waxed. Whenever you want to use the rind, even if you only want to put a little slice into a drink, you must buy only organic fruit or scrub the fruit thoroughly. I use bicarbonate of soda and water. Other people use salt, or vinegar and water, or household soap and water.

lemon-flavoured egg and parmesan soup
stracciatella al sapor di limone

Serves 8
3 free-range eggs
4 tbsp semolina
6 tbsp freshly grated
Parmesan
sea salt and freshly
ground pepper,
preferably white
grated rind of 1
organic lemon
2.3 litres (4 pints)
meat stock (see
page 485)
handful of fresh
marjoram leaves

Stracciatella *is a traditional soup from Rome. Here I mix in a little grated lemon rind for a fresher touch.*

Beat the eggs lightly in a bowl. Add the semolina, Parmesan, salt and pepper and the grated lemon rind. Beat thoroughly with a fork.

Heat the stock to simmering point. Pour a couple of ladlefuls over the egg mixture, whisking with a fork or a balloon wire whisk.

Turn the heat down to low and pour the egg mixture into the stock. Cook for 5 minutes, whisking the whole time. Taste and adjust the seasoning. The egg mixture will curdle and form soft flakes. Ladle the soup into individual bowls and add the washed and dried marjoram leaves.

zabaglione with strawberry purée
zabaione con la purè di fragole

Zabaglione is lovely, but I find it very tiresome to have to get up from
the table and retire into the kitchen to make it. I prefer cold zabaglione,
which is also less rich, especially when mixed with the tanginess of
fresh fruit. You can leave the strawberries whole and mix them in just
before serving, but I prefer to purée them beforehand. The flavour of
the fruit is better distributed and the zabaglione looks stunning. If you
are careful not to blend the purée in too thoroughly the result is much
prettier, looking like Verona marble, pink and yellow. You can then
decorate it with a few whole strawberries.

Serves 6
**4 free-range egg
yolks
150 g (5 oz) caster
sugar
150 ml (1/4 pint)
Moscato or sweet
white wine
150 ml (1/4 pint)
whipping cream
450 g (1 lb)
strawberries
3 tbsp icing sugar
4 tbsp orange juice**

Beat the yolks with 100 g (3 1/2 oz) of the caster sugar. Add 120 ml
(4 fl oz) of the Moscato and heat, whisking constantly, in a bain-
marie until thick and frothy. Do not boil or the yolks will curdle. Set
aside to cool.

Whip the cream and fold into the zabaglione.

Blend two-thirds of the strawberries with the icing sugar in a food
processor and then press through a sieve to eliminate the seeds.
Marinate the rest of the strawberries with the remaining caster sugar,
the orange juice and the remaining wine for about half an hour.

Fold the strawberry purée into the zabaglione and mix a little so that
the mixture is marbled. Transfer to 6 chilled glasses and decorate with
the marinated strawberries.

preparation
The fruit purée can be made up to 2 days in advance and refrigerated.
It also freezes well. Make the zabaglione and fold in the purée up to 1
day in advance and keep in the fridge. Do not marinate the
strawberries for longer than 2 hours or they will become mushy.

italian shortbread biscuits
la fugascina

Makes 40 biscuits
**300 g (10 oz) Italian
00 flour
150 g (5 oz) unsalted
butter, cut into
small pieces
pinch of sea salt
150 g (5 oz) caster
sugar
2 free-range egg
yolks
grated zest of 1
organic lemon
oil for greasing**

Fugascina *is a dialect name for small* focaccia, *the dialect being that of the province of Novara. This recipe was given to me by a friend, Grazia Lucchese, who makes* fugascina *and* torta di mele – *apple cake – for the Saint's day of her village, Germano, high above Lake Orta. When I asked her when the Saint's day was, she answered:* 'Oh, c'è n'è uno al mese. Se non c'è, lo si inventa'. *('There's one a month. And if there isn't one we invent it.') The children carry all the offerings of food in procession to the church, where, after the Mass, the food is auctioned for the Church charities. Grazia was very proud that her* fugascina *was once knocked down for 40,000 lire, about £18. A stratospheric price, you will agree, when you read the recipe.*

Fugascina *is traditionally flavoured with grated lemon rind, which is the most common flavouring in cakes all over Italy. I sometimes substitute 1 tablespoon of* Vinsanto *or* Marsala *for the lemon rind.*

Make the sweet pastry, flavoured with the lemon rind, in your usual way, either by hand or in the food processor.

Take a large baking tray. Turn it over and lightly grease the bottom all over with oil. I use groundnut oil because it has a high burning point. The reason for oiling the underside of the tray will be apparent when you read on.

Put the ball of pastry on the oiled side of the tray and spread it out with the palm of your hand. Then, to spread it more evenly and more thinly, roll it out with a small bottle filled with hot water. It should be rolled out to a thickness of 3 mm (1/8 inch). Make lines with the blunt edge of a knife to mark out the shape of the biscuits; traditionally they are made into 5 cm (2 inch) squares. Put the tray in the fridge and chill for 30 minutes.

Heat the oven to 190°C (375°F) mark Gas 5.

Bake the *fugascina* in the preheated oven for about 15 minutes until gold.

Now comes the reason for using the bottom of the tray. Stretch a thick cotton thread across the width of the tray at one end, place it between the tray and the *fugascina* and, keeping it taut, pull it along the length of the tray, thus separating the *fugascina* from the tray. Had you used the top of the tray, the raised lip all round would have made this operation impossible.

Cut through the marked lines, and when the biscuits have cooled just a little put them on a wire rack.

autumnal fruit salad
insalata autunnale di frutta

Put the wine, honey, lemon juice and rind, and the spices in a saucepan. Bring to the boil and simmer very gently for 20 minutes.

Meanwhile put the prunes in a bowl. Cover with hot tea and leave to soak for 20 minutes.

Soak the sultanas, apricots and figs or dates in warm water for 15 minutes, then dry thoroughly and cut the apricots and figs into strips. If you are using dates instead of figs, remove the stones and cut into smaller strips. Do the same to the prunes.

Peel the apples and pears, cut into small cubes and put in a saucepan. Pour over the wine mixture and cook gently until the fruit is tender. Add the dried fruit, the almonds and the pine nuts. Cook for a further 5 minutes, stirring every now and then.

Allow to cool in the pan and then transfer to a bowl. Serve cold, with a bowl of cream or yoghurt if you like.

preparation
This pudding must be made at least 1 day in advance (2 or 3 days would be even better) and chilled. This allows time for the flavours to blend.

Serves 10
1 bottle sweet white wine
5 tbsp clear honey
rind and juice of 3 organic lemons
1/2 tsp ground ginger
1/4 tsp ground cloves
1/2 tsp grated nutmeg
1/2 tsp cinnamon
100 g (3 1/2 oz) prunes, stoned
300 ml (1/2 pint) strong tea, hot
100 g (3 1/2 oz) sultanas
100 g (3 1/2 oz) dried apricots
10 dried figs or 100 g (3 1/2 oz) dates, stoned and cut into thin strips
450 g (1 lb) dessert apples
450 g (1 lb) pears
100 g (3 1/2 oz) almonds, blanched, peeled and cut into slivers
60 g (2 oz) pine nuts

For serving
lightly whipped cream or yoghurt

roast turkey with pomegranate sauce
tacchino arrosto al sugo di melagrana

Serves 10–12
**1 small hen turkey
with its liver and
heart, fresh, of
about 3 1/2–4 kg
(7–8 lb) undressed
weight
2 organic lemons
3 cloves
4 dessert apples,
peeled and cut into
small pieces
120 g (4 oz) unsalted
butter
sea salt and freshly
ground black
pepper
150 g (5 oz) pancetta
or unsmoked
streaky bacon
120 ml (4 fl oz) meat
stock
3 large pomegranates
or 4 small ones
2 tbsp brandy**

*Although pomegranates are rarely used in Italian cookery, the fruit does
appear in a few dishes from Venice because of its former trade with
the Middle East. Here is one of them. The apples and lemon inside the
turkey give the meat a delicious sharp taste, emphasised by the
pomegranate juice and the liver sauce.*

Heat the oven to 190°C (375°F) mark 5.

Wash the turkey inside and out and dry very well.

Pierce one of the lemons with a skewer in many places, stick it with
the cloves and place inside the bird. Also put the apples and 45 g
(1 1/2 oz) of the butter in the cavity and sprinkle generously inside
and out with salt and pepper.

Rub 30 g (1 oz) of the remaining butter all over the turkey. Cover the
breast with the pancetta, tie it in place and truss the turkey. Put it in a
roasting tin, breast down, add the stock and roast in the oven for about
2 1/2 hours, basting every 20 minutes or so.

While the turkey is cooking, prepare the sauce. Cut the pomegranates
in half and squeeze them. Strain through a metal sieve and press the
seeds with a metal spoon to extract all the juice. Squeeze the
remaining lemon and strain the juice into the pomegranate juice.

Pour half of the fruit juices over the turkey halfway through the cooking.

Clean the turkey liver and heart, wash and dry thoroughly and chop or
cut into tiny pieces.

A quarter of an hour before the turkey is cooked, remove the pancetta and
the string and replace the turkey in the oven breast side up to brown it.

When the bird is ready, transfer to a heated dish and place it back in
the oven with the heat turned off and the oven door slightly open. The
turkey must cool a little, so that the juices penetrate the meat.

Heat 30 g (1 oz) of the butter in a fairly small saucepan, add the liver
and the heart and sauté gently for 1 minute, stirring constantly. Heat
the brandy in a soup ladle until it is nearly boiling. Pour the brandy into
the pan and put a flame to it. Let the brandy burn away, and when the
flame has subsided add the rest of the fruit juices.

Skim all the fat off the turkey cooking liquid and then add the liquid to the liver sauce. Boil to concentrate the flavour until rich and syrupy. Add the remaining butter a little at a time, while swirling the pan. When all the butter has been incorporated, taste and adjust the seasonings. Pour the sauce into a heated sauce-boat and serve separately. (If you do not like bits in your sauce, pour it through a strainer.)

When you serve the turkey don't forget to put a small amount of the apple stuffing on each plate. It is a perfect accompaniment to the turkey and it is complementary to the sauce.

The chestnuts of Valle d'Aosta, the hazelnuts of Piedmont and Avellino, the walnuts of Sorrento, the pine nuts of Versilia and the almonds of Sicily are among the best in the world. The Italians use them freely and eat them in plenty, by themselves or in combination with meat, fish and vegetables. They are also very usual ingredients in puddings, cakes and biscuits. I have always felt that there are degrees of nobility among nuts. Almonds, for instance, with their exotic flavour, are for grand tables; almond paste has lent itself to artistic decorations as well as to delicate sweetmeats, and it has flavoured rich puddings of Arabic origin. Chestnuts, however, seem to belong to more humble surroundings, eaten roasted around the kitchen fire or in the street straight from the hot brazier.

almonds

Almonds are fruit of the trees that delight us in February with the first spring flowers. But the almonds that grow in Britain are of little culinary interest. Sweet almonds only grow where there is no frost, in the same regions as oranges and lemons. They have many uses in cooking, both as flavouring and, ground, as thickening. Almonds are delicious by themselves, salted to nibble with drinks or coated with sugar as sweets.

Almonds keep for only a year. When the new crop arrives in the shops in the late summer the old almonds should be thrown away; their flavour will have evaporated and their oil might have begun to go rancid. Almonds are sold in their shells at Christmas time to eat at the table, or in their skins or peeled or ground, all the year round, to use in cooking. I always buy unpeeled almonds, since it is easy to tell how old they are by looking at the skin. If their skin is wrinkled, the almonds are old. When you want to peel almonds put them in a saucepan of boiling water and boil for 30 seconds. When they are cool enough to handle, squeeze them between your thumb and forefinger and they will pop out of their skins. To release their flavours pop them in a moderate oven for about 10 minutes. A food processor grinds almonds well. You can stop the machine whenever the nuts are ready for your recipe – coarsely chopped, finely chopped or ground.

chicken and almond soup
biancomangiare

Serves 4
2 free-range or organic chicken breasts
1.5 litres (2 1/2 pints) home-made chicken stock (see page 485)

continued over >>

Biancomangiare *is the original word from which the French* blancmanger *and the English* blancmange *are derived. It means 'white food'. In its original form, going back to the thirteenth century, it was indeed white, as it still is in the modern pudding made with ground almonds, cream and sugar. In the Renaissance all white puddings based on almonds, as well as soups based on almonds and chicken, were called* biancomangiare, *and because they were very popular there are many recipes for them in the cookery books of the period. It was one of the many dishes served at the wedding of Isabella di Aragona and Gian Galeazzo Sforza which took place in Southern Lombardy on 23 January 1489. The menu for that occasion was written in verse by Leonardo da Vinci.*

What follows is my version of one of those fifteenth-century recipes, and I have to say that it is one of the most delectable soups I have tasted. The stock must be home-made, and should have the delicate rich flavour that is best produced by a boiling hen or a capon rather than a roasting chicken. The soup looks marvellous garnished with a few pomegranate seeds, the garnish it would have had in Leonardo's time. If pomegranates are not in season, snip some feathery top of fennel or some wild fennel or some dill and sprinkle it on top of each bowl just before serving.

100 g (3 1/2 oz) almonds
1 tbsp rice flour
pinch of grated nutmeg
150 ml (1/4 pint) double cream
sea salt and pepper
pomegranate seeds, fronds of fennel, or dill
freshly grated Parmesan for serving

Poach the chicken breasts for 15 minutes in a little of the stock.

Heat the rest of the stock.

Blanch and peel the almonds and grind them in a food processor. Add about two-thirds of the cooked chicken breast and grind to a purée, adding a couple of tablespoons of the stock. Spoon the mixture into the stock.

When the soup is boiling, turn the heat down and add the rice flour in a thin stream, while beating with a wire whisk or a fork. Simmer for 10 minutes, then add the grated nutmeg and the cream. Cook for a further 5 minutes. Taste and check the seasoning.

Cut the remaining chicken into small strips.

Ladle the soup into individual bowls and garnish with the chicken strips and the pomegranate seeds, feathery fennel or dill. Serve with plenty of Parmesan on the side.

almond and orange cake
torta di mandorle all'arancia

Serves 6
150 g (5 oz) sweet
  almonds
3 free-range eggs,
  separated
150 g (5 oz) sugar
60 g (2 oz) potato
  flour
1 1/2 organic
  oranges
sea salt
30 g (1 oz) unsalted
  butter

This cake combines two of the most characteristic Italian fruits: oranges and almonds. The recipe is from La scienza in cucina e l'arte di mangiar bene *by Pellegrino Artusi, the greatest cookery book of the nineteenth century. It is still in print today, well past its 100th edition. The use of potato flour –* fécule *– instead of flour, gives a softer dough; it is also ideal for anyone on a gluten-free diet. The tin is heavily buttered, giving a soft rich layer on the surface of the cake; if you use less butter the cake is equally delicious, though not so rich. This delicate cake, perfect on its own, is equally good as an accompaniment to a fruit salad, to soft fruits or to a fruit compote.*

Heat the oven to 170°C (325°F) mark 3.

Blanch and peel the almonds. Dry them and chop them very finely by hand, or use a food processor, but do not blend to a paste. The mixture should be granular.

Beat the egg yolks with the sugar until it forms a ribbon and then add the almonds and the flour. Mix well.

Grate the skin of 1 orange and add to the mixture together with the strained juice of all the oranges. The mixture will be very soft and sloppy.

Now whisk the egg whites with a pinch of salt until stiff and then fold into the mixture, lifting it high with a gentle movement, using a metal spoon.

Grease a 20 cm (8 inch) cake tin with the butter, to give a thick layer all round, and pour the mixture into the tin.

Bake in the preheated oven for about 50 minutes until the cake has shrunk from the sides and feels spongy to the touch. Unmould the cake on a wire rack and cool.

The cake looks pretty dusted with icing sugar, or it can be iced with a soft icing flavoured with 1 teaspoon of orange water.

almond meringues
meringhine alle mandorle

Any cook's fridge or freezer always abounds in left-over egg whites, and this is one of the very best ways to use them. They end up as the prettiest friandises imaginable; with their mother-of-pearl colouring and shine they have a distinctly oyster-shell look about them.

You can use ground almonds if you're pressed for time, but I do not recommend it. I find that ground almonds have lost some of their flavour, just like ground pepper and ready-grated Parmesan cheese.

Toast the almonds in a preheated oven (180°C/350°F/mark 4) for 10 minutes until gold and then grind them in a food processor.

Turn the heat down to 150°C (300°F) mark 2.

Beat the egg whites with the sugar until soft peaks form. (I use a hand-held electric beater and it takes 3–4 minutes. If you use a balloon whisk beater, you will have to work at it for quite a time.) Fold in the ground almonds and the lemon juice and mix until the mixture is quite homogeneous.

Line 2 baking trays with parchment paper and place small blobs of the mixture on the paper at a distance of about 3.5 cm (1 1/2 inches) apart. You can pipe the blobs or use 2 teaspoons. Keep the blobs small as the mixture will spread, and the cooked biscuits look prettiest if no larger than 3.5 cm (1 1/2 inches) in diameter. Bake in the preheated oven until set to the touch and very lightly coloured – about 30–40 minutes. Leave to cool in the oven and then store in an airtight tin.

Makes about 25 biscuits
120 g (4 oz) almonds, blanched and peeled
2 free-range egg whites
120 g (4 oz) icing sugar
1 tsp lemon juice

almond milk
latte di mandorla

Makes 300 ml (1/2 pint)
**120 g (4 oz)
almonds, blanched
and peeled
4 bitter almonds,
blanched and
peeled, or 3 or 4
drops of pure
almond essence
300 ml (1/2 pint)
full-fat milk
2 tbsp icing sugar**

Almond milk was very popular in Italy in the Middle Ages, when it was usually made with water or stock rather than with milk, and used mainly as a thickener in sauces. During the Renaissance it was also served at banquets as a soup, flavoured with other ingredients. I experimented with a few old recipes and came out with this variation of almond milk. This is a thin sauce, which is a lovely accompaniment to poached fruit in place of cream or crème anglaise. In Sicily it is served in bars, refreshingly delicious.

It is also ideal with a fruit bavarois of cherries or of apricots, both fruits blending beautifully with the taste of almonds.

Chop the almonds or process them until they reach the granular stage. Transfer to a bowl, with the essence if using it.

Heat the milk to boiling point, stir in the sugar and pour over the almonds. Cover the bowl with clingfilm and leave to infuse for at least 4 hours.

Set a round sieve over a jug and line it with a piece of muslin. Strain the almond mixture and then squeeze out all the juices into the milk.

Cover the jug with clingfilm and put into the refrigerator. Remove from the fridge and bring back to room temperature before serving.

You can use the squeezed-out almonds in cakes or biscuits; they are still good even though part of their flavour has gone into the milk.

potato and almond cake
torta di patate e mandorle

This deliciously moist potato and almond cake comes from the Hotel Mar y Vent in Bañalbufar on Majorca. Nothing Italian about it. But the way it was served at the hotel, lavishly covered with icing sugar, by itself at the end of the meal was very Italian indeed. It reminded me of all the different *torte* covered with icing sugar that are on display at most bakeries and patisseries in central Italy. Falling in line with British tradition that sweets at the end of a meal should not be eaten dry – something I totally agree with – I have served the cake with various ice-creams or stewed fruit. The cherries on page 346 are ideal, the anise flavour of the fennel seeds blending perfectly with the flavour of the almonds.

Serves 8
200 g (7 oz) old floury potatoes such as King Edward
200 g (7 oz) almonds
1 white bread roll (a small bap is ideal)
6 free-range eggs, separated
200 g (7 oz) caster sugar
grated rind of 1 organic lemon
sea salt
icing sugar for decoration

Boil the potatoes in their skins and then peel and purée them through the small disc of a food mill or a potato ricer.

While the potatoes are cooking, blanch the almonds for 20 seconds in boiling water. Peel them and dry them in kitchen paper. Chop them in the food processor, stopping before they become too finely ground.

Take out the soft inside of the bread roll and crumble it by hand or in the food processor.

Heat the oven to 240°C (475°F) mark 9.

Put the egg yolks in a bowl. Add the sugar, almonds, breadcrumbs, lemon rind, a pinch of salt and the potato purée. Mix thoroughly. Whisk the egg whites until stiff but not dry and fold them gently into the mixture, using a large metal spoon, with a high movement to incorporate air into the mixture.

Butter a 25 cm (10 inch) spring-clip cake tin. Sprinkle a large tablespoon of flour into the tin. Shake the tin to cover all the surface and then tip out the excess flour. Fill the tin with the mixture and place the tin in the oven. Turn the heat down to 160°C (325°F) mark 3 and bake for about 50 minutes to 1 hour, until a cocktail stick inserted into the middle of the cake comes out dry. Loosen the band round the tin and turn the cake onto a wire rack, where it should be left to cool. Serve lavishly sprinkled with sifted icing sugar.

preparation
The cake is best eaten the day it is cooked, but it can be made up to 2 days in advance.

almond crescents
cornetti alle mandorle

Makes about 35 biscuits
150 g (5 oz) unsalted butter
60 g (2 oz) ground almonds
45 g (1 1/2 oz) caster sugar
150 g (5 oz) Italian 00 flour
6 drops pure vanilla essence
icing sugar

These very delicate biscuits are good served with fruit puddings or ice-cream.

Cream the butter, almonds and sugar until pale and fluffy. Stir in the flour with a wooden spoon and add the vanilla essence. (The mixture can also be made in the food processor.)

Roll into sausage shapes, 15 cm (6 inches) long by 1–1 1/2 cm (1/2–2/3 inch) in diameter, on a board sprinkled with flour, and with floured hands. Wrap the sausages in foil and chill for 30–45 minutes.

Heat the oven to 150ºC (300ºF) mark 2.

Cut the sausages into 6.5 cm (2 1/2 inches) long pieces with a sharp knife. Roll lightly in the floured palms of your hands, or on the floured board, and shape into small crescents.

Butter and flour a large baking tray and lay the crescents on it, spacing them at 2.5 cm (1 inch) intervals. Now put the tray in the fridge for 30 minutes or so and then bake until very lightly coloured – about 25 minutes. Allow to cool a little and then transfer to a rack. Do this very gently because these biscuits are very friable. When the biscuits are cold, dredge them with sifted icing sugar and store in an airtight tin between layers of greaseproof paper.

amaretti pudding
bônet

Serves 8
300 ml (1/2 pint) single cream
300 ml (1/2 pint) full-fat milk

continued over >>

This pudding is a really soft dark pudding with a rich flavour and a silky texture. It is a speciality of Piedmont, as its name testifies. Bônet, pronounced 'boonayt', means bonnet, and the pudding is so named because the copper mould in which it is cooked is a round mould shaped like a bonnet. You can use any sort of shape, although a round mould is prettier. I have also made bônet in a ring-mould, filling the hole with cream. The cream is my addition; I find it lightens the pudding and combines perfectly with the almond-caramel flavour.

Heat the oven to 160°C (325°F) mark 3 and place a 1 litre (2 pint) mould in it to heat for 5 minutes. Leave the oven on.

Put the ingredients for the caramel in a small saucepan and bring to the boil over a medium heat. Do not be tempted to stir, leave it alone and the sugar will dissolve. The lemon juice will prevent crystals forming on the edge of the syrup. When the syrup begins to turn dark brown, withdraw it from the heat and pour it into the heated mould. Tip the mould in all directions to coat the sides and bottom evenly. It is necessary to heat the mould because if it is cold, the caramel may set before you can cover the whole surface of the mould with it. Set aside while you make the pudding.

Add the cream to the milk and bring to simmering point. Beat the eggs with the sugar until frothy and light. Pour the milk mixture over the eggs in a slow stream from a height so as to cool the liquid, beating constantly.

Crush the *amaretti* biscuits in a food processor, or with a rolling-pin, and mix into the egg and milk mixture together with the cocoa, the rum and the liqueur. Beat thoroughly, using a balloon whisk rather than an electric hand beater, which would scatter bubbles of mixture all over your kitchen.

Pour the mixture into the prepared mould. Place the mould in a roasting tin and add enough very hot (but not actually boiling) water to come halfway up the side of the roasting tin. Place the tin in the preheated oven and cook for about 1 hour until the *bônet* is set. To test if it is ready, insert the thin blade of a knife into the middle of the pudding. It should come out dry.

Remove from the oven and let the *bônet* cool in the mould. When cold, place the mould in the fridge and leave for at least 3 hours. To unmould, loosen the pudding all round with a palette knife. Place a round dish over the mould and turn the mould over on to the dish. Give a few sharp jerks to the dish and then lift the mould away. Put the

5 free-range eggs
90 g (3 oz) caster sugar
150 g (5 oz) hard *amaretti* biscuits
3 tbsp unsweetened cocoa powder
1 tbsp dark rum
2 tbsp *amaretto* liqueur
300 ml (1/2 pint) whipping cream

For the caramel
60 g (2 oz) caster sugar
2 tbsp water
1 tsp lemon juice

mould back over the *bônet* to protect it and refrigerate until you are
ready to serve it.

Whip the cream and spoon it around the pudding or, if you are using a
ring-mould, fill the central hole with it.

preparation
Bônet is better made 1 or 2 days in advance, for the flavours to blend,
and refrigerated. It can also be frozen, but do not leave too long in the
freezer or the flavour will evaporate.

chestnuts

Chestnuts came originally from around the town of Castanis in
Thessalia, hence their botanical name of *Castanea sativa*, in Italian
castagne. In Italy chestnut trees grow on the Alps, and all down the
Apennines as far south as Calabria. They have a short season, from
October to Christmas, after which the nuts become wrinkled and lose
their flavour.

Peeling chestnuts is a boring and lengthy job. It is easier if your hands
can stand a certain amount of heat: the more heat you can bear, the
quicker the job. First wash the chestnuts. Then, using a small pointed
knife, slit the shell of the chestnuts across the whole of the rounded
side, being careful not to cut into the actual nut. Put the chestnuts in a
saucepan, cover with plenty of cold water and bring to the boil. Cook
until ready, which can vary between ten and 20 minutes, depending on
how fresh they are. To find out, take a chestnut between your thumb and
index finger and press gently: it should be just soft. Lift a few chestnuts
from the water, leaving the rest in the hot water to make peeling easier.
Remove the outer shell, as well as all the inner skin which has an
unpleasant bitter taste, with the aid of a small knife. You will notice any
bad nuts as soon as you begin to peel them by the acrid smell they give
off; the whole nut should be discarded. The chestnuts are now ready to

be cooked in stock or milk, according to the recipe. But nowadays you can forget about all that and buy chestnuts already peeled in vacuum packs. They are excellent and they save hours of work.

Dried chestnuts are sold when the fresh ones are out of season. They have to be reconstituted by soaking in water for at least 8 hours before cooking.

chestnut soup
passato di castagne

I have had many chestnut soups in my time, many of them stodgy, some good and a few excellent. Although this version had long been one of the best I knew, it became the ne plus ultra *as a result of reading Eliza Acton's* Modern Cookery for Private Families. *In that book there is a recipe that is very similar to the one I had known, but with one important extra: Eliza Acton adds cream. It is this that transforms a pleasant but homely northern Italian soup into one that is utterly delectable.*

Put the peeled chestnuts into a saucepan and add the stock. Cook for 30 minutes and then purée the soup through a food mill or in a food processor. Return the purée to the pan and add the cream, salt, pepper to taste and the nutmeg. Cook for 5 minutes and then serve.

Serves 4
450 g (1 lb) peeled chestnuts
1.2 litres (2 pints) light home-made vegetable or chicken stock
150 ml (1/4 pint) double cream
sea salt and freshly ground black pepper
generous pinch of grated nutmeg

chestnut mousse
spuma di castagne

Serves 6–8
400 g (14 oz) peeled
  chestnuts
sea salt
1 bay leaf
piece of vanilla pod
1 cinnamon stick,
  about 5 cm
  (2 inches)
200 g (7 oz) sugar
300 ml (1/2 pint)
  full-fat milk
3 free-range egg
  yolks
4 tbsp dark rum
150 ml (1/4 pint)
  double cream
grated chocolate

You can serve this pudding in individual bowls sprinkled with some grated chocolate on the top or in a lovely large glass bowl. When I perfected this recipe I was lucky enough to have a bottle of 14-year-old rum liqueur in the house, and I used this in the mousse. If you don't feel inclined to rush out and buy such a bottle, use dark rum. I am sure you will be quite happy with the result.

Put the chestnuts in a pan with the salt, bay leaf, vanilla pod, cinnamon stick and half the sugar. Pour over enough milk to cover and bring slowly to the boil. Put a lid on the pan and adjust the heat so that the milk simmers without boiling over. Cook very gently until nearly all the milk has been absorbed and the chestnuts are mushy – about 1 hour.

Remove the vanilla and the cinnamon and whiz the chestnuts in a food processor until they are reduced to a smooth purée. Scoop down the bits on the side of the beaker and process again.

Beat the egg yolks with the remaining sugar until pale and forming ribbons and then incorporate gradually into the chestnut purée together with the rum.

Whip the cream and then fold into the chestnut and custard purée. Go on mixing until well blended.

Spoon the mixture into bowls or into a large bowl and cover with clingfilm. Chill until you want to serve it.

Grate enough chocolate to shower over the pudding before serving.

chestnut and cream pudding
dolce di marroni dell'Artusi

Artusi was a nineteenth-century cookery writer and his marvellous book La scienza in cucina e l'arte di mangiar bene, *first published in 1891, is still in print. His chestnut and cream pudding is the ancestor of the long number of Mont Blancs which have come since then and is definitely one of the best.*

Purée the chestnuts in a food mill with the large-hole disc fitted. A food processor is not suitable, as it would mash the chestnuts without aerating the purée. Sift the icing sugar, set aside 2 tablespoons and mix the rest into the chestnut purée together with the rum.

Grate the chocolate in a food processor or through the large holes of a cheese grater. (Hold the piece of chocolate wrapped in foil to avoid it melting from the heat of your hands.) Add to the mixture. Blend everything together.

Choose a large round serving dish and place a saucer in the middle of it.

Now fix the disc with small holes to the food mill. Purée the chestnut mixture through the disc, letting it fall directly on the dish all round the saucer. When all the chestnut has gone through, gently push off the purée that has fallen on the saucer and remove the saucer. Do not squash the purée down, it should stay light and fluffy.

Whip the cream, fold in the reserved sugar and fill the hole with it. Pile any remaining cream into a bowl and hand it round separately.

Serves 6–8
450 g (1 lb) vacuum-packed chestnuts
225 g (8 oz) icing sugar
4 tbsp rum
120 g (4 oz) best quality bitter chocolate
600 ml (1 pint) whipping cream

walnuts

Walnuts are the hardest nuts to find in a good condition because of the amount of oil they contain. At Christmas time they are around in their shells, to go on the table with the other nuts and all the dried fruits. During the year they are sold shelled, but sometimes they are too old to be any good. Buy them from a supplier who has a quick turnover. The half-kernels should be large and intact, of a lovely ivory colour. Old nuts break and as a consequence become rancid more quickly. Before you use them, discard any piece of walnut that is dark in colour and compact in texture. They should be pale ivory with a light texture if they are to have that sweet taste that characterises any dish to which they are added. When old, walnuts first develop a piquant taste that tickles your tongue unpleasantly, and later they become rancid. A single piece of rancid walnut can ruin your dish. Keep them in an airtight jar in the fridge or freezer. Some recipes call for the nuts to be peeled, as the skin is bitter. Blanch them in boiling water for half a minute and then remove as much skin as you can with the help of a small sharp knife. While you peel them you can easily detect any piece which should be thrown away.

walnut cake with mascarpone cream
torta di noce alla crema di mascarpone

Serves 8–10
6 free-range eggs, separated
250 g (9 oz) caster sugar
3 or 4 drops pure vanilla essence
250 g (9 oz) walnuts
sea salt
butter and dried breadcrumbs for the tin

For the topping
2 free-range eggs, separated
60 g (2 oz) caster sugar
500 g (1 lb 2 oz) mascarpone

I must confess that I am not a keen cake-maker. I seldom have one in the house, and when I do I usually forget to eat it. But I do like a sweet ending to a good meal, and that is why I include a select number of good puddings among my favourite recipes.

This walnut cake is always good, whether eaten by itself for 'elevenses', at tea-time, with a night-cap – or at any time of the day with a glass of champagne! But it is at its best filled with mascarpone cream (the same cream that I make for the well-known *tiramisú*) and served as a pudding, when it makes a fine ending to the meal.

If you have time, blanch the walnuts for 30 seconds and peel them. It is a fidgety job, but quite important because the skin is bitter (also see note above).

Beat the egg yolks with the sugar until pale yellow and forming ribbons. Add the vanilla essence.

Reserve a few best-looking halves of the walnuts, put the rest in a food processor and process until very coarsely ground. Add to the egg and sugar mixture and beat again.

Heat the oven to 180°C (350°F) mark 4.

Whisk the egg whites with a pinch of salt until stiff but not dry. Fold gradually into the mixture, using a large metal spoon, with a gentle lifting movement, evenly and thoroughly.

Butter a 25 cm (10 inch) spring-clip tin and sprinkle with the breadcrumbs. Cover all the surface with them by rotating the tin and then shake off the excess.

Spoon the mixture into the tin and bake until firm and set, about 50 minutes. When done, turn the tin over onto a wire rack, unclip and remove the tin and allow the cake to cool.

While the cake is cooling, prepare the topping. Beat the egg yolks with the sugar until the ribbon stage. Fold in the mascarpone, a heaped tablespoon at a time.

Whisk the egg white and fold into the mascarpone mixture lightly but very thoroughly. Chill.

About 2 hours before you want to eat the cake, spread the mascarpone cream all over the top, using a large spatula. Decorate with the reserved walnut halves and chill. Bring to the table straight from the refrigerator.

walnut and honey pie
la bonissima

Serves 6
For the pastry
**150 g (5 oz) Italian
00 flour**
**65 g (2 1/4 oz)
potato flour**
1/2 tsp sea salt
**60 g (2 oz) caster
sugar**
**150 g (5 oz) cold
unsalted butter**
**yolks of 2 hard-
boiled free-range
eggs**
1 free-range egg yolk
1 tbsp milk
**butter and flour for
the tin**

For the filling
**150 g (5 oz) walnut
kernels**
**150 ml (1/4 pint)
honey**
**grated rind of 1
small organic
lemon**
4 tbsp dark rum
**2 tbsp dried
breadcrumbs**
1 tbsp caster sugar

For serving
**300 ml (1/2 pint)
crème fraîche or
double cream
(optional)**

This pie is called la Bonissima *and very good it certainly is. The pastry is made with the yolks of hard-boiled eggs and some potato flour. It is a soft and buttery pastry, quite different from the usual* pâte sucrée. *It is a difficult pastry to roll out, but if you do it on a sheet of greaseproof paper, as I explain in the method, you will manage quite easily. Of course, you can make your usual pastry with raw egg yolk and sugar, although the final result would be slightly different.*

The filling is superb, but care must be taken when buying walnuts. Walnuts go off very quickly because of the high content of oil, which becomes rancid when the walnuts are old. Some of the walnut kernels on sale in Britain are not good enough even when they are within their expiry date. Buy the best. Look through the wrapping if you can and check that the kernels are in large pieces and not broken into small pieces and crumbs, a sure sign of age. If, when you open the bag, you find that the walnuts are all in small pieces, take them back to your shop and complain.

If you like to enrich the pie, hand round a bowl of crème fraîche *or double cream with it –* la Bonissima *will become* bonissimissima!

First make the pastry. Sift the two flours and the salt in a mixing bowl. Add the sugar and the butter cut into small pieces. Rub the butter into the mixture with the tips of your fingers until the mixture is like small crumbs. Push the hard-boiled egg yolks through a sieve, or a food mill set with the small-hole disc, directly into the bowl. Work the mixture together and then turn the dough on to a lightly floured surface and gather into a ball as quickly as you can. Wrap the dough in clingfilm and refrigerate for at least half an hour. (If you have a food processor, put the flours, salt, sugar and butter in the bowl, process for a few seconds, then add the hard-boiled yolks, cut into small pieces, and process until a ball forms.)

While the pastry is chilling, blanch the walnut kernels for 30 seconds in boiling water. Remove as much skin as you can, lifting them out of the water a few at a time as they are easier to peel when hot. Put the peeled kernels on kitchen paper to dry. This is a lengthy and rather boring job, but as the skin is bitter, removing it makes all the difference to any dish containing walnuts. But don't worry if you can't remove all the skin. (Put your favourite tape on, or enlist your children to help; it is the sort of job they can do quite well with their nimble little fingers.) Chop the walnuts coarsely, by hand or in the food processor.

Heat the honey in a saucepan and mix in the walnuts and the lemon rind. Cook gently until the mixture is hot and the walnuts are all well coated in the honey. Draw the pan off the heat, add the rum, mix well and leave to cool.

Heat the oven to 180°C (350°F) mark 4.

Butter a 20 cm (10 inch) spring-clip tin and flour lightly all over.

Remove the dough from the fridge and cut off about one-third of it. Put a piece of greaseproof paper on the work-top, shake a little flour over it and roll out a third of the dough over the paper. Lift the paper and turn the circle over on to the bottom of the tin. Peel off the greaseproof paper.

Now roll out strips of dough about 5 cm (2 inch) wide and line the sides of the tin. Sprinkle the breadcrumbs and the sugar over the bottom and then spoon in the filling. Roll out the rest of the dough on to the greaseproof paper and turn it over to cover the pie. Prick it to make little holes for the steam to escape. With the remaining dough make a piping or narrow tape and place around the edges to seal.

Mix together the egg yolk and the milk and brush the top of the pie all over. If you want, make some cut-out shapes with any remaining pastry to decorate the pie. Brush these as well with the egg yolk mixture.

Bake for about 30–40 minutes until the pastry is a lovely golden colour. Cool in the tin and then transfer the pie to a round dish.

preparation
La Bonissima can be prepared up to 2 days in advance.

walnuts, grapes and parmesan
noci, uva e grana

This was my father's favourite end of a meal in the autumn. In spite of his sophisticated tastes in other matters, the food that he loved best was peasant food. I remember him telling me that the dish he usually had at Savini, the famous restaurant in Milan where he often went for supper after an evening at La Scala, was *polenta e baccalà* (polenta and salt cod) or *polenta pasticciata* (polenta baked in layers with béchamel and *luganega*, a coarse-ground sausage). And if truffles were in season, the chef would add a few slices to the polenta; peasant food no longer!

In the real peasant tradition, my father used to eat bread with everything. My children, brought up in England where bread is eaten only with particular foods, were amazed to see *Nonno* eating bread with huge bunches of grapes at the end of the meal. Although I find bread and grapes rather dull, I find the mixture of walnuts, grapes, Parmesan and bread a perfect blend of different flavours, the bread being the unifying note. The grapes should be white and tasty, not the bland variety tasting only of water and sugar too often sold in Britain under the name 'Italia'.

This is the sort of dish you must provide in generous proportions. After all, whatever is left over will not be wasted. Buy 1 kg (2 lb) of walnuts, 1.35 kg (3 lb) of white grapes, a good wedge of Parmesan of at least 450 g (1 lb) and some crusty Italian bread (a *ciabatta* is ideal) or French bread.

Divide the grapes into small bunches. Put the bunches in a colander and place under cold water. Dry them thoroughly with kitchen paper. Put the Parmesan in the middle of a large round dish and surround it with the walnuts and the grapes.

Put the dish in the middle of the table for everybody to help themselves and crack away.

hazelnuts

Hazelnuts keep better than walnuts, although my remarks concerning walnuts still apply. To peel hazelnuts, either put them in a cast-iron frying pan and toast them for a few minutes, shaking the pan, or place them in a hot oven (200°C/400°F/mark 6) spread on a baking tin for 5 minutes. As soon as you can handle them, rub them against each other, or in a rough towel, and blow away the papery-thin skin. Blow into the sink, or out of doors, otherwise you will find bits of skin flying everywhere. Discard any hazelnuts that are partly dark in colour and oily and thick in texture.

chicken bundles stuffed with hazelnuts, ham and cheese
involtini di pollo ripieni di nocciole, prosciutto e formaggio

Of all nuts, hazelnuts have a flavour that goes best with white meat. In this dish their nutty taste, reinforced by the Gruyère, is toned down by the white wine, which must be dry, yet full and fruity, such as a Pinot Bianco or a Pinot Grigio.

Spread the hazelnuts in a baking tray and toast them in a hot oven (200°C (400°F) mark 6) for 5 minutes. Leave them to cool a little and then rub them between your hands, or with a rough cloth, to remove their papery skin.

Cut the cheese into pieces and put it in the food processor with the ham and the hazelnuts. Process until chopped but not reduced to a paste. Scoop the mixture into a bowl and add the nutmeg, a very little salt and some pepper. Mix well.

Lay the chicken pieces flat on a chopping board.

Put aside 1 tablespoon of the butter and melt the rest in a large frying pan, or in a *sauteuse*, in which you are going to cook the bundles. As

Serves 4
30 g (1 oz) hazelnuts
50 g (1 3/4 oz) Gruyère
50 g (1 3/4 oz) ham
pinch of grated nutmeg
sea salt and pepper
8 free-range or organic boned chicken thighs
60 g (2 oz) unsalted butter
1 tbsp oil, preferably groundnut
5 tbsp dry white wine
120 ml (4 fl oz) meat stock

soon as the butter has melted, turn the heat off. Dip a pastry brush into the butter and moisten the inside of each chicken piece. Season with a sprinkling of salt and pepper.

Pick up about 1 tbsp of the stuffing and press it between your hands into an oblong shape. Lay it on the meat and then roll up the meat and secure with a wooden cocktail stick.

Add the oil to the butter and heat. When the foam begins to subside, slide the bundles into the pan and fry on all sides to a lovely deep gold.

Splash with the wine and boil briskly until it has nearly all evaporated. Add the stock and bring to the boil. Turn the heat down to the minimum and cover the pan with a lid. Cook gently for about 15 minutes until the chicken thighs are cooked through.

Transfer the bundles to a heated serving dish. Add the reserved butter to the liquid in the pan a little at a time and cook gently until it has been incorporated. Taste and check the seasoning. Return the bundles to the pan, together with the juices they have thrown off into the dish. Cook very gently for 1–2 minutes so as to allow all the flavours to combine, and then place back on the dish and cover with the sauce.

If you prefer, you can spoon a little sauce on to each plate and then lay 2 bundles on the plate, although this procedure always reminds me of something that Peter Fleming wrote in his delightful book *Brazilian Adventure*: 'The peoples of this world may be divided into two sorts – the portion-minded and the non-portion-minded. The United States of America are portion-minded people to an almost fanatical degree . . . If you order Brussels sprouts you get Brussels sprouts – 7 of them in a little dish. And you are oppressed by the knowledge that everyone else who orders Brussels sprouts will get 7 of them too in an identical little dish. The pleasure of the table ought not to be standardised in this way: it is shameful.' This was written in the 1930s. Now, alas, the habit has set in all over the western world, even in private homes. All of which explains why I always prefer to let my friends help themselves!

chocolate and nut cake
la torta di cioccolato di julia

The recipe for this melt-in-the-mouth chocolate cake comes from my daughter, the Julia of the title. It is one that even I, not a chocolate lover, find irresistible. It is perfect with the ricotta ice-cream on page 325.

Make sure the nuts you buy are not stale; buy them from a reliable shop with a quick turnover. Use eggs that are at room temperature, not straight out of the refrigerator.

Heat the oven to 200° (400°F) mark 6.

Spread the hazelnuts in a baking tray and toast them for 5 minutes. Leave them to cool a little and then rub them between your hands, or with a rough cloth, to remove the papery skin. Do this in the sink or, better still, in the garden, to avoid having little bits of the brown skin flying all over the kitchen.

Put the hazelnuts and the walnuts in a food processor. Cut the chocolate into small pieces and add to the nuts. Pulse the machine on and off until the mixture is of a grainy consistency, not ground fine.

Transfer the mixture to a bowl and then stir in the brandy, cinnamon, milk and sugar. Mix thoroughly. Now add the egg yolks gradually, blending them in very well, and finally add the orange peel.

Butter generously a 20 cm (10 inch) spring-clip cake tin. Sprinkle with flour and then shake off any excess.

Whisk the egg whites until stiff but not dry and then fold them into the chocolate mixture with a large metal spoon, a few tablespoons at a time, cutting through the mixture with a high movement to incorporate more air.

When all the egg whites have been lightly folded in, spoon the mixture into the prepared tin and bake in the oven for about 1 hour. The cake is ready when a cocktail stick inserted in the middle comes out dry. Unclip the band and turn the cake onto a wire rack. Remove the base and leave till cold.

Before serving, sprinkle lavishly with icing sugar. Cream is optional, but it certainly makes the cake even more luscious.

Serves 8–10
225 g (8 oz) hazelnuts
225 g (8 oz) walnuts
225 g (8 oz) best quality bitter chocolate
5 tbsp brandy
1 tsp ground cinnamon
2 tbsp full-fat milk
225 g (8 oz) caster sugar
5 large free-range eggs, separated
1 1/2 tbsp organic orange peel, very finely chopped
icing sugar
pouring cream (optional)

preparation
The cake is better eaten as soon as it is cool. But you can satisfactorily make it up to 1 day in advance.

pine nuts

Pine nuts are the nuts of the Stone Pine, *Pineus sativa*. They are about 5 mm (1/4 inch) long, of a beautiful ivory colour, with a delicious taste of resin mixed with oil. They are used to thicken sauces, as in pesto, or in sweet-and-sour sauces to dress vegetables, fish or fried meats. They are also added to cakes and biscuits. To release their flavour, it is a good idea to heat the pine nuts in a hot oven or in a cast-iron frying pan for a few minutes.

honey, walnut and pine nut sauce
salsa di miele, noci e pinoli

Serves 6
15 g (1/2 oz) pine nuts
30 g (1 oz) walnut kernels
3 tbsp clear honey
3 tbsp home-made meat stock
1 1/2 tbsp English mustard, prepared

In Piedmont, there is an ancient sauce, made with honey and walnut, that is served with il gran bui, a rich dish of mixed boiled meats. My secret here is to add one tablespoon of pine nuts which, with their slightly resinous flavour, counterbalance the sweetness of the honey.

Toast the pine nuts in a cast-iron pan.

Blanch the walnut kernels in boiling water for 30 seconds and then remove as much as you can of the thin skin.

Mix the honey and the stock.

Pound the walnuts and the pine nuts in a mortar, adding 1 tablespoon of the honey mixture. When reduced to a paste stir in the rest of the honey mixture and the mustard. Mix thoroughly. If you have a food processor or a blender you can process the nuts with the honey mixture in it, and then add the mustard.

Serve with boiled chicken, beef or ham, or the *Bollito misto* on page 158.

ice-creams and sorbets

The best end-use for the fruits I have been writing about, apart from eating them on their own, is to convert them into ice-creams or sorbets, something at which the Italians excel.

It seems that the very first sorbets were made by the Saracens, and that after they invaded Sicily in the ninth century AD the Sicilians improved on the techniques they learned from their Arab masters. Caroline Liddell and Robin Weir write in their masterly book *Ices*: 'The first known technical description of making ice-creams comes from the great Arab historian in medicine, Ibn Abu Usaybi'a (1230–1270), who mentioned in his book making artificial ice from cold water and saltpetre.' But centuries went by before we can find any other documentation. The appearance of water-ices was first recorded in the seventeenth century in Naples, Florence, Paris and in Spain. A recipe for water-ices is found in a French book published in Paris in 1674, while in Italy the first recipe for sorbet appeared in *Lo scalco alla moderna* by Antonio Latini, published in Naples in 1694. But the first ice-cream proper was supposedly created by a *chef-patissier* of Charles I of England. This ice-cream was made without eggs, but soon in France and Italy eggs were added to the cream and sugar, thus achieving a richer flavour and a smoother texture. In Italy, the making of ice-creams, sorbets and all sorts of iced concoctions was established in Sicily and southern Italy. It is still there that the best ice-creams and sorbets are made. The base for ice-cream is egg custard while sorbets are, as they always were, fruit juice and sugar syrup. Both were, as they still are, mostly enjoyed in the streets, like pizza. They are seldom actually made at home, although they are often served at home during the summer. They are bought in good *gelaterie* – ice-cream parlours – which show the sign *Produzione Propria* – produced on the premises. The range of flavours is large from the modern *tiramisú* to the most traditional lemon sorbet.

vanilla ice-cream
gelato di crema alla vaniglia

Italian ice-creams are usually made with egg custard, rather than with cream, to which various flavours are added. The custard base makes for a smoother, more velvety texture. This is my basic recipe for ice-cream. You can add fruit purée, coffee, chocolate, almond praline or pounded hazelnut to the custard, or, for a real treat, marrons glacés. Another typical Italian gelato di crema is flavoured with the grated rind of a lemon instead of the vanilla pod. Lemon-flavoured ice-cream is an ideal accompaniment to fresh fruit; try it with sliced peaches, nectarines, strawberries or pineapples.

Heat the milk with the vanilla pod in a heavy-based saucepan until just simmering.

Beat the egg yolks with the sugar until pale and mousse-like. (I use an electric hand beater.) Pour the milk over very gradually, beating the whole time. Put the pan on the heat. At this stage it is best to use a wooden spoon rather than an electric beater or wire whisk, as it helps you to judge the temperature of the custard. Continue stirring until the custard is very hot, but not boiling or the eggs will scramble. When the custard is ready, the sound of the spoon going round will change to a deeper thud and you will feel the custard thicken. Draw it off the heat immediately.

Serves 4
450 ml (3/4 pint) full-fat milk
vanilla pod
4 free-range egg yolks
120 g (4 oz) caster sugar

Straight away put the saucepan into a basin of cold water and continue stirring for about 3 minutes, otherwise the custard will curdle at the bottom of the pan.

When the custard is cold, remove the vanilla pod. Wash and dry it and keep it for one or two more uses.

Freeze the custard in an ice-cream machine according to the manufacturer's instructions. If you have not got a machine, still-freeze it in the freezer. This is a well-behaved ice-cream which does not make ice crystals.

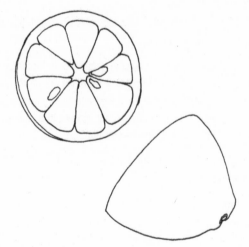

apricot ice-cream
gelato di albicocca

*I have made this apricot ice-cream with raw apricots and with poached
ones. I prefer the second method, because fruit bought in a country where
it does not actually grow does not have enough flavour. The poaching in
syrup and orange juice brings out the little flavour the fruit has.*

*Hand round a dish of almond crescents (page 368) if you wish. They
are very good and they go well with the ice-cream.*

Wash the apricots, cut them in half and remove the stones.

Put the sugar, orange juice and 4 tablespoons of water in a heavy pan.
Bring gently to the boil and simmer for 3 minutes or so, stirring very

Serves 6
**450 g (1 lb) fresh
apricots**
**100 g (3 1/2 oz)
sugar**
juice of 1 orange
**150 ml (1/4 pint)
whipping cream**
1 tbsp icing sugar
**2 tbsp *amaretto*
liqueur**

frequently to dissolve the sugar. Add the apricots to the pan. Cover the pan and cook till soft.

Pour the contents of the pan into a food processor or a liquidiser and process or blend to a coarse purée.

Lightly whip the cream with the icing sugar. Mix in the *amaretto* and the apricot purée. Transfer the mixture to an ice-cream machine and freeze, following the manufacturer's instructions. If you do not have one of these invaluable machines, freeze the mixture to a slush, whisk thoroughly and put back in the freezer until set.

Remove the ice-cream from the freezer and place in the fridge about 1 hour before serving.

preparation
Any fruit ice-cream or sorbet loses flavour if made too long in advance. Try to make it on the day you want to eat it.

firm fruit ice-cream
gelato di frutta

Serves 6–8

For the fruit purée
1 kg (2 lb) fruit, weighed after stoning and peeling if necessary
225 g (8 oz) sugar

continued over >>

This recipe makes the smoothest ice-cream I have ever tasted. I make it with peaches, apricots or plums. You can make the purée 2 or 3 days in advance but, if you can, make the ice-cream on the day you want to eat it, as ice-cream loses flavour and freshness, and begins to make little crystals, after 24 hours.

Cut the fruit into suitable segments and put in a heavy saucepan. Add the sugar and cook very gently until tender. Lift the fruit out of the pan and reduce the liquid until rich and very syrupy. If you are using plums, the liquid will need longer reduction than the other fruits.

Purée the fruit with its liquid in a food processor or blender, or through a sieve or food mill.

For the ice-cream, boil the sugar in the water until it reaches the caramel stage on the sugar thermometer.

While the syrup is boiling, whisk the egg yolks until pale and mousse-like.

When the syrup is ready pour it over the yolks, whisking constantly. Fold into the fruit purée and add enough lemon juice to enhance the flavour of the fruit.

Half-whip the cream and fold gently but thoroughly into the fruit purée. Taste and if necessary add a couple of tablespoons of icing sugar. Remember that iced food needs stronger flavouring, and that sugar helps the ice-cream to achieve the right consistency.

If you do not have an ice-cream machine you can simply put this ice-cream in the freezer and still-freeze it. Remove from the freezer and put it in the fridge about 1 hour before serving.

For the ice-cream
120 ml (4 fl oz) water
60 g (2 oz) caster sugar
2 free-range egg yolks
3 tbsp lemon juice
150 ml (1/4 pint) double cream
icing sugar if necessary

strawberry ice-cream flavoured with balsamic vinegar
gelato di fragola all'aceto balsamico

Strawberries dressed with balsamic vinegar are a classic of Emilia, because the vinegar brings out the aroma with great intensity. The ice-cream is one of my original best recipes.

Wash and hull the strawberries. Dry them with kitchen paper and put them in a food processor with the sugar. Set the processor in motion and add the balsamic vinegar through the funnel.

Transfer the mixture to a bowl, cover it and refrigerate for 2–3 hours. The sugar and the vinegar will bring out the flavour of the fruit. Whip the cream

Serves 4–6
450 g (1 lb) strawberries
150 g (5 oz) caster sugar
1 tbsp balsamic vinegar
150 ml (1/4 pint) whipping cream

to soft peaks and fold into the strawberry mixture. Put in the ice-cream machine, and follow the manufacturer's instructions. If you do not have an ice-cream machine, put the mixture in a container, cover it and put it in the freezer. Stir the mixture once during the freezing. Remove from the freezer half an hour before serving and leave at room temperature.

preparation
This, like any fruit ice-cream, is best eaten within a day of being made.

spumone

Spumone is a frozen concoction of Neapolitan origin. The name, meaning very airy froth, describes an ice-cream made with egg custard, cream and flavourings, as in the following recipe.

zabaglione ice-cream
spumone di zabaione

Serves 6
5 free-range eggs
120 g (4 oz) caster
  sugar
pinch of ground
  cinnamon
120 ml (4 fl oz)
  Marsala
2 tbsp rum
300 ml (1/2 pint)
  double cream
amarettini **or**
  chopped hazelnuts
  for decoration

Separate the eggs and put the yolks in a bowl or in the top of a double boiler. Put 3 of the whites in another bowl.

Add the sugar and the cinnamon to the egg yolks and beat off the heat until the custard becomes pale yellow and forms ribbons. Add the Marsala and the rum, while beating constantly. Put the bowl over a saucepan one-third full of hot water, or put the top on to the bottom half of the double saucepan. Bring the water to the simmer while you whisk constantly – an electric hand beater is ideal for the job. The mixture will become foamy and will nearly double in volume. Put the bowl in cold water and leave it to cool, beating very frequently.

Whip the cream until it forms soft peaks, then incorporate the egg custard into the cream.

Whip the 3 egg whites until they form stiff peaks. Add the whipped egg white by the spoonful to the egg and cream mixture, folding it in gently.

If you have an ice-cream machine, follow the manufacturer's instructions. If not, transfer the zabaglione mixture to a large glass dish and place in the freezer. About 3 hours later remove from the freezer and, with a metal whisk or an electric beater, beat the *zabaglione*. This stirring will break up any crystals that might have formed and make the mixture smooth and velvety. Return to the freezer and leave for at least 4 hours.

You can decorate the *spumoni* with *amarettini* – small *amaretti* – or sprinkle chopped hazelnuts over the top. Serve with almond meringues (*meringhine alle mandorle*) (page 365).

preparation
You can make the *spumoni* 1 day in advance, but no more than that. I find that any ice-cream loses its flavour and freshness if left too long in the freezer.

moulded cream pudding
panna cotta

This is not really an ice-cream. It is an old pudding from Piemonte similar to a classic ice-cream, but served chilled, not frozen. Panna cotta is now becoming as fashionable outside Italy as tiramisú *was ten years ago. But this delicate milky pudding has been around in Piedmont for centuries. It was one of the desserts to appear at the dinner parties of the Royal House of Savoy, later to become the Royal House of Italy. In Piedmont it always was and usually still is served without any fruit – just pure white delectable cream.*

Here I have written a recipe for a panna cotta *with a caramel, which you can however eliminate. Also you can serve some soft fruits or poached plums or cherries with it. The secret of a good panna cotta is to use as little gelatine as possible.*

Serves 6
180 g (6 oz) caster sugar
1 tsp lemon juice
450 ml (3/4 pint) double cream
150 ml (1/4 pint) full-fat milk
piece of vanilla pod
4 tbsp peach *eau-de-vie* or white rum
10 g (1/4 oz) gelatine leaves
2 dozen sweet geranium leaves, if available

First prepare the caramel. Heat the oven to 160°C (325°F) mark 3 and place six 120 ml (4 fl oz) ramekins in it to heat for 5 minutes.

Put 75 g (2 1/2 oz) of the sugar, 3 tablespoons of water and the lemon juice into a small saucepan and bring slowly to the boil. Do not stir. The syrup will heat up very slowly at first and then it will begin to turn very pale gold. It will turn dark brown quite quickly. At that moment withdraw the pan from the heat and pour the caramel into the heated ramekins. Tip the ramekins in all directions for the caramel to slide and coat the surface evenly. Set aside and prepare the pudding.

Heat the cream, milk, vanilla and spirit in a heavy saucepan. Add the remaining sugar and bring slowly to the boil, stirring constantly. Boil for 1 minute. Set aside to infuse for 1 hour or so and then strain the mixture.

Soften the gelatine leaves in cold water and then squeeze them and dissolve them in 4 tablespoons of hot water. Spoon a couple of tablespoons of the cream mixture into the gelatine, stirring rapidly. Now add this mixture to the cream mixture, stirring very thoroughly to incorporate.

Pour the cream mixture into the ramekins. Allow to cool and then cover with clingfilm and chill for at least 2 hours.

Run a palette knife around the side of the ramekins and then unmould on to individual plates. Place the sweet geranium leaves around each mould as if they were the petals of a flower.

preparation
The cream mixture can be prepared up to 1 day in advance. Keep in the ramekins and unmould just before serving.

sorbets

Today's preoccupation with the effects of food on health is not new. In 1784 a Neapolitan doctor, Filippo Baldini, wrote: 'Because of the sugar, the salt and the cold, sorbets give rise to a great number of beneficial effects in our bodies by helping with the digestion of food.'

Water-ices, more than ice-cream, exemplify the Italian taste for pure basic flavours. These are often enhanced by a touch of another flavour that complements the main ingredient. You can add a tablespoon or two of Grand Marnier to your orange sorbet, the juice of half an orange to a strawberry one or a little kirsch to a plum sorbet. The thing to keep in mind is that the fruit juice must be full of flavour. Make sorbets with ripe fruits in full season, and always add some orange or lemon juice to bring out the flavour.

Now that ice-cream machines have become a more common kitchen accessory, the problem of crystallisation need no longer be a worry. I am not a gadget-minded cook, but I cannot think how I lived for so many years without my ice-cream machine. It forms a happy trinity with my food processor and the hand-cranked pasta machine.

orange sorbet
sorbetto all'arancia

This sorbet can also be made with lemons or mandarins to which some lemon juice is added, but not with satsumas as their flavour is not strong enough.

Wash the oranges.

Put the sugar and water in a heavy saucepan. Add the orange rind, without any white pith, of 2 of the oranges, and the lemon balm if you have it in the garden. Bring slowly to the boil, stirring frequently to dissolve the sugar, then simmer for 5 minutes. Allow to cool.

Serves 4
4 organic oranges
250 g (9 oz)
  granulated sugar
500 ml (16 fl oz)
  water
a sprig of lemon
  balm (optional)
1 free-range egg
  white

Squeeze the oranges and add the juice to the syrup. Strain the syrup.

To freeze in a sorbetière. Lightly whisk the egg white and fold into the syrup. Freeze according to the manufacturer's instructions.

To freeze in the freezer. Freeze the orange syrup until it becomes firm round the edge. Whisk the egg white until stiff and whisk into the partially frozen mixture. Use an electric beater if you have one, but put the bowl in the sink and use a lower speed to start off or you will have sorbet flying all over the kitchen. Freeze again and then whisk once more with a metal whisk. Return the bowl to the freezer until the sorbet is really firm.

elderflower water-ice
sorbetto di fior di sambuco

Serves 4
**2 large organic
lemons**
**850 ml (1 1/2 pints)
water**
**275 g (9 1/2 oz)
sugar**
4 large elderflowers

This is a very flowery water-ice which I find quite delicious. Pick elderflowers when they are in full bloom, from bushes in sunny positions; they have a much stronger scent.

Wash 1 of the lemons. Cut a strip of zest, only the yellow part, and put it in a saucepan with the water, the sugar and the elderflowers. Bring slowly to the boil while stirring to dissolve the sugar. Boil for 5 minutes and then draw the pan off the heat. Add the juice of the 2 lemons and leave to cool.

When the syrup mixture is cold, drain it and freeze in an ice-cream machine, following the manufacturer's instructions.

If you haven't got a machine, put the elderflower syrup in the freezer and freeze until the sorbet is firm around the edge. Beat the sorbet using a metal whisk or, better still, an electric beater, until the mixture is smooth. Return to the freezer. Repeat the whisking once more and then freeze until the sorbet is really firm.

basil-flavoured lemon sorbet
sorbetto di limone al basilica

This lemon sorbet, as well as being delicious, looks very pretty, the pale lemon green being speckled with the dark green of the basil. While the flavour of the lemon is immediately identifiable, the basil seems to blend in so well as to be indistinct. Yet it is the basil that transforms an everyday lemon sorbet into a conversation stopper.

It is essential to use leaves from a young basil plant. Old basil plants have a very strong minty flavour, which is wrong for this dish.

Wash the fruit and remove the rind, without chipping into the white pith, and put it into a saucepan. Add the water and the sugar. Bring slowly to the boil and simmer until the sugar has dissolved. Turn the heat up to moderate and boil rapidly for 3–4 minutes. Draw off the heat and allow the syrup to cool completely, and then strain it and discard the rind.

Meanwhile squeeze the lemons and the oranges. You should get at least 500 ml (16 fl oz). Strain the juice and add to the cold syrup, together with the basil leaves. If you have an ice-cream machine, pour the mixture into it and freeze according to the manufacturer's instructions.

If you do not have an ice-cream machine, pour the mixture into a metal bowl and freeze for about 2 hours, until the mixture is half-frozen. Remove from the freezer, put the bowl in the sink (because the mixture might splatter everywhere) and beat with a hand-held electric beater or a whisk. This will break down the crystals. You can use a food processor. Freeze again and then whisk once more. Return the bowl to the freezer until the sorbet is ready.

preparation
Sorbets, especially those based on fruit, lose their flavour if made longer than 24 hours in advance.

Serves 6
8 organic lemons
2 organic oranges
600 ml (1 pint) water
350 g (12 oz) caster sugar
2 dozen large basil leaves, chopped

coffee granita
granita al caffè

Serves 6
**900 ml (1 1/2 pints)
 freshly brewed
 espresso coffee
6 tbsp sugar
200 ml (7 fl oz)
 whipping cream
2 tbsp icing sugar**

This is what you have in a bar during a balmy Mediterranean night.

Heat the coffee, add the sugar and stir to dissolve. Taste and add a little more sugar if you wish. Pour the coffee into freezing trays and, when cold, freeze until solid.

Plunge the bottom of the tray in a bowl of hot water for a few seconds, then break up the coffee ice into chunks and process until it forms small crystals. Return to the trays and place back in the freezer.

Before serving, place 6 long-stemmed wine glasses in the refrigerator to chill.

Whip the cream and stir in the icing sugar to sweeten very slightly.

Remove the *granita* from the freezer. If it is too solid, process again for a few seconds just before serving. Spoon the *granita* into the chilled glasses and top with the whipped cream.

It is difficult to cook an Italian meal without using some wine. Whether the wine is to be red or white, dry or sweet, it must be a decent wine, good enough that you would happily drink it at table. It is no good buying 'cooking plonk'; it will ruin your beef or your fish, and your stomach into the bargain. In this book I have suggested the use of a particular wine only when necessary to the final result.

Except in some puddings, wine should always be brought to the boil and boiled fiercely for 1 or 2 minutes, depending on the quantity, to allow part of the alcohol to evaporate.

Wine is necessary in many dishes to achieve the perfect roundness of flavour. This does not mean that it can be added at will, discretion being one of the guiding rules of a good cook. If, for instance, you are cooking a dish that needs more liquid, yet you have already added all the wine that is recommended, add water rather than extra wine to provide the necessary liquid without the unwanted extra flavour.

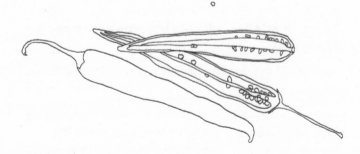

shin of beef stewed in barbera wine
spezzato di manzo al barbera

Serves 4–6
60 g (2 oz) pancetta
1 carrot
1 celery stick, with
    green top if
    possible
5–7 fresh sage
    leaves or 4–5 dried
    leaves
sprig of fresh
    rosemary, 5 cm (2
    inches) long
3 tbsp olive oil
2 tbsp vegetable oil
700 g (1 1/2 lb) shin
    of beef, cut into
    2.5–3.5 cm (1–1
    1/2 inch) cubes,
    trimmed of sinews
225 g (8 oz) boneless
    lean pork, cut into
    same-sized cubes,
    trimmed of sinews
    and excess fat
150 ml (1/4 pint) dry
    white wine
4 large onions,
    thickly sliced
1/2 tbsp sugar
sea salt
300 ml (1/2 pint)
    Barbera wine
freshly ground black
    pepper

Barbera is a robust and full-bodied wine from Piedmont. This rustic dish, rich and full of flavour, is an ideal meat course to serve in the winter.

Shin of beef is the perfect stewing cut because the gelatinous membrane which envelops the nuggets of meat dissolves in the cooking, making the liquid rich and tasty.

Chop together very finely the pancetta, the carrot, celery, sage and rosemary needles and put with the olive oil in a heavy-based casserole. Sauté gently until the vegetables are soft.

Heat the vegetable oil in a large frying pan and, when very hot, add the meat and brown well on all sides. Do not cut short this operation, because it is this frying that gives flavour to the meat, sealing the juices. Remove the meat from the pan and place in the casserole on top of the vegetables.

Heat the oven to 160°C (325°F) mark 3.

Pour the white wine into the pan in which the meat has fried and boil rapidly for 30 seconds. Pour over the meat.

Place the sliced onions on top of the meat and sprinkle with the sugar and salt. Cover the casserole with a tight lid and cook over a low heat until the onion has wilted. Add a generous grinding of pepper.

Heat the red wine, pour over the meat and place the covered pan in the oven for about 2 1/2 hours, until the meat is tender enough to be cut with a fork.

Serve straight away from the casserole or transfer to a heated deep dish.

Polenta is the classic accompaniment, but I can also recommend the bread gnocchi, *Canederli* on page 80. Make them the size of a mandarin. You should not serve any vegetables, but a green salad afterwards might be very welcome to cleanse the palate.

drunk potatoes
patate ubriache

For years we spent a few peaceful weeks at my brother's country house near Lake Bolsena, about 60 miles north of Rome. The house is in a tiny village called Pianiano, which is surrounded by gently rolling hills planted with wheat, corn and vines. Annina, who looks after my brother's house, sits for hours in the village square with the other local women. They all knit incessantly, making jumpers with holes and bobbles in the most garish colours for the boutique owners of the nearby towns. When I am there I join them, and we chat about their knitting, my tapestry work and, mainly, their cooking, which is how I learned about these drunk potatoes.

Not only are they happy to share their recipes, we are also sometimes invited to share meals with them, meals that are of great simplicity, gargantuan quantity and extreme excellence. A typical spread would start with *salame* and prosciutto to whet the appetite, then tagliatelle with a *ragù*, chicken livers being a favourite, then *pollastrelli al forno* – roast chicken (which were still scratching about the day before), perhaps accompanied by these *patate ubriache* and certainly followed by an *insalatina di campo* – a wild salad. Pecorino, and after that a ricotta tart, filled with home-made jam, finish off the meal.

For 5 or 6 people you need 1 kg (2 lb) of good waxy potatoes, cut into 5 mm (1/4 inch) slices. Wash the potatoes in 2 or 3 changes of cold water until the water is clear (this gets rid of the starch). Dry them thoroughly with a kitchen cloth. Make a little *soffritto* in a large sauté pan with 60 g (2 oz) of unsalted butter, 2 tablespoons of olive oil, 2 shallots or 1 small onion, chopped, 1 garlic clove, chopped, and a small sprig of fresh sage. When the shallot is soft, add the potatoes and cook them in the *soffritto*, turning them over frequently so that they take up the taste of the *soffritto*. Remove and discard the sage.

Heat 200 ml (7 fl oz) of dry white wine and 120 ml (4 fl oz) of meat stock and add to the pan. Season with salt and pepper and give the potatoes a good stir. Use a fork as it breaks the potatoes less than a spoon. Cover the pan and cook the potatoes over a low heat until they are nearly done, by which time they should have absorbed nearly all the liquid. Stir occasionally and if they get too dry add a little more hot stock or water. Taste and check the seasoning.

The traditional vinegar of Italy is wine vinegar. Red vinegar is more commonly used than white, although to a certain extent it is a question of taste and of the appearance of the dish.

The main use of vinegar is in salad. Most Italian salads are very simply dressed: with oil, vinegar (or occasionally lemon juice) and salt. The proportion of vinegar to oil can vary according to taste, to the acidity of the vinegar and the type of salad, but usually we add 1–1 1/2 tablespoons of vinegar and 4 tablespoons of oil to a bowl of salad for 4 people. But beetroot, for instance, calls for more vinegar, while tomatoes need far less.

Vinegar is often used in place of wine as a flavouring in the cooking of meat and, occasionally, fish. Meat, rabbit, hare and game are often marinated in vinegar, especially in Umbria, where vinegar diluted with water replaces wine in most recipes. Vinegar is the essential ingredient in a *carpione* or *scapece*, sweet-and-sour dishes made all over Italy. Some cooks add a tablespoon or so of vinegar to pears or plums in the poaching liquid. This may seem odd, but I can recommend it because the vinegar cuts into the sweetness of the syrup.

Another important use of vinegar is as a preservative. The Romans developed the art of preserving food in vinegar and passed their knowledge on to their subjects all over their Empire. Writing in the first century AD, Apicius gave these recipes for preserving turnips: 'First clean them and put them in a vessel and then put on myrtle berries mixed with honey and vinegar.' Or: 'mix mustard and honey, vinegar and salt and pour over the turnips put together in a vessel.'

The quality of vinegar is important. Choose a good French or Italian vinegar which is strong yet has not got the sharp unpleasant acidity of inferior brands. I put a clove or two of garlic in my bottle of vinegar; other people add rosemary or other herbs.

sweet-and-sour shoulder of lamb
spezzatino di agnello in agrodolce

Serves 4–5
850 g–1 kg (1 3/4–2 lb) lean shoulder of lamb, boned and cut into pieces
3 tbsp olive oil
1 large onion, very finely sliced
sea salt
1 tbsp vegetable oil
1 tbsp tomato purée dissolved in 120 ml (4 fl oz) warm milk
3 tbsp sugar
freshly ground black pepper
about 10 fresh basil leaves, torn, or 2 tsp oregano

For the marinade
150 ml (1/4 pint) wine vinegar
6 juniper berries, bruised
3 garlic cloves, squashed
2 bay leaves
sea salt
4 or 5 peppercorns, lightly crushed

Few dishes are more satisfying than a good stew. Shoulder of lamb is an ideal stewing cut because it has enough fat to keep the meat moist and tasty during the lengthy cooking.

In this recipe from Puglia, the heel of the Italian boot, the milk and sugar added to the sauce counterbalance the vinegary marinade, while the basil lifts and refreshes the flavour.

Put the meat and all the ingredients for the marinade in a bowl. Cover the bowl, put it in a cool place and leave for a minimum of 4 hours. Drain and dry the meat.

Gently heat the olive oil with the onion in a heavy pot, preferably earthenware, and add a little salt (this helps to soften the onion without browning it).

Meanwhile sear the meat in a non-stick frying pan with the vegetable oil. If necessary do this in 2 batches, because the meat will brown only in a single layer. Sauté on all sides for a good 10 minutes, stirring very frequently. Then transfer all the meat to the pot containing the onion. Mix well and let the meat take the flavour for 2 or 3 minutes.

Add the dissolved tomato purée and stir well. Turn the heat down to very low and cover the pan, placing the lid slightly askew. This will enable some of the steam to escape, thus concentrating the flavours.

Cook for about 30 minutes, keeping a watch on the meat. Should it get too dry, add a couple of tablespoons of hot water. Strain and heat the marinade and add to the meat with the sugar, salt and pepper. Cook for a further 20 minutes, still with the lid askew, turning the meat occasionally. The lamb is ready when it is very tender; the exact cooking time depends entirely on the age of the lamb. When the lamb is done, add the basil or the oregano.

preparation
The dish can be prepared in advance. It is actually better made the day before and then slowly reheated, either in the oven or on top.

beef braised in wine vinegar
brasato all'aceto

In this old Lombard recipe the joint of beef, the brasato, *is cooked in red wine vinegar instead of the more usual red wine. In northern Italian homes,* brasato *is one of the most popular dishes for serving on Sundays or at dinner parties. It is not the sort of dish you will be able to sample at a restaurant because it requires time, patience and the use of a large piece of meat. But it is ideal at home, however out of fashion it may be nowadays when the home cook so often takes her lead from the restaurateurs. It is a generous dish, equivalent to the British Sunday joint, and it has the advantage that it will not be spoilt if your guests, or your children, are late.* Brasato *is so well behaved that it can even be prepared in advance and slowly reheated in a low oven.*

Prepare the larding. Cut the pancetta into pieces about 10 cm (4 inches) long and 1 cm (1/4 inch) thick.

Mix together the sage leaves, salt and pepper and coat the pancetta pieces with the mixture.

Lard the meat with this mixture by cutting deep slits in it, following the grain of the meat, and pushing the pieces of pancetta into the slits. If you do not have a larding needle, use a chopstick or the end of a clean round pencil.

Prepare the marinade. Mix all the ingredients together in an earthenware pot or a bowl and place the meat in it. Cover the bowl and leave to marinate for 24 hours, turning the meat over as often as you can remember.

Heat the oven to 160°C (325°F) mark 3. Take the meat out of the marinade and dry it thoroughly.

Put the vegetable oil in a heavy frying pan and, when the oil is hot, slip in the meat and brown very well on all sides over a high heat. Transfer the meat to a side plate.

Strain the marinade and add to the frying pan. Deglaze for 1 minute, scraping the bottom of the pan with a metal spoon. Measure the liquid and add enough boiling water to make up to 200 ml (7 fl oz).

Serves 8
- **1.5 kg (3 1/4 lb) chuck steak in a single piece, tied**
- **2 tbsp vegetable oil**
- **1 onion, very finely chopped**
- **3 garlic cloves, peeled and finely chopped**
- **1 salted anchovy, boned and washed, or 2 anchovy fillets, chopped**
- **2 tbsp chopped parsley**
- **1 tbsp chopped fresh sage leaves**
- **2 tbsp finely chopped celery leaves**
- **2 tbsp olive oil**
- **sea salt and freshly ground black pepper**
- **2 tsp brown sugar**
- **6 tbsp double cream**

For the larding
- **50g (1 3/4 oz) pancetta or unsmoked streaky bacon, cut in a single thick slice**
- **8 fresh sage leaves, chopped**
- **sea salt and freshly ground black pepper**

continued over >>

For the marinade
2 tbsp olive oil
juice of 1 large
   organic lemon
150 ml (1/4 pint) red
   wine vinegar
5 or 6 black
   peppercorns

Put the onion, garlic, anchovy, parsley, sage, celery and olive oil into an oval casserole, large enough to hold the meat comfortably but snugly. Put on the heat and cook for a minute, stirring frequently.

Place the meat on this mixture, add the marinade and a little salt and pepper. Bring slowly to the boil. Cover the pan with a lid and transfer to the oven. Cook for 1 1/2 hours. Keep a watch on the meat: it should cook at a very low but steady simmer. Turn the meat over three or four times.

Sprinkle with the sugar and continue cooking, always tightly covered, for a further 1 1/2 hours, until the meat is very tender indeed.

Transfer the meat to a chopping board and allow to cool a little, while you make the sauce.

If the juices in the casserole are too thin, boil briskly to reduce until they are rich and syrupy. Add the cream, stir well and cook for a couple of minutes. Taste and check the salt and pepper and then transfer to a heated bowl and serve with the carved meat.

balsamic vinegar
aceto balsamico

This very special vinegar, made from the cooked and concentrated must of the white grapes of the Trebbiano vine, exists in two forms, one of which can be easily, and relatively cheaply, bought, while the other is almost a collector's item. The first is labelled, simply, *aceto balsamico*, and it is given its characteristic flavour by the addition of a little caramelised sugar. It has a sweet yet vinegary fragrance and a beautiful dark brown colour glinting with gold. This is the balsamic vinegar found everywhere. It is a good product that can be used without qualms in all the recipes I give here.

The other version is called *aceto balsamico tradizionale*, and by law it can only be given this name when it has been aged for at least ten years. This *aceto balsamico* is similar in colour, but its flavour is full and velvety, a perfect balance between sweet and sour, with a more subtle, deeper fragrance. Made on a very small scale in and around Reggio Emilia and Modena, *aceto balsamico tradizionale* is something of a gastronomic cult, not to say an obsession. Pages have been written about it and societies formed to foster it. 'It can be sipped in small glasses, like a very rare liqueur, served on a silver platter so as to give it due honour.' Thus wrote Paolo Monelli in his *Giro Gastronomico d'Italia*, published in 1939, and this is exactly what I did years ago when I went to Emilia to study the mystique at first hand.

The setting for my initiation into the mysteries of this cult was a charming house in the countryside not far from Reggio Emilia. It was the country house of Maria Carla Terrachini Sidoli and her husband Gigi and, apart from the charm of its owners, not to mention the *aceto balsamico tradizionale* made in its attic, it was remarkable for the fact that it remained exactly as it had been when Baron Franchetti, owner of the Ca d'Oro in Venice, built it as a hunting lodge in 1889 and had all the furniture and fittings made expressly for the house. As a result the house, and everything in it, is a perfect example of *art nouveau*.

We were asked for five o'clock and, naturally enough, looked forward to a refreshing cup of cold tea. But as we sat in the garden on that sunny afternoon, with the fertile expanse of the Po valley curling away into the distance, Maria Carla produced a silver tray bearing, not cups and saucers, but tiny glasses, a plate of white bread and a small phial – rather like those used in church for the holy wine – containing the precious liquid. This was the cue for Gigi to launch into a discourse about his favourite occupation, the making of *aceto balsamico tradizionale* in the attic of his hunting lodge.

The start of the process is when the grape must is brought to the boil and reduced. It is then poured into large wooden vessels and any excess acidity is neutralised by the addition of a small amount of marble powder or ash. The must then separates and the clear, pale liquid that will become *aceto balsamico* begins its years of ageing in different barrels. Various woods are used for the barrels: oak, chestnut, mulberry, birch and juniper, and the liquid is transferred from one barrel to another. Typical of the attention paid to detail is the fact that the barrels must be plugged with a stone that comes from a river.

The reason that vinegar-making takes place in Gigi's attic, as it does in the attics of many old *palazzi* in Modena and Reggio Emilia, is that the space under the roof provides the necessary heat yet can be arranged to give plenty of ventilation. In some of these attics the *aceto balsamico* is over 50 years old; enjoyed only by family and friends it is used with great reverence.

So it was that on that sunny afternoon a few drops were poured out of the little phial into our glasses and, on tasting it, I began to understand why this vinegar is treated as an elixir. That *aceto balsamico* had been started in the nineteenth century and had been aged only in barrels made of juniper wood. Its nose was incredibly rich and all-pervading, and I could understand why Lucrezia Borgia was said to have kept on sniffing it – like smelling salts – while suffering from the pains of giving birth to her first son. Therapeutic properties were also attributed to *aceto balsamico* by Rossini who wrote to a friend 'a little vinegar from Modena, with its well known soothing and refreshing effect, succeeded in restoring me to a degree of health and serenity.'

The earliest mention of *aceto balsamico* is found in a chronicle of 1046 written by a Benedictine monk who wrote about the life of Matilde of Canossa. Her father, Bonifacio, heard that the Emperor Henry II wished to taste this famous preparation. 'As soon as he heard of the Emperor's wish, he ordered there to be made a casket and a silver cart with two oxen, and had it brought to the Emperor, who was amazed and full of admiration.' I felt equally moved and grateful when the Sidolis presented me with a phial of this nectar, which I am now using, counting the drops. Not surprisingly, *aceto balsamico tradizionale* is far from cheap. It is used very sparingly, not only because of its cost but also because a few drops are all that are needed.

The recipes I have chosen are made with the ordinary *aceto balsamico*. I never use it to dress a simple salad, nor indeed does any Italian I know, but you can use it for a special salad. I like it, for instance, on cauliflower florets, boiled or steamed, mixed with 4 parts oil, seasoned with a little garlic and 2 anchovy fillets pounded together to a paste. Another treat is to use *aceto balsamico* in a vinaigrette for avocados mixed with extra virgin olive oil and flavoured with salt and pepper.

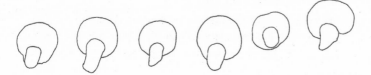

pork fillet with elderberries, almonds and balsamic vinegar
filetto di maiale alla cavalcanti

Serves 4
600 g (1 lb 5 oz)
fillet of pork
45 g (1 1/2 oz)
unsalted butter
2 tbsp olive oil
120 ml (4 fl oz) good
red wine
sea salt and pepper
1 tbsp sugar
pinch of cinnamon
2 tbsp *aceto*
balsamico
1 tbsp ground
almonds
2 tbsp elderberries
1 tbsp capers, rinsed

Ippolito Cavalcanti, Duca di Buonvicino, was not only a fashionable aristocrat and a great gourmet; he also wrote a very remarkable cookery book. Called Cucina teorico-pratica, *the book is a mine of information and a collection of excellent recipes, all in the spirit of the time and place – Naples at the beginning of the nineteenth century, where artists, philosophers, musicians and archaeologists gathered, often over sumptuous meals. Cavalcanti stresses the importance of best-quality ingredients and the right use of spices, salt, stock, alcohol and wine. His recipes are light and inspired, and extraordinarily modern.*

The following recipe is my adaptation of one of Cavalcanti's. The pork is cooked first and then flavoured with the elderberries, capers and almonds. The capers are the liaison in taste between the vinegar and the elderberries, while the ground almonds are used as a thickener, as they were in most antique recipes. I use aceto balsamico *because I find it has the perfect balance between sweetness and sourness necessary for this dish, but a good red wine vinegar will do.*

Trim the pork fillets of their fat, then cut them in half, if necessary, so that they will fit in a large sauté pan.

Heat the butter and olive oil in the pan and add the pork. Sauté until brown on all sides.

Bring the wine to the boil in a separate small pan and pour over the meat with 2 tablespoons of hot water. When the liquid has come back to the boil, add salt and pepper. Turn the heat down so that the liquid will just simmer, cover the pan tightly and cook for 10 minutes until the pork is done. Remove the meat from the pan and keep warm.

Add the sugar and cinnamon, vinegar, almonds, elderberries and capers to the pan and cook, stirring constantly, for 2 minutes.

Slice the meat, not too thinly, and return to the pan for 2 minutes to absorb the flavour of the sauce. Transfer the contents of the pan to a heated oval dish and serve at once.

roast quails flavoured with balsamic vinegar
quaglie all'aceto balsamico

During a holiday in Italy we explored the cooking of Emilia Romagna in some depth. The best meal we had was at a restaurant called Al Portone in Scandiano, a town to the south of Reggio Emilia. You reach the restaurant through a medieval courtyard which, on this April evening, was beautifully floodlit. The restaurant itself is an eighteenth-century building attached to the 12-century *rocca*, the castle that belonged to Count Matteo Maria Boiardo, lord of the provinces of Reggio Emilia and Modena and famous for his epic poem *L'Orlando Innamorato*.

We had a delightful meal, and the evening ended in a long and stimulating conversation with the owners, Paola and Luigi La Carruba. Paola, who does most of the cooking, learnt her *métier* from her mother-in-law, who comes from Parma but is married to a Sicilian. A better gastronomic match would be hard to find. One of the best dishes that evening was a roast guinea-fowl flavoured with *aceto balsamico*. Paola told me that she cooked pheasant and quails in the same way. She pointed out that *aceto balsamico* gives the perfect touch of sweet-and-sour to a sauce for game, especially the smaller feathered game.

Back in London I tried her creation with both guinea-fowl and quails – pheasants were no longer in season. I prefer the quail, partly because the guinea-fowl you buy in Britain are not as moist as the ones in Emilia, so that they become too dry when roasted. Quail are more juicy, and because of their size they cook very quickly, thus having little time to dry up.

If the quails are very small, as they sometimes are these days, you will need two per person.

Heat the oven to 200°C (400°F) mark 6.

Clean and wipe the quails and rub them with salt and pepper inside and out.

Heat the oil in a heavy-based pan and fry the quails over a moderately high heat, turning them over on all sides. This will take no longer than 5 minutes. Add a couple of tablespoons of the stock and place the pan in the oven. Bake for 10–15 minutes, basting twice. Halfway through the cooking, dribble 1 tablespoon of the *aceto balsamico* over the birds. When they are cooked, transfer to a dish and keep warm.

Serves 2
4 plucked quails
sea salt and pepper
2 tbsp olive oil
100 ml (3 1/2 fl oz)
  strong home-made
  meat stock, or
  stock made with a
  good quality meat
  bouillon
3 tbsp *aceto*
  balsamico
30 g (1 oz) unsalted
  butter

Deglaze the pan with the remaining *aceto balsamico* and then add a couple of tablespoons of stock. Bring slowly to the boil and boil for a minute or two.

Cut up the butter and add it little by little to the sauce, stirring constantly. Taste and check the salt and pepper. As soon as the butter has melted, spoon a little sauce over the quail and serve the rest in a heated bowl.

duck breasts with balsamic vinegar
petti di anatra all'aceto balsamico

Serves 6
60 g (2 oz) unsalted butter
1 celery stalk, very finely chopped
1 shallot, very finely chopped
sea salt and pepper
4 tbsp dry white wine
150 ml (1/4 pint) duck stock or other strong meat stock
3 duck breasts, weighing about 350 g (12 oz) each
1 tbsp olive oil
4 tbsp balsamic vinegar

In this recipe the balsamic vinegar is used in the sauce to cut through the richness of the duck, much as brandy, port or Madeira are. I wrote this recipe for duck breasts, as they are easily available in many shops nowadays, though I prefer to buy a duck and remove the breasts, which are enough for my husband and myself. I then make a ragù *for a dish of pasta with the rest of the meat, and I boil the carcass for a bowl of rich, well-flavoured stock. But this needs time, and time is often the least easily available ingredient. So I suggest you buy the French* magrets de canard, *which are now sold in many butchers and better supermarkets. Some of these breasts are quite large, weighing 250 g (9 oz) or more each, which is enough for two people. They are from Barbary ducks, which have leaner meat. These duck breasts go very well with the stewed lentils on page 95, or with the celery purée on page 467. A second* contorno – accompanying vegetable – could be *grilled polenta (page 73), which you can prepare beforehand and just reheat quickly in the oven for 5 minutes.*

I have tried cooking the breasts beforehand and then warming them, cut into slices, in the sauce for half a minute. It does not work, however, because they cook too much and curl up, not looking very attractive.

Heat the oven to 220°C (425°F) mark 7.

Heat the butter with the celery and the shallot in a saucepan. Add 2 pinches of salt. When the vegetables are just soft but by no means brown, pour over the wine and boil until the liquid is reduced by half. Add the stock and simmer gently for about 30 minutes.

While the sauce is simmering away, score the skin of the duck breasts with the point of a sharp knife, deeply enough to penetrate the flesh, and rub with salt and pepper. Grease a roasting tin with the oil and lay the breasts on it, skin side down. Roast for 15–20 minutes, according to how well cooked you like your duck.

Remove the skin from the duck. (It is delicious cut into small strips, fried and sprinkled over a radicchio salad.) Put the duck on a plate and keep warm, covered with foil. Skim off the extra fat from the roasting tin, if there is any. Put the tin over the heat and deglaze with the balsamic vinegar, boiling rapidly for 30 seconds, while scraping the bottom of the pan with a metal spoon. Pour into the sauce, taste for seasoning and transfer to a heated sauce-boat.

Cut the duck breasts into slanting slices and transfer to a warm dish. Spoon over a little of the sauce. Serve the rest of the sauce separately.

preparation
The sauce can be prepared in advance and reheated before the deglazing juices are added. For the duck, see the introduction to this recipe.

olive oil

The olive is the fruit of the *Olea europea*, which has been cultivated in the Mediterranean basin since the third millennium before Christ. The fruit of this ancient tree produces the oil that has always played such a large part in the lives of Mediterranean people. Kings and priests have been anointed with olive oil, Roman athletes oiled themselves with it to make their muscles supple and noble ladies used it to keep their skin soft and fresh. Above all, however, olive oil was used extensively in cooking. The Romans even poured olive oil on their breakfast cereal, which was a kind of polenta.

Today, for those who love the Mediterranean, olive trees are often a reminder of Italian holidays, of walking in the Ligurian hills, of driving along the winding roads of Chianti or past the groves of huge olive trees in Puglia. And these are, indeed, the three regions whose olive oil is the most generally acclaimed. Generally, but not universally, since olive trees grow in all the regions of Italy except Piedmont and Valle d'Aosta, and many regions have their champions who will insist that their oil is the best. In fact there is excellent oil from around Viterbo in Latium, in Umbria and around Lake Garda, the latter being the most northerly area where olive trees grow.

As the fruit must be ripe before it is crushed, there is a considerable variation in the harvesting time between the North and the South. When I was in the Cilento, south of Naples, in late September 1987, the nets were already laid out on the ground ready to collect the olives when the trees were shaken, whereas in Chianti the olives are harvested in late October. The best oil is made within a few days of the olives being picked, and the process of producing the oil takes place without any use of heat or chemicals. Olive oil is pure olive juice, that's all.

In Britain two kinds of olive oil are available: 'extra virgin olive oil' and 'olive oil'. My advice is to keep one bottle of extra virgin for salads and other dressings and a bottle of plain olive oil for frying. In specialist shops and in the best supermarkets you can also buy bottles of estate oil. This is oil that comes entirely from the olives of a single estate, olives that are usually picked by hand and pressed within two days.

The oil most commonly available in Britain comes from Tuscany. It is a fruity and full-bodied oil which can have a tingling peppery taste felt at the back of the palate. The oil from Liguria is sweeter and more delicate, while that from the South, which accounts for 80 per cent of the Italian production, is full-bodied and thick, with a faint almondy taste. I like to use a Ligurian oil or an oil from Lake Garda for delicate dishes, and an oil from Tuscany or the South, which is stronger and more assertive, for salads. Which oil you choose is a matter of personal taste; after trying several you will probably find the one you prefer and stick to it.

the uses of olive oil

The main use of olive oil is in salads. In Italy the word *insalata* – salad – implies raw or cooked vegetables, always dressed and mostly with olive oil, wine vinegar or lemon juice and salt. Other oils are never used in traditional Italian salads.

In the past walnut oil was used in northern Italy by the poor who could not afford the more expensive olive oil. Manzoni mentions this in *I Promessi Sposi*, his novel set in seventeeth-century Lombardy. There were many walnut trees of majestic beauty in Lombardy, and walnut oil was cheap. With the 'economic miracle' of the late 1940s walnut trees came to be seen in a new light, not as a source of cheap and rather poorly regarded oil, but as the provider of a most valuable and highly regarded timber; the wood was ideal for the manufacture of massive suites in the furniture factories of Brianza. So the walnut trees were felled, and now walnut oil has become very expensive and is seen as an exotic product.

Olive oil is also widely used as a cooking fat. It has always been the condiment and cooking fat of central and southern Italy, but it is only since the last war that it has broken through the 'butter line' which ran across Italy between Emilia Romagna and Tuscany. The final victory of olive oil over butter came with the drive for healthy eating. It is also a fat with a high critical, or smoking, point, above which toxic substances are formed. Contrary to what is sometimes said, this characteristic of olive oil makes it a good frying oil. The ideal temperature of the oil or fat for deep frying is 180°C and the smoking point of olive oil is 210°C; only groundnut oil has a higher smoking point. The only snag about using olive oil for frying is its price.

I must finally mention one of the best uses of olive oil, which the Tuscans have taught us, the *battesimo dell'olio* – christening with oil. One, two or more tablespoons of the best olive oil are added to some dishes after they have been cooked, usually at the table. The Tuscans add oil in this way to *la ribollita* – a bean and cabbage soup – and to their *fagioli all'uccelletto* – cannellini beans and tomatoes sautéed in oil (page 451) – to name but two. I add it also to my bread soup (*pancotto*) (page 79) and to most *zuppe* of chick-peas or beans.

About 90 per cent of the recipes in this book could go in this section, since they all contain olive oil. But I put only one because of the unusual use of olive oil in a cake.

apple cake
torta di mele

Serves 8–10
120 g (4 oz) sultanas
150 ml (1/4 pint) olive oil
200 g (7 oz) sugar
2 free-range eggs
350 g (12 oz) Italian 00 flour
1 tsp cinnamon
1 1/2 tsp bicarbonate of soda
1/2 tsp cream of tartar
1/2 tsp sea salt
450 g (1 lb) dessert apples, peeled and cut into small cubes
grated rind of 1 organic lemon

This is an apple cake with a difference, the fat used being olive oil. It is good either for tea or as a dessert, when you can hand round a bowl of softly whipped cream. The cake is better eaten the day after being cooked, so as to allow the flavours to combine and develop. Scrub the lemon thoroughly before you grate it to get rid of any pesticides.

Soak the sultanas in warm water for 20 minutes or so.

Heat the oven to 180°C (350°F) mark 4.

Pour the oil into a bowl, add the sugar and beat until the sugar and oil become homogenised. Add the eggs, one at a time, and beat until the mixture has grown in volume and looks like a thin mayonnaise.

Sieve the flour, cinnamon, bicarbonate of soda, cream of tartar and salt. Add gradually to the oil and sugar mixture, folding them in with a metal spoon. Mix thoroughly and then add the apples and the lemon rind.

Drain and dry the sultanas and add to the mixture. Mix very thoroughly. The mixture will be stiff, with the appearance of pieces of apple and sultanas coated with cake mixture.

Butter and flour a 20 cm (8 inch) spring-clip tin. Spoon the mixture into the tin and bake for at least 1 hour, until a toothpick inserted in the middle of the cake comes out dry.

Remove the cake from the tin and cool on a wire rack.

A similar cake can be made using pears instead of apples, in which case you must substitute almonds for the sultanas. If you like chocolate with pears, replace 2 tablespoons of the flour with the same amount of unsweetened cocoa powder, and add an extra 30 g (1 oz) of sugar to compensate for the bitterness of the cocoa. It is a good cake, too, although as chocolate is not one of my favourite flavourings I prefer the apple version.

olives

Olives, green, black or purple, are a quintessential part of the Italian scene. Although a great proportion of them finish up in the *frantoio* – the press where they are crushed to make oil – there are many recipes that make use of olives, whether in sauces, in salads, stuffed or even stuffed and coated with egg and breadcrumbs and fried. Broadly speaking, I would say that the green olive, with its young, exciting taste is better with rabbit, chicken and lamb, while the darker and richer flavour of the black olive combines better with vegetables or fish.

Olives are eaten preserved. The earliest known recipe for preserving olives was written by Columella, a botanist who lived in the first century AD. He said: 'Scald and drain olives and then place them in a layer in an amphora, covered with a layer of dry salt and a final layer of herbs.' Today, methods of preserving vary between those of the large industrial concern and those of the family, which often remain a secret. These latter are the olives with a faintly bitter yet very refreshing taste that appear in trattorias in the country. They are preserved in brine containing wild fennel, oregano, other local herbs, chilli and garlic. In Umbria orange peel and bay leaves are added, too.

I like to buy olives by the kilo from Greek or Italian shops or, better still, to bring them back from a Mediterranean country. I keep them in jars layered with slithered garlic, chilli and oregano. Covered with oil they are handy to serve with drinks.

black olive purée
puré di olive nere

This purée is very easy to make. It is much nicer than the purée bought in delicatessens such as Tapenade, which contains other ingredients. If you make your own purée you can add capers, anchovies, garlic, herbs etc. later, according to the way in which you want to use your purée.

The only thing you need besides good olives is extra virgin olive oil. The proportion I use is 5 tablespoons of extra virgin olive oil to 450 g (1 lb) of pitted black olives – not tinned or vacuum-packed. Put the olives in the food processor and whiz while pouring the oil through the funnel. I prefer a coarse purée, but this is a matter of taste.

This purée is excellent spread on *crostini* – squares of bread moistened with a little olive oil and toasted in a hot oven for about 8 minutes.

tomatoes filled with rice and black olives
pomodori ripieni di riso e olive nere

Serves 4
150 g (5 oz) long-grain rice
sea salt
150 g (5 oz) black olives, pitted
freshly ground black pepper
3 tbsp extra virgin olive oil
4 large ripe tomatoes
a dozen fresh basil leaves or small bunch of parsley

The rice and olives should be mixed at least 6 hours in advance, so that the rice has time to absorb the flavour of the olives.

Boil the rice in salted water, keeping it very *al dente*: cold rice is better this way. Drain, rinse under cold water and then spread the rice out to dry thoroughly on a dish or tray lined with kitchen paper.

Meanwhile chop the olives. Put them in a bowl and add the rice, the pepper and the oil. Mix well and leave for at least 6 hours. Do not refrigerate.

Wash the tomatoes and cut them in half. Remove and discard the seeds with a pointed teaspoon and squeeze out the water. Scoop out some of the pulp using the same spoon. Reserve the shells. Chop the pulp and add to the rice.

Sprinkle the inside of the tomatoes with a little salt and place them upside-down on a board to drain for at least half an hour.

Dry the inside of the tomatoes with kitchen paper. Check the seasoning of the rice mixture and then fill each half tomato with some of the mixture.

Tear the basil leaves into small pieces, or chop the parsley, and sprinkle on top. Serve at once.

spaghettini with olive purée, anchovy fillets and capers
vermicelli alla puré di olive

We had this at O'Parrucchiano in Sorrento. This restaurant is one of the few remaining delights in a town that has been taken over by mass tourism. The sauce takes no longer to prepare than the pasta takes to cook.

Put the capers in a bowl of warm water and leave them there, to get rid of the vinegar or the salt.

Cook the pasta in the usual way.

Bring the wine to the boil and simmer while you prepare the rest of the sauce.

Heat the oil in a large frying pan.

Chop the garlic, chillies, anchovy fillets and parsley and add to the pan. Cook over a very gentle heat while pounding the anchovies to a paste.

Drain and dry the capers and add to the pan with the olive purée and the wine. Continue cooking very gently until the pasta is ready.

Serves 4
1 tbsp capers
350 g (12 oz)
    spaghettini
sea salt
100 ml (3 1/2 fl oz)
    dry white wine
5 tbsp extra virgin
    olive oil
4 garlic cloves,
    peeled
2 dried chillies
3 salted anchovies,
    boned and washed,
    or 6 anchovy fillets
large bunch of
    parsley
2 tbsp olive purée
    (see page 418)

When the pasta is cooked, add 3 or 4 tablespoons of the pasta water to the sauce. Drain the pasta and add to the sauce. Stir-fry for 1 minute or so. Serve immediately from the pan.

ricotta, olive and gruyère paste
crema di ricotta e olive verde

Serves 6
120 g (4 oz) sweet green olives, stoned
120 g (4 oz) Gruyère
150 g (5 oz) ricotta
cayenne pepper to taste

It is the olives that give this spread a characteristic Mediterranean flavour, while the Gruyère adds a touch of nuttiness. The friend who gave me the recipe serves this paste spread on canapés with drinks.

Buy green olives already stoned, flavoured with garlic and oregano, which go well with the other flavours in the spread. Do not buy stuffed green olives nor the tinned ones.

Put the olives and the Gruyère, cut into pieces, in a food processor and process until smooth. Add the ricotta and process until the spread is homogenised. Transfer to a bowl and add cayenne to your taste, but not too much or it will kill the other flavours.

garlic

Garlic has played a part in many civilisations for over 2,000 years. The Egyptians worshipped garlic as a god, presumably because they were familiar with its medicinal properties. In Roman times, garlic was used mostly in plebeian cooking. The first century AD writer Apicius in his *De Re Coquinaria*, a compilation of Roman and Greek recipes from patrician households, hardly ever lists garlic, while all the other herbs and spices are present. In the Middle Ages, Alfonso, King of Castile, who defeated the Moors and married the daughter of Henry II of England, so hated garlic that he punished anyone who came to court smelling of it.

The fifteenth-century writer Platina, in his *De honesta voluptate ac valetudine* recommends garlic as an antidote for dog bites. It was also reputed to steady the nerves of hysterical people, to combat epidemics and infectious diseases, and to promote the passing of urine. But perhaps its most remarkable function was as a deterrent against vampires. To achieve this desirable end, beautiful young virgins, before retiring for the night, had to secure all windows and doors, place a bible and a crucifix by their bedside and hang at least a dozen bunches of garlic around the room. Apart from its culinary value, garlic is still considered beneficial to health; it is held to purify the blood, clear the skin, aid the digestive processes, lower blood pressure, and so on.

Whatever its real or imagined therapeutic powers, garlic has become an indispensable ingredient of Italian cooking. It is not, however, used indiscriminately; it is used in keeping with the style of the dish. With some dishes you only need a suggestion of flavour while in others an assertive statement is called for. To have only a tinge of flavour, peel a clove of garlic, squash it, put it in melted butter and oil, heat it gently, and remove it from the pan as soon as it becomes pale gold.

To give a subtle yet all-pervading garlic flavour to a dish, boil the garlic in the stock, water or milk for a long time, then purée it and add it to the sauce or the dish. For more flavour, you can cut the garlic in half or into large slices, or you can chop it, the last being the method that releases the most flavour. For a full garlic flavour, sauté it in a *soffritto*

422 **amaretto, apple cake and artichokes**

– frying mixture – until it is just coloured and then add the other ingredients. If you want to make a *soffritto* with onion, garlic and other vegetables, first fry the onion by itself until translucent and then add the garlic. If you put the garlic and the onion in the pan at the same time, the garlic will burn before the onion is soft. Some cooks put a toothpick through the garlic clove so that it can be seen and removed easily whenever they think it has released enough flavour.

New garlic is sweet, tender and plump, and can be used liberally. But garlic ages quickly and its taste becomes sharp. It must then be used sparingly. It is best to cut these older cloves in half and remove the bud inside, as this is by far the sharpest-tasting part. I am wary about using chopped raw garlic, or extracting its juice with a garlic press. The flavour is so pungent that it can kill any other taste. If you want a *soupçon* of garlic in a salad, rub the bowl with a peeled and slightly squashed clove or squash a clove in the spoon and then add the oil to it. After a moment, remove the garlic and dress the salad. To give vinegar a faint garlic flavour I put three or four bruised cloves in a jar and fill it with vinegar. But remember to remove the cloves and put fresh ones in before you refill the jar.

Many recipes could go in this section, but I decided that since garlic is not their main ingredient they should be included under the heading of their principal ingredient. Thus you will find the recipe for chicken with garlic in the poultry section.

Here I can only give you a recipe of a kind: when, at the market, you find a lot of new, mild and sweet garlic, or, as I do, you bring it home from a Mediterranean country, it is better to preserve it under oil than to store it as it is. The climate in Britain is far too humid and the garlic will soon become mouldy. So what you do is peel the garlic cloves, put them in a sterilised jar and then cover them with extra virgin olive oil. You have the garlic and oil all in one whenever you want. Keep the jar in the fridge.

wild garlic green sauce
salsa verde di aglio selvatico

In the early spring the banks of many lanes and streams in Dorset, where I now live, are covered with wild garlic. The little white flowers appear in late April and the air is pervaded by an aroma more often associated with the kitchen than with the countryside. Walk into it and you would think you were preparing aioli. Before it begins to flower I go out and gather bags of this wild garlic with which I make a sort of salsa verde (see also page 427). This sauce goes very well with any dish with which you would serve the classic salsa verde — boiled chicken, brisket, gammon or roast or steamed fish.

Clean the garlic leaves and push them into the beaker of the food processor together with the bread, broken up into morsels. Add the mustard and salt and pepper. Start the motor and whiz for a few seconds before you start slowly pouring the oil down the funnel. Whiz for a few seconds more and then taste and adjust the seasoning.

This sauce keeps well for up to 1 week in the fridge.

Makes about 350 ml
(12 fl oz)
300–350 g (10–12 oz) wild garlic
6 slices good white bread, crust removed
2 tsp Dijon mustard
coarse sea salt
freshly ground black pepper
150 ml (1/4 pint) extra virgin olive oil

battuto e soffritto

See page 488 in The Essentials section.

herbs

There are certain herbs – *erbe odorose* is their mellifluous name in
Italian – that have always played an important role in Italian cooking.

Prezzemolo – parsley – is the most ubiquitous. The parsley used in
Italy is the flat-leaf variety which is sweeter and yet more aromatic; it
is now widely available in Britain. Parsley is often sautéed in the
soffritto – fried mixture – rather than just added at the end, thus
releasing more of its flavour.

The typical herb of northern Italy is *salvia* – sage – the flavour of which
combines so ideally with butter, the cooking fat of the northern regions,
and with veal, Lombardy's most popular meat. A sprig of sage is usually
added to melted butter for the dressing of many different pasta dishes.

Bushes of wild rosemary are a familiar feature of the Mediterranean
landscape. It is a sweeter, more scented variety than the rosemary that
grows in Britain, thanks to the hot sun and the dry atmosphere. It is
also cultivated, and is to be found in any garden, however small. No
roast in Italy is cooked without the obligatory sprig. In her delightful
book *Honey from a Weed*, Patience Gray writes that in the Salento
peninsula, the heel of the Italian boot, rosemary is chopped when in full
flower, steeped in olive oil and used later in a *soffritto*. The rosemary
there, she says, flowers three or four times a year.

Oregano was used extensively in ancient Rome, where it arrived from
the Far East via Greece. It was in Greece that it was christened
origano, from *oros* – mountain, and *ganao* – splendour. And oregano is
still the splendour of the mountainsides of central and southern Italy,
where it has always been used profusely, especially in connection with
tomatoes. It is the herb that is sprinkled on a classic Neapolitan pizza,
and the one most commonly used in a tomato sauce. When you next
buy plum tomatoes try this simple method of preparing them. Peel
them, cut them in half and remove the seeds. Sprinkle them lightly
with salt on the inside and leave them upside-down for about half an
hour. Then dry them and dress them with your best olive oil and
sprinkle them lavishly with oregano. Oregano is also one of the best

herbs for flavouring courgettes: it should be added about ten minutes before the courgettes are done.

Then there is basil. It calls to mind luscious dishes of *trenette* or *piccagge al pesto*, eaten in a Ligurian trattoria under a canopy of vine leaves and washed down with litres of wine from the Cinque Terre. It is there in Liguria that the best basil grows, helped by the ideal climatic conditions: hot sun and humid breezes from the sea. Basil grows successfully in northern countries, but to my mind it becomes something a little different, with a slightly pungent taste reminiscent of mint.

The uses of basil are varied, as it can be added to most foods cooked in olive oil and containing tomato. It transforms the simplest tomato salad. It is good with seafood, and with dentex and red mullet, as well as with aubergine and peppers. Basil is also good added at the end to quickly fried steaks. Only a few leaves are needed, and they should be added at the last minute as basil tends to lose its flavour, and its bright green colour, in cooking. Tear the leaves with your fingers rather than chopping them; when making pesto the leaves should be pounded and not processed by a blade. Basil is the only herb that cannot successfully be dried. I have heard dried basil variously described as tasting like straw or like curry! It can, however, be stored very successfully in jars layered with olive oil or salt, or it can be frozen, leaving the leaves whole.

Marjoram belongs to the same species as oregano and, with basil, it is used a great deal in Liguria, especially in stuffings for vegetables and in *torte di verdura* – vegetable pies.

Parsley, rosemary, sage and marjoram are often used, separately or together to form the basis of a *soffritto*.

There are of course many other less familiar herbs, and a number of these are now back in fashion in Italian cooking. They were out of favour during the eighteenth and nineteenth centuries, perhaps owing to a swing of fashion's pendulum after the important position they enjoyed in the cooking of the sixteenth and seventeenth centuries. In his book *L'arte di ben cucinare*, published in 1662, the great chef Bartolomeo Stefani devoted much attention to recipes containing fresh herbs, edible weeds and flowers. He used many herbs that are only now being rediscovered:

bitter hyssop, rue, scented lavender, the samphire of Shakespearian fame, cucumber-tasting borage and many others.

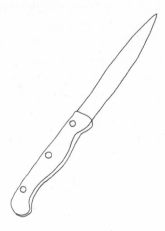

green sauce
salsa verde

Basically this sauce consists only of chopped parsley and olive oil, to which each cook adds what they think best. Sometimes I put a boiled potato instead of the breadcrumbs, leave out the egg, or add a little marjoram instead of the tarragon. What I give here is a guideline to the recipe.

Salsa verde *is the sauce which is usually served with* bollito misto *or any boiled meat or fowl. But I think it is also good spread on hard-boiled eggs or on roasted courgettes or mixed in boiled cauliflower – in which case I leave out the breadcrumbs.*

Put the breadcrumbs in a bowl and pour the vinegar over them. Set aside.

Peel the garlic clove, cut it in half and remove the hard central core, if necessary. This is the part that has a pungent instead of a sweet flavour.

Makes about 200 ml (7 fl oz)
30 g (1 oz) fresh white breadcrumbs
1–1 1/2 tsp red wine vinegar
1 garlic clove
30 g (1 oz) flat-leaf parsley
2 tbsp tarragon
2 tbsp capers
half a dozen cornichons

continued over >>

1 hard-boiled egg,
  shelled
6 anchovy fillets or 3
  salted anchovies,
  boned and rinsed
2 tsp Dijon mustard
150 ml (1/4 pint)
  extra virgin olive oil
pepper
sea salt

Chop the parsley, tarragon, capers, cornichons, hard-boiled egg, anchovies and garlic together. Put this mixture into another bowl.

Squeeze out the vinegar from the bread and add the bread to the mixture in the bowl, working it in with a fork. Add the mustard and then gradually add the olive oil, beating the whole time. Season with a good deal of pepper. Taste and add salt if necessary; the anchovies and capers may have given enough salt to the sauce. You might like to add a little more vinegar; it depends on the strength of your vinegar and how you like the sauce.

The whole sauce can be made in the food processor.

preparation
Salsa verde can be made up to 3 days in advance and kept, covered, in the fridge.

rocket pesto
pesto di rucola

Makes about 350 ml
  (12 fl oz) of pesto
100 g (3 1/2 oz)
  rocket, stalk
  removed
50 g (1 3/4 oz) flat-
  leaf parsley
60 g (2 oz) pine nuts
2 garlic cloves,
  peeled and sliced
coarse sea salt
freshly ground black
  pepper
200 ml (7 fl oz) extra
  virgin olive oil

I never seem to be able to plan the planting of my rocket properly, as it all comes out at the same time. The result being that I have to deal promptly with the surplus. By then the rocket is rather coarse and strong, no longer a favourite in the salad. It is time to make pesto which I use to dress pasta, or mix with ricotta as a dip or a spread on roasted vegetables.

Put all the ingredients, except the oil, in the food processor and whiz. When the herbs are coarsely ground begin to pour in the oil slowly through the funnel. Taste and adjust salt and pepper.

Spoon the *pesto* into sterilised jars. It will keep for 2–3 months.

pesto

Pesto needs little introduction: every Italian cookery book hails it as the best dressing for pasta. This it certainly is, but it must be well made and, oddly enough for such an apparently simple sauce, it is not easy. The Ligurians, who invented pesto, know that; they say that it needs not only the local basil, but also the local touch.

In Liguria, potato and a handful of French beans are cooked with the pasta. The traditional recipes do not contain pine nuts, but modern versions always do, and I find this a successful addition. Use young basil leaves; basil that has been growing for too long acquires an unpleasantly strong taste. The pine nuts must be fresh, i.e. of the current year, and the oil must be a very good olive oil, although an unassertive one. If possible, use an oil from Liguria or from Lake Garda; they are less pungent than an oil from Tuscany or from southern Italy.

The oil must be added slowly, as for mayonnaise, so as to create the right emulsion. Some cooks add walnuts as well as pine nuts, but I prefer to add only pine nuts in order to keep the emphasis on the fresh flavour of the basil. I like to heat the pine nuts in the oven for 3 or 4 minutes, or toast them in a cast-iron pan, to release their aroma. If you have time, make your pesto by hand in a mortar: more juices are released than would be by the chopping action of a metal blade.

The recipes for pesto are numerous. When I make pesto in Britain I add a couple of tablespoons of Greek yoghurt to modify the stronger taste of the basil.

The pasta traditionally used with pesto in Liguria is *trenette* – large tagliatelle, or *piccagge* – another home-made shape. Tagliatelle, either fresh or dried, spaghetti or potato gnocchi are all suitable.

pesto made in the mortar

Enough for 4 helpings
of pasta
**60 g (2 oz) fresh
basil leaves**
2 garlic cloves
**30 g (1 oz) pine nuts
(see note on page
429)**
pinch of rock salt
**4 tbsp freshly grated
Parmesan**
**4 tbsp freshly grated
pecorino**
**120 ml (4 fl oz) extra
virgin olive oil**
**2 tbsp Greek yoghurt
(optional)**

Put the basil leaves, the garlic, pine nuts and salt in a mortar and grind against the sides of the mortar, crushing all the ingredients with the pestle until the mixture has become a paste.

Mix in the grated cheeses and pour the oil over very gradually, beating with a wooden spoon. When all the oil has been incorporated mix in the yoghurt.

pesto made in a food processor or a blender

Pesto can also be made quite successfully in a food processor:

Put all the ingredients, except the cheeses and the yoghurt, in the beaker.

Process at high speed and when evenly blended transfer to a small bowl.

Mix in the cheeses and then blend in the yoghurt, if you are using it.

When the pasta is cooked, reserve 3 or 4 tablespoons of the water in which it has cooked and add to the pesto before dressing the pasta.

Pesto freezes well. Omit the garlic and the cheeses and add them just before you use the sauce.

minestrone with pesto
minestrone alla genovese

The pesto that is added at the end gives this minestrone a particularly Mediterranean taste. Traditionally this pesto is the old-fashioned one, made without pine nuts, although you could quite successfully use the modern pesto if you have some already made in the fridge or freezer. The soup is made only with olive oil and it is prepared a crudo, meaning that all the elements are put together at the same time in the pan when still raw, a much healthier method than first sautéing them.

The quantities here are for 8 people because minestrone is better made in a large amount: it is even more delicious warmed up one or two days later. Minestrone keeps well in the refrigerator for up to 3 days, but it cannot be frozen. Add the pasta and the pesto, in the right proportions, to the amount of soup you want to eat at one meal and chill the rest.

Put the oil, all the vegetables, garlic and stock in a saucepan and bring slowly to the boil. Cook, uncovered, for 1 1/2 hours or so over a very low heat. The soup should just simmer, not boil.

Taste and add salt, if necessary, and the pepper. Add the pasta and continue cooking until ready. The soup should be very thick (the Genoese say you should be able to stand a spoon up in it) but, if it is too thick, add a little water before adding the pasta.

While the pasta is cooking, put the basil leaves, parsley and garlic in a mortar and pound with a circular movement. Add the oil and pound to a paste. Alternatively, make the pesto in a food processor or blender.

When the pasta is cooked *al dente*, turn off the heat and mix in the pesto. Add pepper to taste and leave the soup to rest for about 2 minutes. Serve, handing round the Parmesan in a bowl.

Serves 8

4 tbsp extra virgin olive oil
2 onions, sliced
2 celery sticks with their green leaves, stringed and cut into small pieces
2 carrots, cut into 1 cm (1/2 inch) cubes
2 medium potatoes, cut into 1 cm (1/2 inch) cubes
100 g (3 1/2 oz) shelled peas
100 g (3 1/2 oz) French beans, topped and tailed and cut into 2.5 cm (1 inch) pieces
200 g (7 oz) beet spinach, shredded
a few outside leaves of a round or a cos lettuce, shredded
2 medium-sized courgettes, cut into 1 cm (1/2 inch) cubes
225 g (8 oz) ripe tomatoes, skinned, seeded and coarsely chopped
2 garlic cloves, peeled and sliced
2 litres (3 1/2 pints) vegetable stock or water
sea salt and freshly ground black pepper
150 g (5 oz) tubular pasta, such as small *penne* or *ditalini*
freshly grated Parmesan cheese

For the pesto
30 g (1 oz) fresh basil leaves
15 g (1/2 oz) flat-leafed parsley
1 garlic clove, peeled
2 tbsp extra virgin olive oil

There is, in effect, really no such thing as 'Italian' cooking. Italy, after all, was united politically only a little over 140 years ago, and still to this day the country is by no means united gastronomically. So it seems to me more to the point to speak of Milanese, Venetian, Neapolitan or Sicilian cooking rather than of Italian cooking. It is the regional cuisines that have produced the *pieces de resistance* of Italian cooking, the pizza and *spaghetti al sugo* from Naples, the *bagna caûda* and the *bollito misto* from Piedmont, the risotto with saffron and *ossobuco* from Milan, to mention but a few.

I like, sometimes, to prepare a dinner with a regional basis. In winter my mind and my palate are geared towards northern Italian dishes – a joint of beef braised in Barolo with a steaming golden polenta to mop up the rich sauce, or a warm, comforting risotto with sausages. In the summer I draw more from southern Italian cooking, rich in tomatoes, peppers and fish, simply grilled or steamed. And the wintry, creamy puddings of Turin or Milan will give way to ice-creams from Naples and Sicily and fruit salads.

In the following section I have listed six menus from six regions, the region being the theme. The menus cover six different occasions, from a Bolognese pasta feast for 30 people to a late Roman supper for a couple and four friends, the ideal menu for an after-theatre meal. Or it might be fun to ask your friends to a Tuscan lunch in the middle of London, a lunch in which you will reproduce the food you had when you were on holiday in Chianti or Lucchesia. A bit of a gimmick, perhaps, but food and eating do not always have to be taken too seriously, as my husband and some of my friends have cause to remind me quite often.

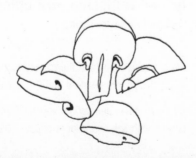

a venetian lunch for 4

risotto with mussels (page 130)
risotto coi peoci

grilled radicchio and chicory
radicchio alla trevisana

cheese and fruit
formaggio e frutta

When I lived in Venice, I used to go every morning to the Rialto market as the fish stalls there are crawling with many different species of crustaceans and slender silvery fish. I would return home with bags of molluscs for lunch and dinner. In the tradition of the local cuisine, rice was the natural accompaniment to the seafood.

The risotto was followed by *radicchio alla trevisana* whenever it was in season. The radicchio was the *radicchio di Treviso*, the best radicchio for grilling, with its slightly bitter flavour brought out by the heat. I have seldom seen *radicchio di Treviso* outside Italy, but I loved grilled radicchio so much that I make it in England with the round *radicchio di Chioggia* that is sold here, together with one or two heads of Belgian chicory, which goes beautifully with it.

The cheese platter would certainly include the delicious Asiago, a semi-fat cheese made principally in the province of Vicenza. Asiago is sometimes available in specialised Italian shops. A bowl of seasonal fruit would make an informal end to the meal.

grilled radicchio and chicory
radicchio alla trevisana

Serves 4
450 g (1 lb) red radicchio
225 g (8 oz) chicory

continued over >>

Wash the radicchio and the chicory carefully. Dry very thoroughly. Cut the radicchio into quarters and the chicory in half, both lengthwise.

Oil the grill pan and lay the vegetables in it. Pour over the olive oil and season with salt and a lot of pepper. Leave for 20 minutes and then cook under a slow preheated grill until the leaves soften, taking care to turn the radicchio and chicory pieces so that they cook all round.

6 tbsp extra virgin olive oil
sea salt and pepper

preparation
You can wash and dry the radicchio and chicory up to 1 day in advance and refrigerate, wrapped in a tea-towel. The vegetables can be grilled a few hours in advance and kept covered, in the kitchen, not in the fridge.

a roman late supper for 6

fennel wedges with olive oil
finocchi in pinzimonio

oxtail and celery braised in white wine
coda alla vaccinara

fruit or ice-cream
frutta o gelato

In Rome the evening meal is often eaten as late as ten o'clock. People stay out till that time, and when they get home they like to sit down to a meal as soon as possible. For this reason I have found that quite a few Roman dishes are suitable to serve when you come home after the theatre or cinema with a few friends.

The first course of this meal is a fresh *pinzimonio*. In a *pinzimonio* everyone is given a little bowl full of the best olive oil. They then help themselves from a dish in the middle of the table, which may contain a variety of raw vegetables but in this case contains fennel, and dip the vegetables in the oil. It is a dish as gregarious and cheerful as the Romans and therefore characteristic of Roman cuisine.

While you and your guests are enjoying the *pinzimonio*, the second course is heated in the oven. It is an earthy peasant dish whose name, *alla vaccinara*, means cooked in the butcher's way, *vaccinaro* being the old name for a butcher in Roman dialect. *Coda alla vaccinara* is served by itself; no vegetables, just plenty of bread.

After these two courses, I would put a bowl of fruit in the middle of the table, although a sorbet might be equally agreeable and just the right thing to help you digest a late meal. In the past the health-giving properties of iced drinks were well known; they were extolled by a certain Filippo Baldini, a professor of medicine, who wrote an essay in 1784 totally devoted to sorbets. For a good sorbet turn to page 395, where you will find a basil-flavoured lemon one, or to page 325, for a delicious ricotta ice-cream.

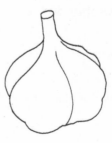

fennel wedges with olive oil
finocchi in pinzimonio

Serves 6
**3 medium to large
fennel bulbs,
preferably the
squat round type**
**sea salt and freshly
ground black
pepper**
**180 ml (6 fl oz)
extra virgin olive oil**
2 dozen black olives

Cut off the top of the fennel and any part of the stalk that is bruised or discoloured. Trim the base, then cut the fennel vertically into quarters. Cut each quarter into wedges, about 2.5 cm (1 inch) thick. Wash, drain and pat dry with kitchen paper. Place the fennel wedges neatly on a dish.

Mix the seasoning into the oil and then divide the oil between 6 small bowls. Pile the olives in the middle of the fennel or scatter them on top. Place the dish in the middle of the table and give each person a bowl of olive oil into which to dip the fennel.

preparation
The fennel can be cut and washed up to a few hours in advance. Wrap in a tea-towel, put the bundle in a plastic bag and keep in the fridge.

oxtail and celery braised in white wine
coda alla vaccinara

Blanch the pork rind in boiling water for a couple of minutes. Drain, refresh under cold water and cut into large strips.

Put the pancetta, oil, parsley, garlic, onion and carrot in a casserole and sauté over a low heat, stirring frequently, until the vegetables are soft but not brown.

Heat the oven to 160°C (325°F) mark 3.

Add the oxtail and the pork rind to the *soffrito* – the vegetable mixture – and sauté these as well, turning them over in the *soffrito*. Heat the wine and pour over the meat. Let it bubble for a couple of minutes while you turn the meat over once.

Heat the stock in the saucepan in which you heated the wine. Stir the tomato purée into the casserole and then add the hot stock. Season with salt and pepper. Cover the casserole and put it in the oven for about 2–2 1/2 hours. Turn the meat over every half hour. Skim off as much fat as you can from the surface of the cooking liquid.

Wash the celery and remove the strings from the outside of the stalks. Cut the stalks into pieces and add to the casserole half an hour before serving. Continue cooking for about half an hour until the celery is done – it should be still just slightly crunchy – and the meat comes away from the bone.

Skim off as much fat as you can from the surface of the cooking liquid. Taste and check the seasonings and serve at once.

preparation
If possible, *coda alla vaccinara* should be prepared 2–3 days in advance and refrigerated so that the fat can be removed easily. In this case do not put the celery in. When cold, remove the solidified fat. Put the casserole on the heat (it doesn't need to go in the oven) and add the celery when the liquid is simmering. You can also freeze the dish, but remember to add the celery when reheating.

Serves 6

225 g (8 oz) pork rind

60 g (2 oz) pancetta or unsmoked streaky bacon, cut in a single thick slice and chopped

3 tbsp olive oil

2 tbsp chopped parsley, preferably flat-leaf

1 garlic clove, peeled and chopped

1 onion, finely chopped

1 carrot, finely chopped

1.5 kg (3 1/4 lb) oxtail, cut into joints

200 ml (7 fl oz) dry white wine

250 ml (9 fl oz) meat stock

2 tbsp tomato purée

sea salt and freshly ground black pepper

350 g (12 oz) celery

a milanese dinner for 8

egg, parmesan and parsley dumplings in stock (page 314)
minestra mariconda

beef braised in vinegar and cream with potato purée
manzo alla california con la puré di patate

panettone with mascarpone
Il pannettone col mascarpone

Lombardy offers quite a number of delicate and attractive-looking soups. These are based on properly made stock, richly yet delicately flavoured, with the right proportion of meat to bone (see the recipe on page 485). *Minestra mariconda*, one of these soups, contains little cheese-flavoured dumplings. I have adapted the recipe from a book, *Il Cucoco Senza Pretese (The Unpretentious Cook)*, a collection of Lombard recipes published in 1834. The original recipe suggests using fish stock for fasting days. What fascinates me in this book is that at the end of each recipe there is a list of costs for each ingredient, and the total. This soup, with quantities for at least 12 people, cost *Lire* 53, equal, today, to 2 1/2 pence!

The California in the name of the meat course is, unexpectedly, a locality to the north of Milan. It is tempting to think that the other one was named by emigrants from Lombardy, but this is unlikely, as California USA was originally a Spanish colony. The cooking of northern Italy is rich in braised meat dishes, and these are traditional for dinner parties and Sunday lunches. They are ideal for a large dinner party because the meat, which is cooked in a single piece, needs little attention and can even be cooked in advance. The best accompaniments are a soft potato purée and a bowl of spinach sautéed in butter and flavoured with freshly grated nutmeg.

For pudding I thought nothing could be more suitable than panettone, the Milanese cake *par excellence*. It used to be eaten in Lombardy only at Christmas time, but now it is eaten in most parts of Italy all year round. This dome-shaped cake has also conquered the world with its light texture and buttery taste. The tall, cylindrical shape created by Angelo Motta in 1921 has given way in the last decade to the original shape of a squat dome, much to the satisfaction of all true Milanese.

This was the sweet bread which became a big seller in the fifteenth century and made Toni, the poor baker, wealthy, and his daughter happy. A local nobleman wanted to marry the beautiful daughter and so he gave her father money to buy the best eggs, flour and butter, as well as sultanas and candied orange and citron. The delicious sweet bread the baker was able to make became known as *pan di Toni* and the prosperous Milanese ladies flocked to Toni's bakery to buy it. Or so it is said! For this is just one of the many stories surrounding the origin of panettone. It certainly is an ancient bread, possibly dating from the Middle Ages. A less romantic, and perhaps more plausible, explanation of the odd name lies in the Milanese penchant for diminutives. Thus *pane* became *panett* and, being bigger than usual, it became panettone.

As a true Milanese, I love my panettone. I like it for breakfast or for tea, or with sweet white wine or *vinsanto*, but I like it best for dinner with another notable Lombard product, mascarpone. When I want to serve it at the end of the meal, I just buy a good panettone, put a few slices in a moderate oven for 10 minutes, and serve it hot with the mascarpone, which voluptuously melts in contact with the hot panettone. You will need a 500 g (1 lb 2 oz) tub of mascarpone. Put it into a bowl and hand it round.

There is now a panettone on the market which contains bits of chocolate as well as the traditional dried fruit. When I eat it by itself I prefer the old-fashioned panettone, but I find that the new chocolate-studded variety is ideal with mascarpone.

beef braised in vinegar and cream
manzo alla california

Serves 8
120 g (4 oz) unsalted butter
2 onions, very finely chopped
2 celery stalks, very finely chopped
2 carrots, very finely chopped
1 tbsp vegetable oil
1.8 kg (4 lb) lean chuck steak or top rump in one piece, neatly tied
120 ml (4 fl oz) red wine vinegar
sea salt and pepper
600 ml (1 pint) single cream

Melt the butter in a deep casserole. Add the vegetables and sauté gently for 10 minutes, stirring frequently.

Heat the vegetable oil in a non-stick pan and seal the meat on all sides. Transfer the meat onto the bed of vegetables.

Pour the vinegar into the non-stick pan and deglaze rapidly. Pour over the meat and season with salt and pepper.

Heat the cream and, when just beginning to show bubbles at the edge, pour into the casserole. Bring slowly to the boil and simmer, covered, over a very low heat for about 3 hours, until the meat is very tender when pricked with a fork. Turn the meat three or four times during the cooking. When the meat is ready, remove to a side plate and keep warm, covered with foil. Skim off as much fat as you can from the surface of the sauce. Purée the sauce in a food processor or liquidiser until smooth. Transfer to a clean saucepan and heat slowly. Taste and adjust the seasoning.

If the sauce is not tasty enough – nowadays some meat contains a lot of water – boil briskly to reduce.

Slice the meat across the grain into 1 cm (1/2 inch) thick slices and lay them, slightly overlapping, in a heated dish. Cover with some of the sauce and serve the rest in a heated bowl.

preparation
The dish can be prepared up to 3 days in advance and refrigerated. Skim the fat off the sauce – it is much easier to do this when the sauce is cold. Slice the meat and reheat very gently in the sauce. The dish can also be frozen.

a sicilian dinner for 6

sweet-and-sour aubergine
caponatina di melanzane

macaroni pie
il timballo del gattopardo

salad of fennel, orange, chicory and olives (page 276)
insalata di finocchi, cicoria belga e arance

sicilian cassata (page 331)
cassata siciliana

Caponatina, one of the peaks of Sicilian cooking, demonstrates very clearly a main characteristic of that cuisine. A simple local ingredient, in this case the aubergine, is taken as the basis of the dish, and it is then embellished and enriched until the end result is an opulent and almost baroque achievement. In some areas of Sicily tiny octopus, or *bottarga* (dried roe of tuna or grey mullet), or even a small lobster are added. In Palermo *caponatina* becomes more Arab in concept by the addition of almond and cinnamon. And to make it even more grandiose, in Catania it is often covered with '*la salsa di San Bernardo*', a sauce based on toasted bread mixed with grated chocolate, toasted almonds, sugar and vinegar. It is a sauce allegedly created by the Benedictine monks in their monastery.

Caponatina, or *caponata*, is usually served as an antipasto, although in that case it would not precede the *timballo* that follows here. In fact, in a truly Sicilian meal the *timballo* would be served first. But I can hardly imagine, in this day and age, anyone wanting to start the meal with such a substantial dish before going on to the main course, and for this reason I have introduced the *timballo* as the *secondo*.

It is indeed a grand *secondo*, being my interpretation of the *timballo* offered in 1860 by the Prince Fabrizio Salina to the notables of the town of Donnafugata in Sicily. This is how Giuseppe Tomasi di Lampedusa describes it in his famous novel, *The Leopard*: 'The burnished gold of the crusts, the fragrance exuded by the sugar and cinnamon, were but preludes to the delights released from the inside of the pie when the knife broke the crust. First came a spice-laden haze, then chicken livers, hard-boiled eggs, sliced ham, chicken and truffles in masses of piping hot, glistening macaroni, to which the meat juice gave an exquisite hue of suede.' I have seldom seen a dish described in such beautiful language and yet with such gastronomic accuracy.

This *timballo* will always be a *tour de force* on the part of the cook. It takes time and a certain knowledge of pastry-making and baking, though the filling is quite easy.

After that I suggest a salad, and when I think of Sicily I immediately think of this one. It is based on the most Sicilian of all produce, the orange. It is a fresh, astringent salad, perfect after the voluptuous *timballo*.

I end the meal with the Sicilian *cassata*. This is the traditional Easter sweet in Sicily, which shares only its name with the industrially made frozen concoction.

sweet-and-sour aubergine
caponatina di melanzane

Serves 6
1.5 kg (3 1/4 lb) aubergines
sea salt
vegetable oil for frying
1 celery head
120 ml (4 fl oz) olive oil
2 onions, sliced
1 tbsp sugar
400 g (14 oz) tomato passata or tinned plum tomatoes, drained and puréed

continued over >>

Peel the aubergines, cut them into 2 cm (3/4 inch) cubes, place them in a colander and sprinkle with salt. Put a weight on top and leave them to drain for at least 1 hour. Squeeze them out, rinse, and dry with kitchen paper.

Heat some vegetable oil to come about 2.5 cm (1 inch) up the side of a wok or a frying pan. When the oil is very hot (it should be hot enough to make a small piece of stale bread turn brown in 40 seconds), slip in as many aubergine cubes as will fit in a single layer and fry until golden brown on all sides, turning them over with a fish slice halfway through the cooking. Adjust the heat if the aubergines begin to burn. Lift them out of the oil and drain on kitchen paper. Repeat until all the aubergine cubes are fried.

Remove the outer sticks and the leaves from the celery head and keep them for another dish. Use only the heart. Remove the coarse outside threads with a potato peeler, if necessary, and cut the sticks into 3.5 cm (1 1/2 inches) long matchsticks. Fry the celery sticks in the same oil as the aubergine until golden and crisp. Drain on kitchen paper.

Heat the olive oil in a clean sauté or frying pan and add the onion, 2 pinches of salt and 1 pinch of the sugar. Cook for about 5–7 minutes, until soft and just coloured. Add the tomatoes, the rest of the sugar, the grated chocolate, a little salt and a generous grinding of pepper. Cook over a lively heat for about 2 minutes and then add the vinegar and the capers.

Stone the olives, cut them into quarters and add to the pan together with the aubergine and the celery. Cook over a low heat for a further 30 minutes. Taste and adjust the seasonings. Spoon the *caponatina* into a serving bowl and allow to cool. Serve at room temperature with plenty of good bread.

Caponatina looks stunning dished out into a large loaf of *pugliese* bread which is cut in half with the soft inner crumb hollowed out. Spoon it into the bread just before serving.

preparation
Caponatina is better made at least 1 day in advance. For 1 day it does not need to be refrigerated. You can prepare it up to 3 days in advance and keep it in the fridge, but remember to bring it back to room temperature before serving, so that the subtle flavour can be fully appreciated.

1 tbsp grated
chocolate
black pepper
150 ml (1/4 pint) red
wine vinegar
100 g (3 1/2 oz)
capers, rinsed
90 g (3 oz) sweet
green olives

macaroni pie
il timballo del gattopardo

Serves 6
30 g (1 oz) dried porcini
75 g (2 1/2 oz) unsalted butter
90 g (3 oz) *luganega* or other sweet, coarse-grained, pure pork sausage, skinned and cut into small pieces
150 g (5 oz) boneless free-range or organic chicken breast, skinned and cut into 1 cm (1/2 inch) cubes
120 g (4 oz) free-range or organic chicken livers, trimmed and cut into small pieces
150 ml (1/4 pint) dry white wine
sea salt and pepper
pinch of ground cloves
pinch of ground cinnamon
generous pinch of grated nutmeg
1 tbsp truffle paste
60 g (2 oz) prosciutto, thickly sliced
120 g (4 oz) cooked garden peas
60 g (2 oz) freshly grated Parmesan
300 g (10 oz) *penne* or short macaroni

continued over >>

First make the pastry. Sift the flour with the salt into a mound on a work surface. Make a well in the middle and add the egg, the egg yolk, 2 tablespoons of water and the sugar. Mix lightly, then add the butter. Blend together by pushing small pieces of dough away from you, using the heel of your hand. If the dough is too dry, add a little more cold water. Gather the dough into a ball and wrap in foil or clingfilm lightly dusted with flour. Chill in the refrigerator for at least 1 hour. The pastry may also be made in a food processor.

Soak the dried porcini in a cupful of hot water for 30 minutes. Lift them out carefully and rinse gently under cold running water. Dry them and cut them into small pieces. Strain the soaking liquid through a sieve lined with muslin.

Put 45 g (1 1/2 oz) of the butter and the *luganega* in a small heavy frying pan and sauté for 7 minutes, breaking the sausage up with a fork. Add the chicken breast and sauté for 2 minutes, stirring frequently, then mix in the chicken livers. Cook for 2 minutes or so, then add the wine and boil fast for 1 minute to evaporate the alcohol. Add salt and pepper to taste and about 4 tablespoons of the porcini soaking liquid.

Reduce the heat and cook until nearly all the liquid has evaporated. Add a couple of tablespoons of hot water and continue cooking for about 5 minutes, stirring occasionally. The meat should cook in very little liquid but should not be allowed to cook dry. Check the seasonings.

Meanwhile melt 15 g (1/2 oz) of the remaining butter in a small heavy saucepan. Add the chopped porcini and cook over a low heat for about 2 minutes. Add the cloves, cinnamon, nutmeg and salt and pepper to taste, and a couple more tablespoons of the porcini soaking liquid. Cook, stirring occasionally, for 5 minutes, then pour the sauce into the pan with the sausage and chicken mixture. Mix well and cook for a further 5 minutes. Transfer the contents of the pan with all the cooking juices to a bowl, add the truffle paste and mix well. Cut the prosciutto into thin short strips and add to the bowl together with the peas and all but two tablespoons of the Parmesan. Mix well. Set aside for the flavours to combine.

Now cook the pasta in plenty of boiling salted water until very *al dente*. It will finish cooking later, in the oven.

While the pasta is cooking, heat the stock. Blend the remaining butter with the flour and add it bit by bit to the simmering stock. Do not add the next teaspoonful of the butter mixture until the previous one has been completely incorporated. When all the mixture has been added, withdraw the pan from the heat and set aside.

Drain the pasta and turn it into a large bowl. Toss with the stock and butter mixture.

About 1 hour before you want to cook the dish, remove the dough from the refrigerator and allow to become pliable at room temperature.

Heat the oven to 220°C (425°F) mark 7.

Generously butter a 20 cm (8 inch) spring-clip cake tin.

Roll out about one-third of the dough into a 20 cm (8 inch) circle on a piece of greaseproof paper. Turn the sheet of paper over on to the bottom of the tin and peel off the paper. Rolling the dough out on to greaseproof paper makes it much easier to transfer. Roll out half the remaining dough into a wide strip and use this to line the sides of the tin. Seal the joints with cold water. Sprinkle the remaining Parmesan and breadcrumbs over the base. Cover with a layer of pasta and then a layer of filling. Build up these alternate layers until you have used up all the ingredients. Cut the eggs into segments and push them here and there into the filling.

Roll out the remaining dough into a circle on greaseproof paper as before and cover the pasta. Seal the dough lid to the side strip. Brush the top of the pie with the egg yolk beaten with the milk and 1 teaspoon of salt. If you wish, make a few decorations with the dough trimmings, brush with egg yolk and milk glaze and fix to the top of the pie. Pierce the top with the prongs of a fork in several places to let the steam escape. Bake for about 10 minutes, then turn the oven down to 160°C (375°F) mark 3 and bake for a further 25 minutes.

Remove from the oven and leave to stand for about 10 minutes. Unclip the tin and carefully transfer the pie on the tin base to a serving dish. Don't try to lift the pie off the bottom of the tin; being heavy, and still hot, it could easily break.

200 ml (7 fl oz) strong meat stock
1 tbsp white flour
3 tbsp dried breadcrumbs
2 hard-boiled eggs, shelled
1 free-range egg yolk and 2 tbsp of milk for glazing

For the pastry
250 g (9 oz) plain flour
1 tsp sea salt
1 free-range egg plus 1 free-range egg yolk
100 g (3 1/2 oz) caster sugar
120 g (4 oz) unsalted butter, diced

preparation

The pastry dough can be prepared up to 3 days in advance and refrigerated. It can also be frozen. The filling can be made up to 1 day in advance and refrigerated. The *timballo* must be assembled no longer than 30 minutes before being baked.

a tuscan lunch for 12

chicken liver canapés
crostini alla toscana

tuscan roast pork with cannellini beans and tomatoes sautéed in oil
arista alla toscana con fagioli all'uccelletto

seasonal salads
insalate di stagione

broad beans and pecorino cheese, or a platter of cheeses
fave e pecorino

sienese fruit and spice cake with vinsanto
panforte e vinsanto

For about ten years in the seventies we had a little house on a hill in Chianti and spent many happy holidays there. Then one morning when I was shopping in Gaiole, our local village, I realised to my dismay that there were no fewer than seven British cars in the little village square. Chianti had become Chiantishire! We decided that somewhere which had become the playground of the British upper class was not for us, so we sold Cornia, our house, and bought a flat in Venice, where the residents, at least, are Italian.

While we were in Tuscany we had many pleasant times with the locals, always over a glass or two, or more, of *vinsanto*. Sometimes we had lunch with them, and my menu here is typical of that sort of occasion. There is, I must confess, one fewer course in my menu than in those authentic Tuscan feasts because I have omitted the tagliatelle that used to follow the antipasto.

I give a recipe for the *crostini* that are part of the antipasto, but you should also serve two or three of the following dishes: a platter of salame, prosciutto, mortadella and other pork meats with a bowl of figs or a dish of slices of yellow melon as accompaniment, some *bruschetta* (page 78) and/or a rustic salad of lentils cooked with all the *odori* (onion, garlic, celery and herbs), garnished with rocket and dressed only with the best olive oil.

The main course, the *arista*, can be served hot or cold; in Tuscany, traditionally, it is served cold. The strange name of this dish is a mystery. Many cookery writers, myself included, have subscribed to the theory that it comes from an episode that took place at a banquet during the Ecumenical Council in Florence in 1439. A Greek patriarch who was there, having tasted the dish, is supposed to have expressed his approval by exclaiming '*Aristos!*' – the best.

The story, however charming, has proved to be unfounded, since the dish *arista* is mentioned in a novella written by Franco Sacchetti some hundred years before the Council.

Another odd name is that of the *fagioli all'uccelletto*, *uccelletto* meaning little bird. Many theories have been advanced as to its origin. The only one I find convincing is that beans prepared in this way are the traditional accompaniment to *uccelletti*, which the Tuscans are passionate about shooting and inordinately fond of eating. *Fagioli all'uccelletto* can also be made *in bianco* – without tomato. The two versions are equally good.

The salad I leave to you, but whatever it is, make a lot and dress it with plenty of extra virgin olive oil. My recipe is on page 491. Another good dish is the tomatoes with basil on page 208.

If your lunch takes place in the spring, you can put on the table a bowl of young broad beans and a whole Tuscan pecorino cheese. Do not bother to pod the beans. Let your guests do it and invite them to cut a wedge of pecorino to eat with the beans. It is a perfect marriage as long as the broad beans are really young and tender.

If broad beans are already past their best, serve the pecorino with other Italian cheeses. At the same time put on the table two *panforti*, the deliciously spiced and honeyed cakes from Siena. Although I have made *panforte* at home, I am convinced that the ready-made panforte available in many Italian shops is better. Pass round a glass of sweet *vinsanto*, as the Tuscans do on such an occasion.

chicken liver canapés
crostini alla toscana

Remove the fat, gristle and greenish bits from the chicken livers. Wash, dry and cut the livers into small pieces.

Put the oil in a saucepan and, when just hot, add the celery, shallot, garlic and parsley and cook for 5–10 minutes until soft. Add the chicken livers and cook very gently – they must not fry – until they have lost their raw colour. Mix in the tomato purée and cook for 1 minute. Raise the heat, pour over the wine and reduce until nearly all the wine has evaporated. Lower the heat and add a little salt and plenty of pepper. Simmer gently for 10 minutes.

Remove the pan from the heat and add the capers and anchovies. Transfer the mixture to a chopping board and chop coarsely. If you use a food processor, be very careful not to reduce the mixture to a purée. Return the mixture to the saucepan and add the butter. Cook slowly for 2 minutes, stirring constantly.

Cut the French bread into slices and brush with olive oil. Toast in a hot oven, 200°C (400°F) mark 6, for 6–7 minutes until crisp. When cool, spread with the chicken liver mixture and serve.

Note: the bread can be moistened with chicken stock mixed with *vinsanto*, instead of oil.

preparation
The chicken liver mixture can be made up to 1 day in advance. Cover and refrigerate.

Serves 12
400 g (14 oz) free-range or organic chicken livers
4 tbsp olive oil
1/2 celery stalk, very finely chopped
1 shallot, very finely chopped
2 small garlic cloves, peeled and chopped
3 tbsp fresh parsley, chopped
1 tbsp tomato purée
6 tbsp dry white wine
sea salt and freshly ground black pepper
1 tbsp capers, rinsed and chopped
4 anchovy fillets, chopped
30 g (1 oz) unsalted butter
1 or 2 French bread sticks
3 tbsp extra virgin olive oil

tuscan roast pork
arista alla toscana

Serves 12
**6 garlic cloves,
peeled**
**4 rosemary sprigs,
about 10 cm (3 1/2
inches) long**
2 tsp fennel seeds
sea salt and pepper
**2 kg (4 1/2 lb) boned
and rindless loin of
pork (boneless
weight)**
4 cloves
**120 ml (4 fl oz) olive
oil**
**150 ml (1/4 pint) dry
white wine**

Ask the butcher to give you the bones of the joint and to tie the joint into a neat roll.

Chop together the garlic, rosemary and fennel seeds, add salt and pepper and mix well. Make small deep incisions in the meat, along the grain, and push some of the mixture into the meat. Pat the rest of the mixture all over the meat and stick with the cloves. Rub with half the oil and place the joint in a bowl. Allow to stand for 4–5 hours, outside the fridge, covered with a plate.

Heat the oven to 180ºC (350ºF) mark 4.

Put the meat and the bones in a roasting tin and pour in the rest of the oil. Roast in the oven for 2–2 1/2 hours, basting every 20 minutes or so. The meat is ready when it is very tender.

Turn the oven up to 220ºC (425ºF) mark 7 for the last 10 minutes to brown the meat, then transfer it to a wooden board. Remove and discard the bones.

Remove as much fat as you can from the surface of the cooking liquid. Deglaze the tin with the wine and 150 ml (1/4 pint) of hot water, boiling briskly while scraping the bottom of the tin to loosen the tasty nuggets of residue. Reduce to about a third. This is a very concentrated juice that can also be eaten with the meat when it is cold. In that case, remove the fat which will have solidified on the top and you will find a delicious soft jelly underneath.

If you want to serve the pork hot, remove the string from the meat, carve and place neatly on the serving dish. Spoon the deglazing liquid over it.

preparation
Like any other roast joint, if you want to serve it hot you cannot cook it ahead of time. If you prefer to serve the *arista* cold, as the Tuscans do, you can cook it up to 2 days in advance and refrigerate it, well wrapped in foil. Remove from the fridge at least 3 hours before serving to bring it back to room temperature.

cannellini beans and tomatoes sautéed in oil
fagioli all'uccelletto

Put three-quarters of the oil, the sage, rosemary and garlic in a pot,
preferably an earthenware one of the type you can put directly on the
heat. Sauté until the herbs begin to sizzle.

Meanwhile chop the tomatoes coarsely and then add them to the pan.
Season with salt and pepper and cook until the oil separates, about 20
minutes. Now rinse and drain the *cannellini*. Add to the pan and
continue cooking for about 15 minutes, until everything is well blended.

Before serving, pour over the remaining olive oil and check the seasoning.

preparation
The dish can be prepared up to 2 days in advance. Cover and
refrigerate and gently reheat, or bring back to room temperature if you
want to serve the dish cold with the cold *arista*.

Serves 12
8 tbsp extra virgin
  olive oil
2 sprigs of fresh
  sage
2 sprigs of fresh
  rosemary
4 garlic cloves,
  chopped
450 g (1 lb) ripe
  tomatoes,
  preferably plum
  tomatoes, blanched
  and skinned
sea salt and pepper
4 tins *cannellini*
  beans, 400 g (14 oz)
  size, or 1.5 kg
  (3 1/2 lb) cooked
  beans

a bolognese feast for 30

baked macaroni with sausage and garlic (page 192)
maccheroni gratinati con la luganega e l'aglio

baked green lasagne
lasagne verdi al forno

penne with four cheeses
penne al quattro formaggi

baked tagliatelle with ham and peas
tagliatelle gratinate al prosciutto cotto e piselli

green bean and tomato salad (page 272)
insalata di fagiolini e pomodori

fennel and parmesan salad
insalata di finocchio al parmigiano

morello cherry jam tart (page 347)
crostata di conserva di amarena

walnut and honey pie (page 376)
la bonissima

Bologna is the home of many of the best pasta dishes and pasta is the ideal food for a large party. Thus you will find that this Bolognese pasta feast avoids those two torments, the pre-prandial banishment to the kitchen and the nagging worry as to whether the dish will taste the way it should. The pasta dishes I have chosen are all baked ones, which means that they can be prepared in advance. You can even taste and correct them in advance and thus be sure of bringing to the table just what you had in mind. You only need to heat them in the oven before serving them. By the time everyone begins to help themselves the dishes will have been out of the oven long enough for the flavours to blend. And as these four pasta dishes go well together, four small portions can happily share the same plate. Put a few bowls full of freshly grated Parmesan here and there for your guests to help themselves.

After that you need a few different salads, but please, serve them after and not with the pasta. Not only does pasta need no accompaniment (especially true in the case of these dishes based on cream and béchamel), but also the sauces would jar with the acidity of the vinegar and the fruitiness of the oil in the salad dressing. And if you clear the table of the pasta dishes and bring in the salad bowls it will help to give the feeling of another course – and more food!

The green salad should be a mixture of round or cos lettuce, lamb's lettuce, chicory, endive and radicchio. On page 491 you will find the recipe for my kind of *insalata verde*. Make two large bowls of green salad because everybody will take some.

With the green salad I suggest you serve two or three other salads. The green bean and tomato salad (page 272) is a classic. Another classic is the courgette and tomato salad on page 271, which you might prefer if the courgettes in the shops are better than the beans. The other salads I would recommend are the celeriac, chicory and radicchio on page 270 or the tomato, cucumber and pepper on page 282, depending on the season.

The fennel and Parmesan salad is the perfect transition between the salads and the cheeses to follow, or to be eaten with them. Serve at least four different cheeses, with plenty of good bread. In Italy we never serve butter with cheese, and it would be wrong to put butter on the table when you serve the cheese with the salad.

For pudding I would choose two sweets based on fruit and two traditional sweets from Emilia Romagna, a sharp morello cherry tart and a rich walnut and honey pie, for which you will find the recipes on pages 347 and 376. Instead of morello cherry jam, I have sometimes used damson jam, which is delicious when – as so often – it is home-made. Whatever you use, the jam must be sharp and fruity.

Prepare a cleansing, refreshing sweet based only on fruit, such as your favourite fruit salad, any seasonal fruits and one or two of my fruit desserts. Choose the Sharon fruits with lime juice (page 342), the oranges and kiwi fruit (page 352) or the peaches with raspberry sauce (page 340), according to the season.

baked green lasagne
lasagne verdi al forno

First make the *ragù*. Heat the butter and oil in a saucepan and cook the pancetta for 2 minutes. Add the onion, and when it has begun to soften add the carrot, celery, garlic and bay leaves. Cook for a couple of minutes, stirring constantly. Add the tomato purée and cook over a low heat for 30 seconds. Put in the minced steak and cook briskly for 3–4 minutes, until the meat has lost its raw colour, stirring with a fork to break up the lumps. Splash with the wine and boil for 2 minutes or so, until the liquid has almost evaporated. Fish out and discard the bay leaf and pour in the stock. Mix well, season, and simmer, uncovered, for about 2 hours, adding a little warm water if the sauce gets too dry. The heat should be at its lowest, so that just a few bubbles break the surface of the sauce.

To make the béchamel sauce, heat the milk until it begins to bubble at the edge. Meanwhile melt the butter in a heavy-based saucepan over low heat. Blend in the flour, stirring vigorously. Now draw the pan off the heat and add the hot milk, a few tablespoons at a time. You must let the flour mixture absorb each addition thoroughly before going on to the next stage.

Serves 8–10
lasagne verdi **made
with 3 eggs, 350 g
(12 oz) Italian 00
white flour and
200 g (7 oz) cooked
or frozen leaf
spinach, or 500 g
(1 lb 2 oz) dried
*lasagne verdi***
1 tbsp vegetable oil
150 g (5 oz) freshly
grated Parmesan
30 g (1 oz) unsalted
butter, melted

For the ragù
60 g (2 oz) unsalted
butter

continued over >>

100 ml (3 1/2 fl oz) olive oil
100 g (3 1/2 oz) pancetta or unsmoked streaky bacon, finely chopped
2 small onions, finely chopped
1 carrot, finely chopped
2 celery stalks, finely chopped
2 garlic cloves, finely chopped
2 bay leaves
2 tbsp tomato purée
450 g (1 lb) lean chuck or braising steak, minced
300 ml (1/2 pint) dry white wine
300 ml (1/2 pint) meat stock
sea salt and freshly ground black pepper

For the béchamel sauce
1.5 litres (2 1/2 pints) full-fat milk
150 g (5 oz) unsalted butter
120 g (4 oz) Italian 00 flour
sea salt
3 pinches of grated nutmeg

When all the milk has been absorbed, return the pan to the heat. Add salt to taste and bring to the boil. Cook over the gentlest heat for 10 minutes, stirring frequently. You can put the pan over a flame disperser or in a bain-marie to save the worry of frequent stirring. Add the nutmeg and check the seasonings. The sauce should have the consistency of thin double cream.

If you are making your own lasagne, turn to page 27 for making the pasta dough, and to page 28 for cutting the lasagne. If your lasagne are home-made, bring a large saucepan of salted water to the boil. Add the vegetable oil. Place a large bowl of cold water near the cooker and lay some clean and dry tea-towels nearby. When the water boils, drop in 5 or 6 rectangles of pasta and stir with a wooden spoon. Cook for about 1 minute after the water has come back to the boil, then lift each sheet of pasta out with a fish slice and plunge it into the bowl of cold water. Lift it out and lay it on the tea-towels. Repeat this operation until all the pasta is cooked. Pat the top of the cooked lasagne dry.

If you are using bought lasagne, cook according to the directions on the packet.

Heat the oven to 200°C (400°F) mark 6.

Butter a 35 x 25 cm (14 x 10 inch) ovenproof dish generously. Spread 2 tablespoons of the *ragù* over the bottom, cover with a layer of lasagne and spread over a little *ragù* and some béchamel. Sprinkle with grated Parmesan. Cover with another layer of lasagne and repeat until all the ingredients are used, finishing with a layer of béchamel. Sprinkle with the remaining Parmesan and dribble the melted butter all over the top.

Bake in the oven for 15–20 minutes, until the top has formed a golden crust. Allow the dish to settle for at least 5 minutes before serving.

preparation

The dish can be prepared totally up to 1 day in advance and refrigerated, covered with clingfilm. The meat sauce can be made up to 3 days in advance and refrigerated. It also freezes well.

penne with four cheeses
penne ai quattro formaggi

Drop the pasta into rapidly boiling salted water.

While the pasta is cooking, cut the Gruyère, Bel Paese and mozzarella into small pieces.

Heat the oven to 200°C (400°F) mark 6.

Drain the pasta when it is still slightly undercooked and return it immediately to the saucepan. Add half the butter, the Parmesan, all the other cheeses and 2 or 3 pinches of cayenne. Mix thoroughly.

Smear an ovenproof dish with a little of the melted butter and transfer the pasta into it. Dribble the remaining butter all over the top and bake for about 15 minutes.

preparation
The dish can be prepared up to 1 day in advance, but only dribble the butter on top just before you put the dish in the oven, and bake for a little longer to heat the pasta through.

Serves 8–10
700 g (1 1/2 lb)
  penne or other
  tubular pasta
sea salt
90 g (3 oz) Gruyère
90 g (3 oz) Bel Paese
150 g (5 oz)
  mozzarella
120 g (4 oz) unsalted
  butter, melted
75 g (2 1/2 oz)
  freshly grated
  Parmesan
cayenne pepper

baked tagliatelle with ham and peas
tagliatelle gratinate al prosciutto cotto e piselli

If you are making your own tagliatelle, do this first, following the instructions on page 27, and then prepare the sauce.

Melt a knob of butter in a frying pan. Add the shallots and a pinch of salt and sauté until soft. The salt helps to release the moisture from the shallots, thus preventing them from browning.

Meanwhile cut the ham into thin short strips and add to the shallots. Cook for a minute or so and stir in the peas. Let them *insaporire* – take up the flavour – for a minute or two and then pour in the cream. Bring slowly to the boil and simmer for 5 minutes. Add salt and pepper to taste. The sauce is now ready.

Serves 8
tagliatelle made with
  4 eggs and 400 g
  (14 oz) Italian 00
  flour, or 500 g
  (1 lb 2 oz) dried
  egg tagliatelle
60 g (2 oz) unsalted
  butter
2 shallots, very finely
  chopped

continued over >>

sea salt
300 g (10 oz) best
   ham, unsmoked
450 g (1 lb) cooked
   garden peas or
   frozen *petits pois*,
   thawed
600 ml (1 pint) single
   cream
pepper
60 g (2 oz)
   Parmesan, freshly
   grated
120 ml (4 fl oz) full-
   fat milk

Cook the pasta in plenty of boiling salted water. Drain when very *al dente*, but do not overdrain. Return the pasta immediately to the cooking pot and dress with the remaining butter and the cheese. Spoon over the sauce and toss thoroughly.

Heat the oven to 200°C (400°F) mark 6.

Choose an oven dish large enough for the tagliatelle to spread loosely and not pile up too thickly. Butter the dish generously and fill it with the pasta. Just before you want to put the dish in the oven, heat the milk and dribble a few tablespoons all over the dish. (This is to keep the tagliatelle moist while baking.) Bake for about 15–20 minutes, until hot all through.

preparation
The dish can be prepared, apart from the milk, up to 1 day in advance and refrigerated, covered with foil. Add the milk before baking and bake for a little longer to heat the pasta properly. This dish does not freeze well.

fennel and parmesan salad
insalata di finocchio al parmigiano

Serves 8–10
6 fennel bulbs
8 tbsp extra virgin
   olive oil
4 tbsp lemon juice
sea salt and pepper
120 g (4 oz) good
   fresh Parmesan

The best Parmesan for this salad is a young cheese. You can also use grana padano, *which is cheaper than the authentic Parmesan properly known as* parmigiano-reggiano. *The best fennel is the kind with round bulbs as it is sweeter than the long fennel.*

Remove the stalks and any outside brown leaves from the fennel. Cut the bulbs vertically into quarters and then cut them across into very thin strips. Wash in plenty of water, drain and dry well.

Put the fennel in a salad bowl and dress with the oil, lemon, salt and pepper. Do not put in too much salt, since you have to add the cheese, which is salty. Toss thoroughly and taste. Leave for about 30 minutes.

Cut the Parmesan into slivers and lay on top of the fennel.

The fennel can be sliced and washed the day before and kept in the refrigerator. It should be wrapped in a clean tea-towel or a small clean pillow-case.

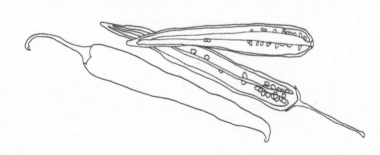

I have always been fascinated by the thought of what people used to eat in the past. My interest in this was once more aroused when I was researching my book *Gastronomy of Italy*, since I had to consult many cookery books written though the centuries to see what ingredients were used. So, for this book, I decided to include a menu from each of the four periods which contributed most to modern Italian cooking, plus one 'Futurist' menu.

The first menu, because it is the earliest, had to be from the only book of Roman recipes, *De Re Coquinaria* by Apicius. It is not known for certain whether Apicius was in fact the author of the book, or whether it was a later compendium of recipes attributed to Apicius.

It was during the Saracen-Sicilian period, some four centuries later, that the foundations of European cooking were laid. The Saracens brought to Italy many spices and vegetables, some of which had previously been known to the Romans. And, even more important, it was in Sicily that these new foods and new methods of cooking came into contact with the indigenous produce and the methods of the earlier civilisations of the Greeks and the Romans. Unfortunately very little writing about cookery has survived from this period, and so I jumped 1,000 years from the Roman era to the Renaissance.

In the fourteenth and fifteenth centuries the great awakening of the mind in Italy was many-sided. Cookery, such an intrinsic part of human life, could not be overlooked, and cookery books began to be written at that time. The recipes in these books have totally captivated me, and I have adapted a certain number to our palates and habits, as you will see throughout this book. I have been fascinated by the similarity of some recipes to modern ones, thus being able to retrace a few favourites to their original source.

These Renaissance cookery books were written by chefs or stewards of grand houses, or of the Vatican, who wrote about the ingredients, how to deal with them, the layout of the kitchen and of the table, the linen, the service, in fact everything connected with cooking and eating. Some books also include menus of the dinners that were prepared for visiting monarchs, ambassadors and prelates. One such is the menu of the dinner prepared by Bartolomeo Scappi for his master, Cardinal Lorenzo Campeggi, who was entertaining Charles V 'when his Caesarean Majesty entered Rome in April 1536'. Campeggi's villa was in Trastevere, which was then a suburb of Rome. Many important Romans used to have splendid villas in the suburbs where eminent visitors to the Pope would spend the night before their audience with His Holiness. Not that these dinners were an ascetic preparation for the awesome meeting of the morrow. Rather, they were a celebration of the excellence and opulence of their host's table, as Scappi's menus testify.

Another fascinating chronicler of glorious meals was Cristoforo di Messisbugo, steward to the fabulously wealthy Cardinal Ippolito d'Este, a brother-in-law of Lucrezia Borgia. Messisbugo's book is not only a recipe book but also an important contribution to social history. He is considered the founder of *haute cuisine*, which France later made its own. I find his recipes rather complicated, however, and I prefer to work from the *Opera* of Scappi.

My other favourite Renaissance writer is Bartolomeo Stefani, chef to another rich and powerful family, the Gonzagas of Mantua. Stefani's simplicity, and his use of herbs in preference to spices, make him a very modern cook, with a light, fresh approach. You will find my adaptation of his pudding, *torta bianca alla bolognese*, on page 472.

The other important period in Italian gastronomy was at the time of Bourbon Naples. Naples became a great cultural centre when the excavations at Pompeii began, in the middle of the eighteenth century, and for some 100 years thereafter it was a Mecca for musicians, literati, artists and young aristocrats from all over Europe. Its *joie de vivre*, its climate and the beauty of its position conspired to make Naples a magnet for the erstwhile jet-set. In 1820, when King Ferdinand entertained the Emperor and Empress of Austria and Prince Metternich, a party was thrown at Capodimonte for 1,000 guests. As Sir Harold Acton writes in his book *The Bourbons at Naples*, 'There were relays of banquets with the rarest fish and the most exquisite viands served in abundance, and any foreign wine asked for was obtainable. The Viennese guests were in ecstasies

over Neapolitan *sfogliatelle*, a fine-flaked pastry melting in the
mouth, "such stuff as dreams are made on".'

One reason why Naples has contributed much to my cooking
(another being my love of Naples) lies in three cookery books written
with a strong emphasis on the cooking of the south. They are *Il
Cuoco Galante* by Vincenzo Corrado, published in 1778, *L'Apicio
Moderno* by Francesco Leonardi, published in 1790, and *Cucina
teorico-pratica* by Ippolito Cavalcanti, published in 1847. Corrado's
book has a fascinating section on vegetables, with some perfect
recipes, and one on *timballi* and *pasticci*. In fact the recipe for the
main course in the Neapolitan menu comes from this section.
Leonardi's work is a vast encyclopaedia in six volumes, ranging
from the history of Italian cooking to many recipes from foreign
countries. He spent some years in Paris and in Russia, where he
became chef to Catherine the Great. Cavalcanti was a wealthy
aristocrat, but nonetheless he wrote a book that was not only for
the rich, incorporating as it does much wise advice and many
simple recipes.

The next period, and locality, which I consider fundamental to Italian
cooking is the nineteenth century in northern Italy, or more precisely in
Piedmont and Lombardy. The cooking of these two regions was greatly
influenced by Austria, which dominated Lombardy for more than half a
century, and by France. Everything French was the *dernier cri*, to the
extent that the wealthy Milanese, who used to spend periods of the
year in Paris, would take their chefs to learn *haute cuisine* directly from
French masters. Fortunately we have quite a few books written at the
time, one by Giovanni Vialardi, who was *chef pâtissier* to the first king
of Italy. But the most important book written then, and still considered
the Italian masterpiece in this genre, is *La Scienza in Cucina e l'Arte di
Mangiar Bene* by Pellegrino Artusi. This book, which by 1963 was in its
800th edition, is still the best-selling cookery book in Italy. It is indeed
a joy to read as well as to cook with, and quite a few of my recipes
are derived from Artusi's.

I have taken gastronomic liberties with most of the recipes I have
chosen, to make the dishes more feasible and more acceptable to
modern palates. But whenever I have added or substituted an

ingredient I have always kept in mind the period when the recipes were originally written, and never brought in any ingredient that was not used at the time.

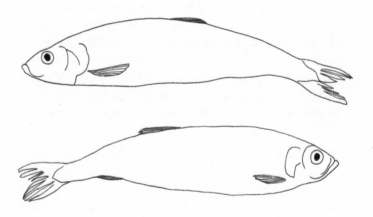

an ancient roman dinner for 8

squid in the pan
in loligine patina

roast pork with coriander
porcellum coriandratum

purée of celery
Aliter olus molle

fresh fruit
frutta

The three recipes in this menu come from *De Re Coquinaria*, a collection of Roman recipes compiled during the time of the first Roman Emperors. These recipes to a certain extent constitute the foundations of European cooking, and therefore of American cooking as well.

The authorship of *De Re Coquinaria* is uncertain. There were three gastronomes called Apicius who lived during those years, all so famous for their love of food that by the end of the first century AD the name Apicius had already become the accepted name for the wealthiest Roman gourmets. The Apicius who lived under Tiberius killed himself when he saw his fortune coming to an end. He had spent most of his great wealth on good living and was afraid that the 10 million *sestertii* that remained would place quite unacceptable limits on his way of life. So he arranged his last banquet, and took poison.

The recipes in *De Re Coquinaria* were transcribed anonymously in the third or fourth century AD, and they are the only sure source, however vague, of the eating habits of that period. The book is divided into ten chapters, covering the whole culinary range from wines and syrups to fish, truffles and sauces. The recipes, however, are extremely succinct, with no indication of proportions for the ingredients, and no cooking times or methods. Nor does the book contain information on the laying of the table or the order of the courses.

What we do learn from the book is which ingredients were used and in what combination of tastes. The love of the ancient Romans for spices and herbs is immediately evident. Whether these were used to disguise unpleasant flavours or for love of spicy and highly flavoured food we cannot know – probably both.

The first course of my menu, the squid, is flavoured with rue, a herb that has almost disappeared from modern cooking. Oddly enough, I recently came across a recipe for spaghetti with a rue sauce, created by the great chef Angelo Paracucchi for his restaurant Locanda dell'Angelo near Lerici. Rue has a rather bitter and very aromatic flavour that can swamp everything else. It has to be used with great discretion. It is impossible to buy, but it grows well in any soil and is one of the most decorative plants I know, with its silvery-bluey leaves and compact bush shape. The American John Edwards, who adapted Apicius' recipes, suggests using fresh rosemary instead.

The *secondo* had to be pork, the favourite Roman meat. Cooked in this way, with sweet ingredients juxtaposed with fresh coriander, it is particularly succulent. The accompaniment for the pork is celery, yet another Roman favourite. They must have loved its fragrance, because they used it not only in cooking but even more in garlands and wreaths.

I could not find any sweet that caught my fancy, the few in the book being rather boring custards or omelettes. This is, in fact, quite understandable, since the Romans preferred to eat fruit, which they knew how to produce to perfection.

squid in the pan
in loligine patina

Serves 8
1.8 kg (4 lb) squid
6 tbsp extra virgin olive oil
120 ml (4 fl oz) dry white wine

continued over >>

'Crush pepper, rue, a little honey, broth, reduced wine and oil to taste, when commencing to boil bind with roux.' (Marcus Gabius Apicius)

The best squid to buy for this dish are those caught around the Cornish coast; they are large and very tasty and they need the lengthy cooking that makes this recipe so perfect.

Ask your fishmonger to clean and skin the squid. If he is not prepared to do so (I feel that in that case I should advise you to find another fishmonger), proceed as follows. Hold the sac in one hand and pull of the tentacles with the other hand. All the contents of the sac will come out too. Cut the tentacles above the eyes. Squeeze out the small bony beak in the centre of the tentacles. Peel off the mottled skin from the sac and the flaps. Remove the transparent backbone from inside the sac and rinse the sac and tentacles thoroughly under running water. Drain in a colander and then dry with kitchen paper. Cut the sacs into 1 cm (1/2 inch) strips and the tentacles into small pieces. The squid are now ready for cooking.

Choose a large heavy sauté pan or, better still, a large earthenware pot. The squid should cook spread out, rather than piled up. Heat the oil, add the squid and sauté gently for 5 minutes. When the squid have released their liquid, turn the heat up to evaporate and cook for 2–3 minutes, stirring frequently. Splash with the wine and let it bubble away for a couple of minutes.

Now turn the heat down and mix in the chopped herbs, the garlic and the honey. Cover with the fish stock and bring to the boil. Taste for salt and add some if necessary. (Fish stock is sometimes already salted.) Season with plenty of pepper. Put the lid firmly on the pan or cover with foil tied under the rim of the pan. The squid must cook tightly covered so that the steam is kept in. They must also cook over the gentlest heat. I use a flame disperser. They should be ready in 40–50 minutes, depending on their size. Test for doneness by pricking the squid with a fork; it should offer no resistance to the prongs.

Scoop out the squid, place on a heated serving dish and keep warm, covered with foil. Put the flour in a small bowl and add a few tablespoons of the cooking liquid to make a paste. Blend the paste into the pan and cook for a few minutes, stirring constantly. Check the seasonings. Pour the sauce over the squid and serve with plenty of crusty bread. The dish can be served hot, though not too hot, but it is also excellent at room temperature.

preparation
The dish can be prepared totally up to 1 day in advance and chilled in a covered container. Do not serve straight from the fridge.

1 tbsp finely chopped rosemary needles
1 tbsp finely chopped rue, if available
2 large garlic cloves, sliced
1/2 tbsp clear honey
500 ml (16 fl oz) (scant measure) fish stock (see page 486)
sea salt and freshly ground black pepper
1 tbsp flour

roast pork with coriander
porcellum coriandratum

Serves 8
4 tbsp olive oil
1.5 kg (3 1/4 lb)
  boneless rolled leg
  of pork
2 tbsp fresh
  coriander, chopped
1 tsp dried oregano
2 tsp fresh dill,
  chopped
8 peppercorns
1 tbsp rock salt

For the sauce
300 ml (1/2 pint)
  meat stock
200 ml (7 fl oz) red
  wine
1 tbsp red wine
  vinegar
1 small onion,
  chopped
2 tbsp pine nuts
3 tbsp sultanas
1 1/2 tbsp honey
4 tbsp olive oil
sea salt and pepper

'Roast the pig carefully; make a mortar mixture in this way: pound pepper, dill, oregano, green coriander, moisten with honey, wine, broth, oil, vinegar and reduced must. All of this when hot, pour over. Sprinkle over with raisins, pine nuts and chopped onions and so serve.' (Marcus Gabius Apicius)

Heat the oven to 225°C (425°F) mark 7.

Put 2 tablespoons of the oil in a small roasting tin and coat the meat in the oil. Put the tin in the oven and roast for 15 minutes.

Meanwhile pound together in a mortar (or a heavy pudding basin) the coriander, oregano, dill, peppercorns and rock salt, moistening with the remaining oil. When the 15 minutes are up turn the heat down to 180°C (350°F) mark 4. Spread the herb mixture over the meat and replace the meat in the oven. Cook for 1 1/2 hours, basting every quarter of an hour or thereabouts.

For the sauce, put all the ingredients in a saucepan and boil, uncovered, for 40 minutes. The liquid should boil slowly, so that by the end of the 40 minutes there will be plenty left but it will have a rich, concentrated flavour.

When the meat is done, transfer it to a side dish and cover it with foil. Do not worry about it getting cold. Any roast must be left out of the oven before eating for 10 minutes at least, to allow the juices to penetrate the inside of the joint. Skim off as much fat as you can from the surface of the cooking juices in the tin. Deglaze the roasting tin with a couple of tablespoons of boiling water and then pour everything into the sauce, scraping down all the bits of herbs.

Carve the meat into 1 cm (1/2 inch) slices and spoon a little sauce over the meat. Hand the rest round in a sauce-boat.

preparation
The sauce can be prepared up to 3 days in advance and refrigerated in a covered container. Reheat slowly before you add the deglazed cooking juices.

purée of celery
aliter olus molle

'Cook celery in soda water, squeeze water out, chop fine. In the mortar crush pepper, lovage, oregano, onion and mix with wine and stock, adding some oil.' (Marcus Gabius Apicius)

Remove all the strings from the celery stalks. I find a potato peeler better than a knife for this job. Scrub and wash the stalks and cut into 5 cm (2 inches) pieces.

Bring a saucepan of salted water to the boil. Add the celery and cook for 5 minutes after the water has come back to the boil. Drain very thoroughly. Chop the celery to a coarse purée. You can use a food processor, although it tends to make the celery too mashed up.

Put all the other ingredients in a saucepan and bring to the boil. Simmer for 10 minutes and then stir in the celery. Cook for a further 10 minutes, stirring frequently. If the purée seems too thin, turn the heat up to evaporate some of the liquid. Taste, check the seasoning and serve as an accompaniment to the pork.

preparation
The purée can be prepared up to 1 day in advance and refrigerated in a covered container. Reheat slowly in a heavy saucepan into which you have put 1 tablespoon of olive oil.

Serves 8
2 celery heads
sea salt
2 tbsp olive oil
1 onion, finely
  chopped
1 tbsp lovage,
  chopped, or 2 tsp
  celery seeds,
  pounded
1 tbsp dried oregano
120 ml (4 fl oz)
  white wine
225 ml (8 fl oz)
  vegetable stock

a renaissance dinner for 6

a lenten spinach pie
torta d'herbe da quaresima

stewed fish
pesce in potaggio

boiled cauliflower with oil
cavolfiore all'olio

ricotta and cream cake
torta bianca alla bolognese

In 1989 the Victoria and Albert Museum held a special event called '*Una Notte in Italia*' and, as part of this, I gave a cookery demonstration. Because of the historical overtones of the venue I decided to show how to prepare a Renaissance dinner. My dinner was, of course, conceived as a twentieth-century meal and not as a proper Renaissance meal, when each course would have contained many different dishes, all placed on the table at the same time.

The recipe for the *torta d'herbe da quaresima* comes from one of the first culinary books to appear in print, the *Libro Novo* by Cristoforo di Messisbugo. The torta is a typical example of the cooking of the sixteenth century, when sweet and savoury ingredients were combined to form a perfect harmony. Sweet ingredients were included in Renaissance, and Roman, recipes in order to enhance the flavour of the food, which sugar does, rather than to sweeten it. Buy Italian spinach, the kind that is in bunches, or very young leaf spinach. The large beet spinach is not suitable.

My choice for the second course is a fish dish, from two recipes by the great Bartolomeo Scappi, who flourished between 1540 and 1570 and was chef to Pope Pius V. The fish Scappi suggests is pike, carp or eel, all great favourites at the time. At my demonstration I used lovely chunks of eel, but I've also made this recipe with hake or halibut steaks, and it works well. I expect it would also be quite good with salmon steak. Most salmon is farmed nowadays and I find its taste not good enough for it to be simply steamed or grilled.

Next in this dinner I would serve a simple salad of boiled cauliflower taken from the *Brieve racconto di tutte le radici di tutte l'erbe e di tutti i frutti* by Giacomo Castelvetro. Castelvetro was born in Modena in 1546 but wrote this booklet in England, where he took refuge after he was banned from Italy, having incurred the wrath of the Inquisition through his leanings towards Protestantism. He dedicated his *Brieve racconto* to his patron, Lucy, Countess of Bedford. The book, which has now been translated into English by Gillian Riley, is not a cookery book but a eulogy of the fruits and vegetables of his native country. There is in Castelvetro's writing all the nostalgia and passion for something once enjoyed, now lost. When I first came across this book in 1975 in the Biblioteca Comunale in Milan I was taken back to the time when I first arrived in England in the early 1950s and the only vegetables were cabbages and lettuces in the summer plus, of course, potatoes and carrots. Nothing has changed, I thought, in 400 years!

Most of the vegetables are cooked in the simplest ways, such as the cauliflower in this recipe. 'We have in this season,' Castelvetro wrote, 'cauliflowers, which take pride of place for goodness and beauty among all the other species of the cabbage family. First cooked in lightly salted water, they are dressed with olive oil, salt and pepper.'

If you want to add a little 'body' to this course, serve some boiled new potatoes, even if they could not have figured in a Renaissance menu. Potatoes, which of course came originally from the New World, were hardly eaten in Italy until the nineteenth century.

The sweet, a very delicate soft cake, in effect a cross between a cake and a pudding, is derived from a recipe by Bartolomeo Stefani. Stefani was chef to the Marquis Ottavio Gonzaga of Mantua during the seventeenth century. His fascinating book, *L'Arte di Ben Cucinare*, was published in Mantua in 1662 and has now been reprinted in a facsimile edition by Arnaldo Forni. As well as recipes it contains instructions and advice, information and menus, ending with the menu of an extraordinary banquet served by his patron to Queen Christina of Sweden when she stayed in Mantua on her way to Rome.

The description of the room and table décor make fascinating reading. In the middle of the table there stood a sugar sculpture of Mount Olympus, with the altar of faith, on top of which were two putti holding a royal crown over the Queen's coat of arms. At each end of the table there were four orange trees, with fruit and leaves made of jelly. Between the trees stood two colonnades made of sugar, designed by an architect, one with 12 Corinthian columns and the other with 12 Doric columns. Between the column of one row there stood sugar statues of early warriors, while between the others there were statues of 'the most virtuous men who have ever lived'.

The dinner began with strawberries and marzipan sweetmeats shaped like birds. Fruit was always served first during the Renaissance, because it was supposed to help the digestion. After 400 years this belief is gaining favour again; many dieticians advise eating fruit half an hour before the beginning of a meal. *Plus ça change* . . .

a lenten spinach pie
torta d'herbe da quaresima

Serves 6

For the pastry
**45 g (1 1/2 oz)
caster sugar
1/4 tsp powdered
saffron or 10
saffron strands
250 g (9 oz) Italian
00 flour
1/2 tsp sea salt
120 g (4 oz) unsalted
butter
2 free-range egg
yolks
1 1/2 tsp rosewater**

For the filling
**30 g (1 oz) raisins
30 g (1 oz) sultanas
1.35 kg (3 lb) fresh
bunch spinach, or
700 g (1 1/2 lb)
cooked, or frozen
spinach
sea salt and pepper
4 tbsp olive oil
30 g (1 oz) walnut
kernels
3 dried figs
1 tbsp sugar
1/4 tsp ground
cinnamon
1/2 tsp grated
nutmeg
60 g (2 oz) grated
Parmesan
1 tbsp dried
breadcrumbs**

For the glazing
**1 free-range egg yolk
1 tbsp milk
pinch of sea salt**

*'Take washed spinach and put it in a pot and throw in 4 ounces of oil
and sauté it well and chop it and put it in a pot with 4 ounces of sugar
and 1 ounce of cinnamon and a quarter of pepper and 6 ounces of
raisins and 1 pound of figs, cut thin, and half a pound of sultanas and
shelled and peeled walnuts and mix everything together well . . . And
then you will prepare your case and you will cook following the order
of the other Lenten pie.' (Cristoforo di Messisbugo)*

First make the pastry the way you usually do, by hand or in the food
processor. Pound the sugar and saffron together and mix well into the
flour and salt before rubbing in the butter. Mix in the egg yolks and the
rosewater. When the dough is ready, wrap it in clingfilm and chill for at
least 30 minutes. Soak the raisins and sultanas in a cupful of hot water
for 15 minutes or so. Drain and dry thoroughly.

Trim, wash and cook the spinach without putting any water in the pan.
The water that clings to the leaves is enough. Add 1 teaspoon of salt.
When the spinach is tender, drain, and as soon as it is cool enough
squeeze well between your hands. Sauté it gently in the oil for 10
minutes, stirring frequently to let it *insaporire* – take up the flavour.
Chop it coarsely and transfer to a bowl.

Blanch the walnut kernels in a little boiling water for 20 seconds. Drain
and remove as much as you can of the bitter skin. Dry the kernels and
chop finely, together with the figs. Add to the spinach in the bowl.

Drain and dry the sultanas and the raisins and add to the bowl. Mix in
the sugar, cinnamon, nutmeg, salt and pepper. Add the Parmesan,
reserving 1 tablespoon, and mix very thoroughly with your hands.

Heat the oven to 190°C (375°F) mark 5.

Butter an 18 cm (7 inch) spring-clip tin and sprinkle with flour.

Roll out about one-third of the pastry dough into a circle to cover the
bottom of the tin. Roll out strips of dough and line the sides of the tin.
Sprinkle the bottom with the dried breadcrumbs and the remaining
Parmesan. Spoon the spinach mixture into the tin and cover with a disc
of rolled-out pastry. Seal the edges and brush with the egg yolk into
which you have stirred the milk and salt. If you like, and if you have

any pastry left, cut out some pretty shapes, place on top of the pie and brush with the egg yolk glaze. Pierce the top here and there with a fork to allow the steam to escape.

Bake for 30 minutes then turn the heat down to 180ºC (350ºF) mark 4 and bake for a further 10–15 minutes, until the pastry is lovely and golden. Serve warm or at room temperature, but not hot.

preparation

The whole pie can be made up to 2 days in advance and refrigerated. It can also be frozen successfully, but do not leave in the freezer for longer than 2 weeks or the flavours will evaporate. Remove from the fridge at least 3 hours before serving.

stewed fish
pesce in potaggio

'Cut the fish into thick rolls and cook it with white wine, vinegar, spices and water and cook it as for the trout in Chapter CXVI. It can be served hot or cold.' (Bartolomeo Scappi)

Heat the oven to 200ºC (400ºF) mark 6.

Put the fish in an oven dish into which it will fit in a single layer.

Heat the wine and vinegar with the spices, seasonings, onion and bay leaves. Add 225 ml (8 fl oz) of water and bring to the boil. Boil for 2 minutes and then pour it over the fish. Cover the dish with foil and cook in the oven until ready, about 15–20 minutes, depending on the thickness of the fish steaks.

Transfer the fish to a serving dish and keep warm.

Strain the cooking liquid into a saucepan and reduce over a high heat by about half. Add the sugar, ground almonds and herbs, then bring to

Serves 6
6 fish steaks, about 200 g (7 oz) each
225 ml (8 fl oz) dry white wine
2 tbsp red wine vinegar
1/4 tsp powdered saffron or 10 saffron strands
1/4 tsp ground ginger
sea salt
15 peppercorns, bruised
1 onion, stuck with 3 cloves
2 bay leaves

continued over >>

2 tbsp sugar
45 g (1 1/2 oz)
  ground almonds
2 tbsp mixed
  chopped herbs:
  rosemary, sage,
  thyme, marjoram,
  mint
2 tbsp chopped
  parsley
30 g (1 oz) unsalted
  butter

the boil, turn the heat down and simmer for 10 minutes or so.

Add the butter in little lumps and, when it is all incorporated, transfer to a sauce-boat and serve.

preparation

Fish should always be cooked just before it is eaten. If you are using whole almonds, which is better than buying them ready ground, you can grind them up to 3 days in advance and refrigerate, or you can prepare them up to 2 months in advance and freeze.

ricotta and cream cake
torta bianca alla bolognese

Serves 6
300 g (10 oz) ricotta
1 tbsp rosewater
300 ml (1/2 pint)
  double cream
120 g (4 oz) sugar
1/2 tsp cinnamon
4 free-range eggs
icing sugar, sifted
unsalted butter to
  grease the tin

'You will take 4 pounds of fat ricotta pounded in the mortar splashed with rose water, adding 12 fresh eggs, 8 ounces of sugar, half an ounce of cinnamon, pounding everything together well and when well swollen, you will grease a pan with butter. You will put in the mixture and you will cook it slowly in the oven and you will serve it hot with sugar on top.' (Bartolomeo Stefani)

Heat the oven to 180°C (350°F) mark 4.

Pass the ricotta through a food mill or a sieve and mix in the rosewater. Do not use a food processor, as this would not aerate the ricotta. Fold in the cream, the sugar and the cinnamon. Beat the eggs lightly in a bowl and add gradually while beating constantly.

Generously butter a 20 cm (8 inch) spring-clip tin and line the bottom with greaseproof paper. Butter the paper and spoon the mixture into the tin. Bake in the preheated oven for 50 minutes or until a cocktail stick inserted in the middle of the cake comes out just dry. Remove from the tin and peel off the paper.

Serve warm, sprinkled with plenty of icing sugar.

The mixture can be prepared up to 5 or 6 hours in advance and refrigerated. If necessary you can even make the cake the day before, although it is nicer just warm.

an eighteenth-century southern italian dinner for 6

mussels italian style
cozze all'italiana

baked macaroni with chicken breast and prosciutto
timballo di maccheroni alla pampadur

apple snow in a ring
mela in tortiglié

It was in Naples in the eighteenth century that what are now the two most Italian of all Italian foods, pasta and tomatoes, became part of everyday eating. In the eighteenth century the Neapolitans, until then known as *mangiafoglie*, leaf-eaters, adopted the traditionally Sicilian pasta and made it their own. And it was in the fertile plain of Campania that the tomato, which first arrived in Europe in the wake of the Conquistadores, found at last the ideal habitat and became the perfect *pomodoro*. It was also during that period that the best Italian cookery books were published in Naples and Rome rather than in the north of Italy, as had been the case previously.

The first two recipes I have chosen for this menu are typically Italian. The *primo* is a favourite dish to this day, and it is often still made as in this Leonardi recipe. Francesco Leonardi was a Roman who finished his successful career as chef to Catherine the Great. He was very knowledgeable about foreign methods, techniques and produce, but he also recorded Italian regional cooking of traditional simplicity, as in this recipe for mussels.

Contrary to what most Italians would do, I have decided to serve a pasta dish as a main course. But this *timballo* is no everyday pasta dish. It is a rich and delectable concoction which the creator of this recipe, Vincenzo Corrado, dedicated to Madame Pompadour, the 'Pampadur' of the title. Corrado was the first author who assimilated the terminology of French gastronomy, which by then had gained supremacy over all other cuisines. He also tried to graft French techniques into the local cuisine. Yet the Italian feeling for simplicity and purity of ingredients is there, especially in the chapter devoted to '*Il Vitto Pitagorico*', vegetarian food, in which most of the recipes are functional and very appealing to modern palates.

The third book, *Cucina teorico-pratica*, from which I have taken the pudding, was written by Ippolito Cavalcanti, Duke of Bonvicino, at the beginning of the nineteenth century. The pudding interested me especially because I could see in it a connection with English nursery food. Perhaps Cavalcanti had the recipe from one of the many English ladies who spent the winter months in Naples. Cavalcanti gave apple snow an appealing shape and decorated it with *erbaggio*, sugar shapes mainly green in colour. I have used chopped pistachio nuts to replace the *erbaggio*. It is a good pudding, and one your friends will love for its familiar flavour, albeit under an elegant disguise.

You must start with a very dry apple purée. If your purée is too wet, put it in a saucepan and heat it, stirring the whole time, until you have achieved a stiff consistency. I give the quantity of the purée, not of the apples, because it depends so much on what apples are used. Many of my readers will want to use their windfalls from the garden, which are usually better than bought fruit, but with windfalls you never know how much waste there will be. Cavalcanti, in spite of his wealth and rank, had a very down-to-earth approach, as can be seen in the fascinating appendix to his book. He gives practical and thrifty advice and I am sure he would have approved of the use of windfalls when there are any.

mussels italian style
cozze all'italiana

'Put in a pan over the fire a little oil, parsley, onion and a point of garlic, everything well chopped, then moisten with half a glass of white wine, reduced by half, and a little water from the mussels, opened in the usual way, let them boil a little and add the mussels, well washed and drained, season with ground pepper, give it a boil and serve with slices of bread underneath.' (Francesco Leonardi)

Scrub the mussels under cold water. Discard any mussel that remains open after you tap it on a hard surface. Tug off the beards, knock off any barnacles and rinse in several changes of water.

Heat the oven to 200°C (400°F) mark 6.

Cut the bread into fairly thick slices and lay the slices on a baking tray.

Pour the oil into a large saucepan in which you will be able to cook the mussels later. I prefer to use a wide sauté pan in which the mussels can spread out and cook more quickly. If your pan is not large enough use 2 pans, dividing the ingredients in half, but increasing the amount of oil by 1 tablespoon, and of the wine by 2 tablespoons.

Using a pastry brush, moisten the bread slices with a little of the oil from the pan. Put the baking tray in the oven and bake for 6–8 minutes. Turn off the oven, but leave the bread in it to keep warm.

Chop the parsley, onion and garlic together and add to the pan with the oil. Turn the heat on and sauté for 1 minute. Add the wine and the pepper and cook briskly for a couple of minutes to evaporate the alcohol. Transfer the mussels to the pan. Put a lid tightly on the pan and cook until all the mussels are open, which will take 4–5 minutes. Shake the pan often. Discard any unopened mussels.

As soon as the mussels are open, turn the heat off. If you are using an earthenware pan, bring it to the table, otherwise transfer the mussels and all the juices to a heated terrine, or ladle the mussels directly into individual soup bowls. The toasted bread must be placed in the soup bowls so that the mussels are ladled over it. Serve at once.

Serves 6
1.8 kg (4 lb) mussels
1 Italian *ciabatta* or French loaf
100 ml (3 1/2 fl oz) extra virgin olive oil
1 large bunch flat-leaf parsley
1 onion
3 garlic cloves
200 ml (7 fl oz) dry white wine
black pepper

preparation

Mussels cannot be reheated. You can scrub and clean them and leave them in a covered bowl up to a few hours in advance. The bread can be toasted up to 2 days in advance, wrapped in foil and refrigerated. Remove from the fridge at least 2 hours before serving.

baked macaroni with chicken breast and prosciutto
timballo di maccheroni alla pampadur

Serves 6
100 g (3 1/2 oz) unsalted butter
1 tbsp olive oil
1 rosemary sprig, about 7.5 cm (3 inches) long
450 g (1 lb) boneless pork loin
120 ml (4 fl oz) dry white wine
sea salt and pepper
250 g (9 oz) free-range or organic chicken breasts
150 g (5 oz) prosciutto, medium sliced
450 g (1 lb) large *penne* or macaroni
60 g (2 oz) freshly grated Parmesan
3 tbsp dried breadcrumbs

continued over >>

'Have the macaroni cooked in beef stock. Cooked and cooled, it is dressed with roast pig juices and roast capon breasts chopped, chopped prosciutto, pepper and grated cheese; and like that it is placed on the dish and covered with a sauce of yolks of eggs, Parmesan, butter and cream flavoured with cinnamon and, this sauce set in the oven, it is served.' (Vicenzo Corrado)

Choose a small heavy-based casserole into which the pork will just fit. Put in 30 g (1 oz) of the butter, the oil and the rosemary and turn the heat to medium high. As soon as the butter begins to colour, add the pork and brown well on all sides. This will take about 10 minutes.

Turn the heat up to high and pour over the wine. Reduce by half and then turn the heat down to low so that the liquid simmers gently. Sprinkle with salt and pepper. Cover the pan with a sheet of greaseproof paper and put the lid on slightly askew. Cook for about 1 1/2 hours, turning the meat over every 30 minutes and adding a little water if the pork is cooking dry. When the meat is very tender remove from the pan and reserve for another meal.

Add a couple of tablespoons of warm water to the pan and bring to the boil, scraping the bottom of the pan with a metal spoon to free the cooking residue. Measure the liquid and if necessary add enough water to make up to 120 ml (4 fl oz).

Heat 30 g (1 oz) of the remaining butter in a non-stick frying pan. Add the chicken breasts and sauté very gently until done, about 15 minutes, turning the breasts over halfway through the cooking. Season with a little salt and pepper and add a couple of tablespoons of water if necessary. Transfer the chicken breast and their juices to a food processor together with the prosciutto, cut into pieces. Process until coarsely ground, not a smooth purée. If you do not have a food processor chop coarsely by hand. Transfer the mixture to a bowl and add the pork juices. Mix thoroughly.

3 free-range egg yolks
300 ml (1/2 pint) single cream
1/2 tsp ground cinnamon

Heat the oven to 200°C (400°F) mark 6.

Cook the pasta in plenty of boiling salted water. Drain, turn immediately into the bowl with the meat mixture and add the remaining butter and half the Parmesan. Mix very thoroughly and then taste and adjust the seasoning.

Butter an oven dish and sprinkle all over with the dried breadcrumbs. Turn the dish upside-down and shake off the excess crumbs. Transfer the pasta into the dish and level it down gently.

In a bowl mix together the egg yolks, cream, remaining Parmesan, cinnamon, a little salt and a generous amount of pepper. Spoon this sauce over the pasta and place the dish in the oven. Bake for about 15 minutes until a golden crust forms on the top. Remove the dish from the oven and allow to stand out of the oven for 5 minutes before serving, to allow the flavours to combine.

preparation
The dish can be prepared without the topping up to 1 day in advance. Cover tightly and refrigerate only in hot weather. Spoon over the egg and cream mixture before baking and bake for 10 minutes longer to allow the cold pasta to heat through.

apple snow in a ring
mela in tortiglié

Serves 6
600 g (1 1/4 lb)
    apple purée,
    sweetened
1 vanilla pod
3 tbsp Maraschino,
    Alchermes, Rosolio
    or Crème de Cassis
1 tsp cinnamon
grated rind of 1
    organic lemon
3 egg whites
75 g (2 1/2 oz) sugar
2 tbsp chopped
    pistachio nuts
200 ml (7 fl oz)
    whipping cream

'You will make an apple jam, I mean a compote of apple, being enough for 12 persons, 3lb; you will mix in one or two pinches – or perhaps more – of rosolio liqueur, citron, cinnamon and vanilla, according to your taste, and you will arrange the jam on a suitable dish with the utmost care, round and round like a snail; you will whisk 4 egg whites until stiff mixing in 1lb of sugar; you will cover the ring with this meringue with the blade of a knife, and you will sprinkle it again with sugar and with coloured sugar crystals; and you will place it with hot cinders underneath and with a little live coal above and when the meringue will have formed a crust and will have taken a lovely colour, you will serve it cold.' (Ippolito Cavalcanti)

The apple purée must be dry or it will not keep its ring shape. It should be sweet, to your taste, keeping in mind that it will be covered by a meringue.

Split the vanilla pod in half. Scrape out the seeds, and add them to the purée with the liqueur, cinnamon and lemon rind. Taste and check for sweetness and flavouring.

Whisk the egg whites until stiff. Reserve 2 tablespoons of the sugar and add one third of the remainder to the egg whites. Continue whisking and then add half the remaining sugar. Whisk well; the meringue will be beautifully glossy and silky. Now sprinkle the rest of the sugar over the top and fold it into the meringue gently with a metal spoon.

Take a round ovenproof dish and shape the purée into a ring. If your purée is really stiff you can use a forcing bag with a large fluted nozzle attached. My purée has never been that stiff, because, I expect, the delicious apples from my garden are not of the right sort. But you can try; it would certainly make the sweet look prettier.

Heat the oven to 150°C (300°F) mark 2.

Cover the apple purée with the meringue, using a thin metal spatula. I never smooth it down too neatly, because I don't like dishes that look too 'manicured'. Sprinkle with the reserved sugar and then with the chopped pistachios. Bake in the oven for 15–20 minutes, until the meringue is set and just coloured.

Leave to cool and then chill. Before serving, whip the cream and use some to fill the hole in the middle. Serve the rest of the cream separately, if you wish.

preparation
The purée can be totally prepared up to 3 days in advance and kept in the fridge in a closed container. The meringue must be prepared and baked no more than 1 hour before serving or it will become soggy.

a nineteenth-century northern italian dinner for 8

vegetable soup
zuppa alla santé

pot-roasted chickens with rice
pollastri al riso

sautéed mushrooms with oregano and garlic (page 296)
funghi al funghetto

a buttery marquise from lombardy
bavarese lombarda

As I was browsing through my nineteenth-century cookery books when planning this menu, I could retaste in my imagination most of the dishes of my childhood in Milan. Plenty of soups, warming casseroles, large rich braised joints, stewed vegetables and rich puddings. Not much Mediterranean flavour in this type of cooking, but rather it is one looking northwards towards Austria with its rich stews and France with its buttery sauces. This is still, fundamentally, the cuisine of northern Italy, into which in the past 30 years the cooking of the south has instilled its lighter and fresher approach.

At home, no dinner was considered a proper dinner by my father if it did not start with a soup. And a proper soup, at that, rich and nutritious and '*non quel consommé che si beve in tazze, e sembra una specie di the*' ('not that consommé that you drink in cups, like some kind of tea').

The soup in this menu is very representative of a soup served at Milanese dinner parties of the period: lighter than a minestrone yet with similar characteristics of flavour and reinforced with bread so that it becomes thick. If you want to make it more elegant, serve small croûtons instead of the large croûtes.

The recipe comes from *Il Cuoco senza Pretese* (*The Unpretentious Cook*), published in Como in 1834. Unfortunately the name of the author is not given. Most of the recipes in this chatty book give precise quantities in pounds and ounces, which were the measures in use in Lombardy before the metric system was adopted around 1860. At the end of each recipe there is a list of costs. This *zuppa alla santé* cost 35 lire – 17 pence. The list in this case does not include the stock, since every self-respecting household always had some stock ready. The recipe speaks for itself in its simplicity. I can only add that it must be made with good stock.

The main course is my adaptation from a recipe that appears in *Trattato di Cucina* by the Piedmontese Giovanni Vialardi, published in 1854. It is a large tome, illustrated by the author and divided into 19 chapters embracing all culinary subjects. One of the chapters, for example, is dedicated to cooking suitable for children and contains a recipe for a '*Pappa*' – pappy food – for a child of three or four hours, 'lacking his or her mother's milk or because of the late arrival of his or her wet nurse'. The recipe is too long, I'm afraid, to find room here. Vialardi's style is rather dull, but his recipes are good, and his drawings for the presentation of the dishes are extremely interesting and very artistic. He was, in fact, a *chef pâtissier* to the first king of Italy, greatly influenced by Carême and other French masters.

The dish in this menu does not need a master for its preparation, nor for its presentation. It is simple enough for any respectable cook and it is very good. Vialardi suggests serving the chicken with a garnish of asparagus or mushrooms. Try my sautéed mushrooms on page 296.

The pudding is one of my favourite recipes by Pellegrino Artusi, possibly the greatest Italian cookery writer, who, although a northerner, was the first to see, late in the nineteenth century, some movement towards the unification of the cooking of Italy following its political unification. The marquise in the menu was indeed often made in Milanese families, as it still is today. Considering the amount of butter it contains and the longevity of many members of past generations of my family, I begin to wonder about the harm butter is supposed to do! This is indeed a rich sweet which I find irresistible, with its subtle eggy flavour enhanced by virtue of the eggs being hard-boiled. At home we children called it, simply, '*Il dolce squisito*'.

vegetable soup
zuppa alla santé

'*Cut into thin slices, and not too long, a few celery stalks, carrots, savoy cabbage, turnips and leeks and fry them in butter for a short time, and then pour them into the broth to finish cooking, and use them later to moisten the bread.*' (from Il Cuoco senza Pretese)

Heat the oven to 200°C (400°F) mark 6.

Melt the butter in a stockpot. Place the bread slices on a baking tray and, using a pastry brush, moisten one side with a little melted butter. Place the tray in the oven for 8 minutes. Turn the heat off and leave the bread in the oven

Peel and wash the potato, turnip, onion and carrot, keeping them, and all the following vegetables, separate from each other for the moment. Cut into short matchsticks and dry with kitchen paper. Wash the celery stalks, remove the thread and cut into matchsticks. Thoroughly wash

Serves 8
100 g (3 1/2 oz) unsalted butter
8 slices pugliese bread or other good country-type white bread
450 g (1 lb) vegetables: potato, turnip (if available), onion, carrot, celery
2 leeks, white part only
100 g (3 1/2 oz) Savoy cabbage leaves

continued over >>

sea salt and pepper
1.5 litres
  (2 1/2 pints)
  stock (see
  pages 485 or 487)
freshly grated
  Parmesan

and trim the leeks. Cut them into matchsticks and the cabbage into thin ribbons.

Add the potato, turnip and onion to the stockpot and sauté for 5 minutes over a slow heat. Season with a pinch of salt, which will prevent the vegetables browning. They should just soften a little.

Now add the carrot and celery and cook for 3 minutes, still very gently, stirring frequently. Finally add the leek and the cabbage and gently sauté them too, for a minute or two, turning them over and over. While the vegetables are cooking, bring the stock to the boil. Pour the stock over the vegetables, add pepper and cook for 5 minutes or until the potato and turnip are cooked. The other vegetables can be crunchy, but undercooked potato or turnip are definitely unpleasant. Taste and check the seasonings.

Put the toasted bread in individual soup bowls and ladle the soup over it. Serve at once, handing the Parmesan round separately.

preparation
If necessary, the soup can be prepared up to 3 days in advance and refrigerated in a covered container. In this case you must turn the heat off as soon as the broth is boiling. Reheat the soup and simmer gently until the vegetables are ready.

pot-roasted chickens with rice
pollastri al riso

Serves 8
120 g (4 oz) unsalted
  butter
1 tbsp olive oil

continued over >>

'Cook two young chicken . . . but do not lard them, cooked tender, juicy, of a beautiful colour and serve them with good rice or tagliatelle underneath. Release the cooking juice, purée it through a sieve, defat it, and reduced as a sauce, pour it over . . . They are served with a garnish of asparagus and mushroom.' (Giovanni Vialardi)

Heat the oven to 200°C (400°F) mark 6.

Put half the butter, the oil, vegetables and parsley in a heavy casserole into which the two birds will fit snugly. Cook for 10–15 minutes over a low heat, turning the vegetables over quite frequently.

Meanwhile wash the chickens under cold water and pat dry with kitchen paper. Season each cavity with salt and pepper and with the chopped herbs. Place the chickens over the bed of vegetables, pour over half the stock and season, if necessary, with salt and pepper. Cover with a piece of foil and with the lid. Place the casserole in the oven and cook until the chickens are done, about 1 1/2 hours. Test by piercing a thigh with a skewer. The liquid that runs out should be clear.

Put a large saucepan of water on the heat for the rice.

Carve the chickens into neat pieces and place on a dish. Cover loosely with foil and keep warm in the oven with the heat turned off.

Skim off as much of the fat floating on the surface of the cooking juices as you can. Turn the cooking juices with all the vegetables into a food processor or a blender and blend to a smooth purée. The purée should have the consistency of single cream; if it is too thick add a little of the reserved stock. Taste and check the seasoning. Transfer the sauce to a bowl and keep warm in a bain-marie, i.e. by placing the bowl in a saucepan half full of boiling water and covering with a lid.

Cook the rice in the boiling water to which you have added 1 1/2 tablespoons of salt. When the rice is *al dente*, drain well and return immediately to the pan in which it has cooked. Toss with the remaining butter, season with Parmesan and with a few grindings of pepper and then add a few tablespoons of the sauce to coat the rice thoroughly.

Transfer the rice to a large heated serving dish, making a well in the middle. Place the chicken pieces in the well and spoon over the rest of the sauce. Serve at once.

preparation
The chicken can be cooked up to 2 days in advance and refrigerated in a covered container. Carve the chicken before reheating. Reheat in the oven and then make the sauce.

2 small carrots, cubed
2 onions, sliced
2 celery sticks, cut into strips
small bunch of parsley
2 fresh free-range or organic roasting chickens, weighing about 1 kg (2 lb) each
sea salt and pepper
2 tsp fresh rosemary and fresh sage leaves, chopped
450 ml (3/4 pint) good meat or chicken stock
300 g (10 oz) long-grain rice
6 tbsp freshly grated Parmesan

a buttery marquise from lombardy
bavarese lombarda

Serves 8
about 150 g (5 oz)
Madeira cake
6 large free-range
eggs
180 g (6 oz) unsalted
butter, at room
temperature
180 g (6 oz) icing
sugar, sifted if
necessary
12 drops of pure
vanilla essence
100 ml (3 1/2 fl oz)
white rum, such as
Bacardi

'This pudding, named differently by different people, could well be called "the sweet plat du jour" since it is so often served and so much enjoyed in so many families.' (Pellegrino Artusi)

First make the cake, either according to your usual recipe, or following mine for a fatless sponge on page 492. A Genoese sponge or a Victoria sponge are also suitable. Use a loaf tin for a better shape of marquise.

Gently lower the eggs with a spoon into a saucepan of boiling water and cook them for 7 minutes exactly. The timing is important because the yolks must be just soft in the middle. Put the saucepan under cold water, leave for 2 minutes and then peel the eggs. Cut them in half and scoop out the yolk (you can use the whites, chopped up, in a salad).

Cut the cake into 5 mm (1/4 inch) thick slices and lay half the slices on a serving dish.

Cream together the butter and the cooked egg yolks and then add the icing sugar, reserving about 3 tablespoons for the decoration, and the vanilla. Blend very thoroughly, using a wooden spatula, or use a food processor for the whole operation.

Pour the rum into a bowl. Moisten the prepared cake with the rum, using a pastry brush. Cover the cake with the cream, spreading it evenly all over. Now place the rest of the cake over the cream and moisten it well with the rum. Cover with clingfilm and chill for at least 3 hours. Just before serving, remove the clingfilm and sprinkle the reserved icing sugar all over the top, using a sugar sifter or pressing it through a fine sieve with a metal spoon.

preparation
Artusi recommends leaving the marquise 'on ice' for 3 hours. I prefer to make it the day before. You can even make it 2 or 3 days in advance. It keeps very well in the fridge.

the essentials

The following recipes are basic recipes of Italian cooking, plus a handful of others which could not easily be included in any of the previous sections.

meat or chicken stock
brodo di gallina o di carne

A good stock depends entirely on the quality of the meat used. Chicken stock should be light and delicate, but not bland. A boiling chicken gives a tastier and less fatty stock, which is what you want, but boilers are hard to come by nowadays, so that you may have to buy a free-range or organic roasting chicken. Ask the butcher for the feet and head, which help the flavour.

Cut off and discard the last joint of the feet, scrub the feet well and put them in a stockpot. Remove any feathers from the head, wash it and add it to the pot. Remove and discard the fat you may find in the cavity of a roaster. Wash the chicken and put it in the pot with the rest of the ingredients. The cardamom seeds give the stock a very flowery taste.

Add enough cold water to cover everything by about 5 cm (2 inches) and cook over a very low heat until the stock is ready. Remove the scum which rises to the top at the beginning of the cooking. The surface of the liquid should just be broken by an occasional bubble. The best stock is made from liquid cooking at 85°C. Halfway through the cooking add about 1 teaspoonful of salt. (It is always better to add very little salt to stock, in case you want to reduce it. If you add what might seem the right amount of salt in the first place, the reduced stock would be much too salty.) After 2–2 1/2 hours, remove the chicken and strain the stock.

When cold, remove the fat from the surface and chill.

Makes about 1 1/2–2 litres (2 1/2–3 1/2 pints) stock
1 chicken or 1 kg (2 lb) of beef and veal pieces
1 carrot
1 onion, stuck with 1 or 2 cloves
2 celery sticks
1 ripe tomato
1 leek
a bunch of parsley, leaves and stalks
1 garlic clove
1 bay leaf
2 cardamom seeds
sea salt

For a good meat stock, buy a selection of beef and veal pieces and scraps, with some bones attached. You can add 2 or 3 chicken wings, if you like, or any other bits you have in the freezer, except pork or lamb. Add the flavouring vegetables and cold water as for the chicken stock and simmer for at least 3 hours, as instructed in the previous paragraph.

I serve the chicken or the meat itself, hot, for a family meal, surrounded by some boiled vegetables. As dressing I use, simply, the best olive oil. This does not always find favour with the British, many of whom are addicted to strong sauces and garnishes. Alberto Denti di Pirajno, though in other respects an anglophile, commented on this failing in his book *Il Gastronomo Educato*: 'Dr Johnson defines a sauce as something eaten with food to improve its flavour. It would be hard to believe that was written by a man with the intelligence and culture of Dr Johnson if we did not know he was English. Still to this day his compatriots, unable to give flavour to their food, call on the sauces to supply their dishes with that which they do not have. This explains the gravies, jellies and the prepared extracts, the bottled sauces, chutneys and ketchups that populate the tables of these unfortunate people.' Strong words from one of the greatest gastronomes among writers and the greatest Italian writer among gastronomes.

fish stock
brodo di pesce

Makes 1.75 litres (3 pints) stock
1.35 kg (3 lb) white fish bones and heads
3 tbsp olive oil

continued over >>

For a good fish stock you must use only white fish. With any luck your fishmonger will give you some sole bones and heads, haddock, hake, etc. Make up the rest with some inexpensive fish such as whiting. Cut off and discard the gills in the heads of the fish as they would give the stock a bitter taste.

Rinse the fish. Heat the oil, vegetables and garlic in a stockpot and sauté gently for 7–8 minutes. Add the fish to the pan and sauté for

5 minutes to *insaporire* – give it flavour. Add 3 litres (5 pints) of cold water, the peppercorns, parsley, bay leaves and salt. Bring to the boil and skim well. Simmer for 15 minutes, then pour in the wine and simmer for a further 15 minutes. Strain through a large sieve lined with a piece of muslin. Cool, then skim again if necessary and blot off any surface fat, using kitchen paper.

Transfer the stock to a clean pan and reduce over a high heat until you have only 1.75 litres (3 pints) left.

1 large onion, quartered
2 carrots, thickly sliced
a handful of fennel tops
2 celery stalks, thickly sliced
2 tomatoes, quartered
6 garlic cloves, unpeeled
a dozen peppercorns
4 sprigs flat-leaf parsley
2 bay leaves
1 tsp sea salt
300 ml (1/2 pint) dry white wine

vegetable stock
brodo vegetale

A good vegetable stock is just as useful a standby in the kitchen as a meat stock. It can be used for many vegetable risotti, for stewing vegetables, for adding to soups and sauces and even for drinking on its own when you feel the need for something simple and soothing. Once upon a time, when the seasons were observed, the vegetables used were those in season. Now that everything is 'in season' all year round, use the freshest and preferably the local vegetables, as they have more flavour. But do not use cabbage as that would give the stock the wrong taste. The indispensable vegetables are onion, celery, carrot and leek; I have used an orthodox selection in this recipe.

Makes about 1.5 litres (2 1/2 pints) stock
3 celery sticks
4 carrots
2 leeks, the white and green part
1 onion, stuck with 1 clove
2 tomatoes
1 courgette
bunch of greens, such as beet spinach or lettuce leaves, but not spring greens
2 garlic cloves
large bunch of parsley, leaves and stalks
fresh herbs
2 bay leaves
peppercorns
cooking salt

Peel and wash the vegetables and cut them into pieces. Put them in a large stockpot with the herbs and the peppercorns. Cover with 2 litres (3 1/2 pints) of cold water, add half a tablespoon of cooking salt and bring to the boil. Simmer slowly for at least 2 hours. Strain and taste and, if necessary, boil rapidly to reduce to make the stock more full of flavour.

preparation
Stock keeps in the refrigerator for about 3 days, after which it must be brought back to the boil and boiled for at least 5 minutes. Or it can be

frozen. I put some stock into ice bags and freeze it. It is handy to use, since you can take out only one or two cubes at a time – one cube equals about one tablespoon.

battuto e soffritto

Battuto, literally 'beaten', in a culinary context means chopped so fine as to appear pounded. A *battuto*, consisting traditionally of chopped pork fat and/or pancetta, onion garlic, parsley, celery and carrot, is the starting point for most Italian recipes for sauces, meat dishes and soups. The traditional *lardo* – pork fat – is now often replaced by lighter types of fat, olive oil being the most popular. The *battuto* is used a *crudo* – raw – in some dishes, in a bean soup, for instance. It gives a fresher, less rich flavour to the dish and is certainly a healthier method. Usually, however, the *battuto* becomes a *soffritto* by being sautéed in some kind of fat.

Soffritto means 'underfried': the *battuto* is subjected to a slow, careful underfrying, as a result of which 'a cook achieves part of that unmistakable taste which can be identified as Italian,' as Marcella Hazan so aptly puts it.

There are three secrets of a good *soffritto*. Firstly the *battuto* should be finely chopped. Secondly the *soffritto* should cook very gently, while being watched by careful eyes, with a hand ready to stir whenever any of the ingredients begins to catch. The third secret is that when the first ingredient to be sautéed is onion you should add a pinch of salt to it at the beginning. The salt releases the moisture in the onion, thus preventing it from frying too quickly.

béchamel sauce
salsa besciamella

Béchamel is a good sauce in its own right and it is also the basis of many other sauces. For this reason it is important to be able to make a good smooth béchamel. I find it best to cook béchamel for at least 10 minutes so as to kill the bitter, metallic taste of uncooked flour.

The density of béchamel can vary according to its use. I prefer to make a thin sauce when I use the béchamel in combination with pasta. A thick sauce is needed whenever the béchamel is to be used as a binder for stuffings, rissoles, etc.

Makes about 450 ml (3/4 pint) sauce
600 ml (1 pint) full-fat milk
60 g (2 oz) unsalted butter
45 g (1 1/2 oz) Italian 00 flour
sea salt
nutmeg

Heat the milk until it just begins to bubble at the edge.

Meanwhile melt the butter in a heavy-based saucepan over a low heat. Blend in the flour, stirring vigorously. Now draw the pan off the heat and add the hot milk, a few tablespoons at a time. You must let the flour mixture absorb each addition thoroughly before going on to the next.

When all the milk has been absorbed and the sauce is lovely and smooth, return the pan to the heat. Add salt to taste and bring to the boil. Cook over the gentlest heat for 10–15 minutes, stirring frequently. I prefer to use a flame disperser or to put the saucepan in a larger saucepan containing 5 cm (2 inches) or so of simmering water. Now add a grating of nutmeg, which is the most usual flavouring.

I sometimes like to change the flavouring according to what I want to use the béchamel with. For a plain pasta with béchamel I infuse 2 garlic cloves in the milk. If I want the béchamel as a base sauce for fish, for instance, a bay leaf would go in the milk.

roast potatoes
patate arrosto

Serves 6
**24–30 small new
potatoes, all perfect
3 tbsp olive oil
4 garlic cloves
salt and pepper
1 sprig of fresh
rosemary, or 2 bay
leaves, or 1 tsp
fennel seeds,
pounded**

This is my unorthodox method of roasting potatoes.

Scrape the potatoes. Wash them in a basin of cold water and dry
thoroughly.

Heat the oven to 200°C (400°F) mark 6 and place an oven dish in it to
heat up.

Pour the olive oil into a large frying or sauté pan into which the
potatoes will fit in a single layer, and add the garlic. Place the pan on a
medium high heat and when the garlic becomes pale gold, remove it.
Slip in the potatoes and fry them for 7–8 minutes, shaking the pan
frequently, so that they form a golden crust all over.

Transfer the potatoes and the little oil left at the bottom of the pan to
the oven dish. Season the potatoes with salt and pepper and add the
herb of your choice. Cover the dish with its lid or, tightly, with foil. Bake
until the potatoes are done, about 30–40 minutes.

preparation
Potatoes cooked this way keep warm in the turned-off oven for a good
half hour.

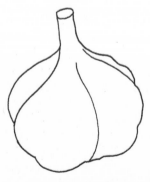

green salad with herb dressing
la mia insalata verde

Buy a selection of the following salads: Cos and round lettuce, Belgian chicory, lamb's lettuce, Little Gem, curly endive and a radicchio head for colour. I am not very keen on Lollo Rosso, but if you like it use a few leaves. I would never add Webb or Iceberg, as they have the wrong texture and a cabbagey taste that does not go with the other salads.

Serves 6–8

Having picked, washed and thoroughly dried the salad, cut the leaves into shreds or small pieces; only lamb's lettuce should be left whole. I find the current fashion for serving large whole leaves totally wrong for two good reasons. First, you cannot possibly toss the salad well enough to coat it properly with the dressing; second, one or two leaves will fill your plate – especially if the salad is served on small side plates – when you would have liked to help yourself to more variety. To this basic selection, add a bunch of rocket. I shred rocket so that its peppery flavour can be detected in every mouthful.

Now for the dressing of my choice. I use herbs from the garden: 2 leaves of sorrel, 2 or 3 leaves of spring borage, a few basil leaves, a dozen blades of chives, lovage leaf and a little fresh oregano or marjoram. All the herbs are chopped with a little garlic – 1 small clove for 8 people is more than enough. Before you chop the garlic, cut it in half and, if there is one, remove the green inner core, which has a strong and sharp flavour.

Put the chopped herb mixture in the salad bowl and add about 2 tablespoons of good red wine vinegar, 2 teaspoons of sea salt and a generous amount of black pepper. Now add gradually about 8 tablespoons of extra virgin olive oil, while beating with a fork. The proportion of vinegar to oil depends on personal taste, on the fruitiness of the oil and on the acidity of the vinegar; my quantities are a rough guide. I sometimes like to add 1–1 1/2 teaspoons of Dijon mustard, not an Italian habit, but one I am delighted to borrow from France.

Add about half the salad to the bowl, toss thoroughly and then add the rest of the salad. The secret of a good salad is to be patient and mix it with the dressing very well, otherwise the first people to help themselves will have dry rabbit food, while the last will have a soup.

preparation

The salad leaves can be prepared up to 1 day in advance and kept in the refrigerator, wrapped in a clean cloth. The herb dressing must be prepared up to 1 hour in advance to allow the flavours to blend, but the salad must be tossed at the last minute.

fatless sponge
pan di spagna

Makes a cake of about 180 g (6 oz)
2 free-range eggs, separated
60 g (2 oz) caster sugar
50 g (1 3/4 oz) Italian 00 flour
1/2 tsp sea salt

Preheat the oven to 180°C (350°F) mark 4.

Butter a 600 ml (1 pint) loaf tin generously, dust with flour all over and shake off the excess.

Whisk the egg yolks with the sugar until pale yellow and forming soft peaks. Use an electric hand beater if you have one, but not a food processor, which does not work for this recipe. Sieve the flour with 1/4 teaspoon of the salt at least twice, letting the flour drop from a height to aerate it.

Put the egg whites and the rest of the salt in a very clean bowl and whisk until stiff but not dry.

Scoop out a couple of tablespoons of the egg white and drop them over the egg yolk and sugar mixture. Sprinkle with 2 tablespoons of the flour and delicately fold into the yolk mixture with a metal spoon. Repeat, adding a little of each at a time and folding them in until all the egg white and flour have been incorporated. Use a light movement, raising the spoon high so as to aerate the mixture. Stop folding as soon as the mixture becomes homogeneous.

Pour the mixture into the prepared tin and bake for about 30 minutes until the cake is springy to the touch and has shrunk from the sides of the tin.

Loosen the cake from the sides of the tin with a palette knife and turn on to a wire rack.

Leave to cool completely and then wrap with foil or store in a cake tin.

preparation
This cake is best used within 1 day of making, although it can be made well in advance and frozen, wrapped in foil. Allow to defrost completely before using.

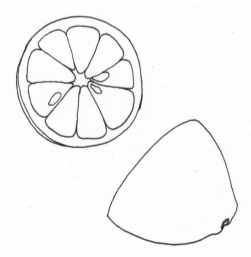

index